Contemporary America

Contemporary States and Societies

This series provides lively and accessible introductions to key countries and regions of the world conceived and designed to meet the needs of today's students. The authors are all experts with specialist knowledge of the country or region concerned but have been chosen also for their ability to communicate clearly to a non-specialist readership. Each text has been specially commissioned for the series and is structured according to a common format.

Published

Contemporary Russia
EDWIN BACON with MATTHEW WYMAN

Contemporary South Africa
ANTHONY BUTLER

Contemporary America (3rd edn)
RUSSELL DUNCAN and JOSEPH GODDARD

Contemporary China
ALAN HUNTER and JOHN SEXTON

Contemporary Japan (2nd edn)
DUNCAN McCARGO

Contemporary Britain
JOHN McCORMICK

Contemporary Latin America
RONALDO MUNCK

Forthcoming

Contemporary India
KATHERINE ADENEY and ROBERT WYATT

Contemporary France
HELEN DRAKE

Contemporary Europe
B. GUY PETERS

Also planned

Contemporary Asia
Contemporary Germany
Contemporary Italy
Contemporary Spain

Contemporary America

Third Edition

Russell Duncan
and
Joseph Goddard

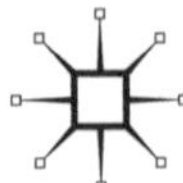

First edition 2003
Second edition 2005
Third edition 2009

Published by
PALGRAVE MACMILLAN

Palgrave Macmillan in the UK is an imprint of Macmillan Publishers Limited, registered in England, company number 785998, of Houndmills, Basingstoke, Hampshire RG21 6XS.

Palgrave Macmillan in the US is a division of St Martin's Press LLC, 175 Fifth Avenue, New York, NY 10010.

Palgrave Macmillan is the global academic imprint of the above companies and has companies and representatives throughout the world.

ISBN 978–0–230–57689–6 hardback
ISBN 978–0–230–57690–2 paperback

This book is printed on paper suitable for recycling and made from fully managed and sustained forest sources. Logging, pulping and manufacturing processes are expected to conform to the environmental regulations of the country of login.

A catalogue record for this book is available from the British Library.

A catalog record for this book is available from the Library of Congress.

10 9 8 7 6 5 4 3 2 1
18 17 16 15 14 13 12 11 10 09

Printed and bound in Great Britain by
CPI Antony Rowe, Chippenham and Eastbourne

Contents

List of Figures, Maps, Illustrations, Tables, and Boxes

Figures

Maps

Illustrations

Tables

Boxes

Acknowledgments to the Third Edition

This edition deals with the changes in American society during the last four years and the promise of a transformational moment in domestic and foreign policy that has come with the election of Barack Obama. The authors are grateful for the support of publisher Steven Kennedy and the staff of Palgrave Macmillan who have shared their enthusiasm for the descriptive and analytical approach we have used in *Contemporary America*. We are especially indebted to Stephen Wenham and Keith Povey for their keen advice in the present volume. Ben Greig, who first listened to the proposal for the first edition of the book, back in 2002, continues to bolster our work. Special thanks go to our colleagues at the University of Copenhagen for their widespread encouragement during the comprehensive rewriting and updating since 2005. We would also like to thank the five anonymous peer reviewers for their careful readings, comments, and suggestions. Russell Duncan has the overall editorial responsibility for the book and particular responsibility for Chapters 1, 2 and 5–10. Joseph Goddard has primary responsibility for Chapters 3 and 4. This volume is a product of the Contemporary America Project at the University of Copenhagen. As always, the authors dedicate this edition to our families.

RUSSELL DUNCAN
JOSEPH GODDARD

The authors and publishers are grateful to the following for permission to use copyright material: *Orlando Sentinel* for Cover Illustration; Press Association/AP for Illustrations I.1, 1.4, 2.1, 2.4, 3.1, 3.2, 4.2, 6.1, 6.2, 7.2, 8.1, 8.3, 10.1, 10.2; Momatiuk-Eastcott/Corbis for Illustration 2.2; Corbis for Illustration 4.1; Polfoto for Illustrations 4.3; Timepix for Illustration 1.2; Getty for Illustration 1.3; Joe Horsey for Illustration 3.3; US Navy-AFP/Getty Images for Illustration 9.2;

Illustrations 5.1, 5.2, 5.3, 6.3, 7.1, 9.1 are by Russell Duncan. Thanks also to the Library of Congress and National Archives and Records Administration for help with public domain images. Every effort has been made to trace all copyright holders of third-party materials included in this work, but if any have been inadvertently overlooked the publishers will be pleased to make the necessary arrangement at the first opportunity.

List of Abbreviations

ABA	American Bar Association
ACLU	American Civil Liberties Union
AFDC	Aid to Families with Dependent Children
AFL	American Federation of Labor
BIA	Bureau of Indian Affairs
CIA	Central Intelligence Agency
CIO	Congress of Industrial Organizations
CNN	Cable News Network
DHS	Department of Homeland Security
EOP	Executive Office of the President
EPA	Environmental Protection Agency
ESA	Endangered Species Act
EU	European Union
FTC	Federal Trade Commission
FED	Federal Reserve Banking System
FBI	Federal Bureau of Investigation
GATT	General Agreement on Tariffs and Trade
GDP	Gross Domestic Product
GNP	Gross National Product
IMF	International Monetary Fund
INS	Immigration and Naturalization Service
IRS	Internal Revenue Service
JCS	Joint Chiefs of Staff
NAFTA	North American Free Trade Agreement
NASA	National Aeronautics and Space Administration
NATO	North Atlantic Treaty Organization
NPS	National Park Service
NRA	National Rifle Association
NSA	National Security Advisor
NSC	National Security Council
NYSE	New York Stock Exchange
OMB	Office of Management and Budget

PAC	Political Action Committee
PBS	Public Broadcasting System
SDI	Strategic Defense Initiative
SEC	Securities and Exchange Commission
TANF	Temporary Assistance for Needy Families
UN	United Nations
WTC	World Trade Center
WTO	World Trade Organization

Map 0.1 The United States of America: States and State Capitals

Introduction

The year 2008 ended and 2009 began in alternating moods of depression and joy as the global economy continued its downward trend and one of America's most unpopular presidents ever was replaced by a young optimist with an educated wife and two small children (see Illustration I.1). It was almost as if a paradigm shift had occurred in world fears and hopes: ambivalently worrying what could be done to

Illustration I.1 Inauguration of Barack Obama, 20 January 2009

On 20 January 2009, US Supreme Court Chief Justice John Roberts administered the oath of office to President Barack Hussein Obama. Obama selected the same bible used by President Abraham Lincoln in 1861 and swore to uphold and defend the Constitution of the United States against all enemies foreign and domestic. Pictured with Obama (47 years old) is his wife Michelle (44) and daughters Malia (10) and Sasha (7). Visible just behind Chief Justice John Roberts is former President George W. Bush, Laura Bush, and former President Bill Clinton.

(Ron Edwards/AP/Press Association Images, 2009)

raise the economy and cheering that the new face of America would rally the world to better days. Barack Obama represented what might be possible, still, in America, and the world – a coming together, a new beginning, a redefinition. This story of failure, struggle and redemption conveys the myth and reality in the American chronicle of change and continuity.

Since the seventeenth century, Americans have maintained a frontier mentality, experiencing unprecedented social mobility while its people searched the questions of "Who are we?" and "What kind of country will we be?" In the nineteenth century, slavery confronted freedom before a Civil War resolved the question of civil liberties and political democracy – even if it took another century and a half to establish both *de jure* and *de facto* realities for those universal principles. Certainly the election of Barack Obama indicates the vitality of American democracy and progress toward universal freedom and equality.

The American character as played out through the contours of a short history is marked by the central ideas of equality and possibilities. Americans insist that possibilities – dreams – can be realized through freedom, democracy, and merit. Because Americans have an ethos of individual achievement (and individual failure), they often reject efforts to make everyone more equal via a leveling of incomes through taxation and social programs. *Contemporary America* explores the fairness and unfairness of such an ethos. Americans can be the most tolerant and overly friendly people on earth. Their entire history as an "immigrant nation" demands compromises among a diverse population of interests. Americans can also be arrogant, intolerant, and unyielding when they think they are preserving the very character of their community or nation against conspiracies of the unenlightened.

There are profound contradictions in the American dream. Historian Eric Hobsbawm wrote that despite "the human wastage (that) is the other face of American capitalism, . . . the USA promises greater openness to talent, to energy, to novelty than other worlds" (Hobsbawm, 2003). For over a century, the United States has been one of the world's most affluent nations; but it compares unfavorably with other industrialized, democratic countries in the areas of poverty, murder, HIV cases, inequality, greenhouse emissions, health care, and life expectancies. Its universities excel, but its elementary schools rank just below average in international studies. Americans work about 350 hours more per year (9 weeks) than their European counterparts. Americans are patriotic, religious, and conservative in their values, but the scale of dissent over most issues illustrates basic disagreements and changing priorities among the people. As the dynamic change from Bush to Obama illustrates, the United States can rapidly take up new directions and policies as it adjusts to contemporary events.

Much of what has happened in the history of the United States is based upon the European imagination of a New World. Europeans imagined America before they discovered it and, in the years since discovering it, they have been trying to define what it is that makes it different. Christopher Columbus never understood that he had located a new continent or continents in 1492, but died steadfastly believing that he was somewhere in eastern Asia. Others spoke of the discovery of an Atlantis, a lost continent that had long filled the European imagination. In the sixteenth century, explorers from many nations – some using a new map, *Amerika,* named for the Italian explorer Amerigo Vespucci – canvassed the coast of the New World, sailing into inlets, collecting souvenirs, and being astonished at what they did or did not find there. But whatever Europeans believed – and they believed many things – they were overcome with the possibilities of what could be gained from possessing a part of America.

The idea of building something new on new land, of having the freedom to do so, of looking toward the future and not the past, of accepting the progress of change over the stasis of continuity, and of individual rebirth/recreation, inspired European adventurers and became the story of the American people. During the Age of Discovery, Europeans tried to define the dream that might be; during the Age of Reason, philosopher John Locke made what has proven to be a long-lasting appeal to innocence: "in the beginning, all the world was America."

The American Dream and American history stem directly from these European dreams and imaginings. From its discovery until the present day, America-the-place as well as America-the-idea has been discussed as opportunity. It has been seen as a "safe haven" where conditions could be altered in favor of whoever needed change. Immigration, economic opportunity, and the chance for individual redefinition are central components of the American Dream. Egocentric and religious, most Americans have believed that a divine Providence guided the nation. In the first years of the twenty-first century, nothing had changed the American belief in the country's exceptional status. With the end of a Cold War putting an exclamation point on the success of American individualism, and as immigrants continue to pour into the country, Americans still believe that every person in the world is a potential American citizen.

Americans are taught from childhood that anything or everything is possible. This American Dream is a decidedly bourgeois notion and it is formulated upon the belief that government will not limit individual ambitions, either by restrictive laws or by using transfer income to gain an equality of outcome for others. Americans have consistently and overwhelmingly resisted any equality other than the equality of opportunity to achieve merit, and, thereafter, the rewards that merit brings.

So why haven't these dreams of equality and freedom been realized in contemporary America? Is there a basic hypocrisy in the gap between what America stands for and what it is? For many of its critics, the United States is a nation built on the avarice of rich white Protestant males who laid waste to the environment of a pristine continent, killed the native inhabitants, enslaved Africans, warred against all peoples who stood in the way, suppressed women and ethnic minorities, abused the working class, and cannibalized European culture into a vulgar materialism spread by Hollywood and McDonald's. Despite the truths inherent in these criticisms and the widespread knowledge of such actions, non-white and non-Protestant immigrants of both sexes continue to arrive, chasing the hope of a better life under the promise of opportunity. Philosopher Reinhold Niebuhr called the distance between the dream and reality "the irony of American history" (Niebuhr, 1952). That irony, as we hope this book will show, cannot be reduced to – though neither does it exclude – hypocrisy.

Understanding the USA in the twenty-first century requires a historical background that is not suited to a mere timeline or a few brief paragraphs. Chapter 1 provides an overview of the nation's history and introduces the main themes of the American experience. Chapter 2 examines the contours of a vast country by looking at it through the lens of its main regions, environmental concerns, and immigrant groups. Chapters 3 and 4 detail governing political institutions and explain the importance of constitutional provisions and the division of powers. Chapters 5 through 7 explore American society and culture, delving into family, class, race, and gender, while discussing culture, religion, crime, education, and welfare. Chapter 8 examines the US domestic and international economy and the changing character of the American workforce. Chapter 9 focuses on America's place in an increasingly globalized world and on current issues and events set in context by a brief review of the historical evolution of US foreign policy. Chapter 10 supposes future trajectories. A picture of continuity and change, singularity and diversity, individualism and community, and conflict and consensus are common denominators to all chapters in trying to explain the lifeways in contemporary America.

1

History

American history is long, reaching back to at least 10,000 years ago when the first group of humans struggled into the interior of a continent to become Native Americans. United States history is short – just 230 years old – and it is not difficult to find people alive today who remember World War I, who, in turn, had known slaves and slave owners who could tell them firsthand about the 1840s, and who had known people who had traded with Native Americans or who had shaken hands with Thomas Jefferson. Five people linked together cover the entire lifespan of the United States, a nation born in modern times with a fast and furious history. Writer William Faulkner succinctly described this notion in *Intruder in the Dust*: "yesterday today and tomorrow are Is: Indivisible: One" (Faulkner, 1948: 194). It is difficult to find another nation – if even one exists – whose citizens celebrate their Founders the way Americans do. Annually, books on the American Revolution pour off the presses and onto bestseller lists. Politicians are always asking rhetorically, then explaining, what George Washington or Thomas Jefferson would have done today. It does not seem to matter that those two leaders died some time ago. Historian Bernard Bailyn's assessment and accusation that "Americans live remarkably close to their past" is a good starting point for understanding the contours of America's belief in history-as-present-tense (quoted in Rothschild, 2004).

One thousand years before Europeans stumbled upon America, agriculture was established in the present-day US southwest and Pueblo Indians built their houses into high cliffs to protect themselves from their enemies, the Apaches. The Makah in Washington state had a highly-developed culture based on salmon fishing. By 1492, the year of Christopher Columbus's "discovery" of America, approximately

10 million – some claim 100 million – people lived in what would become the United States and as many as 50 million more lived in Canada, Mexico and southward.

On the eve of discovery, Europe had been transformed by the rise of nation states, which were influenced by the twelfth-century Crusades' stimulation of commercial activities and an interchange of technology. Trade revolutionized commerce, changed the system from barter to coinage, and built banking houses, joint-stock companies, and cities. The Renaissance emphasized discovery and science and the Protestant Reformation stressed individual freedom, tore at the power of the Roman Catholic Church, and ignited competition and wars among Christians.

European nations competed to control trade. Each needed a strong military and a rich treasury, which could be achieved through a favorable balance of trade, war and conquest, and colonies whose settlers fed raw materials to the manufacturing centers in the mother country. As nations sponsored enterprises to capture the New World, Native Americans were brought into a web of commercial relations that encircled the globe, becoming producers and consumers in a developing world market system.

To provide items for trade, American Indians voluntarily took more from the ecological system to supply the furs Europeans wanted in exchange for copper pots, ornamental beads, whiskey, and woolen shirts. While trade transformed cultures, disease wiped them out as the accumulated knowledge of the tribes was lost when the elders died and the death of the medicine men broke the spiritual edifice of Indian life. Contact with whites killed 90 percent of all North American Indians as typhoid, influenza, smallpox, and tuberculosis took their toll. As the devastation accelerated, many hoped for salvation by accepting the Christ thrust at them by missionaries. This trinity of trade, disease and Christianity placed Native Americans on the edge of oblivion.

The Rise of a Nation

Colonial America, 1508–1763

America was born in violence and change as Europeans fought Native Americans and each other for control of the land. World markets determined the course of development in America in terms of shipping ports, agricultural production, industry and workforce. The

English established a line of colonies from Maine to Georgia. Jamestown, Virginia (1607), was payrolled by a joint-stock company and soldiered by professional mercenaries. Soon, the settlers were growing tobacco for the European market. In 1619, a Dutch ship sold twenty Africans into indentured servitude in Virginia and the British, French, Spanish and Dutch empires grew rich from the profits of the international slave trade. As cash crops expanded and developed in the colonies, the demands for workers increased and plantation owners embraced slavery. By the time of the American Revolution in 1776, one of every five Americans was a slave.

In 1620, religious dissenters, who wanted to separate forever from the Church of England, landed in a place they called Plymouth Colony. Indian tribes quickly developed trading ties with these Pilgrims and introduced them to corn, beans, turkeys, squash, and potatoes. Legend has it that the Native Americans and the newcomers celebrated a huge feast in 1621 – the story behind the purest American holiday, Thanksgiving.

Other dissenters – in a group of 1,000 people aboard 17 ships – who wanted to reform and purify the Church of England arrived in Massachusetts in 1630. These Puritans were engaged in an "errand into the wilderness" to establish a utopian religious community, a model for England and the world. Puritan leader John Winthrop defined the colony "as a city upon a hill. The eyes of all people are upon us" (Winthrop, 1989: 41). Perfectionists, the Puritans demanded order, even if they trampled on concepts of freedom or equality. They were so intent on living righteously in an evil world that they became intolerant and, in 1692, the excesses of the infamous Salem, Massachusetts, witch trials – marked as they were by community hysteria, the fear of women, rural–urban conflicts, and, simply, cultural change – highlighted the failure of the Puritan errand.

American ideology owes much to Puritan patterns. Witch hunts fit neatly into the conspiracy theories of runaway government or internal communist threats and Americans still believe the US is God's nation. Insisting that hard work is its own reward, the Puritan work ethic is essential to American individualism. A university education remains the best path to the American dream, something the Puritans supported by founding Harvard University in 1636.

Between 1660 and 1763, the colonies developed differently. The population rose rapidly as a result of a steady immigration, slave importation and natural increase. There was a baby boom as families formed earlier due to the availability of land and need for labor. In England, the average marrying age for women was 23 years old; in

America, it was 19. With colonial women giving birth to an average of seven children, the population reached 100,000 in 1660; by 1775, 2.5 million, one-third of them native-born. Rising numbers led to rising expectations. Additionally, slavery enriched the colonists as the northern colonies gained from the carrying trade and the southern colonies from the products produced.

Historian Edmund Morgan called slavery the central paradox of American history and he convincingly linked the rise of liberty and equality in America and the soothing of class conflict to slavery. The more that Euro-Americans enslaved Africans, the more liberty expanded for whites (Morgan, 1995). Colonists transplanted European social hierarchies to the colonies, but as skin color began to mark caste, lower class whites demanded an expansion of voting rights and landholding privileges. Regardless of their economic standing, most whites came to view themselves as a "middle class" because there were always browner or redder peoples below them.

From 1734 to 1755, an evangelical revival swept through the colonies on the heels of Jonathan Edwards's sermons about "Sinners in the Hands of an Angry God," and Methodist cleric George Whitefield's colony-by-colony salvation tour. The Great Awakening was the first all-American cultural event and it appealed to the Protestant sense of individual responsibility and anti-authoritarianism. This revival led many colonials to question the authority England was exerting over the colonies.

The American Revolution and the Constitution

While the colonies grew, Britain engaged in a struggle for supremacy with Spain and France. In the Great War for Empire, 1754–63, Britain gained Canada, all French possessions east of the Mississippi River, and Florida. With her rivals effectively neutralized, Britain tightened control over the colonies. Parliament increased taxes as a way to pay the enormous debt of £140 million accrued from the war and from stationing 10,000 soldiers along the frontier to protect the colonists from Indian attacks.

The taxes took many forms and the colonists responded bitterly to each and every one of them. Staging riots and breaking laws, colonists claimed the "rights of Englishmen" to "no taxation without representation." Colonials advanced a conspiracy theory put forward by English Whigs during the Glorious Revolution of 1688 and Thomas Jefferson argued that taxes and other recent events proved, "a deliberate, systematical plot of reducing us to slavery" (quoted in Wood, 1969: 331).

Jefferson was just 33 years old when, as a delegate from Virginia to the Second Continental Congress in Philadelphia, he wrote The Declaration of Independence in 1776 (Box 1.1). The idea of revolution was not new, but the acts of a people, in an orderly manner, explaining and justifying their rights to throw off oppression and

Box 1.1 Excerpt from The Declaration of Independence

When in the course of human events, it becomes necessary for one people to dissolve the political bands which have connected them with another, and to assume among the Powers of the earth, the separate and equal station to which the Laws of Nature and of Nature's God entitle them, a decent respect to the opinions of mankind requires that they should declare the causes which impel them to the separation.

We hold these truths to be self-evident, that all men are created equal, that they are endowed by their Creator with certain unalienable rights, that among these are Life, Liberty, and the pursuit of Happiness. That to secure these rights, Governments are instituted among Men, deriving their just powers from the consent of the governed. That whenever any Form of Government becomes destructive of these ends, it is the Right of the People to alter or to abolish it, and to institute new Government, laying its foundation on such principles and organizing its powers in such form, as to them shall seem most likely to effect their Safety and Happiness. Prudence, indeed, will dictate that Governments long established should not be changed for light and transient causes; and accordingly all experience hath shown, that mankind are more disposed to suffer, while evils are sufferable, than to right themselves by abolishing the forms to which they are accustomed. But when a long train of abuses and usurpations, pursuing invariably the same Object evinces a design to reduce them under absolute Despotism, it is their right, it is their duty, to throw off such Government, and to provide new Guards for their future security . . .

We, therefore, the Representatives of the United States of America, in General Congress, Assembled, appealing to the Supreme Judge of the world for the rectitude of our intentions, do, in the Name, and by Authority of the good People of these Colonies, solemnly publish and declare, That these United Colonies are, and of Right ought to be free and independent states; that they are Absolved from all Allegiance to the British Crown, and that all political connection between them and the State of Great Britain, is and ought to be totally dissolved; and that as Free and Independent States, they have full Power to levy War, conclude Peace, contract Alliances, establish Commerce, and to do all other Acts and Things which Independent States may of right do. And for the support of this Declaration, with a firm reliance on the Protection of Divine Providence, we mutually pledge to each other our Lives, our Fortunes, and our sacred Honor.

Thomas Jefferson, 1776

establish a new government was unprecedented. Jefferson was the first philosopher to place sovereignty, not just rights, in the people. The people had the power to create the government and the people had the power to tear it down. The war for independence lasted until 1783 when the colonial forces under General George Washington, with crucial aid from France, prevailed. America became the first European colony to separate from its mother country.

After a brief period of ineffective government, in 1787, a convention of delegates wrote a document that British Prime Minister William Gladstone later praised as "the most wonderful work ever struck off at a given time by the brain and purpose of man" (quoted in Kammen, 1987: 162). The Constitution of the United States of America set up a federal system which shared power with the states and, ultimately, with the people. Because Americans feared central power, it took two years of intensive lobbying to convince the people and the states to ratify the Constitution. In 1789, the new government met in the nation's capital, New York City, and acclaimed George Washington president. Europeans looked on in wonderment but were quickly distracted when Frenchmen stormed the Bastille. Acknowledging America's role in fomenting these events, the Marquis de Lafayette sent Washington the key to that prison.

In 1793, England declared war on France. Washington immediately invoked American neutrality, an uneasy action that bubbled through the presidencies of John Adams, Thomas Jefferson, and James Madison. Americans were busy at home. Political parties had formed, dividing the supporters of stronger national power in the Federalist Party from the supporters of state power, Democratic-Republicans. By 1800, population had increased to 5.3 million, three new states had been added to the union, the value of exports was $71 million compared to $20 million in 1790, 20 colleges had been established, there were 200 newspapers, and the technology of the cotton gin had increased production of "white gold" from 1.5 million to 36.5 million pounds in a decade – and with it, the demand for slaves. The country was split between a free labor system in the North and a slave system in the South. Symbolizing the intersection of two differing social systems, Congress relocated the nation's capital in 1800 to the District of Columbia – an area set free of the boundaries of any state – and named the city, Washington. The war between England and France continued to disrupt the economy and the passions of the people. In 1812, after the British seized American ships and impressed American sailors into the British navy, President Madison declared war on England. The war was basically a drawn contest with the peace treaty ratified in 1815.

Westward Expansion and Reform

The nineteenth century was marked by the violence, power, and labor of territorial expansion (Map 1.1). In 1803, President Jefferson doubled the size of the United States by purchasing the Louisiana Territory from Napoleon. The US purchased Florida from Spain in 1819. By 1821, eight new states had entered the union as equals to the older states. The northern states had abolished slavery, but Southerners held tightly to their property and way of life. Slavery increasingly disturbed Northerners, who saw it as a stain on the nation's otherwise "heroic" narrative. Thomas Jefferson, a slaveholder, had once offered an apology that the institution was a necessary evil. Jefferson likened slavery to holding "the wolf by the ears." You don't like it, but you don't dare let it go (quoted in McPherson, 1982: 39). The principal American philosopher for freedom and equality clung to his slaves throughout his life.

Whites coveted western lands and as wagon trains rolled out of Eastern cities, the Indians were killed or confined to reservations. By 1838, all the eastern tribes had been forced west of the Mississippi River and, in the most famous atrocity, 15,000 Cherokees were forced to relocate from Georgia to Indian territory in Oklahoma. 4,000 died along this "trail of tears." Complicating the land struggles, the area from Texas to California was owned by Mexico, which had won its independence from Spain in 1821. In 1836, American settlers living in Texas revolted against Mexican rule, declared a Lone Star Republic, and asked to join the union. Nine years later, President James K. Polk, a fervent expansionist, proclaimed that the country should fill its natural boundaries and reach its "Manifest Destiny" (Illustration 1.1) of stretching from the Atlantic to the Pacific oceans. The US absorbed Texas and, from 1846 to 1848, made war on Mexico, won, and took all Mexican land north of the Rio Grande.

Polk bullied England into ceding the entire Northwest (part of Oregon territory), establishing the division with Canada. With the 1853 purchase of a strip of Mexican land, the US reached its present size, excluding Alaska, Hawaii, and various small offshore possessions. And yet, many Americans were not satisfied and believed that Manifest Destiny demanded more.

In addition to the issue of slavery in the territories, rapid growth brought on other discussions about the moral and social fabric of the nation. Reformers advocated individual and institutional uplift. Workingmen's associations pulled laborers together. Most middle-class women sought power by supporting a notion of separate spheres

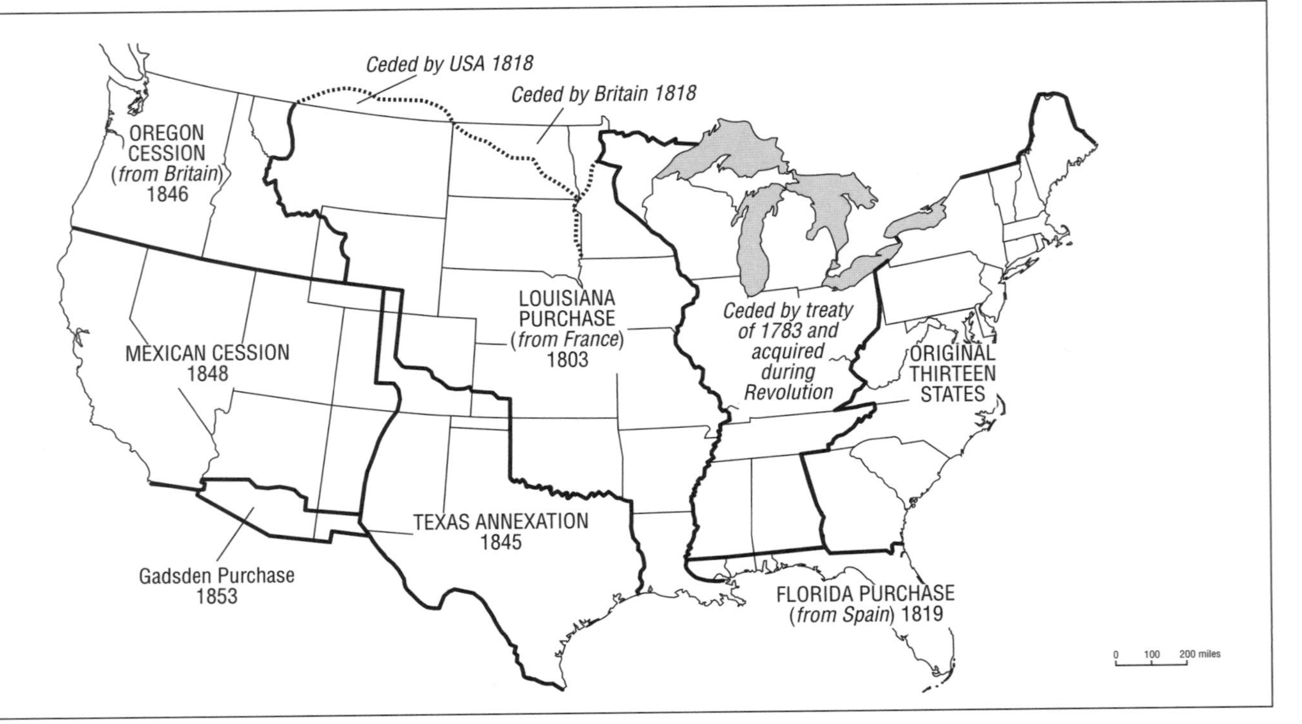

Map 1.1 US Territorial Expansion

Illustration 1.1 American Progress

Alternatively called "American Progress" or "Manifest Destiny Crosses the Plains," this 1872 illustration by John Gast captures the frontier myth of expansion. Columbia – the female symbol for the spirit of America – accompanies the explorers, covered wagon pioneers, communication and transportation systems, and pioneer farmers as they move westward. Indians, buffalo, and other "wild beasts" retreat in the face of "civilization."

(Library of Congress)

which argued that women should stay in the home and let men deal with the world. Other women argued for equality in all matters.

Margaret Fuller's *Woman in the Nineteenth Century* (1844) helped inspire the first Women's Rights Convention (1848) at Seneca Falls, New York, where the delegates declared "All men and women are created equal." A new religion, Mormonism, competed for converts with Shakers, Quakers, Adventists and others. A temperance movement linked poverty with "Demon Rum" and called for bans on alcohol.

The Industrial Revolution reshaped the workplace and the market economy in the North to the demands of industrial capitalism, an agrarian empire was rising in the West, and a cotton kingdom ruled the South. The North and West were becoming less Anglo-American and more Euro-American as immigrants poured in. Inventors conquered time and space, knitting the country together with steamboats, railroads, and telegraph lines. Cities grew rapidly, especially New York City, whose population exceeded 200,000 in 1830, 1.1 million in 1860, and 4.8 million in 1900.

In politics, the nation had been in the Founders' hands until 1828 when the Federalists were replaced by a group that soon called itself Whigs, and the Democratic-Republicans became the Democratic Party. Whigs resembled Federalists in favoring stronger national power over all aspects of the economy. The Democrats had a wider base but were weakened by their support of slavery. In 1854, the Whigs were replaced by the Republican Party, which organized on a platform of antislavery. The Democratic and Republican parties – although greatly changed – have anchored the nation's two-party system ever since.

The American Civil War

In 1860, the election of the Republican antislavery advocate Abraham Lincoln so enraged and frightened the South that before he could take office in March 1861, there were seven – soon 11 – fewer states in the union. The Confederate States of America formed a nation composed of South Carolina, Mississippi, Louisiana, Texas, Florida, Alabama, Georgia, Virginia, Arkansas, North Carolina, and Tennessee. While many in the North encouraged Lincoln to let the states depart in peace, Lincoln held firmly to his conviction that the union could not be dissolved.

The crises were many. A constitutional crisis arose over the sovereignty question of state versus national power, of a written commitment to liberty and slavery, and of how to convert territories into states. A social crisis inherent in having the population double every 25 years since the 1700s and the reformist, humanitarian impulse of the abolitionist movement to improve the lot of slaves, women, Native Americans and immigrants split communities. Economic interests questioned whether the transcontinental railroad should connect California with a southern or a northern terminus – the route picked was important to spread either slavery or free labor – and debated whether slaveowners had the right to take slave property into the free states. A religious crisis raged over whether the country's manifest destiny was of a slave or a free nature – causing a split in Protestant churches as abolitionists could not tolerate being in the same denomination as slaveholders, and vice versa. A moral crisis cast the shadow of hypocrisy over the contradiction in human bondage and the words of the Declaration of independence that "all men are created equal."

And then war came. The fighting lasted four years and took 620,000 American lives. It was a modern war with huge armies, rifled weaponry, forced enrollments and widespread civilian casualties. It took four years before the North's industrial prowess and continued large-scale immigration wore down the Confederacy. Two of Lincoln's speeches during the war – his "Emancipation Proclamation" and his "Gettysburg Address" (Box 1.2) – joined the Declaration of Independence and Constitution as the most revered and memorized expressions of American freedom, equality, and new beginnings. The "Gettysburg Address" uses biblical language, a progression of tenses from past to present, birth and rebirth metaphors, and Lincoln's contention that if America fails, freedom will fail. With his elegant language and strong leadership, Lincoln displaced Washington as the greatest American of all time, a position he still holds in yearly polls.

Box 1.2 The Gettysburg Address

Four score and seven years ago our fathers brought forth on this continent, a new nation, conceived in Liberty, and dedicated to the proposition that all men are created equal. Now we are engaged in a great civil war, testing whether that nation, or any nation so conceived and so dedicated, can long endure. We are met on a great battle-field of that war. We have come to dedicate a portion of that field, as a final resting place for those who here gave their lives that that nation might live. It is altogether fitting and proper that we should do this. But, in a larger sense, we can not dedicate – we can not consecrate – we can not hallow – this ground. The brave men, living and dead, who struggled here, have consecrated it, far above our poor power to add or detract. The world will little note, nor long remember what we say here, but it can never forget what they did here. It is for us the living, rather, to be dedicated here to the unfinished work which they who fought here have thus far so nobly advanced. It is rather for us to be here dedicated to the great task remaining before us – that from these honored dead we take increased devotion to that cause for which they gave their last full measure of devotion – that we here highly resolve that these dead shall not have died in vain – that this nation, under God, shall have a new birth of freedom – and that government of the people, by the people, for the people, shall not perish from the earth.

Abraham Lincoln, 1863

The Rise to Power

Of Race and Frontiers

With the war over, the national government consolidated its power and Americans changed a key verb. Before the war and in recognition of the power of the states, people used the plural form: "The United States are . . . ." After the war, with the nation achieved, they substituted the singular form: "The United States is . . . ." In 1867, the US purchased Alaska from Russia. The government sought to reconstruct the South in the national image. Three constitutional amendments (13th, 14th, 15th) – during the period called Reconstruction – freed the slaves, provided citizenship, and gave the vote to black men.

Southern whites responded by requiring literacy tests and poll taxes for voting, leasing convicts to private individuals, refusing to allow blacks to sit on juries, and organizing the Ku Klux Klan. In 1877, Southern resistance had exhausted government efforts and led President Rutherford B. Hayes to end Reconstruction and announce that the South would be left alone to deal with its "negro problem." By the 1890s, lynch mobs killed over a hundred African Americans a year. Then, in 1896, the US Supreme Court ruled that "separate but equal" school rooms, hospitals, libraries, hotel accommodations, and streetcars were in the spirit of the Constitution. The nation was officially segregated.

During the last quarter of the nineteenth century, the country filled up as the government helped itself, railroad interests, and homesteaders to the land Indian tribes had believed to be theirs "as long as the wind blows, as long as the grass grows, as long as the rivers flow" – as ran the official phrasing used in treaties granting property rights to Indian tribes. The first transcontinental railroad connecting San Francisco with New York City was completed in 1869, spurring further migration westward. The government's resolve to finish the Indian wars was accelerated by an event that occurred during the nation's centennial celebration. In late June 1876 along the Little Big Horn River in Montana territory, a brash army colonel set out to destroy a group of Native Americans. Surprised by one of the largest concentrations of tribes in the history of the West, George Armstrong Custer and his command of some 250 men were killed by the forces of Sitting Bull, Crazy Horse and Rain-in-the-Face. Whites cried for revenge, and, to destroy Indian resistance and culture, army snipers helped professional hunters kill nearly 30 million buffaloes. The Indian wars ended with the surrender of Geronimo and his group of Apaches in 1886.

The West belonged to the white man. Laws allowed homesteaders to settle on 160 acres, without cost, if they would cultivate the land. Many families built little houses on the prairie and began farming. Railroad companies received enormous subsidies in the form of land grants – 10–40 square miles of land for each mile of railroad built, an area equal to one-sixth of all Western lands. Timber and mining companies were soon cutting and digging everywhere. During the cowboy era, herds of cattle were driven from the grazing fields in Texas to stockyards and slaughterhouses in the Midwest.

In 1893, historian Frederick Jackson Turner put forth his "frontier thesis" that the experience of isolation and the availability of free land had shaped American democracy and institutions (Turner, 1966). Turner inscribed the frontier as the crucible where the American traits of individualism and acquisitiveness originated and he described the central place frontiers occupy in the American imagination. The rhetoric of the frontier continues in contemporary America as leaders speak of foreign policy or business challenges as new frontiers to be explored, conquered, and made safe.

The Gilded Age

By 1900, the United States had 258,000 miles of track, one-third of all the railroad mileage in the world. Railroad companies merged with investment banking firms and large corporate law firms to help create modern managerial capitalism. John D. Rockefeller's oil company and Andrew Carnegie's steel factories led the way by integrating production processes to control all aspects of the production of a single product (vertical integration) or to gain a monopoly over a single step in production (horizontal integration). In fact, developments sped along so fast that the industrialists and bankers, who saw themselves as "industrial statesmen," seemed to be "robber barons" to the general public. Writer Mark Twain called the period *The Gilded Age* (1873) because the rise of huge industry, big cities, and commerce looked golden; but to scratch off the gold revealed only the ugliness of base metal.

The philosophy of the marketplace reflected the era's conservative tone as economic policy followed free market principles. This *laissez-faire* approach stressed self-sufficiency and self-interest in a climate of limited governmental intervention, excepting tariff protection in international trade. The American creed of equal opportunity contributed to this, but so did the belief in natural selection and evolutionary change put forth by Charles Darwin and adapted into a philosophy that natural laws govern people's place in society – labeled by Herbert Spencer as "survival of the fittest." Then, William Graham Sumner summarized these beliefs by arguing that the acquisition of private property was the most important goal for individuals. Andrew Carnegie promoted this "Gospel of Wealth" and agreed that any government interference – such as welfare – hindered progress and hurt society because in any free society operating under evolutionary principles, wealth and power would naturally go to those most deserving of it.

As they have done throughout their history – in alternating cycles of liberal reforms and conservative retrenchments – Americans looked at their country and adjusted it. A new type of investigative journalism led the way, with social commentary and photographs, such as Jacob Riis's *How the Other Half Lives* (1890), Lincoln Steffen's *The Shame of the Cities* (1904), and Upton Sinclair's *The Jungle* (1906). Americans searched for order, called for government action, and considered solutions to reform community in the face of unprecedented immigration, industrialization, and urbanization. Their solutions helped ameliorate the problems of cities and city people, focused on maintaining white supremacy, and were wide-ranging and pragmatic attempts to redistribute wealth, expand social services, and put more people into the middle class.

The interests of farmers seemed to be crushed as the rural lifestyle of the nineteenth century gave way to the roaring urban machinery of the twentieth. In 1890, the same year that industries first earned more profits in the US than farmlands, farmers formed the Populist Party, the largest agrarian-based political party in US history. Populists favored an expansion of the money supply as a way to redistribute wealth, a graduated income tax so that the more you made the more you paid, nationalization of railroads in order to lower prices for farm products, voting reforms – including the secret ballot – to ensure democracy, and an eight-hour work day to protect laborers. In 1892, Populists had some success in electing candidates, but failed to elect a president or to control Congress. Meeting the usual fate of strong third parties in American history, the Populist party died in 1896, a result of fusion politics. Its ideas, however, lived on, and some were transformed into law during the Progressive Era.

The Progressive Era

Between 1890 and 1920 millions of non-English-speaking peoples from Southern and Eastern Europe immigrated through the new federal immigration facility built in 1892 on Ellis Island in New York harbor. No one could help but notice, towering over them from a

Illustration 1.2 The Statue of Liberty

During the Great Depression, many questioned the Statue of Liberty's promise of abundance and the capacity of America to provide for its own "tired. . . . poor. . . . [and] huddled masses." Renowned photographer Margaret Bourke White made this shot of "Lady Liberty" in 1930.

(Margaret Bourke White/Time Pix)

smaller island, the Statue of Liberty (Illustration 1.2). This "Mother of Exiles" had been a gift from France. Set in place in 1886, a plaque placed in the base proclaimed:

> Give me your tired, your poor,
> Your huddled masses yearning to breathe free
> The wretched refuse of your teeming shore
> Send these, the homeless, tempest-tossed to me,
> I lift my lamp beside the golden door.

By 1910, six American cities had populations exceeding one million people. Conditions were appalling as massive overcrowding led to problems of sanitation, sewage, and garbage control. Economic competition flared up between the newcomers and those who had arrived earlier as every new wave of immigrants worked for whatever wages they could get, with wages kept low by the constant arrival of new workers. As laborers competed, the racial and ethnic clashes of the Old World reemerged in the form of xenophobic stereotypes of this group as "lazy" or that one as "violent" or the next one as "stupid." Newly-arrived immigrants sought out others of their own national origin and created ethnic enclaves in various cities: "Little Italy," "Little Norway," "Little Russia," or "Little Poland."

Activists, called Progressives, instituted reforms. Social reformers, like Jane Addams, wanted improvements in housing, labor, and health conditions that would reduce class tensions and improve neighborhoods. Structural reformers improved streetcar lines, railroads, state prison systems and established a comprehensive school system for all white ethnic groups. State legislators increased income taxes and taxed corporations for the first time. Labor legislation installed inspectors to ensure factory safety, regulated the work days of women and children, and ordered a minimum wage. By 1916, most states had accepted the old Populist demands for election reforms: the secret ballot, initiative, referendum, recall, and direct election of US Senators.

Women's organizations grew to national prominence. Feminists Elizabeth Cady Stanton, Susan B. Anthony, and Alice Paul demanded women's suffrage and persuaded the country to bring this about by ratifying the 19th Amendment (1920). Victoria Woodhull advocated "free love" – an effort to separate ideas of sex for pleasure from those of sex for procreation – and Margaret Sanger distributed birth-control information. Charlotte Gilman's *Women and Economics* (1898) challenged the right of men to the best jobs and supported the need for women's organizations, a position taken up again in the 1960s by Betty Friedan and the National Organization for Women.

Believing that African Americans must pull themselves up by their bootstraps, the most powerful black leader in America, Booker T. Washington, reluctantly accepted segregation, while he pushed vocational education as the best way to advancement. His approach has been labeled "accommodation." Others reacted to the black experience of discrimination and continuing lynchings by advocating the confrontation and integration approach of W. E. B. DuBois, who helped found the National Association for the Advancement of Colored People (NAACP) in 1910. Still others pursued the separatist approach of black nationalist Marcus Garvey, whose Universal Negro Improvement Association (1919–27), stressed a heroic African past and called for all blacks to return to Africa where they would establish their own country.

By 1900, the United States was the richest country in the world. It produced more than one-third of the world's coal, iron, and steel. Its navy ranked third behind Britain and Germany. And yet, America reflected a nervousness as patriots watched European imperialists devour Africa – one sure way to get more customers and raw materials that business interests demanded. Applying Darwinian and manifest destiny ideas to nations, Americans viewed themselves and their country as a superior race/nation which had the right to expand over lesser peoples/nations in the survival of the fittest. In 1898, in a war with Spain, the United States took the Philippines, Puerto Rico, and Guam, and established a base at Guantánamo Bay, Cuba, as a symbol of its hegemony over the independent island nation. A flag cult arose as Americans began the ritual of standing for the playing of *The Star-Spangled Banner* and as students recited the "Pledge of Allegiance" (Box 1.3) every day in school. Americans left Africa to Europe, settled for dominance in the western hemisphere, and pursued an Open Door policy of free trade in Asia.

From Isolation to Superpower

World War I and the 1920s

From 1901–09, Theodore Roosevelt helped establish the modern regulatory state, put power in the office of the president and defined foreign policy by dividing the world into what he called "civilized"

Box 1.3 The Pledge of Allegiance

> I pledge allegiance to the flag of the United States of America, and to the Republic for which it stands, one nation [under God], indivisible, with liberty and justice for all.
>
> 1897

Note: Congress added the words "under God" in 1954. When, in 2002, a federal court ruled the words unconstitutional by provisions separating church and state, President George W. Bush defiantly responded: "no authority of government can ever prevent an American from pledging allegiance to this one nation under God" (quoted in Oppel, 2002). Two years later, the US Supreme Court reversed the lower court by citing the Pledge as a patriotic oath, not a prayer (CNN.com, 2004).

and "uncivilized" nations: the civilized ones defined as white and Western. Roosevelt is famous for seizing land in Panama and building a canal to increase trade and security by linking the Atlantic and Pacific oceans. He set limits on corporate greed by using the power of his office to champion reform, partly by prosecuting monopolies and partly by safeguarding and conserving wilderness areas. The two men who followed him as presidents, William Howard Taft and Woodrow Wilson, championed even stronger roles for the federal government.

Though protected by two broad oceans and a big navy, with a peaceful northern border and a weak neighbor to the south, the United States could not isolate itself from world affairs, especially following the outbreak of war in 1914 among the main European powers. In 1917, after German submarines increased their attacks on ships carrying US passengers, including the *Lusitania* – which was busy supplying Britain with war munitions – America officially entered World War I. Protest was so strong that Congress enacted an Espionage Act to curb dissent. Draconian measures banned the teaching of the German language and the playing of Beethoven. Thousands of Americans had their civil rights abused by over-zealous patriots and the US Supreme Court declared that freedom of speech could be limited if there was "a clear and present danger."

After the war, President Woodrow Wilson supported a League of Nations, but ultimately failed to convince his countrymen to join it. Americans experienced their largest-ever race and labor riots before the government restored order. After years of Progressive reform, Americans seemed desperate to put "America First" and for a "return to normalcy" – two phrases made popular by President Warren G. Harding, heralding business expansion and smaller government.

For many Americans, the 1920s was an era of prosperity. The period has been described variously as: the "Jazz Age," the "Roaring Twenties," or the "Era of The Lost Generation." It was a hedonistic age marked by the pursuit of pleasure, pushed along by the rise of advertising and radio, stimulated by the writings of Sigmund Freud and F. Scott Fitzgerald, and changed by a revolution in manners and morals, movies, automobiles, and a "me generation" that stressed a live-for-today attitude. Aviator Charles "Lucky" Lindbergh thrilled everyone when, as a young man in the most technologically advanced machine yet made, an airplane, he made a solo flight from New York to Paris, circling the Eiffel Tower and landing victoriously among 100,000 Frenchmen. Young women – "flappers" – threw off the Victorian fashions, cut their hair short, and reached for rayon stockings, silk panties, makeup, short dresses, a dance partner, a cigarette, and a beer. They sought "youth" and drank, even though the 18th Amendment (1919) prohibited the "manufacture, sale, or transporting of intoxicating liquors" anywhere in the United States. People flouted the law and bought from bootleggers – increasingly gangs of organized mobsters such as Chicago's Al Capone and his 1,000-man army of machine-gun-carrying thugs – until the 21st Amendment (1933) recognized the inevitable and nullified Prohibition.

Perhaps more than any single individual, efficiency expert Frederick W. Taylor, the spirit behind Henry Ford's automobile assembly lines, symbolized the 1920s. Manufacturing speed, standardized packaging, and a belief that there was only "one best way" led writer John Dos Passos to call the innovator "Speedy Fred," the man who died "with a watch in his hand" (Dos Passos, 1979: 48). In 1907, an automobile cost over $2,000; Taylor's methods reduced the costs to $300 in 1924. American males – and a few liberated females – bought their dream machines on credit. Cars changed American patterns of mobility, settlement, and leisure time.

These changes brought Protestant Anglo-Saxon America to invoke its jeremiad and reassert itself with a fundamentalist movement which surged across the land to root out the devil and other communists. The Russian Revolution of 1917 led to a "Red Scare" in the US, a fear that hurt labor and prompted a 25-year-old official in the Federal Bureau of Investigation (created in 1908) named J. Edgar Hoover to root out Bolsheviks. For his zeal and ability, Hoover was promoted to FBI director, a post he held from 1924 to 1972. The Ku Klux Klan rose up again, this time with approximately 5 million dues-paying fanatics in its ranks. The 1924 Immigration Act set quotas on immigration that favored white European Protestants over all other aspirants. The next year, in Tennessee, the world watched a court case to see if a young biologist, John Scopes, would be sentenced to jail for breaking a state law prohibiting the teaching of evolution to high-school students. The court found Scopes guilty and Europeans generally labeled American fundamentalism a backwoods and backwards philosophy.

Meanwhile, business was booming. In 1928, presidential candidate Herbert Hoover announced: "We in America today are nearer to the final triumph over poverty than ever before in the history of any land. . . . [P]overty will be banished from this nation." One year later, on 29 October 1929, the stock market crashed and the Great Depression stalked the land. By January 1933, the economic situation entered its cruelest year with thousands of people dying from starvation and nearly 12 million others unable to find work [See Illustration 1.3].

Illustration 1.3 "There's No Way Like the American Way"

Photographer Margaret Bourke White captured the pathos of the 1930s in racially-segregated bread lines, unemployed men and women, and the myth of the American Dream. For the people standing in line, the advertisement with the smiling, white, nuclear family in the new car drove home the ways inequality and discrimination made the Great Depression more devastating for the majority of African Americans.

(Margaret Bourke-White/Getty Images)

A New Deal and the Second World War

No president in the twentieth century had a greater impact on American life than Franklin Delano Roosevelt (FDR). Voters elected him four times and he ruled a dozen years in the White House, 1933–45. FDR used optimistic radio chats to persuade listeners that, "The only thing we have to fear is fear itself." His New Deal economic recovery plan was a pragmatic approach – profoundly conservative and profoundly revolutionary – to help people find hope and paychecks. In his first "hundred days" in office, FDR sent over 100 pieces of reform legislation to Congress and, in so doing, created the American welfare state – a stark contrast to the long-standing Jeffersonian maxim that "the government which governs best, governs least." Still, the Great Depression ended only after the start of World War II in Europe in 1939.

With the public refusing to take part in another European war, the United States once again declared its neutrality but supplied the British. Then, on Sunday, 7 December 1941 – in Roosevelt's phrasing, "a date that will live in infamy" – the Japanese attack on Pearl Harbor naval base rushed America into war. The power of the national government soared as it established wage and price controls, rationed products, decided what would be produced, and raised income taxes. Americans migrated to the cities and moved west, especially to California. Women and African Americans entered the workforce in large numbers as over 16 million men joined or were drafted into the military. FDR declared it illegal to discriminate in hiring for government jobs and Congress passed a Fair Employment Practices Act. By 1944, America produced twice as much war material as Germany and Japan combined. Government spending increased from $8 billion a year in 1936 to $98 billion in 1945. In the Pacific, US forces fought an island-by-island campaign, before developing and dropping the two atomic bombs on Japan that ended the war. Three hundred thousand Americans died in the Second World War even though the country's major contribution was weaponry.

The Cold War

The 1950s

With the war over and colonial empires crumbling, the world entered into a "Cold War" increasingly divided into blocs led by the Soviet Union and the United States. Americans reached a consensus that Soviets were evil atheists out for world domination and concluded that the United States was the only country capable of stopping them. As the United States accepted the superpower role it still maintains, the country moved from a dependence on conventional armies to a strategy of sophisticated airpower, long-range missiles, nuclear submarines, and thermonuclear warheads.

After a decade of economic depression followed by a four-year war where personal spending was limited and where savings accounts bulged with $140 billion, Americans began to consume. Millions of veterans used the new "G. I. Bill" to get university degrees, and in the process, increased the numbers of US research universities. As the middle class expanded and prospered, they became more homogenized and seemed to reach a basic consensus about values and culture. Sociologist David Reisman's *The Lonely Crowd* (1950) described this as a loss of individualism and the change to a new conformity of doing what others expected. The primary expression of wealth was the baby boom of 1945–57 which saw the birthrate soar to 25 births per 1,000 people – about 4 million babies a year. Larger families promoted a demand for housing construction and the automobile allowed for far-flung suburban communities. By 1960 the majority of Americans lived in the suburbs, commuted on the new interstate highway system, and bought what they needed in shopping malls.

To renew themselves, Americans turned to religion and listened to radio evangelists like Billy Graham who preached that true Americans were Christians, not "godless Communists." In 1954, Congress added the words "under God" to the Pledge of Allegiance, and the next year put the words "In God We Trust" on every piece of currency. Christianity demanded order and pressured women to return to the domestic sphere to raise "decent" children. Thousands obeyed, but thousands more were reluctant to give up the freedom and equality provided by a paycheck. The "two-income family" lifted the status of working women and increased disposable income so that most white Americans lived in what economist John Kenneth Galbraith called *The Affluent Society* (1958). The white poor, Native Americans, migrant laborers and most African Americans continued to struggle.

In *Brown* v. *Board of Education* (1954), the Supreme Court ordered the integration of the nation's schools. The next year, protestors in Montgomery, Alabama, refused to ride the segregated city bus lines and found a leader in Martin Luther King, Jr. Latinos and American Indians began to protest their poverty and second-class citizenship in the richest country on earth. A growing youth culture turned to jazz, marijuana, and Rock-'n'-Roll to challenge the conformity in the suburbs.

During the 1950s, Americans became hysterical over "Reds." Congress used the House Un-American Activities Committee (HUAC) – which was formed in 1938 to explore whether or not the New Deal welfare programs were "creeping socialism" – to uncover conspiracies against the American way of life. HUAC's Richard Nixon headed the investigation into the stealing of atomic secrets by foreign spies. Actor Ronald Reagan accused Hollywood of harboring communists, and the "Red Scare" accelerated after Senator Joseph McCarthy claimed that communists had infiltrated the government. As McCarthyism and the Korean War increased the American paranoia over communist expansion, voters in 1952 elected US Army General Dwight D. Eisenhower to the presidency. Eisenhower calmed fears by denouncing McCarthy and encouraging economic growth.

He believed in the partnership between government and business, and he held to a philosophy: "What is good for General Motors is also good for our country." The government invested in weaponry and big businesses profited in what Eisenhower critically termed the "military-industrial complex." Things were booming like never before.

The 1960s

The decade opened with a presidential election between Republican Vice-President Richard Milhous Nixon and Democratic Senator John Fitzgerald Kennedy (JFK). Both were anti-communists who had supported McCarthy's witchhunt. Nixon appealed to conservative Protestants and Kennedy, a Catholic, fought to downplay rumors that he was controlled by the Pope. Nixon pushed for television debates – and got them. But television was kinder to Kennedy, whose camera presence won the election.

At his inauguration, Kennedy challenged Americans to "ask not what your country can do for you, ask what you can do for your country." His womanizing – including Marilyn Monroe – was not high media drama in days when the press seemed more capable of separating private actions from public discourse. Kennedy's domestic program, the "New Frontier," raised the minimum wage, built low-cost housing for the poor, sponsored a redevelopment program for poverty-stricken Appalachia – the mountainous area of twelve states from southern New York to northern Alabama – and appointed more minorities to federal jobs than anyone had done before. Yet, JFK insisted on balancing the budget instead of spending on social welfare programs and even though he supported the efforts of Martin Luther King, Jr., his administration could not be counted on to stand up to determined Southern white racism.

It was in foreign policy that Kennedy made his mark, even after a bad start. A CIA-planned invasion of Cuba failed, and a few months later the world awoke to a new barrier – and a Soviet victory – the Berlin Wall. Emboldened, Cuban President Fidel Castro and Soviet leader Nikita Khrushchev put missiles in Cuba in October 1962. Kennedy responded by threatening nuclear war if the missiles were not removed. When Khrushchev capitulated, Kennedy's popularity rose. Americans also admired Kennedy's establishment of the Peace Corps because it fit into the historical missionary zeal of bringing democracy and "American know-how" to developing countries. They liked his determination to win the space race by putting a man on the moon before the decade ended and supported, but could not foresee the consequences of, his order sending 16,000 combat advisors to Vietnam. Then, on 22 November 1963, a sniper – or, according to a proliferation of conspiracy theories, snipers – assassinated him in Dallas, Texas.

JFK-the-martyr myth immediately rose up in the American imagination as a shining promise of what might have been. His beatification eased the way for his successor, Lyndon Johnson, to declare a "war on poverty" and to promote his "Great Society" programs for raising the lot of the underprivileged. Minority groups were already resisting their exclusion from the affluent society. In the farms of the West where workers labored long days for poor pay and no benefits packages, Cesar Chavez organized migrant Chicano laborers into the United Farm Workers Union. The African American Civil Rights Movement hit high gear, and mass protests created turmoil and brought world opinion to bear on discrimination and racism. Martin Luther King used non-violent moral pressure, but others, like Malcolm X and the Black Panthers, increasingly believed that violence could be a revolutionary tool. From 1964 to 1968, race riots erupted across urban America. In this climate of anger and fear, further assassinations followed: Malcolm X (1965), Martin Luther King, Jr. (1968), and presidential candidate Robert Kennedy (1968). Domestic violence combined with the demoralizing war in Vietnam to destroy the Great Society.

The nation divided sharply along generational, philosophical, gender, and racial lines. When it became clear that the Vietnam War had drifted into genocide and that there were limits to American power, anti-war protests further split society as women, environmentalists, blacks, Latinos, gays, American Indians, hippies, and students demanded change. Johnson was beseiged by the incessant chanting outside the Oval Office: "Hey, Hey LBJ! How many kids you kill today?" and "Two, Four, Six, Eight, We don't want to integrate!" and "Power! Black Power!" He did not run for re-election.

The 1970s

Richard Nixon was back, promising "peace with honor" in Vietnam and a return to "law and order" at home. Americans – whom Nixon called "the Great Silent Majority" – elected him to the presidency in 1968 and 1972. He eventually pulled American troops out of Vietnam, but only after a savage escalation of bombing forced the peace. Nixon also made overtures to Russia and China and foreign policy entered an era of détente. In domestic affairs, he promoted a

"New Federalism" to reduce the role of the national government by returning power to the states and placed thousands of police in America's streets to reestablish domestic order.

The scandals came quickly. Daniel Ellsberg, a Pentagon official, leaked top-secret documents, the Pentagon Papers, to the *New York Times.* The *Washington Post* uncovered a story about the 1972 burglary of the Democratic National Headquarters in the Watergate building. The first story revealed the misinformation campaign and outright lies the Johnson administration told the American people about Vietnam. The second story revealed that Nixon had known about the burglary and had covered it up. The Senate investigated the matter, television turned it into high drama, and when Congress threatened to impeach him, Nixon resigned. Watergate was a triumph for a liberal press, the checks and balances system and the American people, but it also increased American fears of conspiracy and mistrust of government. With the years of social turmoil and assassinations, the nation's first war defeat, a stagnant economy with high inflation, and two presidents dishonored for lying, the American people suffered a crisis in confidence.

Usually the elected vice-president becomes president when a vacancy occurs out-of-sync with the normal election cycle, but, before Nixon resigned, Vice President Spiro Agnew had been found guilty of tax evasion and had stepped down. Nixon selected Gerald Ford to fill Agnew's position, effectively making Ford the only "appointed" president in US history. Still, the people felt better to have a man known to be scrupulously honest at the helm. Ford made Americans laugh when he declared upon taking office, "I'm a Ford, not a Lincoln" – a word-play on a common automobile and a luxury car (Lincoln Continental), as well as the obvious connection. Americans were prepared to suspend judgment when the unthinkable happened – Ford issued an executive pardon, freeing Nixon from criminal prosecution. While Ford explained it as a way to end "our long national nightmare," most Americans saw the action as yet another misuse of executive privilege (Ford, 1974). Runaway inflation and recession marked the post-Vietnam years.

In 1976, Georgia Governor Jimmy Carter defeated Ford by making a single campaign promise never to lie to the American people. In domestic affairs, Carter could not stop inflation, which rose to 14 percent as unemployment topped 7 percent for the first time since the Depression. An energy crisis hurt the economy when Islamic oil-producing states cut oil exports in protest of US-Israeli actions in the Middle East. Two disasters also indicated governmental failures.

In 1978, at a housing development in Niagara Falls, New York, called "Love Canal," hundreds of people suffered when dioxin – one of the deadliest poisons ever made – rose up from the toxic waste dump nearby. The next year, at Three Mile Island in Pennsylvania, a nuclear power plant released radioactive gases into the atmosphere. As disasters piled up and the economy continued to tumble, Carter spoke to the nation about a "crisis in the American spirit," and of "self-indulgence and overconsumption" to the point that "Human identity is no longer defined by what one does but by what one owns" (Carter, 1979). Whereas Carter had hoped to inspire the nation to overcome its "malaise" and redeem itself, the media and the American people faulted presidential actions and a lack of leadership as mainly responsible for America's woes.

Carter did better in the global arena, deftly handling a treaty returning the canal zone to Panama, officially recognizing the People's Republic of China, brokering the peace between Egypt and Israel that ended their 30-years' war, and campaigning worldwide for human rights. But those successes were overcome in the long year of 1980 when Iranian revolutionaries held 52 Americans hostage in Tehran after the overthrow of the US-backed Shah. Carter's diplomatic efforts failed and the American people fumed over Muslim terrorists and Arab oil embargoes. When Carter seemed to be locked in the White House doing nothing, his popularity tumbled. When he tried a rescue mission with helicopter gunships, a dust storm in the desert spoiled the attempt, and Americans blamed him personally.

The Reagan Era

Rising prices, energy shortages, hostages, and social turmoil, fed into the rising right-wing resurgence. In 1979, in the United Kingdom, the conservative Margaret Thatcher was elected prime minister. In 1980, in the United States, voters opted for the governor of California, a former actor in second-rate movies, a charismatic cowboy who was threatening war with Iran if it did not return the hostages. Ronald Reagan beat Carter by a landslide electoral college vote of 489–49 after promising to return Americans to confidence by stressing patriotism and revitalizing the military. At 69, he was the oldest president the country had ever elected, his grandfatherly chuckle charmed voters, and his acting ability gained him the sobriquet "the Great Communicator."

On inauguration day, Iran released the hostages – there had been a secret deal. Reagan continued his aggressive stance, labeling the

Soviet Union "an evil empire" and vowing to intervene militarily if anyone threatened US interests. This high-risk strategy made the world uneasy while it strengthened American confidence. Reagan approved expensive high-tech projects, got the military budget increased from $136 to $244 billion – four times the amount spent per minute during the Vietnam War – and promoted a "Star Wars" defense system in outer space to protect the US against a nuclear strike by another power. But Reagan's approach did not bring peace or security. When he sent marines into Lebanon in 1983 as part of a peacekeeping force, terrorists used a truck bomb to kill 239 of them. Reagan withdrew the soldiers. In 1985, Muslim fundamentalists held various Americans hostage, hijacked airplanes, killed an American tourist on a cruise ship near Crete, and bombed an American nightclub in Munich. Frustrated by the inability to hold any country responsible, Reagan sent an airstrike against Libyan leader Muammar Qadhafi for his support of terrorists.

Reagan was more successful in stopping Cuban-led insurgency in Grenada. He also approved of CIA help to the "Contras" – a rightwing group in Nicaragua trying to overthrow an elected socialist government. Worried that the US might be getting involved in another Vietnam, Congress ordered all funding to the Contras stopped. At that point, Lt. Colonel Oliver North – a deputy to the National Security Advisor – devised a plan to use the money from a secret arms deal with Iran to fund the revolution in Nicaragua. Patently illegal, the press called the events "Irangate" – echoing the Watergate scandal – and a congressional investigation revealed a presidency out of control, one managed so loosely that non-elected officials could subvert the orders of Congress. Reagan said he knew nothing of it and the matter faded away.

Reagan's domestic policy rolled back the social welfare programs begun in the New Deal and expanded during the Great Society. Individual responsibility and free market capitalism were revived. Social commentators spoke of "lifestyle choices" as a way to explain away poverty, failure, and multiculturalism. Reagan got tax breaks for the rich and called for an increase in capital punishment, harsher penalties for drug use, more prisons, and bigger police departments.

In 1988, Reagan's two-term vice president, George Bush, easily defeated the Democratic nominee Michael Dukakis. Bush spoke of a "kinder, gentler" America while he maintained Reagan's economic policies. He benefited from breathtaking events in Eastern Europe: the Berlin Wall came down, Germany reunited, and Soviet President Mikhail Gorbachev's reform policies led to the collapse and breakup of the Soviet Union into national states. The Warsaw Pact no longer existed and Eastern Europe moved toward free-market capitalism, something Bush called "the New World Order."

In August 1990, Iraq invaded Kuwait, only to be surprised at the quick and determined response of Bush, who by January had deployed over 500,000 American troops to the Persian Gulf. The quick victory in "Operation Desert Storm" boosted his popularity at home. But the economy slowed and, wanting to balance the budget, Bush sought to reduce government domestic programs while reneging on his 1988 campaign promise, "Read my lips! No new taxes!" The American public resisted any further cuts in health care and the tax increase infuriated conservatives. In the election of 1992, 19 million disgruntled voters supported a third-party candidate, Texas computer billionaire Ross Perot. This split in the conservative vote elected the Democratic nominee, a young lawyer and governor from a small Southern state, who played saxophone on MTV: William Jefferson Clinton.

The 1990s

Coinciding with Clinton's presidency, the US economy entered its longest period of expansion, unemployment fell to historic lows, inflation bottomed out, crime rates plunged dramatically, civil disorders nearly ceased, and world leaders generally approved of the change in leadership styles and rhetoric. Clinton's election lifted the first baby-boomer into the Oval Office, leaving behind the personal memories of the World War II generation. The president's wife, Hillary Rodham, had a law degree from Yale University, a daughter Chelsea, an established career, and was an equal partner in political strategy. The Clintons would share the presidency and put forth an ambitious agenda to increase health care, fix the economy, end deficit spending, erase discrimination, reduce violence, and give more power to the states.

Immediately, Clinton was in trouble. With his first order as Commander-in-Chief, Clinton removed the ban on homosexuals enlisting in the armed forces. The backlash by military leaders and homophobic Americans was so great that the president had to compromise to a "Don't ask, don't tell" policy, meaning that recruiters would not ask about sexual preference and gays should not reveal themselves (quoted in Tindall and Shi, 1996: 1545). Simultaneously, the disclosure that the Clintons had received insider treatment in a real-estate deal was coupled with lawsuits charging the president with sexual misconduct while he was Governor of Arkansas. Suddenly, everyone had a story to tell about Clinton's womanizing. In the midst of a hailstorm of allegations, Clinton appointed his wife to chair the committee to change the health care system to a universal benefit package for all Americans. Critics charged nepotism and asked "Just who does *she* think she is?" Health care reform was defeated because a coalition of opposition groups, including doctors, hospitals, and small business owners, thought they would lose profits or have to pay the bulk of the health premiums in an expanded benefits system.

By 1994, media attacks on the Clintons created enough of a backlash to elect a Republican majority in the House and Senate for the first time since the 1950s. House Republicans, led by Speaker Newt Gingrich, pushed a "Contract With America" which would offer tax cuts, put term limits on politicians, expand the death penalty, restrict welfare, and pass a constitutional Amendment to balance the budget. The Senate refused to agree to the Contract and the president vetoed the Republican budget proposal because it sliced Medicare payments, reduced environmental protection, and cut taxes too much. Because the House has the constitutional power over the government's purse, without an approved budget there is no money. Twice, in efforts to force Clinton to sign the budget, Gingrich allowed the government to shut down, delaying all payroll checks to civil-service employees, the military, and politicians. Gingrich miscalculated as the public supported the president and blamed Congress. As coincidence often affects politics, Timothy McVeigh, an extremist in Oklahoma City who wanted to strike a blow against big government, exploded a truck bomb at the federal building killing 169 people, including a dozen children in a day-care center. The American people rallied to the president.

Additionally, the stock market was booming and military involvement abroad was limited to peacekeeping missions in Africa (Somalia, Rwanda) and Eastern Europe (the former Yugoslavia). With the 1996 election approaching, Clinton announced his intention to balance the budget by 2002 and adopted the Reagan plan of returning power to the states. Clinton was a fabulous talker and his ability to read the mood of the American people provided the margin for victory over Republican Bob Dole.

Gender played a huge factor in the election as women favored Democratic policies, particularly the pro-choice stance on abortion. Clinton responded by appointing more women to high positions than anyone had done before, including Attorney General Janet Reno,

Supreme Court Justice Ruth Bader Ginsberg, and Secretary of State Madeleine Albright.

Political analyst Joe Klein defined the "Clinton conundrum" as "solid policy and brilliant politics obscured by the consequences of tawdry personal behavior" (Klein, 2002: 21). Clinton could not restrain his libido and found himself in real trouble when a 21-year-old intern, Monica Lewinsky, told a friend that she had been having sex with the president and that she had a sperm-stained dress to prove it. Clinton went on national television, looked the country straight in the face, and stated, "I did not have sexual relations with that woman, Miss Lewinsky" (quoted in Campbell, 1998). When he later admitted that he had lied under oath, the House voted for impeachment and the Senate trial dragged on for a month. The American people were titillated but forgiving. By a majority of nearly 80 percent in most polls, the people disapproved of the trial. The Senate voted 50-50 for conviction. Since a two-thirds majority, 67 votes, is necessary to remove a president, the vote was a victory for Clinton. Americans wanted to continue the era of hope that the post-Cold War promised, an end of history in terms of ideological strife and a focus on prosperity and globalization for all.

The Twenty-First Century

It was not to be. The presidential election of 2000 was a close contest which pitted George Walker Bush, the Republican Governor of Texas and son of the man Bill Clinton defeated in 1992, against the sitting vice president, Albert Gore. Gore won the popular vote nationally by a narrow margin but Bush won enough states – and thereby electoral votes – to gain the White House. The election was disputed because of voting irregularities in Florida. After both Bush and Gore filed lawsuits to contest the vote, the United States Supreme Court, in a political decision based on the justices' preferences, issued a 5–4 judgment declaring that Bush had won in Florida. The White House belonged to the Republicans.

Because of the way Bush gained the presidency, Democrats felt cheated and were polarized, while Republicans believed the system had proven its worth. The Religious Right believed there had been a divine intervention and they looked forward to the next four years of conservative power. They would not be disappointed. Bush appointed two conservative Supreme Court justices and filled the Department of Justice with lawyers of whom the Religious Right approved. But before Bush could focus on further changes in domestic policies, his attention was diverted to foreign policy by the terrorist attacks of 11 September 2001. His first term was overwhelmingly focused on what was immediately dubbed "The War on Terror." In 2002, at the first Fourth of July celebration after the assaults of 11 September, Bush called up the past in the present by making reference to the American Revolution: "We love our country only more when she's threatened. . . . All Americans can draw a straight line from the free lives we lead today to that one moment, when the world changed forever. From that day in 1776, freedom has had a home and freedom has had a defender" (quoted in AP, 2002). Citing Jefferson and the familiar touchstone of freedom, Bush struck the essential chord of memory in the American experience. The American people rallied behind the president.

In 2004, Bush was reelected because most Americans agreed with his approach to defeating tyranny and terrorism at home and abroad. Voters also believed that on the issue of character, Bush was closer to the mainstream than was his Democratic opponent John Kerry. Bush won the election handily and claimed a "mandate" to pursue his programs. He stressed the nation's character by citing its historical, religious, and political struggles in the defense of freedom. In his second inaugural address, Bush emphasized the theme of an "ownership society": the idea that people have a stake in their communities and should control their own destinies. Vice President Dick Cheney – who became the most influential vice president in American history – agreed with these sentiments, explaining that "ownership is a path to greater opportunity, more freedom and more control over your own life, and this goal is worthy of a great nation. Everyone deserves a chance to live the American dream" (quoted in Rosenbaum, 2005). The second Bush administration insisted that the road to a such a society was filled with obstacles, but it could be gained. Overall, the American people have judged his greatest failure to be the War in Iraq. His greatest success was in keeping any further terrorist attacks from taking place on American soil. Many analysts call him the worst president in American history and speak of his failed presidency. Toward the end of his presidency, Bush went to Iraq to praise the progress of the new government there. When an Iraqi journalist stood and threw two shoes at Bush, many people around the world and in the United States felt that he was throwing shoes for everyone (see Illustration 1.4).

In the chapters that follow, *Contemporary America* furthers the explanation of the most recent past – the successes and failures of

Illustration 1.4 President Bush Assaulted in Iraq

On 14 December 2008, President George W. Bush and Iraqi Prime Minister Nuri Kamal al-Maliki held a joint press conference in Baghdad to announce a new security agreement and praise the progress Iraq has made toward democracy since the overthrow of Saddam Hussein in 2003. Taking issue with that purpose, Iraqi journalist Muntader al-Zaidi, stood up, denounced Bush as "you dog," and threw two well-aimed shoes, barely missing an agile president. Mr. Bush was unhurt (Myers and Rubin, 2008). At his trial in February 2009, Mr. al-Zaidi pleaded "not guilty" and called his actions "a natural response to the occupation." The Iraqi court sentenced him to three years in prison (AP, 2009a).

(AP/Press Association Images, 2008)

the Bush years – even while it focuses its attention squarely on the American people and the policies and promises of the Obama era. Obama continues to make sharp departures from his predecessor in policy formulations and overall approaches to matters both domestic and foreign. His approach to governing is substantially different from what came before him. His belief in separating science from religion and in allowing radically different viewpoints to coexist in cabinet meetings represents a significant departure from the ideologically-driven policies of Bush and Cheney. *Contemporary America* explores the contours of change and continuity in the United States now under the leadership of Barack Obama.

2

Land and People

The United States has a diverse and expansive population and geography. In 1790, the first US Census counted 3,929,214 people on 891,364 square miles of land. On January 1, 2009, with a population of 305,629,269 and a total area of 3,679,192 square miles (9,529,063 sq. km), the US is the third-largest country in population and the fourth-largest in size. The continental distance is immense. Between New York City and San Francisco it is 3,200 miles (5,200 km), about the same distance as from New York to London. Alaska alone covers 586,412 square miles (1,518,807 sq. km) and is 2,300 miles (3,700 km) long.

No other nation has a wider range of ethnic, racial, or cultural variations or possesses a physical environment including Arctic tundra, subtropical rainforests, natural harbors, arid deserts, fertile prairies, three continental mountain ranges, active volcanoes, prehistoric swamplands, geysers, great inland seas, multiple networks of lakes and rivers, and three ocean borders. Excepting Hawaii and Alaska, the nation is confined geographically by the same latitudes stretching between northern France and Egypt and is as large as the whole of Europe combined. America's highest point is Mt. McKinley in Alaska at 20,320 feet (6,194 m) and the lowest and hottest point is Death Valley in California–Nevada at 282 feet (86 m) below sea level and a record-high temperature of 134 degrees Fahrenheit (57 C).

The United States has nearly 200 cities with 100,000 or more people and at least 80 percent of the national population lives in urban or suburban areas. This leaves vast open spaces and a feeling of "emptiness." Exemplifying this small population and large land mass, in 2008, 30 of the 50 states had smaller populations than did tiny Denmark, with 5.5 million people. Additionally, the population density of the US is 33 people per square kilometer as compared to

Japan's 340, Britain's 252, Germany's 236, and China's 142 (CIA, 2008). Table 2.1 indicates the actual and relative sizes of the United States and selected states within the United States in comparison with other countries.

Table 2.1 Country and State Comparisons

Entity	*Area (sq. miles)**	*Population** (millions)*
Russia	6,592,817	140.1
China	3,705,392	1330.0
India	1,147,950	1148.0
Canada	3,851,794	33.2
Mexico	742,486	110.0
USA	3,539,227	305.6
France	210,668	64.1
Afghanistan	250,000	32.7
Texas	267,277	24.3
Spain	192,819	40.5
Iraq	167,556	28.2
California	158,869	36.8
Germany	135,236	82.4
Japan	152,411	127.3
Montana	147,046	1.0
Poland	117,571	38.5
Vietnam	125,622	86.1
New Mexico	121,598	2.0
Italy	113,521	58.1
Philippines	115,124	96.1
Arizona	114,006	6.5
UK	93,278	61.0
Ghana	88,811	23.4
Oregon	97,132	3.8
South Korea	38,023	48.4
Portugal	35,382	10.7
Maine	33,741	1.3
Denmark	16,359	5.5
Taiwan	13,892	22.9
Maryland	12,297	5.6

* 1 square mile equals approximately 2.6 square kilometers.
** Population is rounded to the nearest 100,000.

Source: CIA Factbook, 2008.

The Land

The landmass of the contiguous 48 states (see Map 2.1) is framed by the Pacific Ocean and Sierra Nevada mountain range on the west and the Atlantic Ocean and Appalachian mountain range on the east. The Gulf of Mexico and Rio Grande river mark the border with Mexico; the St. Lawrence seaway and the Great Lakes establish much of the border with Canada. The country is bisected by the world's third-longest river, the Mississippi (3,740 m/6,020 km), which begins in Minnesota, irrigates and drains half the continent, and pours into the Gulf of Mexico just south of New Orleans. The United States is further dissected by the Rocky Mountains, a high range stretching southwards from Alaska to New Mexico.

With the exceptions of Alaska, the Pacific Islands, Puerto Rico, and the southern portions of Florida, Texas, and California, the United States is in the temperate zone and enjoys four distinct seasons. All US cities outside Alaska experience hot summers. The warm water of the Atlantic Gulf Stream spawns hurricanes and thunderstorms from Texas to Maine, and hot weather in the country's midsection combines with flat land to produce over 1,000 tornadoes every year. With global warming, the frequency and power of hurricanes has increased, as Hurricane Katrina showed in 2005 when it destroyed homes and lives as it drowned the city of New Orleans. At frequent intervals, too much rain or snow raise the level of the Mississippi-Missouri-Ohio river system, flooding areas to create lakes hundreds of miles wide. In winter, an arctic or "Canadian" jet stream blows from west to east, dipping as far as the middle of the United States and bringing severely cold weather and heavy snows to the northern states.

East of the Rockies and along most of the Pacific coast, the United States has adequate to above-average rainfall, punctuated in recent years by moderate periods of drought. This combines with the rich soil of the Midwest, the South, and California to provide a bountiful agricultural production in grains, fruits, and vegetables. Where the rainfall is less, but still sufficient to grow grass, cattle farmers and cowboys operate massive livestock businesses on a monotonous landscape.

Natural Resources

The country has vast natural resources in almost everything, including timber, oil, natural gas, coal, iron ore, bauxite, uranium, gold, copper, and silver. It also controls nearly 12,500 miles (20,000 km) of coastline

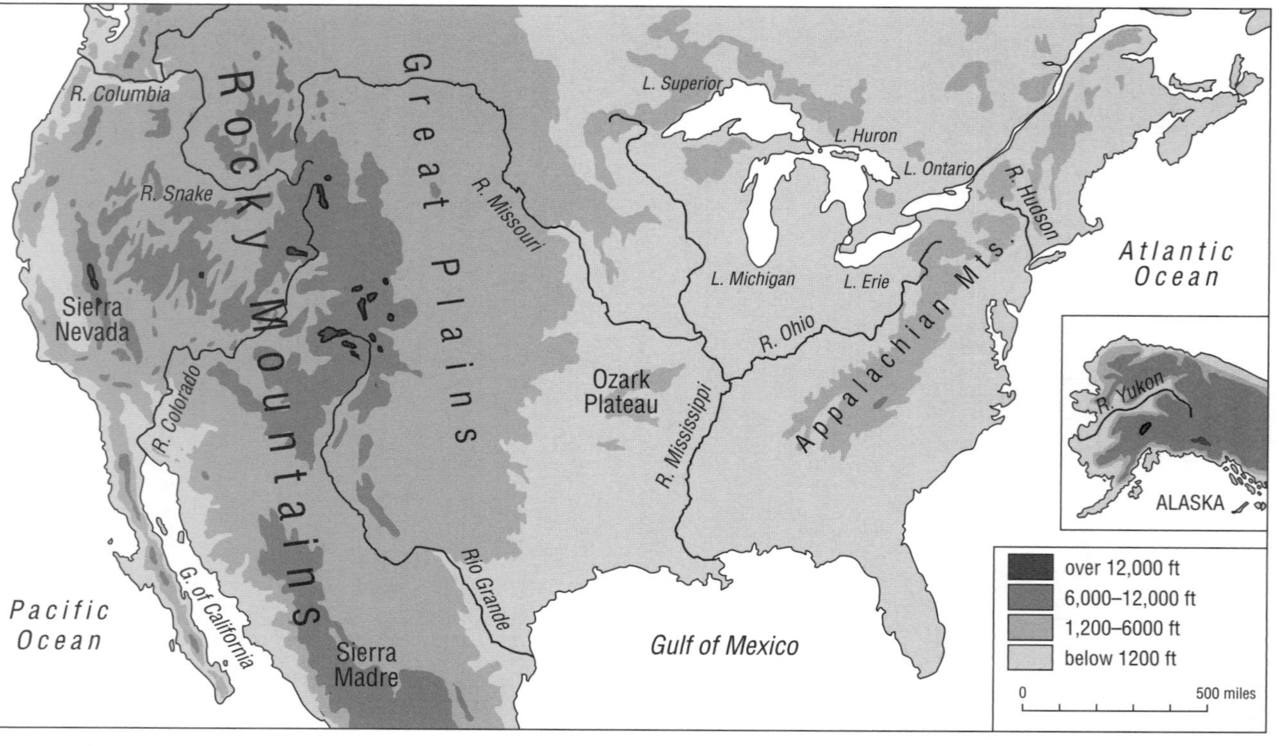

Map 2.1 Major Topographical Features

from which to import and export products and to send out fishing fleets. For over 200 years, Europeans wrote to relatives about what seemed to be limitless forests and of their own handiwork in using an axe for taming the wilderness. Today, US timber companies clear-cut whole areas of woodlands and fight with environmentalists over the destruction of old growth forests, most of which are protected by law. The companies also plant more trees than they cut each year, ensuring a growth cycle which renews the forests every 20 years.

America has rich reservoirs of oil, found mostly along the Gulf of Mexico in Texas and Louisiana, but also in Oklahoma, Pennsylvania, and elsewhere. The biggest oilfield is in Alaska and a trans-Alaskan pipeline carries the crude oil to coastal shipping and refining firms. Still, the American love for the automobile means that the country consumes far more oil than it produces and is the world's major importer of petroleum. Copper and silver are mined primarily in Nevada, New Mexico, and Colorado. The vast iron ore deposits in Wisconsin and Michigan and the world's largest coal mines – in West Virginia and Pennsylvania – ensure that the country's steel mills are well supplied. Two-thirds of the world's known uranium deposits are located under the Navajo Indian reservation in Arizona. The United States uses the uranium for its military and to power over 100 nuclear power reactors in 31 states.

With this wealth in resources causing a mindset of unlimited abundance, Americans have often run roughshod over the land, depleting the soil, overkilling animals, polluting the environment and wasting resources. Fur traders and soldiers slaughtered millions of bison; by 1889, fewer than 1,000 animals remained alive. Old growth forests were lost through logging practices that scalped whole areas, strip mining in open mines scarred the earth, the dumping of chemicals into waste heaps caused health problems, and rivers and lakes became so polluted that whole ecosystems were changed.

The EPA and Global Warming

In 1970, the Nixon administration established a national policy for the environment and created the Environmental Protection Agency (EPA). The EPA tries to achieve a balance between population size and resource use and sets national standards for the emissions of greenhouse gases, supports anti-pollution activities, regulates the disposal of toxic wastes, monitors noise levels, pesticide use, ocean dumping, and issues Environmental Impact Statements on the possible consequences of new building sites. The EPA's 18,000 employees research and set national standards for water and air quality, test compliance, and issue sanctions against any corporation, individual, state, or Indian tribe which violates the standards.

Twenty-five percent of all greenhouse gases causing global warming are currently spewn from US sources – not a surprising number given that US factories produce twenty-five percent of the world's industrial products. In 2001, the Senate failed to ratify the 2000 Kyoto Protocol on Climate Change after President Bush announced that he would not support the measure. The world viewed this as an act of bad faith because Clinton administration representatives – led by then-Vice President Al Gore – had agreed to reduce pollution under the protocol. Bush disputed the consensus by scientists worldwide that with increasing levels of carbon dioxide, it is "very likely" that global warming will continue to accelerate (see Illustration 2.2). Twelve US states and thirteen environmental groups filed legal challenges. In 2007 the US Supreme Court ruled that the EPA has offered no reasoned explanation for its refusal to decide whether greenhouse gases cause or contribute to climate change" (Sherman, 2007). Bush continued to dally.

Al Gore has become the most distinguished voice for a cleaner environment, continuing his longtime advocacy for ecological reform, begun in his 1992 book, *Earth in the Balance*. In 2006 he had a best-selling book and Academy Award winning documentary film, *An Inconvenient Truth: The Crisis of Global Warming* (see Illustration 2.1). In 2007, the Nobel committee awarded him the Peace Prize for his work. At the awards ceremony in Stockholm, Gore warned (Gore, 2007):

> So today, we dumped another 70 million tons of global-warming pollution into the thin shell of atmosphere surrounding our planet, as if it were an open sewer. And tomorrow, we will dump a slightly larger amount, with the cumulative concentrations now trapping more and more heat from the sun. . . . As a result, the earth has a fever. And the fever is rising. The experts have told us it is not a passing affliction that will heal by itself. . . . We, the human species, are confronting a planetary emergency – a threat to the survival of our civilization that is gathering ominous and destructive potential even as we gather here. But there is hopeful news as well: we have the ability to solve this crisis and avoid the worst – though not all – of its consequences, if we act boldly, decisively and quickly.

With Barack Obama and a new Congress, perhaps the United States will lead the war against global warming, reforming its policies and encouraging China and India to higher standards. A week after taking

Illustration 2.1 Al Gore and the Fight to Stop Global Warming

In 2006, former Vice President Albert Gore starred in *An Inconvenient Truth* – an informational film about global warming and what to do about it. The film won an Academy Award for best documentary filmmaking. Gore's book by the same name was translated into many languages and, as in the photo above, Gore toured many nations to advocate increased vigilance in the fight to cut back on carbon dioxide emissions. In 2007, the Nobel committee cited Gore as "the single individual who has done the most to create greater worldwide understanding of the measures that need to be adopted" to stop global warming. For those efforts, Albert Gore received the Nobel Prize for Peace.

(Itsuo Inouye/AP/Press Association Images, 2007)

office, Obama announced his support for more stringent automobile emission control limits.

National Parks

In 1871, Congress established the nation's first national park, Yellowstone, in Montana and Idaho; and in 1890, Yosemite in California. In 1903, President Theodore Roosevelt overrode Congressional criticism to set aside millions of acres of national lands, thereby enlisting the government into conservation. Congress created the National Park Service (NPS) in 1916 to administer lands put into the public trust. In 2006, the NPS controlled 84 million acres

(34 million hectares) in 391 parks and had 273 million visitors. In addition to the NPS, each of the 50 states has a state park system for recreational and conservation purposes, for a total of more than 5,000 state parks nationwide.

The largest national park is Wrangell-St. Elias National Park in Alaska, at over 13.2 million acres (5.3 million hectares), established in 1978 during the Carter administration. Generally, Democratic presidents have supported programs protecting public lands; Republican presidents resisted the creation of more parks and wanted existing reserves opened to private exploitation. Two recent presidencies are illustrative of this difference. The Clinton administration banned road-building and commercial logging on 60 million acres (24 million hectares) of forests, increased the size of many national parks, established 11 new national monuments and adopted tougher standards for automobile emissions. The Sierra Club and the Wilderness Society praised Clinton and hailed 2000 as the best year for conservation since the Carter administration (Booth, 2001).

On the other hand, Bush opened parks and Indian reservations for oil exploration, power plants, logging, and mining. He was especially keen on oil production in Alaska's National Wildlife Reserve, which contains an estimated 10 billion barrels of oil buried under the fragile tundra ecosystem. Bush believed that the economy, jobs, and national security trumped most environmental concerns (see Illustration 2.2). In his last budget, Bush asked for $379 million in budget cuts for the National Forest System and wildlife management – a drop of 75 percent from 2001.

Another issue is the decrease in biodiversity as thousands of animals and plants are now extinct and the rate seems to be increasing to as many as two hundred species a year. Americans are concerned that the loss of biodiversity might threaten the planet but they concentrate more on the environmental movement. Congress passed a Clean Air Act (1970) and Water Pollution Control Act (1972) to ban pesticides, require unleaded gasoline and levy huge fines for dumping waste. Thousands of laws nationwide provide environmental protection.

In addition to the land set aside for parks, the federal government has designated more than 93 million acres (37 million hectares) as National Wildlife Refuges. These refuges protect animals and plants, restrict sightseeing, and prohibit fishing, hunting, and rock collecting. In 1973, Congress passed the Endangered Species Act (ESA) to provide guidelines for the protection of certain species. One of the more recent successes has been the recovery of the American Bald Eagle, one of the world's largest soaring birds and the longtime symbol of the American nation. When Europeans arrived in the New World, there were an estimated 500,000 nesting pairs present. Hunters and the widespread use of pesticides reduced the population to 500 pairs before the ESA listed the bird as its top priority. By 2004 there were 7,678 mating pairs. While the survival of the bald eagle is a striking success story, only 44 species have been removed from the endangered list in three decades and 572 remained or were new on the list in 2008 in the US with 1,143 worldwide (FWS, 2008).

Since 1980 the Environmental Protection Agency (EPA) has operated a Superfund program to clean up the nation's toxic waste dumps. The program was funded by a billion-dollar-a-year tax on the industrial corporations responsible for the pollution. From 1994 to 2006, Republican-dominated Congresses reduced the tax and cut the budget. With the Superfund lacking money, the Bush administration began to limit cleanup operations, including the New Jersey dumping ground for Agent Orange, the cancer-causing defoliant used during the Vietnam War. Bush's environmental policies led one columnist to quip: "Mother Nature has been known to tremble at the sound of the president's approaching footsteps. He's an environmental disaster zone" (Herbert, 2002). Up next for the United States is what to do about the older nuclear reactors and bombs that need to be decommissioned.

The People

Native Americans

When Europeans arrived in America, they found it already occupied. Through European eyes, the Native Americans were living upon the land but did not possess or use it according to biblical injunctions to "Be fruitful, and multiply and replenish the earth, and subdue it; and have dominion . . . over every living thing that moveth upon the earth" (Genesis 1:27–8). Religious immigrants saw the land both as a place where danger lurked and as a source of redemption and wealth. Soon Euro-Americans were using Royal grants, legal deeds, squatters' rights, vigilante justice, and military force to subdue the "Red Man" and the land.

In contemporary America, a few million people are descended from the Native Americans, but the vast majority of all Americans can trace a part or the whole of their ancestry to Europe. It can be asserted that Europe's primary export for the last 400 years has been people and

Europeans have been especially prolific in rapid ecological change and in reproducing societies which mirrored their own. As soon as they had transplanted colonies, those began to transform through the interplay of other immigrant cultures, the land, and climate.

The people who became Native Americans migrated across the Bering Straits from Asia to settle on land unclaimed by precedent or legal deed – or even by humans at all. These Asians advanced yearly ten or so miles until they stretched out in different groups across the North American continent. As time and distance separated them from their roots in Mongolia and Siberia, these immigrants accommodated their cultures to the land and became "Indians" – as the early Europeans called them.

Their cultures also changed rapidly with European contact as Indians and Europeans together became Americans. Prior to the arrival of the European horde, thousands of Indian tribes were widely distributed across America. The Anasazi culture of Colorado built a thousand homes into cliffs at Mesa Verde and Chaco Canyon; the Adena-Hopewell culture were mound builders living in Ohio; in New Mexico, the oldest continuously occupied town in the United States is the Acoma Pueblo village near Santa Fe; at Cahokia, near St. Louis, the Mississippi culture built a massive pyramidal city of 10,000 inhabitants that had to be abandoned due to overcrowding and pollution problems about the time of Columbus's voyages; from Canada to Georgia, the Iroquoian peoples hunted, farmed, and warred against their neighbors for supremacy over the land.

In the twenty-first century, over 2.2 million people identify themselves primarily as American Indians or Inuit; millions more have native ancestors. Indians are assimilated into the national culture even if one-quarter of them reside on land set aside exclusively for their tribe. The other three-quarters live in urban or suburban areas nationwide. Generally, an individual must have at least one-fourth blood quantum measurement to be classified as "Indian" under tribal and US government rules. Many tribes allow exceptions of various types, with the Cherokee, for example, believing that a person either is or is not a Cherokee – blood cell counts being less relevant than identity and culture.

There are 562 officially recognized tribes/clans, with 1.4 million people living on 66 million acres of reservation land (Map 2.2) (BIA, 2008). In the last 20 years, more than ten million acres have been added to existing or new Indian reservations. Tribal affairs are run by elected chiefs and tribal councils who act in ways similar to mayors and city councils. Tribal councils hear complaints, settle disputes, and

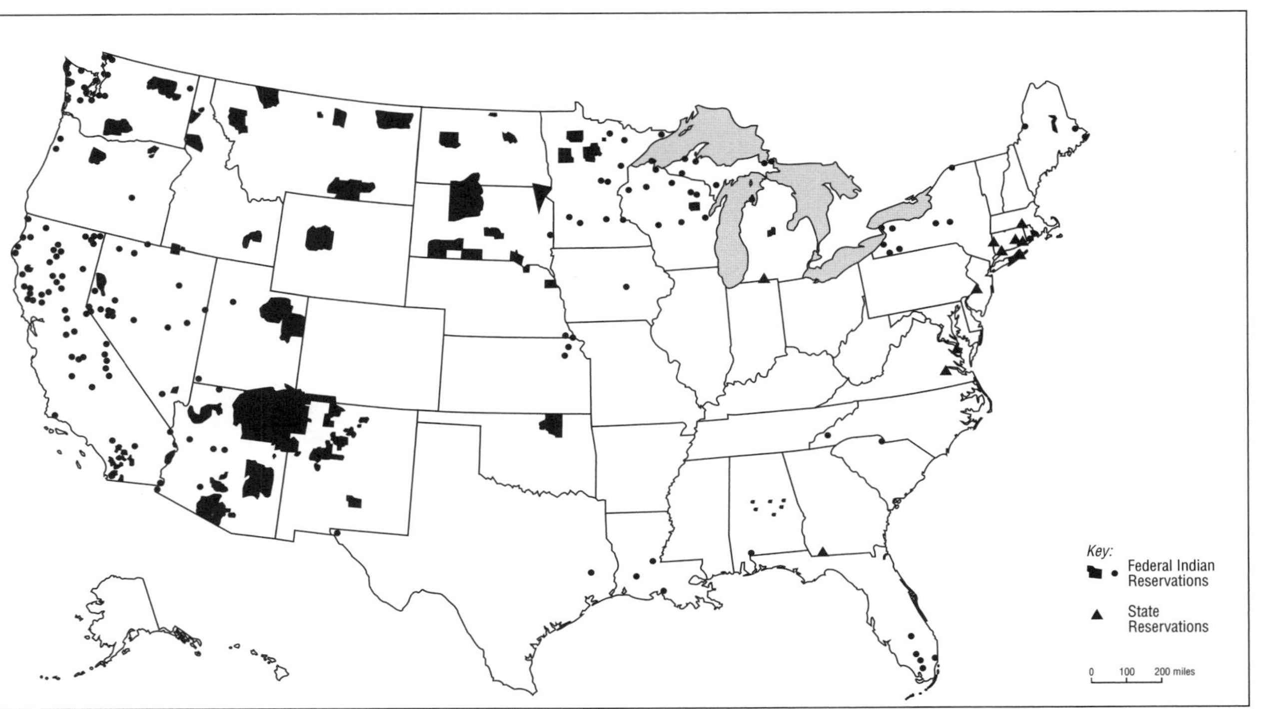

Map 2.2 American Indian Reservations

Source: www.census.gov/dmd/www/pdf/512indre.pdf

decide how to spend the money earned by tribal enterprises or distributed to them by the federal government under the Department of the Interior's Bureau of Indian Affairs (BIA). In contemporary America, 32 tribes oversee community colleges on their reservations. Forty-eight tribes are involved in oil or natural gas production and 50 operate various types of mines. Many tribes have opened casino gambling parlors, built tourist hotels and golf courses on reservations to attract capital for jobs and improvements. Some tribes manage all the profits for the collective communities and others transfer money directly to tribal members.

Despite these success stories, most Indian tribes are located on isolated reservations where tourists rarely travel. Their members remain poorly educated and impoverished. They have social problems that far exceed the national average in rates of alcoholism, low life expectancy, high unemployment, and inadequate health care. In 2004, overall reservation unemployment was 43 percent as compared with the 5.5 percent national average; and of those employed, 33 percent earned wages below the poverty line (NCAI, 2004).

While Indians are proud to be Americans, the major disputes with the federal government are over the sense of Indianness that is tied to the land. Without the land, some have said, there are no Indians. Many of the disputes are over who has the right to the natural resources. Public dams redirect water supplies and conservation policies restrict the number of fish which can be caught. Both of these infringe on traditional patterns and Native Americans have mostly won lawsuits over water and fishing rights. Other land disputes concern the rich mineral deposits and oil under reservation lands which have been leased to private corporations or, in the name of national security, have been mined under contracts with the US Bureau of Land Management. For example, in January 2002, the Bush administration reversed a Clinton administration ban on mining gold on the ancestral lands of the Quechan tribe in California to allow a 1,600-acre open pit mine in a desert area (Madigan, 2002). In contemporary America, the US government allows private contractors to operate coal-burning power plants on or near sacred lands, as Illustration 2.2 shows.

African Americans

African Americans as a group do not share the common defining experience of voluntary immigration to the United States which most other Americans share; instead, their ancestors were kidnapped or sold into slavery and forced to adapt to a country with established

Illustration 2.2 Smoke Signals on the Navajo Reservation

The Navajo Indian Reservation is the largest Indian nation in population and land size, with 250,000 people living on 27,000 square miles in the states of New Mexico, Arizona and Utah (see Map 2.2) – an area larger than 10 of the 50 states. With two coal-fired power plants already in operation, the 2008 proposal to build a third one brought the federal government, private business, and traditional Navajo beliefs into conflict. Divisions exist within the Navajo nation between traditionalists who believe that Mother Earth and Father Sky are being violated and the tribal council which says the plant will provide $52 million in revenue and bring 400 jobs to the reservation while increasing energy supplies to a needy Southwest. The EPA approved the building of the plant despite protests by traditionalists and environmental activists. Pictured above is the Four Corners Power Plant, which the EPA annually ranks as the dirtiest CO_2 emitter in the United States.

(Momatiuk-Eastcott/Corbis)

racial hierarchies. This substantial difference still affects race relations as other racial and ethnic groups – other assimilated citizens – feel themselves more authentically American because of the original intent of their ancestors to make a new and better life for themselves from the one they were leaving behind. It is important to remember that the United States had no feudal past and thus no established peasantry. For African Americans, the continent of origin, slavery and its confrontation with America's stated moral vision, and the long-standing status as the nation's central minority set them apart. For many

African Americans, who believe that each new immigrant group succeeds only at their expense, the recent surge in immigration hampers the efforts toward equal citizenship.

After decades of struggle, the Civil Rights Movement of the 1950s and 1960s mobilized the African-American community in line with the actions and words of leaders such as Martin Luther King, Jr. ("Agitate, Litigate, Legislate!") and Malcolm X ("By any means necessary!"). While still facing discrimination by private individuals, in job promotions, and by financial institutions, much has changed as Blacks have succeeded in wiping away all rules and regulations that denied equality before the law. Much of the split in American society is now as much a function of class as race, with a large portion of African Americans still, using King's words, "wrapped in an airtight cage of poverty in the midst of an affluent society" (King, 1963: 81).

In the contemporary United States, 41 million people identity themselves as African Americans. Being African American is more than visual as blacks define themselves as much by self choice and societal definition as by ancestry. Social definitions count. For example, Americans consider white women capable of conceiving black babies, but generally deny that black women can have white babies. Another example: Haitians have defined anyone with one part of white blood as "white," which is just the opposite of the long-standing American insistence that one drop of black blood made a person "black."

Whether defined in racial, ethnic, or cultural terms, Americans have long experienced a phenomenon just beginning in many societies in the world: the ability to blur the differences between culture groups and fuse them into a national group. Many would like to see the old racial classification pentagon of white, black, red, yellow, and brown, and cross-cultural definitions such as Muslim, Hispanic, Asian-American, or Jew, deleted for a post-racial or post-ethnic idea of simply being "American" or not. Intermarriages push different groups closer to this idea as does the concept of "symbolic identity," which allows a feeling of ethnicity or race as a sub-region of the whole.

Regions

While the United States of America is a nation, its name indicates the simple fact that it is a union of different states. Each state has a particular personality based upon its peculiar history of settlement and immigration as well as according to its geography. Americans often describe their country by regions. There is a general, but not complete, agreement over which states belong to which regions and, of course, regions contain subregions which are also contested. We have divided the country into five basic areas which generally conform to a contemporary understanding.

The South

As the area closest to Columbus's discovery, the South (Map 2.3 and Table 2.2) has cities dating from the struggles of Spain, England, France, and American Indian tribes for dominance in the New World.

The oldest permanent European settlements in the United States are the Spanish cities of San Juan, Puerto Rico (1508), and Saint Augustine, Florida (1565), the English settlement at Jamestown, Virginia (1607), and the French city of New Orleans, Louisiana (1718). Indian tribes were mostly removed west of the Mississippi River by the 1840s, but the Cherokee Indian Reservation in the Appalachian Mountains in North Carolina remains the largest Indian land-base east

Map 2.3 The South

Table 2.2 The South

State, District, Territory, or Commonwealth	*Date joined US*	*Area (Sq. Miles*)*	*Population (July 2008 est.)*
Georgia	1788	58,977	9,685,744
South Carolina	1788	31,189	4,479,800
Virginia	1788	42,326	7,769,089
North Carolina	1789	52,672	9,222,414
Washington, DC	1791	68	591,833
Kentucky	1792	40,411	4,269,245
Tennessee	1796	42,219	6,214,888
Louisiana	1812	49,651	4,410,796
Alabama	1817	52,237	4,661,900
Mississippi	1817	48,286	2,938,618
Arkansas	1836	53,182	2,855,390
Florida	1845	59,928	18,328,340
West Virginia	1861	24,231	1,814,468
Puerto Rico**	1898/1917	3,508	3,954,037
US Virgin Islands***	1917/1927	171	109,840

* 1 square mile equals approximately 2.6 square kilometers.

** Of these, an estimated half (two million) of all Puerto Ricans live in the US and their numbers are distributed among the states in which they live. Puerto Rico is a commonwealth whose people are citizens of the United States. Puerto Ricans are neither allowed to vote in US presidential elections nor are they required to pay income taxes, unless they live inside US national boundaries.

*** The US Virgin Islands are unincorporated territories which were purchased from Denmark in 1917. Citizens of the Virgin Islands became non-voting citizens of the United States in 1927.

Source: US Census Bureau (2008h) US Population Estimates; CIA (2008).

of Oklahoma. The “father of his country” George Washington, the author of The Declaration of Independence Thomas Jefferson, the principal writer of the Constitution James Madison, and the nationalist who claimed the entire western hemisphere for American hegemony, James Monroe – four of the first five presidents – were Virginians. In contemporary America, two of the five most recent chief executives, Jimmy Carter and Bill Clinton, are Southerners.

Much of the South’s regional identity comes from its way of life based upon the legacies of slavery and racism, its failed attempt to separate from the United States, and its warm climate. Spanish remains the official language in Puerto Rico and the Southern drawl – a speech pattern which mixes African and Scottish influences – is widespread. This creates a real as well as psychological division that defines the South.

Since colonial times the South has delivered staple crops – tobacco, cotton, rice, sugar – to a world market. The earliest settlers were mostly English and Scottish Protestants (and Spanish Catholics in Puerto Rico and French Catholics in Louisiana) who imported Africans and set up a hierarchical society with slaveholding aristocrats at the top and black slaves at the bottom. White Southerners developed a pro-slavery argument based upon genetics, history, religion, and anti-capitalism. They used scientific theories to argue that whites were superior, that the classical democratic city of Athens and the republican city of Rome incorporated slavery, that the Bible sanctioned slavery, and that the system was a positive good when contrasted to the outrages of Northern manufacturing capitalism with its degradation of white workers. The Confederate States of America (1861–5) consisted of all the states in this region, plus Texas, excepting only Kentucky and West Virginia, which seceded from Virginia in 1863 to form a new state. Precisely because the South lost and the slaves were freed, Southern identity is still marked by the "Lost Cause" and by the intimate interaction and family ties of blacks and whites.

Jimmy Carter's 1970 election as governor of Georgia and his subsequent 1976 election to the presidency marked the South's rise to regional power. Until then the region operated mostly as an internal colony of the North, supplying cheap labor and raw materials to feed the nation's growth. For the last half century, the "New South" has been part of the "Sunbelt" – a broad cross-regional area from Virginia to California – which continues to enjoy high immigration, massive job growth, and sunny, hot weather. Illustrating its political strength, Sunbelt candidates have won every presidential election since 1964.

While Washington, DC, is a decidedly Southern city, the key city in the modern South is Atlanta, Georgia. Immigrants – particularly those from Vietnam and Mexico – have changed the dynamics of the Southern population as has the return migration of African Americans from Northern cities since the 1970s. Foreign industries invest heavily in building factories in Southern cities in exchange for tax relief, pollution waivers, and non-unionized workers. The National Aeronautics and Space Administration (NASA) and the Defense Department are significant contributors to the Southern economy, with the main space launch pad at Cape Canaveral, Florida, the nuclear research lab at Oak Park, Tennessee, the principal Army bases in North Carolina and Georgia, and the Marine Corps training facility at Parris Island, South Carolina. Of course, sunshine promotes the South's huge tourism business, with more than a thousand miles of beaches and resorts, pristine islands protected against development, and many large amusement parks, including Florida's Disneyworld, Epcot Center, Busch Gardens, and Universal City Studios themepark. Prominent universities such as Emory, Georgia Tech, Duke, Vanderbilt, Virginia, Georgetown, and North Carolina help the South past its long-time image of slow-talking and slow-thinking, even while the region remains the most religious, least educated, and lowest paid area in the country.

The North

The North (Map 2.4 and Table 2.3) has long been associated with core American values of religious freedom, cultural diversity, liberty, capitalism, democracy, work and education. Most of the prominent symbols of American nationalism – apart from those in Washington, DC – are located in the North. The buildings in which congresses wrote the Declaration of Independence and Constitution are in Philadelphia, Pennsylvania. Massachusetts has the landing spot of the Pilgrims – Plymouth Rock – Puritan graveyards, and the houses and churches where patriots planned the American Revolution. The Statue of Liberty, Ellis Island Immigration Museum, and United Nations stand in New York harbor.

Puritan beliefs in the middle-class values of hard work, education, individual uplift, democracy, religiosity, and America as a "city upon a hill," defined an American ideology. English Puritans built homogenous communities in the sub-region of New England: Massachusetts, Connecticut, New Hampshire, Vermont, and Maine. Yet, the arrival of Swedes, Germans, Dutch, Catholics, and other dissenters throughout the Mid-Atlantic sub-region of New York, New Jersey, Maryland, Pennsylvania, Rhode Island, and Delaware foreshadowed the future of American cultural pluralism.

With the exception of Vermont, all the states in this region have direct access to big Atlantic harbors from which trading and fishing ships have always operated. Additionally, with the Appalachian Mountains pushing the fall line near the coast, northern cities benefit from water power available to supply electricity and run factories. The industrial revolution which began in England first arrived in Boston and then spread across the North. Textile and flour mills, factories making interchangeable parts for weapons, shipbuilding and insurance firms have long been mainstays of the region. By the mid-nineteenth century, the United States led the world in the number of merchant ships – and these operated almost entirely out of Northern

Map 2.4 The North

ports. As trade was orchestrated from this region, banking houses such as J. P. Morgan, Chase Manhattan, and the New York Stock Exchange financed America's business expansion and built New York City (NYC) into the world's leading financial center.

As NYC established itself as the main port for immigrants from Europe, various waves of ethnic groups gave the North an even more polyglot society. "Chain migrations" reached into Europe as one immigrant family from a single town would cause a linkage, pulling scores of relatives, friends, and former neighbors to America. Starting in 1892, immigrants were processed at Ellis Island before most of them settled in neighborhoods of their own cultures. Here the immigrants found people, language, food and historical knowledge which kept alive Old World cultures while they made the transition to the overarching American culture. Today, people from all over the world, even those who could never imagine themselves as Americans, identify with New Yorkers.

Iron and oil deposits in Pennsylvania led to the rise of Andrew Carnegie's steel company and John D. Rockefeller's Standard Oil

Table 2.3 The North

State	*Date joined US*	*Area (Sq. Miles*)*	*Population (July 2008 est.)*
Delaware	1787	2,396	873,092
Pennsylvania	1787	46,058	12,448,279
New Jersey	1787	8,215	8,682,661
Connecticut	1788	5,544	3,501,252
Massachusetts	1788	9,241	6,497,967
Maryland	1788	12,297	5,633,597
New Hampshire	1788	9,283	1,315,809
New York	1788	53,989	19,490,297
Rhode Island	1790	1,231	1,050,788
Vermont	1791	9,615	621,270
Maine	1820	33,741	1,316,456

* 1 square mile equals approximately 2.6 square kilometers.

Source: US Census Bureau (2008h) US Population Estimates; CIA (2008).

monopoly. Pennsylvania, New Jersey, and New York surpassed Massachusetts as centers of heavy industry. Industries, trade, and the finance capitalism of the region means that even though the North is geographically smaller, it is more densely populated and much more urban than the other regions. NYC is the nation's largest city and a sprawling urban network – a megalopolis – connects Boston to Washington, DC.

The Northeastern universities are renowned and include the oldest American university, Harvard (1636), as well as Yale, Princeton, Brown, Columbia, Dartmouth, M.I.T. and literally hundreds of others. Education is big business, employing millions, and supplying a useable product, knowledge, to American undergraduates and to the foreign nationals who make US graduate programs excel. Universities also provide many of the innovations in scientific and technological advances.

The Midwest

The Midwest (Map 2.5 and Table 2.4) is an extension of the North and was settled by immigrants streaming westward from northern states in the aftermath of the American Revolution and War of 1812. After the 1848 European revolutions restored conservative monarchies, many Northern Europeans saw the chance to get a farm, work, and to be free by immigrating to the United States. The Midwest has huge populations descended from Germans, Irish, Norwegians, Swedes, Danes, Finns, Poles and Ukrainians.

Map 2.5 The Midwest

Residents still see the region as the "heartland" of America, mostly untainted by the history of slavery in the South and overcrowded moneychangers and capitalists in the Northeast and Middle Atlantic states. Midwesterners are known for their honesty and down-to-earth directness and they speak a dialect best described as "flat." They view themselves as liberals who conserve American values. Beginning in 1862, the Homestead Act allowed families to claim 160 acres of land (equal to one-quarter of a square mile) by living on it. The area expanded rapidly. As Russian immigrants came into the region, they brought wheat seeds from the Steppe, which quickly took to the soil and gave the region its major crop.

Bordering Canada or the Mississippi River system, the Midwest is further serviced by direct access to the largest freshwater lakes in the world, the Great Lakes, which provide drinking water as well as shipping links to the Atlantic Ocean. The land has gentle hills east of the Mississippi and an increasing flatness west of the river. This is farming country, the agricultural breadbasket, meatpacking, and dairyland

Table 2.4 The Midwest

State	*Date joined US*	*Area (Sq. Miles*)*	*Population (July 2008 est.)*
Ohio	1803	44,828	11,485,910
Indiana	1816	36,420	6,376,792
Illinois	1818	57,918	12,901,563
Missouri	1821	69,709	5,911,605
Michigan	1837	96,705	10,003,422
Iowa	1846	56,276	3,002,555
Wisconsin	1848	65,499	5,627,967
Minnesota	1858	86,943	5,220,393
Kansas	1861	82,282	2,802,134
Nebraska	1867	77,358	1,783,432

* 1 square mile equals approximately 2.6 square kilometers.

Source: US Census Bureau (2008h) US Population Estimates; CIA (2008).

of the nation. It is also a region of great industrial and manufacturing cities, including Chicago, Detroit, Cleveland, Cincinnati, St. Louis, Minneapolis-St. Paul, Indianapolis, and Milwaukee. Heavy factories near these cities produce automobiles, chemicals, steel – and pollution. In the 1980s, the Great Lakes ecosystem was heavily fouled and the Cuyahoga River running through downtown Cleveland frequently caught fire due to its high oil and chemical content.

Between the World Wars, the cities of the Midwest (and North) proved an irresistible magnet for African Americans emigrating from the South to the promise of better lives. As the economy expanded after World War II, blacks continued to arrive in large numbers. The competition for jobs and housing led to ugly racial incidents and to the establishment of inner-city ghettos with maximum crowding and high crime rates. By the 1980s, the Midwestern automobile and steel industries had come under pressure from foreign competitors. Critics labelled the region the "Rust Belt" when many companies collapsed, workers were laid off, and millions relocated to better opportunities and less polluted cities in the Sunbelt. Still, the agricultural prowess of the region kept it in business until the industries could rebound.

During the 1990s, and until the effects of the financial crisis began to be felt in 2008, the Midwest prospered from the resurgence of the automobile industry and the success of urban renewal projects as economic highs brought prosperity, better jobs, more police protection, and lower crime rates which made the cities attractive again. Cleveland built the Rock-'n'-Roll Hall of Fame next to two new sports stadiums and a technology museum adjacent to where the cleaned-up Cuyahoga River flows into Lake Erie. Chicago remains central to the region as the third largest city in America and center for the nation's commodities exchange.

The West

The West (Map 2.6 and Table 2.5) is the region of big states and small populations. Even with the recent decade of rapid growth coming

Map 2.6 The West

Table 2.5 The West

State	*Date joined US*	*Area (Sq. Miles*)*	*Population (July 2008 est.)*
Texas	1845	267,277	24,326,974
Nevada	1864	110,567	2,600,167
Colorado	1876	104,100	4,939,456
Montana	1889	147,046	967,440
North Dakota	1889	70,704	641,481
South Dakota	1889	77,121	804,194
Idaho	1890	83,574	1,523,816
Wyoming	1890	97,818	532,688
Utah	1896	84,904	2,736,424
Oklahoma	1907	69,903	3,642,361
Arizona	1912	114,006	6,500,180
New Mexico	1912	121,598	1,984,356

* 1 square mile equals approximately 2.6 square kilometers.

Source: US Census Bureau (2008h) US Population Estimates; CIA (2008).

from Mexico, Texas is relatively unpopulated outside the major cities of Dallas-Fort Worth, Houston, San Antonio, and Austin. This is also "Indian Country" with sizeable populations of Native Americans both on and off the reservations. Because the West – except Texas – came into the Union after the American Revolution created a nation and the American Civil War decided what sort of nation it would become, it is often said to be defined by its lack of history and its newness. And yet, the West looms large in the popular perception of Americans as movies tell the tales of immigrant wagon trains across the frontier, the adventures of cowboys, and the wars between the US cavalry and the Native Americans. The West of the imagination is also vast in territory and it is that open space, the frontier – still waiting to be filled – that continues the expansive dreams of the country.

The West is dryer than the rest of the country with many parts of it described as the Great Plains and the Great American Desert. It contains a vast open landscape and dramatic scenery including the Grand Canyon in Arizona (Illustration 2.3), the Badlands in South Dakota, the largest cave in the United States at Carlsbad Caverns, New Mexico, ancient Mesa Verde Cliff Dwellings in Colorado, and petrified forests made up of trees turned into stone. Since the 1920s, when engineers built giant dams on the region's rivers – such as Hoover Dam on the Colorado River in Nevada – the cities of Phoenix, Arizona; Las Vegas, Nevada; and Albuquerque, New Mexico, have

Illustration 2.3 Grand Canyon National Park, Arizona

Centuries of erosion created the Grand Canyon National Park in Arizona. Ansel Adams took this photograph from the South Rim.

(Ansel Adams Collection, RG 79, Records of the National Park Service, NARA)

grown large as irrigation systems provided a more accommodating environment. Even where there are great forests and lakes in the Rocky Mountains, the region is marked by hot, dry summers and lightning storms that set off forest fires every year. In this heat and drought, Americans turn up their air-conditioners and spread what little water they can spare over their lawns. This adds to the demand for electricity, increases calls for nuclear power, puts further pressure on precious water supplies, and endangers wildlife.

The West has a different ethnic mix than the rest of the country because of the large numbers of Native Americans, a history that saw much of the land taken from Mexico, and the recent influx of millions of Chicanos from Mexico – adding to the large resident Latino population. For years, most white Americans saw the West as too rocky and dry for successful farming operations and the wagon trails that rolled west from St. Louis were all headed for the Pacific Rim states. Except for Texas and the states of Nevada, and Colorado which were settled by prospectors mining gold, silver, lead, and copper, the Western states as well as Washington, Alaska, and Hawaii are the latest additions to the United States. Utah was settled by Mormons following leader Brigham Young to territory outside the United States, founding what is perhaps the country's most culturally homogenous city: Salt Lake City (1847). The Mexican War brought Mormons back under US control by the land transfer agreed to in the peace treaty.

Much of the land in the West is owned or administered by the federal government. Indian reservations, most of the nation's national parks, and large areas of national mineral and forest reserves keep populations thin, as do the deep canyons and rugged landscapes of the Rocky Mountains. Private individuals also control vast areas of the West. For example, CNN founder Ted Turner owns 1.3 million acres (0.52 million hectares) on eight ranches in Montana, New Mexico, and Nebraska, swears to hold the land as an undeveloped trust, and grazes the nation's largest buffalo herd on prairie grass. Most white Westerners disagree with Turner and want US land policies aimed less at conservation and more at development. These citizens have been politically influential in the rise of the New Right, which has demanded more states' rights and less federal government intervention. In the 2008 presidential campaign, most of these white conservatives still voted Republican, sending all but 19 of the Western states's 91 electoral votes to John McCain; but this represented a gain for the Democrats from 2004 when George Bush swept every western electoral vote.

The Pacific Rim

The states and Pacific island territories in this region (Map 2.7 and Table 2.6) are tied by their common orientation to the Pacific Ocean. The US Navy, Marine Corps, and Air Force have some of their largest

Map 2.7 The Pacific Rim

strategic bases in these states, with the facility at Pearl Harbor, Hawaii, being the best known. The histories of the Pacific Rim states differ dramatically but their commerce is interwoven and is oriented more toward Asia than to Europe. Alaska has a large Inuit population, Hawaii has a large Polynesian population supplemented by at least 25 percent of Japanese ancestry, and California is the primary port of entry for Asian immigrants to the United States. California was taken from Mexico in 1848, Oregon and Washington were ceded from Britain in 1845, Alaska was purchased for $7 million from Russia in 1867, Hawaii was wrenched from independent Hawaiian control in 1891, Guam was ceded by Spain in 1898, and American Samoa was incorporated by mutual agreement in 1929. For many Americans, Alaska's huge territory and tiny population marks it as the "last frontier" within the boundaries of the United States – and the state and national governments control 99 percent of Alaskan land.

Table 2.6 The Pacific Rim

State	*Date Joined US*	*Area (Sq. Miles*)*	*Population (July 2008 est.)*
California	1850	158,869	36,756,666
Oregon	1859	97,132	3,790,060
Washington	1889	70,637	6,549,222
Guam**	1898/1950	217	175,877
American Samoa***	1929/1967	90	64,827
Alaska	1959	615,230	686,293
Hawaii	1959	6,459	1,288,198

* 1 square mile equals approximately 2.6 square kilometers.

** Guam is an unincorporated territory whose inhabitants are US citizens without the right to vote in US elections. Guam has an elected legislature of its own. The large US Navy base at Guam provides most of the island's economy. (*Source*: CIA, 2008 est.)

*** American Samoa is an unincorporated, unorganized territory whose citizens are US nationals, but not US citizens. American Samoa has a non-voting representative in the US Congress. The US administration is the main employer, followed by an American tuna firm, and tourism. (*Source*: CIA 2008 est.)

Source: US Census Bureau (2008h) US Population Estimates; CIA (2008).

Historically, the Spanish settled in California and sponsored expeditions into the entire Southwest. The cities of Santa Barbara, Monterey, San Francisco, San Diego, and Los Angeles began religious missions which claimed the land for Spain and the people for the Catholic Church. The year California was ceded from Mexico, settler John Sutter found gold near Sacramento and the "gold rush" that followed brought so many settlers – from 15,000 in 1848 to 260,000 in 1852 – that by 1850, California was a state. Its favorable climate, location and scenic beauty guarantee a continued population growth.

In contemporary America, California contains fully 12 percent of the total American population and Los Angeles rivals NYC as the nation's biggest city. Its most famous industry, Hollywood, glues Americans together via mass culture. In 2000, California's non-white population surpassed the white population for the first time since 1860 as Hispanics and Asian immigrants flooded into the state in the 1990s. California leads the nation in the manufacture of high-tech equipment and aircraft. Up the coast in Seattle, Washington, Bill Gates, runs his Microsoft computer juggernaut.

The Pacific Rim states are mountainous and sit atop geological fault lines or alongside active volcanoes. Earthquakes are common and volcanoes sometimes erupt, spewing lava and starting forest fires. The Hawaiian Islands in the mid-Pacific are actually the tops of volcanoes. The Pacific Ocean provides an enormous harvest of fish and the states' large rivers are full of salmon and shellfish. Washington and Alaska employ thousands in the salmon industry. Huge agricultural areas – excepting Alaska – grow large portions of the nation's fruits and nuts. There are vast forests of fir trees and the logging industry is lucrative from northern California to Alaska. The California Redwood or Giant Sequoia is the world's largest species, growing to a height of 400 feet (121 m), having a diameter of 30 feet (9 m), and being approximately 4,000 years old. Besides protecting the Giant Sequoias by federal law, the US government has control over a forest area of approximately 45,000 square miles in California, Oregon and Washington – an area equal in size to the entire state of Pennsylvania.

Immigration

The movement of peoples from other nations into the United States has been unsurpassed and the country continues to be the preferred destination for most immigrants (Figure 2.1 and Table 2.7). Since 1607, immigrants have come with their own ideas of what they would do if they could claim a piece of land for themselves. America's population doubled every 25 years in the nineteenth century and every 50 years in the twentieth century. In 1965, one of every 20 Americans was foreign-born. In the twenty-first century, one person in eight (38 million people) – of whom 645,000 were US military veterans – were born in another country (MPI, 2007; Ho and Terrazas, 2008). The consistently strong immigration has kept America younger than many other nations. The estimates for 2050, for example, put the US median population age at 35 years old, in comparison to a 52-year-old Europe and an even older China.

Beyond the original colonists, early immigrants and the 400,000 Africans brought as slave laborers during what might be called the first wave of immigration, there have been eras marked by the influx of different groups. Between 1820 and 1890, 10 million "Old Immigrants" came. These peoples were overwhelmingly English, German, Irish, and Scandinavian. The Irish came from different religious and economic backgrounds as they fled persecution for their Catholicism and starvation from the widespread potato famine. From 1890–1924, Europeans from Eastern and Southern Europe poured into New York. These "New Immigrants" – many of them of Italian, Polish, Hungarian,

Figure 2.1 Immigrants to the United States by Decade, 1821–2007 (in millions)

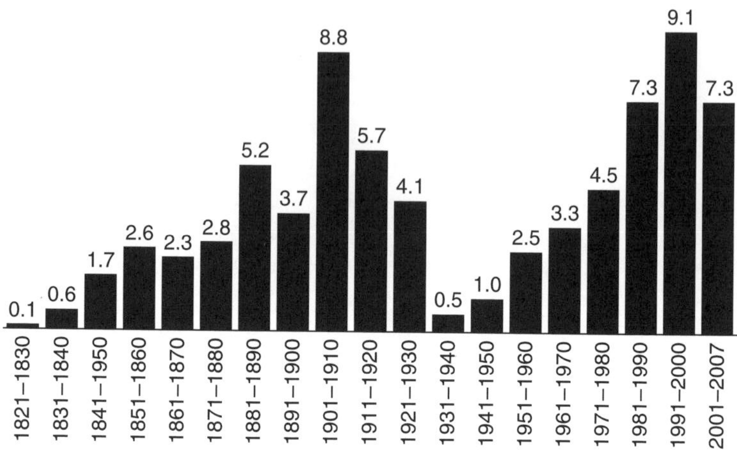

Source: US Immigration and Naturalization Service (INS), (2000) table 1; Center for Immigration Studies, (2008) figure 1.

Russian, Czech, Greek, and Middle Eastern origins – were mostly unlettered, poorer, religiously different, and politically unwanted in their countries of origin. But whatever their economic status or home culture – and surviving the multitude of hatreds and fears from among the "Old Immigrants" – these individuals quickly gathered themselves into a new and somewhat homogenous group recognized as Americans. This does not mean that assimilation was easy; many immigrants struggled to hold onto, even to reestablish, the world they left into the world they entered. Probably most immigrants kept one foot in each world, forming a transnational culture whose economic interactions shaped the minority experience in the United States. The current wave of immigrants, overwhelmingly from Latin America and Asia, is once again changing the way America defines itself and is defined by others.

The immigration policy of the United States has been both inclusive and discriminatory. There have been efforts to bar some groups and stop immigration entirely. Critics say that immigrants have a profoundly harmful effect on a high-tech society if they are poor and under-educated, and union representatives sometimes complain that immigrant labor keeps down wages while increasing welfare payments. When the economy is growing, the call is for more immigrant workers; but financial downturns lead quickly to

Table 2.7 Immigration by Country of Origin, January 2000–March 2007

	Country	*No. of Immigrants*
1	Mexico	3,583,000
2	India	629,000
3	China	568,000
4	Philippines	396,000
5	Guatemala	303,000
6	Former USSR	292,000
7	Cuba	261,000
8	Korea	255,000
9	El Salvador	249,000
10	Dominican Republic	224,000
11	Honduras	211,000
12	Colombia	192,000
13	Vietnam	155,000
14	United Kingdom	150,000
15	Brazil	124,000
16	Haiti	122,000
17	Canada	116,000
18	Japan	113,000
19	Peru	113,000
20	Jamaica	101,000
21	All Others	2,101,000
	Total	10,258,000

Source: Camarota, S. (2007).

fundamental questions about immigration policy and the very nature of America.

Immigrants have sometimes faced a "100 percent Americanism" backlash by xenophobes who want everyone to speak the same language, to be of a certain ancestry, and to have an accepted religion and cultural folkways. Even the way people dress has come under criticism. Catholics, Jews, and others have been singled out in the past but are generally accepted in modern America. Since 11 September, bias has grown against Muslims – much of it fanned by radio talk shows – but the vast majority of Americans have always rejected neo-Nazi or Ku Klux Klan ideology and they continue to favor the individual variations of a multicultural society. Most Americans realize that first-generation adult immigrants rarely break free of their old habits or become fluent in English; but their children do assimilate and often with a vengeance that rejects the "foreign" ways of their parents. By the third generation, very few children can speak the foreign language of their grandparents. More than any government action or voluntary help programs, popular culture and intermarriages turn immigrants into Americans.

The National Origins Act of 1924 limited immigration to a quota system based upon country of origin. The act favored Northern and Western Europe and reduced total immigration from over 800,000 to 164,000 a year. The Great Depression, World War II, and the Cold War had a great impact on policy, which has been in flux ever since. In 1965, the quota system was revised, as Congress allowed a more equitable distribution of immigration visas by hemispheres, totaling 290,000 a year and stressing the reunification of families instead of job qualifications. The Immigration Act of 1986 granted general amnesty and, sometimes, citizenship – to those who could pass the tests about general US history and laws – to illegal immigrants who would register. In 1990, Congress raised the number of legal immigrants per year to 700,000. The 2000 Immigration Act allowed "commuter green cards" to people living in Mexico or Canada but are in the US daily or often on work-related business. The result has been a surge in the numbers of women, rich business people, and two new immigrant majorities: Latinos (including Hispanics) and Asians.

Latinos is an inclusive term for anyone from Central and South American origins; Brazilians who speak Portuguese are Latinos, but not Hispanics. Hispanics are so-called because they speak Spanish as their first language. Before World War II there were just 3 million Latinos in the US, mostly in the southern parts of the Sunbelt and among the Puerto Rican community in NYC. In 2008, there were more than 47 million Latinos, the majority of whom are Chicanos – as immigrants from Mexico identify themselves. Latinos are as completely integrated into US society as everyone else. Illustration 2.4 shows Los Angeles Mayor Antonio Villaraigosa campaigning with Barack Obama in 2008.

Many Latinos provide substantial support to communities in their country of origin. For example, in the first half of 2008, Chicano immigrants sent approximately $12 billion south of the border (Lazo, 2008). Additionally, because the Chicano experience is unique in that they come from an adjacent nation which owned much of the land now claimed by the US, the newest wave of immigrants is made up of transnational commuters who frequently travel back and forth between, and feel immense loyalty to, their country of birth and their country of residence. When these groups establish themselves in America, they tend to settle together among relatives and friends they have known most or all of their lives. Chain migration has always

llustration 2.4 Antonio Villaraigosa and Barack Obama

On 8 July 2008 Los Angeles Mayor Antonio Villaraigosa signified his support for Democratic Presidential Nominee Barack Obama with a fist bump. Both men were addressing the League of United Latin American Citizens convention in Washington, DC. Villaraigosa had campaigned for the nomination of the first Latino to run for president of the United States, Governor Bill Richardson of New Mexico, later transferring support first to Hillary Clinton, then to the eventual Democratic nominee.

(Jae C. Hong/AP/Press Association Images, 2008)

happened, but the new phenomenon seems to be the relocation of whole towns to US suburbs. For example, of the 3,000 people living in the Mexico town of Ejido Modelo in 1984, half had resettled together in the Atlanta suburb of Eastpoint by 2001. According to transplanted resident Sigifredo Rodriguez, "When I walk the street, I see all of my people. Sometimes I feel like I'm in my own country." Transnational Patricia Doñan adds, "Once you're accustomed to being here, you don't really miss your town because everybody from your town is here" (quoted in Duncan, 2004).

The rapid rise in the percentage of Hispanics has caused concern. Political Scientist Samuel Huntington warns that this "persistent inflow of Hispanic immigrants threatens to divide the United States into two peoples, two cultures, and two languages" (Huntington, 2004b). Huntington argues that the American idea and policies toward immigration have been symbolized by the Ellis Island immigration facility – or even John F. Kennedy Airport in NYC – where immigrants come into America from across an ocean. Mexican immigration differs because of Mexico's contiguity with the United States, the demographic scale which includes legal and illegal immigration of so many people with a similar language, Spanish, as opposed to a diversity of languages in the past. And while no other immigrant group could ever claim original title to American soil, the area from Texas northward to Utah and westward to California was part of the Mexican homeland until 1848. Former Mexican President Vicente Fox called Mexican emigrants "heroes" and called himself "president of 123 million Mexicans, 100 million in Mexico and 23 million in the United States" (quoted in Huntington, 2004b).

Asian Americans are designated as a group not by language, culture, history, or ethnicity, but by the fact that they arrive from Asia. There is little cohesion among the group as Vietnamese, Indians, Chinese, Japanese, Indonesians, Koreans and others have little to bind them together. In the past, discriminatory immigration laws prohibited the Chinese from immigrating in 1882 and the Japanese in 1924. The Japanese attack on Pearl Harbor, the Korean and Vietnam wars, and the rise of communist, modern China maintained fears of Asians. In the 1980s, Congress voted monetary compensation to the thousands of Japanese-Americans concentrated into work camps during World War II. With a reduction of racism during the Cold War period, nearly half of all immigrants to America since 1965 have been Asians who initially settled together in Pacific Rim states and big cities in the Sunbelt. In San Diego, the world's largest community of Vietnamese immigrants lives in "Little Saigon" and makes up a major part of the more than 250,000 first-generation Vietnamese-Americans living in California and the 1.1 million nationwide.

Asian immigrants have been dubbed the "model minority" by the press because of their work ethic, low crime rate, focus on education, rapid acquisition of English, and quick assimilation into the broader culture. In fact, Asian Americans – notably Japanese, Chinese and Indians – now score higher than all other groups on standardized exams, attend the finest universities in numbers out of proportion with their percentage of the population, and earn higher salaries than Euro-Americans.

The government agency which oversees immigration is the Department of Homeland Security (DHS) – its forerunner, the Immigration and Naturalization Service (INS), was incorporated into the DHS in 2003. The DHS was created and given cabinet-level status to strengthen security as part of the war on terrorism. With a total budget of $51 billion in 2009, the DHS is a huge employer, including the 30,000 immigration officers who patrol the borders of the United States

(DHS, 2009). Agents monitor visas, investigate visitors, test and administer naturalization oaths – over one million each year of the twenty-first century – arrest and deport illegal aliens with disqualifying factors (DHS, 2008b). The DHS oversees temporary visas (171.4 million in 2007), the most common being tourist, business and student permits. Additionally, the DHS monitors the out-migration of foreign-born immigrants; since 1965, 20 percent of all immigrants to the US returned to their country of origin (DHS, 2008b). Asylum seekers and refugees also apply to the DHS for permission to stay in the US. The biggest group was the more than one million Vietnamese, Laotians, and Cambodians applying from 1975-93 in the wake of the US war with Vietnam. In 2007, DHS Border Patrol agents arrested 960,756 people – mostly Mexican nationals – trying illegally to cross into the United States (DHS, 2008a). Despite these efforts, an estimated 8–10 million illegal immigrants are living in America (Huntington, 2004a).

Government policy is often contradictory in the way it treats illegal immigrants. The 1996 Immigration Law requires that foreigners facing deportation be jailed while they are processed – from murderers to students who overstay their student visas. Conversely, illegals who are not apprehended are protected by a federal law requiring schools to educate all children, irrespective of their status. The government provides anti-discrimination rights and insists on minimum wage and safety guidelines to protect illegal immigrants from unfair hiring practices by employers. Of course, the law is one thing and practice is another; many illegal immigrants are afraid to challenge employers for fear of being deported, and will take less than a minimum or competitive wage in order to remain at work in the United States. Georgia and many other states offer welfare benefits and hospital services on a need basis, not by legal status. Other states take a harder line; for example, California has barred state money for education, health care or other services for illegal aliens – though this has in part been overturned by the courts.

Obviously, the US immigration system is broken and needs fixing. It has been broken for a long time. In just the five-month period from January to May 2007, 1,100 different immigration bills were considered by state legislatures nationwide, even though immigration law is primarily a federal perogative. The US Congress does not seem to know what to do, but the American people, by overwhelming majorities, say they want two things: (1) a tough enforcement policy, and (2) leniency for the millions of illegals already in the US (Jacoby, 2006). The debate focuses on unauthorized Mexican immigrants and border management. Americans must compromise over competing concerns to strike a balance between national security and national cohesion, between economic impact and human rights issues, between compassion for immigrants and constitutional law and order.

Politics intersects with immigration reform. In 2006 and 2007, with Congress and the President deadlocked over how to solve the problem – amnesty, permanent citizenship, crackdowns on employers, work visas, renewable permits, deportation, stronger border controls, security fences, and imprisonment – millions of pro-immigrant protestors marched through American cities in the largest mass protests in US history (see Illustration 4.2). Congress was unable to agree on a new immigration reform act. Bush, who had supported a form of amnesty/work permits, reacted to political pressure from the nativist element in the Right Wing, by ordering the militarization of the border, with thousands of additional immigration agents, the National Guard, enhanced electronic security systems and the building of a 2000-mile-long high-tech fence to secure the border. Many Democrats also supported these measures, in various ways, due to their own beliefs or in response to the wishes of their constituents. Sociologist Alan Wolfe noted that for a nation that defines itself as a liberal democracy built by immigrants, "There is something ugly about criminalizing illegal aliens, rounding them up, and deporting them" (Wolfe, 2006).

Early in his presidency, Obama formed a policy group to devise an immigration reform bill that will balance his assertion that "we are a nation of laws as well as a nation of immigrants" (Park, 2009). While the Obama administration and Congress continue to discuss a new immigration law, it seems certain that with a natural increase of four million births a year and a strong immigration from Asia and the Americas, the United States will continue its historic pattern of expansion and diversity. The country's wealth and power depends on the nation's ability to attract and assimilate foreigners. The land and resources are sufficient to accommodate a much larger population. Both the internal birth rate and immigration sources favor non-white groups as a more culturally diverse and multi-racial America continues to grow. African Americans, American Indians, Asian Americans, and Latinos are increasing at double and quadruple the rate of white ethnics. With his name and background radiating the politics of the new immigration, Barack Hussein Obama praised the immigrants and the Dream: "For all the noise and anger that too often surrounds the immigration debate, America has nothing to fear from today's immigrants. They have come here for the same reason that families have always come here, for the same reason my father came here – for the hope that in America, they could build a better life for themselves and their families" (Obama, 2008c).

3

Government

Although Americans disagree over how strong government should be, they expect action in a crisis. Signalling a gung-ho pragmatism, President Obama stated that "The question we ask today is not whether our government is too big or too small, but whether it works" (Obama, 2009b). Four years earlier, President George W. Bush had sketched a more minimal role for government and more responsibility for individual people: "By making every citizen an agent of his or her own destiny, we will give our fellow Americans greater freedom from want and fear, and make our society more prosperous and just and equal" (Bush, 2005).

American governing structures are typified by deliberate divisions of power. The federal government is split and shared among three branches, comprising the Presidency, Congress, and the federal courts system, each with specific areas of responsibility. Yet, they were not set up to control fully their own spheres. The division of power is complicated by checks and balances, amounting to mutual surveillance and limitation, while allowing the federal government to make, enact, and interpret laws. A further division of government exists in the overlapping relationship of federal and state governments. Each state resembles the federal government, with separate executive, judicial, and legislative branches. Beyond this, governmental power fractures again to create local, county, or district levels of authority. The separation of powers and the checks and balances give many access points to individuals or groups who are not always represented by the principle of majority rule. Access allows a plurality of interests to be heard and appeased, holding the diverse peoples together under the Constitution, which has been formally amended only 17 times since the inclusion of the first ten amendments as the Bill of Rights in 1791.

The Constitution

The Constitution is the founding document of American government. The division of power in this federal system is determined both by the Constitution and through a mix of practical compromises made during the 230 years since the republic was founded.

In the formative years of the nation, the idea of apportioning authority was seen as the best method of ensuring benevolent government. When the American Revolution ended in 1783, the Founders – including Benjamin Franklin, John Adams, James Madison, and Alexander Hamilton – needed to establish a system to do the business of government. This meant creating institutions to run what was even then a vast territory along the Eastern seaboard from Massachusetts to Georgia, and beyond to the Mississippi. Preserving order and protecting the nation from external threat were uppermost in their minds. At the same time, each state believed itself to have established its own identity in colonial times and wanted a system to protect its sovereign power while limiting national power. The Founders developed a double plan, which they embodied in the Constitution and the Bill of Rights. The Constitution (Box 3.1) sets out the structure of the federal government, explaining how it should carry out its business. The Bill of Rights, appended during the ratification process, guaranteed protections under law for state and individual rights. Essentially, three sets of sovereignty were confirmed: federal, state, and popular.

The debate over government power reflected the differing concerns of the states. Larger states, such as Virginia, would get more influence simply through the size of their populations. Smaller states, such as New Jersey, wanted the numbers in the legislature to be the same for all states, regardless of size. The Founders agreed to mesh the interests of small and large states by establishing a bicameral legislature, collectively called Congress, and consisting of a House of Representatives and a Senate. The number of representatives each state placed in the House – above a minimum of one representative per state – would be in direct proportion to its percentage of the total national population. In the Senate, each state would be equally represented by two senators.

This compromise gave over-representation to the small states, because no matter how low a percentage of the national population, they would have two senators and one representative. Presidential elections have always been influenced by this advantage as the numbers of electors each state has in the Electoral College matches its total number of representatives (proportional according to decennial Census population) and senators (always 2). This arrangement puts territorial sovereignty above popular sovereignty. It should be noted that Americans do not vote for their president directly and nationally. Instead, they vote indirectly and by state, with votes transformed into Electoral College delegates. The victorious candidate in each state – except in Maine and Nebraska, where votes are split – wins all the state's electoral delegates. Because there are 538 electors – 100 senators, 435 representatives, and 3 delegates from the District of Columbia – it takes 270 votes to win an election. In 2000, even though getting 400,000 fewer less votes than Al Gore, George W. Bush won the Electoral College by 271–267. In 2008, Barack Obama beat John McCain by nine million popular votes, by 28 states to 22, and by a 365–173 vote in the Electoral College.

Division of Powers

The Constitution, as originally devised, divided power between law-making, law-enforcing and law-interpreting branches: Legislative, Executive and Judicial. This separation of powers limited each branch of government to its own specific area of authority. The Executive branch had the power to administer laws and to represent the state in foreign affairs. The Congress was designed to pass laws, with its authority split between the House and the Senate. Through its control of the budget and taxation, the House focused on domestic policy. Because treaties with other nations need approval or refusal, the Senate would oversee foreign policy. The Founders imagined the Supreme Court as the weakest branch and did not define it or the federal court system in clear terms. The judiciary would act as a court of appeal to mediate among different legal interpretations, and, eventually, to decide the constitutionality of government actions.

The division of government into three branches along with strict written definitions of the range of federal and state power worked to soothe fears of a rogue executive or of a conspiracy by a legislative majority to take away fundamental rights. In fact, although executive,

Box 3.1 The Constitution of the United States of America, a Summary

Preamble

We the People of the United States, in Order to form a more perfect Union, establish Justice, insure domestic tranquility, provide for the common defence, promote the general Welfare, and secure the Blessings of Liberty to ourselves and our Posterity, do ordain and establish this Constitution for the United States of America.

Articles

- I Legislative Branch. Sets a bicameral legislature, membership and election rules, privileges, areas of authority and limitations.
- II Executive Branch. Sets election and eligibility stipulations for President, the powers of the presidency, relations with Congress and impeachment.
- III Judicial Branch. Establishes Supreme Court and sets jurisdiction.
- IV Federalism. Provides mutual recognition and citizenship rights, creation, and governance of new states.
- V Amendment Procedures. Establishes procedure for amending the Constitution.
- VI Supremacy Clause. Establishes Federal laws over State laws. Prohibits religious tests for officeholders.
- VII Ratification. Provides conditions for initial ratification of Constitution.

Bill Of Rights [Amendments 1-10 (1791)]

- 1st Underlines freedom of religion, speech, press and assembly
- 2nd Confirms right to bear arms
- 3rd Prohibits quartering of military troops in private houses in peacetime

→

legislative and judicial authority overlap on most issues, Americans split the functions of government so dramatically that no branch occupies the central space on the field of power. This situation strongly contrasts with most parliamentary systems, where the biggest party or governing coalition forms the government, appoints and directs the executive, and controls chief judicial appointments.

Even the layout of Washington, DC, makes obvious the separation of powers by physically separating the three branches in a long, acute triangle. The large buildings command a view of the Mall, the grassy three-mile long (5 km) rectangle in the heart of the city, yet no branch has an uninterrupted view of the other two. Both spatially,

→

4th	Prohibits unreasonable searches and seizures
5th	Freedom from double-jeopardy or self-incrimination
6th	Rights of accused to speedy jury trial, witnesses, and lawyer in criminal trials
7th	Right to jury trial in civil cases
8th	Prohibits cruel and unusual punishments; requires reasonable bail
9th	Retains unlisted rights for the People
10th	Reserves unlisted powers for the States or the People

Subsequent Amendments

11th	Limits lawsuits between states (1795)
12th	Revises presidential electoral college system (1804)
13th	Abolishes slavery (1865)
14th	Grants citizenship to ex-slaves. Provides for *due process* and *equal protection* (1868)
15th	Protects voting rights regardless of "race, color or previous condition of servitude" (1870)
16th	Authorizes federal income tax (1913)
17th	Provides for direct election of US Senators (1913)
18th	Prohibits the manufacture or sale of alcohol (1919)
19th	Grants voting rights for women (1920)
20th	Sets accession dates for President and Congress. Establishes presidential succession (1933)
21st	Repeals 18th Amendment (1933)
22nd	Sets two-term limit for President (1951)
23rd	Grants electoral votes to citizens of Washington, D.C. (1961)
24th	Prohibits poll taxes in federal elections (1964)
25th	Revises presidential succession procedure (1967)
26th	Lowers voting age to 18 (1971)
27th	Sets timing limits on congressional pay raises (1992)

Note: For full text see: Appendix

and conceptually, their gaze meets outside the locale of individual power.

The constitutional separation of powers creates a checks and balances system with each branch dependent on the others. Although these checks and balances will figure prominently in a later discussion of what each branch can or cannot do, their overlapping nature makes it difficult, if not impossible, for unrestrained power to accrue to any one branch. As demonstrated in Figure 3.1, each branch can check the actions of the other branches. This balance of power encourages compromise as the most effective strategy for getting things done.

Figure 3.1 The System of Checks and Balances

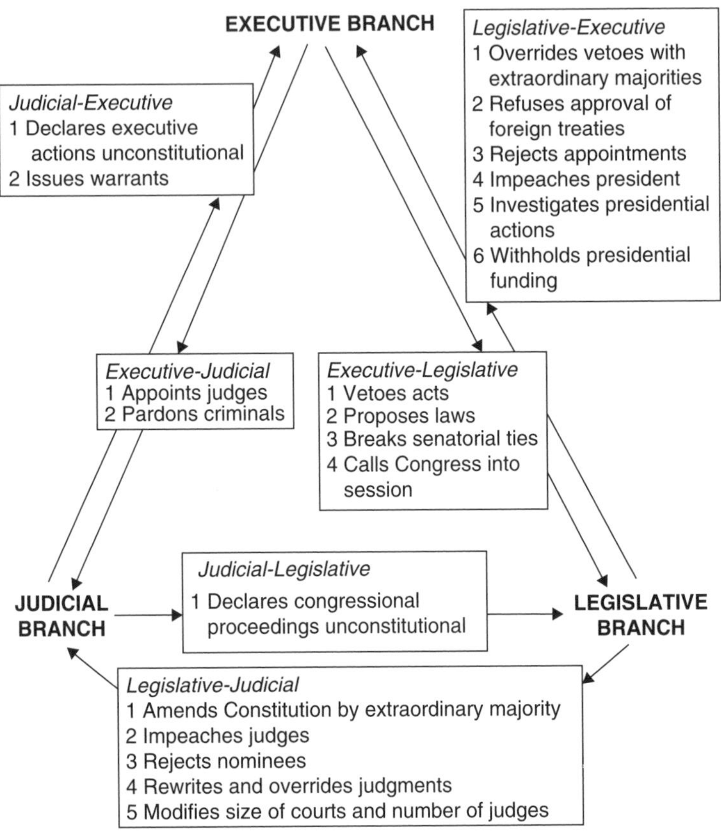

The Federal System

The original idea of the relationship of the states and the federal government is contained in Article 5 of the Constitution. Additionally, the 10th Amendment states: “The powers not delegated to the United States by the Constitution, nor prohibited to it by the States, are reserved to the States respectively, or to the people.” In contemporary America, the reality is quite different. Constitutional arrangements satisfactory for a small republic of four million people in thirteen semi-sovereign agricultural states do not meet the needs of 300 million people living in an integrated, service-based, post-industrial economy. Defining what is local, state, and national is much more difficult and any clear-cut division of power is vague.

Modernization has replaced the static relationship of power with a dynamism that makes federalism as much a process as an institution. The process of federalism has accelerated over the last century, and has moved power consistently from the states to the national government, despite occasional rhetoric to the contrary. This process has been helped by the generality of the Constitution and amendments, leaving room for interpretation when times or circumstances change. Box 3.2 outlines federalism as process, showing how the enumerated powers of the government have been changed by delegated powers.

Historians have described federalism metaphorically as Layer Cake or Dual federalism, Marble Cake federalism, New federalism, "New" New federalism, and Rhetorical or Kaleidoscopic federalism. These metaphors seek to present a picture of how power is shared, separated, checked, and balanced.

Layer Cake, or Dual, federalism evokes an image of separate and somewhat equal layers of sovereignty between the federal and state governments. Like a layer cake, the powers of the national government are contained within its single layer, over and above the powers in the layer of state government, which are over and above the layer of local governments. Each layer is distinct in its sovereign powers. The United States clearly matched this model from 1790–1865, and continued to be influenced by it until 1932.

Marble Cake federalism best illustrates the period 1933–69. In this model, state and national power swirl around each other, rising and falling and being supreme according to where you slice the cake. Power is not set firmly above or below, but is cooperative and fluid, allowing for expansion and contraction of federal power and programs according to the beliefs of a specific president and congress. In 1933, during the worst year of the Great Depression, President Franklin Roosevelt greatly expanded the role of the federal government with his "New Deal" program of welfare, social security, and jobs. In 2009, President Obama made strong strides in the same direction.

In 1969 President Richard Nixon put forward a policy he called "New Federalism." Nixon believed that the government's main role was in foreign policy and that, in domestic affairs, the federal government had become too intrusive in everyday lives. He wanted to allow the states more power and diversity in deciding how much to spend and on what to spend it. The Nixon administration pushed a states' rights position just as Americans were discovering the conspiratorial and imperial workings of Nixon and his henchmen in the Watergate affair and Vietnam. Still, this model of New Federalism matched the people's fears that the national government had gotten too big and

Box 3.2 Federalism as Process

18th Century

Interstate Commerce: Article I Section 8 grants Congress the right to regulate commerce between the states. As the American domestic economy expanded, congressional power was magnified.

Necessary and Proper Clause: Article 1 Section 8 contains the "elastic clause" which empowers Congress to "make all laws which shall be necessary and proper" to govern. For instance, the Constitution enumerates the power of Congress to raise taxes. The elastic clause allows Congress to establish a bureaucracy, the Internal Revenue Service, to fulfill this obligation.

19th Century

Supremacy Clause: Article VI declares the Constitution to be the "Supreme Law of the Land," trumping the powers of state constitutions. However, it was only in cases such as *Marbury* v. *Madison* (1803), and *Fletcher* v. *Peck* (1810) that the supremacy of federal law was accepted and made enforceable. As the final adjudicator of the law, the Supreme Court has the potential to be the most powerful branch, if it chooses to exercise this potential.

Citizenship: At the end of the Civil War, the 13th Amendment freed the slaves, the 14th provided citizenship to black males, and the 15th promised the vote, thereby transferring the power over citizenship and voting from the states to the national government.

20th Century

Business Regulation: The Progressive Era brought about an increased regulation of industry and industrial ownership. The federal government began to exercise greater control over the economy to ensure fair prices and high quality products in a competitive environment.

Trust in Government: World War I, the Great Depression, and World War II redefined the government's role in managing national economic and human resources for a common purpose. The successful outcome of the wars and the Depression-era legislation provided public support for expanded government.

Stronger Government: The Cold War struggle in space, nuclear armaments, and world power, aided the public perception and need for a stronger federal government to direct the national defense.

Global Village: The communications revolution of internet computers decreased the importance of distance and frontiers and let corporations, not national governments, dominate trade and commerce. Nixon and Reagan returned some power to the states.

21st Century

The War on Terror and the Rise of the National Security State: Increased governmental power through inter-agency cooperation, enhanced surveillance, and public support for security measures. Emergence of executive directed "unitary government." Massive defense-led increases in government spending.

self-indulgent. After a hiatus during the term of Jimmy Carter, administrations since Ronald Reagan's in 1981 enacted a "New" New Federalism which provided less monetary support, more tasks and thus more control to the states.

In the 1990s, Bill Clinton pioneered a subtle change in the model. Called Rhetorical federalism by political scientists, Clinton downsized the federal government by allowing the states to decide how to spend money transferred from the national treasury to them. While the federal government decreased or eliminated specific program funding to the states, it still mandated technical and policy regulations asserting its will without costing it dollars in such areas as communications, transportation, education, and environmental protection.

Bush continued to devolve power to the states, even while the events of 11 September 2001 and the new Department of Homeland Security strengthened the federal government's role in welfare and police power within each state. The Bush administrations encouraged the view that federal powers should be focused and coordinated by the executive. Overstretched federal budgets helped pay for the "War on Terror," Iraqi reconstruction, and to fund federal tax cuts – leaving the states responsible for welfare programs without funding to implement them.

How these models are applied determines whether state or nation provides each particular public service and, of course, who pays for it. The incoming Obama administration promised greater activity, less arm-twisting, and coequality from the executive and the federal government. Pointing to the future, Obama was eager to ensure that "we will once again be true partners in the work of rebuilding our economy, strengthening our states, and lifting up our entire country" (Obama, 2008a).

Just like the federal government, every state has a written constitution establishing governing practices within its borders. This is not surprising since the original 13 states were in place before there was a United States and their representatives framed the US Constitution. The states mirror the federal division of powers, with popularly elected governors, bicameral legislatures (except Nebraska), and separately functioning court systems topped by state supreme courts. In some larger states, State senators and representatives are virtually full-time legislators. In others, state senators and representatives are part-time and return home from the state capitols once legislative sessions are over to attend to their regular jobs (NCSL, 2008b). States decide on taxes, maintain their own police forces, and set laws for people living within state boundaries. Most states limit executive power by having the people elect state government cabinet members and judges – even state supreme court justices – unlike the federal Constitution, which leaves those selections to the president and confirmation by the Senate. Thus, there is often more internal anarchy in state government as the officials within the executive branch are responsible to the people who elected them and not necessarily to the political party of the governor.

Local government at the county and municipal level is much more idiosyncratic. The US Constitution does not provide a guide for how states should distribute their internal power and the tradition of local autonomy, resulting from the existence of self-governing communities in colonial times, thrives. Across the country, there are over 80,000 units of local government. Mayors, city councils, and city courts – all elected – have responsibility and power in geographically-defined municipalities. County commissioners decide policy, enforce the law, and provide services to areas outside of city borders. Tribal councils with tribal police set policies in Indian country. Elected school boards direct school districts which establish local curricula, and have decision-making and spending powers over local property taxes. Big cities often straddle state boundaries and state power relationships, spreading cooperative local jurisdictions interstate. Many other types of government entities exist, from wildlife protection areas to military bases.

The Branches of Government

The Executive Branch

President Harry S. Truman (1945–53) remarked that his days in office were spent persuading people who should have known better what they ought to do (Neustadt, 1990). Embedded in Truman's lament is the complaint that the presidency is not as powerful as is sometimes supposed, meaning that the chief executive often has to be chief lobbyist. Presidential influence relies on hard constitutional and legal sources of power, softer, personality-based powers such as persuasion and likeability, and pure contingencies. Reagan portrayed a grandfatherly demeanor and a camera presence that caused him to be dubbed "The Great Communicator." Clinton had an affability and boyish charm that few could resist. They contrast sharply with the tough images put forth by the "imperial" presidents of the 1960s, Kennedy, Johnson, and Nixon. George W. Bush relied mostly on an expansive interpretation of the power of the office of the president, folksy language, sophisticated photo opportunities, and high profile press conferences, efficient advisors, and a war against terrorism to promote his programs. Obama combines reforming zeal with the smart use of media his predecessors had pioneered.

Other than in moments of national emergency, there is a mismatch between what a president can actually do and what most people think he can do. A president is limited by the separation of powers and the system of checks and balances as well as by the watchdog attention of the world media. Furthermore, Congress may be controlled by the opposition party; and even when it is not, as with the 111th Congress (2009–11), a president cannot be sure that members of his own party will support him because they often choose district or nation over party. Wars and economic crises influence his range of options as the American public will blame or support him in sometimes unpredictable ways. While any increase in national power certainly strengthens the power of the presidency, short-term issues can wreck a president's ability to influence legislation or conduct foreign policy. Power rises and falls. Franklin Delano Roosevelt (FDR) had enormous power as his energetic resolve coincided with the national emergencies of Depression and World War II – emergencies which demanded and warranted extensions of government responsibility into the daily lives of American citizens.

Whereas no one before or after FDR served more than two terms, the American people elected FDR president four times. Congress, fearing a concentration of power and wanting to prevent this from happening again, voted for term limits. The 22nd Amendment, ratified in 1951, limited any single president to two four-year terms. Underlining how power is divided, neither a president nor his cabinet officers are members of Congress. In fact, the vice-president is the only member of the Executive branch who can cast a vote on legislation – and only in the Senate if his vote is necessary to break a tie.

With only a few years to make a difference, a newly-elected president usually has enormous momentum and Congressional goodwill to get his programs enacted. Barack Obama's 2008 victory promised new directions through unified government, but recent history suggests nothing is certain. Bill Clinton saw his post-inaugural momentum seep away, due to the defeat of his health care reforms, flip-flopping support for gays in the military, and after reelection, the Lewinsky affair – and impeachment. George W. Bush started with less goodwill due to his polarizing 2000 victory, even though he insisted "I'm a uniter, not a divider." Before his first year in office ended, the War on Terror showed that Americans rally around the flag and the person of the President in a crisis. The war in Iraq increased Bush's power and led to his 2004 reelection victory in which Bush declared: "I earned political capital, and now I intend to spend it" (Bush, 2004a). World events, the economy, competence, the media, popularity, and personality, combine to enhance or limit the constitutional power of a president.

The legal power of the presidency comes from the enumerated, inherent, and delegated powers provided by law and precedent. Article II of the Constitution sets forth the presidential powers in approximately 500 words, including the role of Commander-in-Chief of the armed forces and senior diplomatic officer, the authority to appoint federal officers, ministers and Supreme Court Justices, and the power to pardon criminal offenders. Additionally, the president is required annually to inform Congress about the state of the Union. He is expected to initiate legislation in the nation's interests and to serve as the chief executive office of the corporate whole of the United States as well as being the chief bureaucrat formally responsible for every action of government agencies.

While the American people might hope that all presidents would follow Truman's famous maxim, "The buck stops here," they expect political finger-pointing and even admire a person's ability to wriggle out of bottom-line responsibility. While Nixon, Carter and Ford were blamed for almost everything they did or did not do, Reagan's talent to elude blame was so pronounced that nothing seemed to stick to him – "the Teflon President" – and Clinton proved so politically astute as to be labeled "Slick Willie" and "the Comeback Kid." George W. Bush's mistake in believing that Saddam Hussein had weapons of mass destruction and links with Al Qaeda, the enormous budget deficit and ballooning national debt, and the loss of three million jobs did not stop his reelection. Barack Obama acknowledges that voters expect their leaders to project a sense of adeptness and confidence.

In addition to the powers enumerated in the Constitution, presidents have gathered or accrued powers, which have been buttressed by the Supreme Court rulings that "inherent powers" reside in the duties and responsibilities of the Chief Executive. Presidents need such authority to make decisions concerning territorial, economic, and demographic growth. George Washington expanded presidential power by taking on a ceremonial role as Head of State, receiving foreign diplomats, signing treaties, and "embodying" the nation. Thomas Jefferson's purchase of Louisiana (1803) was an obvious example of the exercise of inherent powers, as the Constitution nowhere mentions the right to buy territory. This loose interpretation of presidential prerogative set a precedent for future land deals. Abraham Lincoln pushed the limits of Constitutional powers by calling forth and increasing the size of the militia in 1861 and denying the citizens' rights to *habeas corpus.* Teddy Roosevelt claimed it as the president's duty to be anything that the needs of the nation demanded, unless expressly prohibited by the Constitution or Congress – including the building of the Panama Canal, making executive agreements with leaders of other countries, and establishing regulatory agencies.

Delegated powers are responsibilities transferred to the president by Congress, often in times of crisis or in his role as head of the bureaucracy. An example of crisis delegation was Roosevelt's "New Deal" program, whereby the Congress temporarily relinquished its lawmaking role to give the executive the kinds of power usually reserved for a president in wartime. FDR swiftly enacted a public works program to relieve unemployment. Other delegated powers are less intentional and reflect the president's role as chief administrative officer. Presidents appoint the heads of all federal agencies and thereby create policy according to the political and ideological stance of the appointee on issues such as racial justice, law enforcement, or use of natural resources. Usually these appointments are not as biased as Bush's selection of Attorney General Alberto Gonzalez, who then promoted or fired attorneys based on ideological beliefs. Barack Obama's nomination of Steven Chu and Carol Browner as Energy Secretary and Climate and Energy Czar respectively signaled a stricter regulatory regime for the environment than under the Bush administration, which favored business over environmental issues.

Presidential power also increased during the Cold War as the role of war manager led to a more imperial presidency (Schlesinger, 1973). That power receded with revelations of corruption concerning Vietnam and Watergate, a non-elected president (Ford), and Carter's powerlessness to stop double-digit inflation or return the hostages from Iran. With the end of the Cold War, presidential power softened again before the attack on the World Trade Center stiffened presidential authority, giving George W. Bush the opportunity to rebuild the imperial presidency – or, at the very least, a strong and unitary executive with fewer limits (Brinkley, 2009). The global economic crisis which began in 2008 tests the resolve of Obama to resist the emergence of a twenty-first century imperial presidency based on interventionist economic policy. Illustration 3.1 shows a meeting of the five living presidents in January 2009.

Illustration 3.1 Five Presidents

On 7 January 2009, outgoing President George W. Bush hosted a conclave of still-living presidents to meet with and offer advice to incoming President Barack Obama in the Oval Office. Pictured from left to right are George Herbert Walker Bush (1989–93), Barack Hussein Obama (2009–), George Walker Bush (2001–09), William Jefferson Clinton (1993–2001), and James Earl Carter, Jr. (1976–81). Ronald Wilson Reagan (1981–89) died on 11 June 2004.

(J. Scott Applewhite/AP/Press Association Images, 2009)

Simultaneously, the role of the media in sanctioning or condemning presidential actions affects his strength. After the Watergate affair, reporters, who had traditionally shown discretion in regard to presidents' private lives, were willing to tell all. The media frenzy surrounding Clinton's extra-marital escapades entertained audiences with open discussions that would not have been acceptable before the collapse of media deference. Disgraced President Nixon described executive failure in 1977: "Anybody who is in that [presidential] office who does something that reduces respect for the office makes America a little weaker, a little less admirable, and most important, a little less able to be the leader of the free world" (Birt and Frost, 2002). The postmodern presidency emerged and was christened with synonyms: Imperiled, Protean, Diminished, Rhetorical, and Shrunken. To be president was to be fragile and assailable from all directions. The occupant of the Oval Office became more ordinary. But this situation also played into the hands of experts and spin doctors who could use the media to gain public sympathy even while reporters were tearing at personal lives and language blunders (Kurtz, 1998). Modern presidents recognize the media's influence: Reagan, Clinton, Bush, and Obama were masters of the photo opportunity and the effective use of choreographed images.

A president needs a large staff to manage the duties and personnel of the Executive branch, which currently totals more than three million employees. The Executive Office of the President (EOP) is composed of over 1,500 people specializing in various fields. The president's most trusted advisors make up an informal group called the White House Staff. The Chief of Staff is a facilitator who buffers the president, acts as his most savvy political advisor, literally manages the president's schedule, and decides who gets to see the president and when. The vice-presidency has evolved from "stand-by equipment," as Vice President Nelson Rockefeller quipped in the late 1960s, to become more important during the last three administrations. Ex-Vice-President Dick Cheney was immensely influential in almost every policy decision of the 43rd presidency. Whether Vice President Joe Biden will wield as much influence in the 44th remains to be seen. The National Security Council (NSC) is the executive's most influential group in dealing with internal and external security. It includes the vice president, secretaries of State and Defense, and various senior members of the armed forces and intelligence communities. The Office of Management and Budget (OMB) deals with the president's program, recommends the federal budget, and oversees federal spending programs.

Beyond the EOP, thousands of administrative jobs change hands with every new president. Senior bureaucratic positions in domestic and foreign affairs are filled by presidential nominees who give the president extensive support and influence over national affairs. The president's cabinet is made up of a second body of advisors who are appointed by the president – and confirmed by the Senate – to head federal departments. The significance of the cabinet changes according to the managerial style of the president, but the US does not practice a cabinet-style government of collective responsibility and decision-making common to many parliamentary democracies. The power of the Department heads for Trade, Housing, Energy, Education, Defense, State, and so on, stems directly from the president. Cabinet members are not elected (explaining why Secretary of State Hillary Clinton resigned her senatorial seat), even if many have established political power bases of their own. Critics have claimed that the cabinet is simply an advisory body with real decisions being made within the EOP and appointments made to showcase diversity rather than competence. This charge may be unfair, given the talent residing in the current body.

The presidency is resilient and the world is unstable enough to provide opportunities for power to rise or fall according to circumstance. The presidency provides a focal point for the American people and the world – a central and unified institution in the body of one person. The Constitution originated this role for the executive, but years of discovering inherent rights and adding delegated powers have created a much more powerful office than the Founders imagined or desired. The prominence of the office is reflected by its central position in media attention and public consciousness. In this lies its weakness: the presidency can lead to unrealistic public expectations in its power to deal with all situations. Traditionally, the American public has been impatient with presidents who have failed to win wars and bring troops home, to create growth, or to stop inflation. A collision of these factors translated into public approval ratings of the president's performance at below 30 percent towards the end of Bush's second term (*WP*, 2009).

The Legislative Branch

Congress is a bicameral legislature made up of 435 representatives and five delegates (commonly called congressmen or congresswomen) in the House of Representatives and 100 senators in the Senate. The Constitution sets two-year terms for representatives and six-year terms for senators. Every even-numbered calendar year, the entire membership of the House and one-third of the Senate stand for re-election. This election cycle makes the House more chaotic as representatives are always on the campaign trail for the next election. The staggered election cycle in the Senate means that even if all the incumbents were to be defeated and replaced by new faces – a highly unlikely scenario – two-thirds of the body would be experienced and provide a certain measure of stability to the national government.

The legislative process is hampered by different term lengths, leading to a more divided government because voters vote at intervals of two years – a very long time in politics. So, the president, senators, and representatives are expressions of the electorate's will at different times. Thus, a majority in one election can turn into a minority in the next election. Midterm elections – two years after a presidential election – frequently serve as "presidential plebiscites," where the voters confirm or condemn presidential actions by electing or defeating members of his party. In contrast to parliamentary systems, a midterm defeat for a president's party does not translate into a formal vote of no confidence in the president.

It has been quite normal for American government to be divided, with different parties controlling different elected branches. Divided government and different term lengths weaken the role of the parties, making cooperation necessary. This creates strong pressures towards bipartisanship, where representatives and senators make decisions and durable compromises on policy across party lines. In 2009, however, the Democrats gained control of all three elected branches, making bipartisanship less important and party loyalty more vital in lawmaking. Democrats seemed likely to have enough Senate seats to control debate after Senator Arlen Specter declared that he was switching to the Democratic Party (see Illustration 3.2).

The working atmosphere varies as the House "bustles" and the Senate is "clubby." House rules are much stricter overall with debating time

Illustration 3.2 Senate Judiciary Chairman Arlen Specter

In January 2006, the Senate Judiciary Committee chaired by Republican Arlen Specter held confirmation hearings on President Bush's last Supreme Court nominee, Samuel Alito. In April 2009, citing personal and political reasons for his actions, Specter switched allegiance to the Democratic Party. Sitting left to right are Sen. Specter, R-Pennsylvania; Sen. Patrick Leahy, D-Vermont; Sen. Edward Kennedy, D-Massachusetts; Sen. Joseph Biden, D-Delaware; Sen. Herb Kohl, D-Wisconsin (partially hidden); and Sen. Dianne Feinstein, D-California.

(Gerald Herbert/AP/Press Association Images, 2006)

severely limited while the Senate allows unlimited time unless 60 senators vote for a debate-ending "cloture motion." The sheer number of people in the much larger House chamber explains some of the difference, as does the effect of term lengths on the internal community of politicians. Because their six-year terms grant them protection from wild swings in public opinion and because of their enhanced stature in representing an entire state instead of a congressional district within a state, senators view issues more nationally. States are more diverse than congressional districts and senators are used to combining disparate opinions into a majority opinion. Their relative few numbers, more genteel working culture, long terms, and statewide electoral mandates give them far more media attention than representatives who must usually decide – with their re-election hanging in the balance – between local issues and national opinion. The House chaos reflects the members' close attention to current, rather than long-term, public opinion.

The dilemma for legislators is whether to follow long-term trends in opinion or to mirror the electorate's present and immediate views. John F. Kennedy noted that a politician's wish to be re-elected might push him to "flatter every public whim and prejudice . . . to put public opinion ahead of public interest" (Safire, 1978). Often voters hold contradictory opinions, believing one thing at any given moment and something quite different over the long-view. For example, in the abstract, most Americans concur that action should be taken to reduce the socioeconomic differences visible between people; but they overwhelmingly oppose specific, concrete actions which could affect their own personal lifestyles. Popular support for the death penalty may waver over the long term, yet sudden heinous crimes such as the 1995 Oklahoma City bombing of a US federal building, the 2001 destruction of the World Trade Center, or the 2002 Washington region sniper attacks caused significant increases in favor of capital punishment (DOS, 2002).

However their members vote, both the House of Representatives and the Senate are fully involved in making the law and making sure the bureaucracy implements and enforces the law. In lawmaking, the House is more specialized and the Senate is generalist. The prime responsibility of the House of Representatives is initiating legislation for the collection and distribution of money through its control over taxes and spending. The Senate is specifically charged with approving or rejecting all presidential appointments and treaties with foreign countries. The original powers of Congress as enumerated in Article I of the Constitution are shown in Box 3.3.

Box 3.3 Constitutional Powers of Congress

- Levy and collect taxes
- Borrow money for the public treasury
- Make rules and regulations governing interstate and foreign commerce
- Make uniform rules for the naturalization of foreign citizens
- Coin money, state its value, and provide for the punishment of counterfeiters
- Set weights' and measures' standard
- Establish bankruptcy laws
- Establish post offices and post roads
- Issue patents and copyrights
- Set up a federal courts system
- Punish piracy
- Declare war, raise and support armies, provide for a navy
- Call out the militia to enforce federal laws, suppress lawlessness or repel invasions
- Make all laws for the seat of government
- Make all laws necessary to enforce the Constitution

Source: Dept. of State, http://usinfo.state.gov/products/pubs/outusgov/ch4.htm

The work of the House and Senate is coordinated along lines of party affiliation. The legislative agenda of a chamber is set by the leader of the party with the greatest numerical representation – called the majority party – and the working agenda of each of the committees is generally set by the longest-tenured committee member representing the majority party. Party leaders go to considerable lengths to enforce voting discipline among their members, and they are often successful due to their ability to provide campaign money, information, and expertise.

All the same, party affiliation is not always the decisive factor for American politicians. Representatives vote to improve the economy of their home district by, for example, building a military base, establishing a national park, or constructing a dam. This is called "bringing home the pork" or "pork-barrel" legislation – that is, keeping the home folks fed. The amount of pork and the constant electioneering let voters focus on politicians as individuals rather than as party members, personalizing elections in such a way that congressional elections take on more of a candidate-centered rather than a party-centered approach. This strengthens the independence of elected officials and means that party leaders must woo their own members on every issue.

Committees are at the heart of lawmaking. Legislators spend much more time involved in process, in the production of the actual wording of the law – based on debate and expert help – than they do voting in chambers. Woodrow Wilson contrasted committee work with full House proceedings as the difference between "Congress at work," and "on public exhibition." Committee work is a slow and unglamorous process.

The large number of representatives enables a division of labor which produces specialists within policy fields; the small number of senators translates into fewer and broader committees. On any given day, there are close to 200 committees of various types – standing, select, joint, and conference – operating. The 20 or so standing committees in each house are a fixed feature of congressional life, in that they are involved both in the formulation of law and the feedback of its effects from the bureaucracy (Departments and Agencies implementing the law). They also exert oversight over specific areas of policy implementation, such as the Senate Committee on Foreign Relations. Select committees are temporary, created with a single task in mind. When the task is over, the committee dissolves. Joint committees include members from both houses, such as the Joint Economic Committee. For a bill to become a law, both houses must agree to the exact wording and details. Conference committees, including both senators and representatives, are set up specifically to reconcile differences in legislation passed in each of the houses. The need for discussion based on specialist knowledge of particular issues means that committees often have to set up subcommittees. The House Livestock and Horticulture Subcommittee with 20 members, for example, is a subcommittee of the 50-member House Agriculture Committee. Subcommittees discuss the specifics of a law and conduct hearings with expert witnesses to ensure that the detailed drafting of a law is consistent with intended policy outcomes. Committees are essential to the legislative process. Figure 3.2 shows how a bill becomes a law.

To begin the lawmaking process, ideas for legislation come from any branch or level of government, interest group, community, or individual. To initiate the legislative process, the idea must be sponsored by a member of Congress who formally introduces it on the floor of the House or Senate as a "bill." Each bill is assigned to a relevant committee.

The work of a committee is structured by its Chair – the senior member of the biggest party – who is attuned to the political desires of his party. Chairs have considerable power and decide which bills to

Figure 3.2 The Lawmaking Process

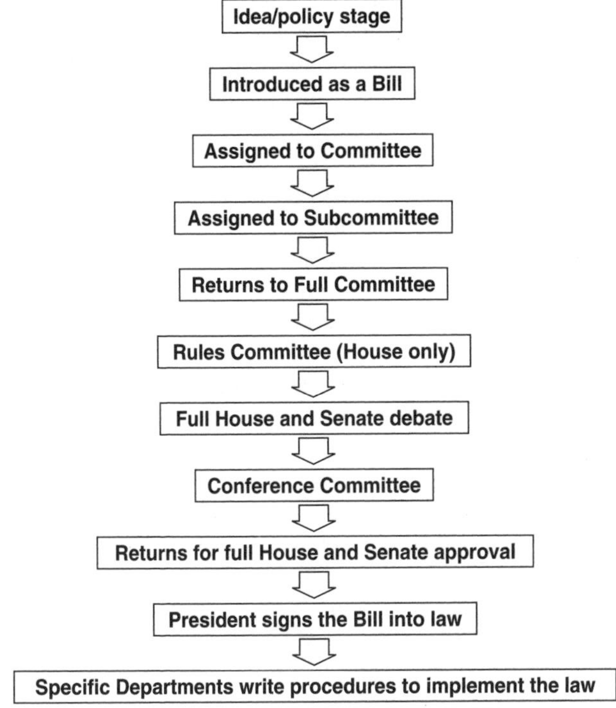

Note: Bills go through the stages shown in Figure 3.2 above in both houses (Rules Committee excepted). This figure shows the route of a successful bill. At any stage, the bill can fail and be dropped. Even when it survives the Congress, a president can veto the bill and return it to Congress for revision or oblivion. Congress can then overturn the veto by a two-thirds majority vote.

consider or ignore – there are far more bills introduced than committees can handle. Thus the majority party controls the legislative agenda both through the committees and through the leadership offices of Speaker of the House and of the Senate's president "*pro tempore*" (for the "time being" – the vice-president is the formal president of the Senate). The Speaker and Senate president decide on legislative priorities and appoint committee chairs from members of their own party.

The strength of party affiliation and the influence of the House Speaker or Senate president can be overestimated. Committee Chairs can exert significant independence, a result of the seniority principle and consequently having worked within committees for a long time and of a feeling of collegiality among all committee members. Powerful chairs who realize they have reached the limits of their political careers offer majority leaders little leverage. In 1994 the seniority principle was broken temporarily. Newt Gingrich – then Speaker of the House – passed over senior members for younger members whose Conservative ideological stance matched his own, cementing him as the most powerful Speaker for a generation. In late 1998 the seniority system re-emerged following Gingrich's demise. In 2007 Nancy Pelosi became the first woman to hold the job.

Subcommittees study bills and listen to advice from experts both in and out of government. Once convinced of the merits of a bill, the subcommittee reports to the full committee which, when satisfied, reports it ready for debate by the full House or Senate. In the House, the Rules Committee sets rules and time limits for debate. After debate and changes, members vote on the bill. Unless there are compelling local or ideological reasons not to, members usually rely on their party's advice and vote accordingly. If voted down in either chamber, the bill is dead; if passed, the bill goes to a Conference Committee to iron out differences between the bills passed in different chambers. The bill is sent back to both houses for one, last time. If approved, it goes to the president for final approval, which he usually gives, signing it into law. If the president does not like the bill and less than 10 days remain in the legislative session before recess, he can kill the bill by refusing to sign it. This is called a "pocket veto." The president can also veto the bill and return it to Congress, where it is either modified and returned to the president, or simply dies. If it can get the support of at least two-thirds of Congress, the legislators override the president's veto. The bill now becomes law and is called an "act." Committees have the right of oversight – keeping a watchful eye – to ensure that the act is applied as it was meant and that its effects match legislative intent.

The legislative process is deliberate and slow most of the time. However, Congress can act promptly during times of national crisis or when popular opinion clearly backs a certain course of action. In 1933, FDR and Congress sped through over 100 pieces of legislation in the famous "Hundred Days." Promising a vast program of change when inaugurated, Obama sought inspiration from FDR's purposeful energy to combat the dire economic circumstances, declaring that "the basic principle that government has a role to play in kick starting the economy that has ground to a halt is sound" (Obama, 2008b).

Congress is not, and never has been, a mirror of American society. Although during the last generation officeholders have become more

Table 3.1 Profile of the 111th Congress (2009–11)

Gender/Ethnicity	*Population (%)*	*Representatives (%)*	*Representatives (No.)*	*Senators (%)*
Male	49	82.3	358	83
Female	51	17.7	77	17
African American	12	9.6	42	1
Latino (Hispanic)	13	5.7	25	3
Asian American	4	1.6	7	2
American Indian	1	0.2	1	0

Source: *Congressional Quarterly*, 2008.

representative of American society in terms of gender and race, there has been less change in terms of education, occupation and income of officeholders. As Table 3.1 shows, white males predominate in the 111th Congress. The average age of representatives is 56 – slightly younger than the 63-year average age of senators.

In all democracies there is tension in the way elected officials view their responsibilities towards the people: should they act as delegates or trustees? Delegates treat the policy wishes of their supporters as instructions. Trustees are freer to follow their own informed views on how to best help their district and nation. Most elected officials mix and match these two approaches. If an issue exerts strong passions among the folks back home, it is almost certain to bring out the delegate; if the issue is not particularly important locally, the representative is more likely to vote in the trustee mode. The national political climate also matters. For example, the ideological rigor of the Republicans' 1994 "Contract with America" encouraged representatives of both sides to vote more along party lines, as did increased polarization and antagonism between the parties during the George W. Bush administrations, and a feeling of steadfastness in defeat among vanquished Republicans in 2008.

Collectively, Congress represents a synthesis of models of government. Candidates are elected by the will of the majority, yet their effect is diluted by the plurality of districts and institutions within the three elected branches. Additionally, the social profile of elected officers, and the vast expense of getting elected, suggests that legislators' lives are far removed from the daily concerns of ordinary citizens.

The pluralist model argues that pressures to reflect the opinions of not only the majority of the voters, but of different vocal minority interests pushes elected officials into a delegate/trustee mix and match of positions. The bifocal – local and national – nature of representation forces lawmakers toward compromise, giving different groups of voters and interests access from a number of directions. Occasionally majority opinion gets decoupled from the policy process, leaving legislators and sectional interests to brew private or "elite" policy outcomes.

The Judicial Branch

In contemporary America the Judicial branch is the equal of the others, but this has not always been the case. The Founders imagined the Court as the "least dangerous" branch and the Constitution devotes just three short paragraphs in Article III to establish the Court and to empower Congress to construct a federal judicial system. The real power of the Court came in the early 1800s when Chief Justice John Marshall used the Constitution's Supremacy Clause to declare the federal courts superior to the state courts. Marshall also established the principle of judicial review to make the Supreme Court the final judge on whether congressional acts, state laws, lower court judgments, and executive actions follow the rules set out in the Constitution.

Using the power of judicial review, the Court is always involved in the most politically sensitive issues, including racial integration, prayer in the schools, abortion rights, handgun control, death penalty decisions, and fairness issues. Most cases before the Court deal with 1st and 14th Amendment freedom and equality protections. For example, in 1989, in the name of the free-speech clause of the First Amendment, the Supreme Court held that it is unconstitutional to punish a person for burning the American flag. No discussion of civil society – of liberties and rights – would be complete without the strong voice of the Supreme Court in the resolution of the issue. This contrasts markedly to most other Western countries, where such issues are dealt with by the elected legislatures.

Judicial activities are divided into separate federal and state jurisdictions. The system of federal courts includes a tripartite division among US District Courts, US Courts of Appeal, and the Supreme Court. The federal courts hear appeals from judgments rendered by lower courts, but mostly they work with original disputes over federal law, suits by or against the federal government, or cases between citizens of different states. The US Supreme Court is predominantly an appeals court which rules on the constitutionality of a law or action, and in that way establishes the law for all courts.

The Supreme Court consists of nine judges – called justices – who are appointed by the president and confirmed by the Senate. Because justices serve for life and because a president can only appoint a new justice when a vacancy occurs, each president's influence is limited. When a justice retires, changes career, or dies, the Justice Department creates a list of likely candidates which will be reduced to a shorter list by senior White House advisors. The president selects his nominee and sends the name to the Senate, where the Senate Judiciary Committee conducts hearings to determine a candidate's background qualifications, approach to the law, and judicial philosophy. Senate approval is not automatic. Even though confirmed in 1991, Clarence Thomas termed confirmation hearings a "high-tech lynching." President Bush's 2005 nominee White House Counsel Harriet Miers, withdrew before the hearings because of resistance to her appointment. Conservative Republicans, including Senate Judiciary Committee member Sam Brownback, were worried by Miers's vague stance on abortion (Stolberg, 2005).

Early in 2009 the Court consisted of members appointed by Ford (John Paul Stephens III), Reagan (Antonin Scalia and Anthony Kennedy), George H. W. Bush (David H. Souter and Clarence Thomas), Clinton (Ruth Bader Ginsburg and Stephen G. Breyer), and George W. Bush (John G. Roberts Jr. and Samuel Anthony Alito, Jr.). Republican presidents who believed in limiting the role of the Federal government and of repatriating responsibility to the states appointed seven of these justices. The Roberts Court – all courts are named after their Chief Justice – is a relatively conservative body which reflects an adherence to individual and states' rights over the national collective (Banks and Blakeman, 2008). David Souter's retirement in 2009 and the nomination of Sonia Sotomayor a Latina, to the bench allowed Obama to leave an imprint on the Supreme Court (see Illustration 3.3).

Judicial politics are dynamic and the Court is active in politics by nature of its selective and interpretive judgments. In deciding a case, justices have considerable discretion and are influenced by ideas of judicial method and judicial philosophy. Judicial method can be traced along a line with procedural ideas at one extreme and substantive ideas at the other. Put simply, a procedural view is based on a justice's strict adherence to accepted rules when formulating judgments. A substantive approach concentrates more on outcomes than process with judgments made for the effects they will have, rather than strictly according to precedent. Justices also must balance judicial restraint against judicial activism. Judicial restraint stems from a philosophy that elected legislators should make the law and that justices should

Illustration 3.3 The (Tilting) Scales of Justice (Kennedy)

Since 2006, the Supreme Court has often split 5–4 with Justice Kennedy holding the swing vote. This cartoon shows that the calibration of the scales of justice depends on the views of the people sitting on the bench. Clarence Thomas, Antonin Scalia, Samuel Alito, and Chief Justice John G. Roberts are pictured in the "RIGHT" scale, Anthony M. Kennedy is the fulcrum in the middle, and Ruth Bader Ginsburg, David Souter, John Paul Stevens, and Stephen G. Breyer are in the "LEFT" scale. With Souter's retirement in 2009, Obama faced the difficult task of selecting a justice who would maintain the balance. He chose Sonia Sotomajor.

(David Horsey, 2007)

closely follow the original intent of statutes. Judicial activism assumes that justices, even though not elected, should make judgments in-line with an ever-changing society. Division and partisanship in the elected branches has complicated matters in recent years as divided government sends mixed signals to the Court. Partisanship also raises the significance of the verdicts, as the Court mediates between elected branches controlled by ideologically-enlivened parties (Clayton and Giordano, in Peele *et al.*, 1998).

The current Court is divided into a conservative group emphasizing restraint and established process on the one hand and incremental change on the other, a centrist element oscillating between deference to and interpretation of the letter of the law, and a faction of judicial activists more concerned about law's spirit (Toobin, 2007). Consensus is difficult to obtain and many verdicts from the Roberts Court split 5–4 in favor of restraint and established process. While unanimity of opinion is not required, lower courts can more easily follow precedent when the Supreme Court is unified. Additionally, the more contentious the issue, the better a unanimous or near-unanimous verdict works to convince the public on a certain point. For example, the 9–0 decision on school desegregation in 1954 convinced Americans that the federal government would enforce integration. 5–4 splits ensure that more cases will arise in hopes of swinging a centrist justice to the other side and overturning the decision.

The Supreme Court has the flexibility and freedom to decide which cases to hear. It selects less than 100 cases a year from the approximately 7,000 cases discussed in Court conferences. If at least four justices agree to hear a case, it is placed on the docket. Choosing its own cases allows the Court to direct the law in areas it wants and ignore it in others – even though the Court often adds cases the administration or national media push strongly. Of course, just how the justices interpret the law depends on their legal philosophy and personal beliefs.

Legal adjudication is based on the principles of constitutional and statute law, and, in their absence, common law (or judge-made law). The adjudication of statute law, especially recent, is less problematical than common law, as the intent of the legislation is usually more obvious, either from the legal text itself, or from the records of the committee or government department primarily responsible for the drafting of the text. Exceptions occur when cases are heard which are based on contradictory or clashing pieces of law. Common law is based on the principle that if there is no existing written or statute law on an issue, the uniformity of the law will be enforced by using earlier judgments – especially those from higher courts – called precedents. The briefness of the Constitution, the large number of states, the plethora of laws which need to be reinterpreted as time and conditions change, and the fact that the US is the most highly-litigious society on earth, give the Supreme Court enormous leverage to shape society through its decisions.

The federal court system also includes 14 appellate courts and 94 district courts with over 800 judges. Presidents have a great impact at these levels, leaving a durable legacy by filling vacancies with personal choices. Democrats Jimmy Carter and Bill Clinton changed the courts dramatically by eschewing middle-class and middle-aged white men and appointing hundreds of women and members of racial minorities. Their choices have made the Judicial branch far more representative of diversity in contemporary America than Congress. George W. Bush underlined the legal philosophy of his nominees, and selected them to "faithfully interpret the law, not legislate from the bench" (OPS, 2004). President Obama's nominees will likely showcase more expansive interpretations of the law and continue recent moves toward greater diversity.

In addition to the president's power to select judges, the Executive branch has other channels into the Judicial branch. The Department of Justice deals with the day-to-day management of judicial affairs. The attorney general, who is appointed by the president, is the nation's chief law enforcement officer. The attorney general is a powerful aide to the president with the authority to set cases selected to push the president's political agenda into the federal courts. The president also has an officer, the solicitor general, who represents the federal government in dealings with the Supreme Court. The solicitor general decides which judgments the government should appeal.

Parallel to the federal system of courts are the state courts, which adjudicate the overwhelming majority of the approximately 90 million lawsuits tried each year. State inferior courts – often divided into city or county jurisdictions – deal with routine cases of traffic violations, divorce, child custody, or other relatively minor and civil suits. State superior courts preside over multi-county districts and convene juries to try criminal cases – such as burglaries, murders, and assaults. Because criminal cases can involve prison terms or capital punishment, a jury of twelve people usually determines the fate of the accused. This use of ordinary citizens connects people to the judicial process, an important element of justice because the social backgrounds of jurors differ widely and provide a cross-section of society, whereas lawyers and judges still generally have middle- and upper-class backgrounds and outlooks.

Each state has its own appeals courts, topped by a state supreme court. States vary in the number of courts and in terms for judges who are either appointed by state governors or elected by the people, in contrast with federal judges. Elected judges who must stand for re-election may feel pressure to follow public opinion, which can lead to popular but legally dubious decisions. Appeals courts are in place to rectify possible errors.

With separate federal and state systems (Figure 3.3), each with three levels of courts, groups who want to change the laws have multiple points of access to present "class action suits" to bring people in similar circumstances together to have a verdict rendered which will

Figure 3.3 The Court System

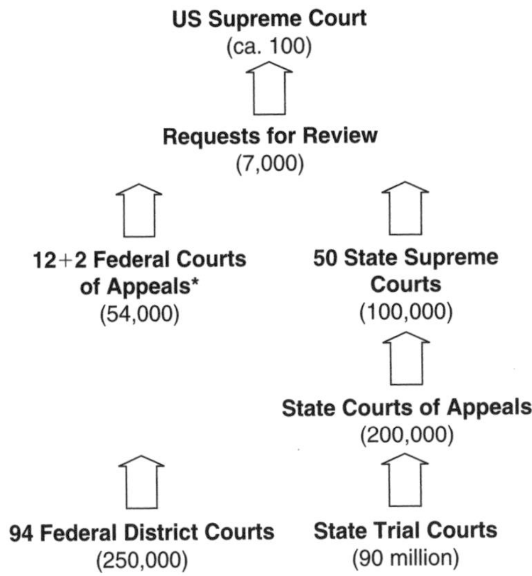

* There are twelve regional United States Court of Appeals, one United States Court of Appeal for the federal circuit, and one United States Court of Military Appeals.

Figures in brackets indicate the approximate number of cases heard since 2000.

Source: US Courts (2001, 2008).

apply to all of them. For example, in 1995 and 1997, women who had had breast augmentation surgery, whether or not they had experienced side effects, pursued and won a single suit against the makers of the silicon implants by claiming health risks that had been concealed by the manufacturers. Tobacco companies have been forced to pay millions of dollars to smokers for concealing the fact that nicotine in cigarettes is addictive and potentially more harmful than enthusiastic smokers realize – due to the tar levels actually taken in rather than recorded in laboratories. Environmental groups have originated cases against factories for polluting air and water resources. Access to the courts requires money and expertise, which favor powerful interests in the private and political realms, but multiple levels of courts give access to groups and citizens who can challenge the laws or the political majority. Ease of access helps explain the high numbers of lawsuits in the United States and the way in which the courts provide cultural glue for the diverse interests of diverse peoples in the United States.

Often the Supreme Court is criticized as an unelected branch of government which has an impact upon people's lives without being accountable. Controversy surrounds some judgments, yet the predominant role of the Court is to guard and mediate the Constitution in the present and to bring about closure. When the government system is challenged, the Supreme Court usually shows its strength by settling the controversy. In *Gore* v. *Bush,* the case that decided the 2000 presidential election, a divided verdict was good enough for the American people. Bush wanted the Court to stop the manual recount of 170,000 contested votes in Florida, even though the Florida Supreme Court had ordered the count to continue, as Gore requested. The US Supreme Court overruled the Florida Supreme Court decision. In its second verdict, 5–4, the Court disallowed a recount of the tainted ballots. Five days later Gore accepted the decision, praised the system, and urged Americans to support president-elect Bush.

In June 2008, in *Boumediene v. Bush*, the Supreme Court ruled by 5–4 that Guantánamo Bay detainees seized in Bosnia in 2002 had the constitutional right to use the federal courts to challenge their continued incarceration. This case confirmed that the rule of law extended to Guantánamo for the third time in four years. Leading the majority opinion, Justice Kennedy remarked that "The laws and Constitution are designed to survive, and remain in force, in extraordinary times" (*NYT*, 2008). In November 2008, Boumediene and four others won their case for release in the Federal District Court in Washington DC. Meanwhile, Barack Obama has promised to close Guantánamo detention center.

American government is a story of motion. The three federal branches are dynamic, and their relative strengths are affected by diverse factors. The executive, legislature, and judiciary compete for influence on the federal stage. The states and the federal government are likewise interdependent and competitive, with power overlapping and flowing between jurisdictions. Legitimacy aggregates from ballot boxes and up to government at all levels: local, state and federal. Importantly, the commuted authority of electors is also in flux, affecting power dynamics elsewhere. This discussion of power flows brings us into the realms of politics, and will be continued in the next chapter.

4

The Political System

The 2008 Election

The presidential election of 2008 held the nation – and the world – transfixed for more than a year. A breathtakingly diverse group of serious candidates fought for the nomination of their parties: Hillary Clinton, John Edwards, Rudi Giuliani, Mike Huckabee, John McCain, Barack Obama and Mitt Romney brought the issues of gender, populism, urban versus rural, religion, hero status, race, age, and Mormonism into the spotlight. Finally two outsiders – 72-year-old war hero John McCain (Republican) and African American Barack Obama (Democrat) faced off in the most extensive and expensive contest ever seen. Would age trump race as a turnoff issue for voters? And could a Republican – any Republican – win with the party's fortunes at its lowest point in a generation? Democrats chose to compete nationally, instead of throwing "billions into an ever-shrinking target slice of the country" in the handful of swing states seen in recent elections (Moser, 2007). The voter turnout in 2008 defied predictions by increasing slightly over 2004, as younger voters, African Americans and Latinos outweighed the decline in Republican constituencies. While Obama's national victory was definitive in Minnesota senatorial recounts rumbled on for months – showing as in 2000 that the distance between ballot boxes and courtrooms is short.

Many pundits agreed that the perfect storm intersected with the perfect candidate. Weary of war, worried about recession, and wanting renewal, Americans were ready to reinvigorate their democracy by electing the young half-Kenyan Barack Obama to the presidency. Obama promised rejuvenation, redemption, and the future, breaking with the polarization of the Clinton and Bush administrations. Obama embodied America, and American self-conception in so many ways: the handsome child of an immigrant, mixed racial origins, an (admittedly atypical) middle class upbringing, upward mobility, a beautiful wife and children, and a can-do attitude which promised a better future. It helped, of course, that Obama's team framed him as offering a fresh slate. Emerging into national politics in 2004, Obama was unconnected to the Clinton presidency or by the fallout after War on Terror patriotism subsided to leave most Democrats compromised by their stance over Iraq. Even though Republican John McCain scrupulously distanced himself from the Bush administration, his military background and "maverick" righteousness was no match for the man who seemed to embody the adage that "No army is as powerful as an idea whose time has come." Obama won by the largest margin in twenty years.

Participatory Democracy

Voters and Voting

American citizens generally register to vote at the local courthouse in their hometowns when they turn 18 years old. Some states require them to give their political affiliation, usually Democrat, Republican, or Independent. Citizens in some states can also register at libraries when they sign up for a lending card, at police stations when they get a driver's license, or by mail when they move outside the city, county, or state. Because Americans move a lot, they must often re-register in a new city or state. Once on the electoral roll, Americans can vote in the many separate or combined elections to pick local dog-catchers, school board members, mayors, members of city councils, sheriffs, draft board members, judges, secretaries of state, lieutenant governors, governors, highway commissioners, state legislators, US Senators and Representatives, and the President of the United States, to name only a few of the elected posts.

In the contemporary United States, the vote is a universal right, whereas in the past voting was viewed more as a privilege. Even though the Constitution declared "We the People," the Founders had real reasons to fear "mob rule" and so restricted voting rights to those who owned property and met residency requirements. "We the People" was an elite idea of representative rule before the agitation by free whites increased in 1828 and led to the expansion of the suffrage and establishment of the Democratic Party. By mid-century, all white men could vote. Black men received the vote in 1870 only to have it removed on a state-by-state basis in the South; women were included in 1920; and American Indians were classified as citizens in 1924. There were important Voting Rights Acts in the 1960s and 1980s which finally ensured that everyone who wanted to vote could vote: except people disqualified for serious breaches of the law.

In addition to deciding on leaders, voters vote directly on the issues. Nearly half the states allow their citizens to vote for or against state laws and 49 states require a popular vote on any change in the state's constitution. When state legislatures put a proposal to the people's vote – instead of deciding matters themselves – the vote is called a referendum. In addition to a legislature's power to call for a referendum, 23 states allow the people to initiate a referendum from the grassroots level without going through a city council decision, state legislature, judicial ruling, or congressional procedure. Advocates for a new law often go door-to-door, collecting signatures on petitions. Once enough signatures are gathered – from 1,000 to 60,000 according to jurisdiction – the "initiative" is placed on the ballot. People vote on such issues as whether or not to raise or lower taxes, decide if alcohol can be sold in their counties, build sports stadiums, reduce penalties for marijuana usage, and allow gay or lesbian adoptions. In 2003, Californians voted to recall incumbent Governor Gray Davis and to replace him with Hollywood superstar Arnold Schwarzenegger in a muscular demonstration of direct democracy (Illustration 4.1). Votes in eleven states approved of state constitutional amendments banning gay-marriage in 2004 and three more in 2008, demonstrating popular support for traditional family constructions (Box 4.1). 36 states held ballot referenda in conjunction with the 2008 election (NCSL, 2008a).

Additional concerns swarm around the question of who votes. In the 1830s Alexis de Tocqueville wrote glowingly of American democracy: "In countries in which universal suffrage exists, the majority is never doubtful, because neither party can reasonably pretend to represent that portion of the community which has not voted" (Tocqueville, 1994). Tocqueville could not have imagined that most Americans would regularly abstain from casting their votes in off year elections at the start of the twenty-first century. Americans have long agreed on the principle that all citizens have the right to vote; but that in no way implies that Americans see voting as a duty. They rather see it as a freedom and an equal opportunity to do with as one wishes. Yet, does it really matter if Americans decide not to vote? The answer is hard to determine. Political scientists acknowledge that individual Americans and various organizations have many ways to participate

Illustration 4.1 Schwarzenegger Wins California Gubernatorial Election

In 1968, Arnold Alois Schwarzenegger immigrated from Austria to America and has come to embody the ideology of the self-made man. In this photograph, Schwarzenegger and his wife Maria Shriver – a member of the American "royal" family, the Kennedys – celebrate his victory as Governor of California. In his inaugural speech, Schwarzenegger declared: "I have an immigrant's optimism. . . . I see California as the golden dream by the sea."

(Kenneth James/CORBIS, 2003)

in and make an impact upon political decisions without ever stepping into a voting booth. Some specialists even believe that voting is one of the least influential forms of political participation available to the people.

Box 4.1 Proposed Marriage Amendment: California, 2008

PROPOSITION **8**

ELIMINATES RIGHT OF SAME-SEX COUPLES TO MARRY. INITIATIVE CONSTITUTIONAL AMENDMENT.

OFFICIAL TITLE AND SUMMARY **PREPARED BY THE ATTORNEY GENERAL**

ELIMINATES RIGHT OF SAME-SEX COUPLES TO MARRY. INITIATIVE CONSTITUTIONAL AMENDMENT.

- Changes the California Constitution to eliminate the right of same-sex couples to marry in California.
- Provides that only marriage between a man and a woman is valid or recognized in California.

Summary of Legislative Analyst's Estimate of Net State and Local Government Fiscal Impact:

- Over the next few years, potential revenue loss, mainly from sales taxes, totaling in the several tens of millions of dollars, to state and local governments.
- In the long run, likely little fiscal impact on state and local governments.

In November 2008, voters in three states approved amendments to state constitutions to define marriage as a union of one man and one woman, thereby joining the eleven states who had so voted in 2004. The summarized text of the 2008 California Proposition is presented in the box above. Amendments to the state constitutions in the fourteen states were provoked by the February 2004 actions of the Massachusetts Supreme Court which ruled that same-sex marriages conformed with the state's constitution. Opponents of "gay marriage" feared that the Massachussetts Supreme Courts ruling would set a precedent nationwide (*source*: California General Election, Official Voter Information Guide, 2008).

Interest Groups

There are two basic forms of participatory behavior for individual or group action: conventional and unconventional. Conventional behavior includes the regular voting and party systems that legitimize existing institutional arrangements. Unconventional participation includes, for example, the disruptive demonstrations against the Bush administration's immigration restrictions in 2006 (Illustration 4.2). In contemporary America, everyday individual political behavior spans the spectrum from the supportive to the disruptive. Opinions are most often expressed through interest groups, not by individual voters. For instance, a member of the American Federation of Teachers (AFT) – a

Illustration 4.2 Pro-immigration Rally, Chicago, 2006

On 1 May 2006 a nationwide day of protest was held, with huge crowds turning out in Chicago, New York, Washington, Las Vegas, Miami, Los Angeles, San Francisco, Atlanta, Denver, Phoenix, New Orleans, and Milwaukee to voice their opposition to congressional proposals calling for more stringent immigration laws and border controls. Perhaps as many as 300,000 demonstrators thronged Union Park, Chicago, in support of the estimated 11–12 million undocumented immigrants living and working in the US who would be affected by the legislation. Americans commonly participate in unconventional political activities, such as the muscular demonstrations of mass opinion shown above.

(M. Spencer Green/AP/Press Association Images, 2006)

union with a qualified membership and specific interests – may abstain from voting in a local, state, or national election but is still intimately involved in the political process through the collective influence of the AFT. Or, take the example of a busy chief executive officer (CEO) who decides not to take an hour off to vote, but influences policy decisions when engaged in management decisions through a business group, such as the National Association of Manufacturers (NAM). The individuals in these two examples have exhibited conventional behavior, but they could also be involved in disruptive actions, through strikes or illegal monopolies or insider trading schemes that affect the entire US economy, damaging confidence in the economy and in the political system's ability to regulate it. Interest group politics are growing while individual voting participation remains modest.

An interest group, often called a lobby, is made up of people or businesses who organize themselves to influence public policy on certain issues. They link civil society and the market to political institutions by supporting or declining to support particular politicians. Legislators are lobbied directly by experts who present them with detailed research or opinion polls and most often contribute money to a politician's (re)election fund. Interest groups have narrow policy focuses, whereby politicians and parties face broad and varied constituencies.

Interest groups are of two types. Open groups allow anyone to join, claim to work for the public good, and have mass memberships consisting of individuals with limited resources. Such open groups include the Sierra Club, dedicated to the preservation of wilderness areas; the American Civil Liberties Union (ACLU), which especially focuses on the First Amendment's protection of freedom of speech; the Christian Coalition, which supports laws against homosexuals and abortions; and the National Rifle Association (NRA), which defends the rights of gun owners. Even the little known group, The National Bowling Association (TNBA), has as its main aims the promotion of "sportsmanship, fellowship and friendship among its 23,000 membership." Its website announces that the TNBA "plays a part in the national movement toward implementation of American democracy, ideals and principles" – evidenced by its influence in desegregating bowling halls since 1950. Membership is open to all bowlers or lovers of bowling of any race (TNBA, 2008). These open interest groups have large and disparate memberships, rely on small membership dues or private contributions to support their lobbying efforts, and more often than not provide voters, instead of dollars, to politicians who support their causes.

The other type of lobby group is the closed interest, which promotes action to benefit very specific organizations or groups of people. These closed groups include labor unions such as the American Federation of Labor (AFL) and the Major League Baseball Players Association (MLBPA), trade and professional organizations such as the AFT representing educators, the American Bar Association (ABA) for lawyers, the American Medical Association (AMA) for doctors, and the Bowling Proprietors' Association of America (BPAA). The BPAA and its associated Political Action Committee (B-PAC) represents bowling alley owners. B-PAC raised over $150,000 (and spent around $130,000) in the 2007–8 election cycle as part of an "aggressive strategy . . . shaping the legislative debate and promoting the issues that are of importance to our members." B-PAC increases the bowling industry's political presence by funding candidates "who are supportive of the bowling industry" (B-PAC, 2008). These closed interests use money and the promise of supplying voters to lobby for candidates who support their interests. In 2007–8, the BPAA put over $82,000 into specific Republican campaign chests for seven senatorial and five house candidates (FEC–BPAA, 2008). The AFT donated well over $10 million, and endorsed Barack Obama's campaign in July 2008 (FEC–ACT, 2008; AFT, 2008). Closed interests, with the exception of unions, usually have small memberships, but their strong financial resources make sure that politicians will listen to their agenda. The concerns of bowlers and bowling proprietors illustrate the push behind the expansion of lobbies in recent years. Both are focused on issues which are too small to be effectively promoted by parties, but that are important to their members and promoted by groups through support, candidate endorsement and campaign cash.

The ideological and socioeconomic contrasts between the parties are also reflected in interest groups. Commercial interest groups like the BPAA more often support the Republicans in the hope of influencing their policy agenda than the Democrats, who gain more support from unions and public interests. Lobbyists come up with ideas for legislation, and provide feedback to politicians on the effects of legislation and of voters' responses to it. The Christian Coalition claims to deliver "tens of millions" of voter guides in election years (CC, 2009); the AFT made contact with more than 4 million people in 2008 (AFT, 2008). Money collected by interests flows towards powerholders, which for the 2007–8 election cycle meant the Democratic Party. Partisan interest is thus tempered by the need to be heard. The influence of interests gained through campaign contributions has come under repeated scrutiny over the last generation.

The existence of interest groups helps to illuminate the pluralist nature of American civil society. Interest groups allow Americans to express their views and preferences constantly, not just in voting booths on election days every two years. They give citizens with particular concerns many points of access to the political process. In a society topping 300 million people divided into thousands of subcultures and many classes with varying religious, educational, and occupational interests, lobby groups expand democracy by granting minority groups a voice to augment the simple arithmetic of a winner-take-all voting system of majority rule. With interest group politics, various minority groups or minority interests can be heard and might succeed on issues that would never survive a majority vote. The darker side is that groups with greater resources in terms of members, expertise, and money have disproportionate influence on policy debates.

Recent decades have seen the rise of think-tanks which link interest groups and policymaking to academia. Think-tanks operate across broad swathes of the political landscape and cover much more policy ground than single interest groups. Think-tanks are funded by private gifts from individuals and organizations, through publishing, grants, and endowments. Prominent think-tanks, like the Brookings Institution (founded 1927) and the Heritage Foundation (founded 1973) employ hundreds of top scholars, assistants, and administrators to produce credible research for governments and media as a way to shape public opinion. Academics use think-tanks to apply research to policy formulation, implementation, and monitoring. Brookings, for instance, produces research and background papers on foreign policy, economic studies, globalization, and governance studies from a liberal point of view, whereas Heritage covers many of the same issues from a conservative perspective. At least twenty other influential think-tanks, including the Institute for Policy Studies, the Progressive Policy Institute, the American Enterprise Institute, and the Cato Institute, have prominent offices in Washington, DC.

Interest groups have the financial resources to push legislation and ensure that they are heard in another way, through litigation. Groups often file "class action" lawsuits in American courts to stop big business or to overturn legislation that does not give every person "equal protection" under the law, as demanded by the 14th Amendment. Some scholars argue that the use of lawyers to trump the will of a legislature is hardly democratic; others contend that lawsuits and interest groups help ensure that all citizens are heard and that the law is applied fairly.

Political Parties

Over and above the interest groups, political parties gather the electorate into large coalitions of voters that affect the governing structure of the country. Parties and their candidates support ever-changing plans for the administration of government in order to balance order, freedom, and equality for the people, and to provide national security for the state. Parties propose and nominate candidates and offer general policy platforms to help voters make choices. The Democratic and Republican parties dominate the political landscape; yet they are not alone. Many smaller parties exist but their influence is normally limited, as the winner-takes-all electoral system disregards the votes of losing candidates. For most people, voting rationally means voting for Democrats or Republicans.

Since the 1860s the stability of the Republicans and Democrats as structuring organizations for civil society has been remarkable. The longevity of the parties indicates a high degree of flexibility on issues and the ability to transform themselves to meet changing circumstances and attitudes. Otherwise, the rise of strong third parties, such as the Reform Party in 1992 would supplant them. The elections of 1896, 1932/1936, and 1980 were transforming elections for the two parties as they fused ideas from other/lesser parties into their platforms and switched constituencies. Republicans in 1896 dropped the mantle of reform and equality that had been Abraham Lincoln's legacy, and became the conservative party of big business interests. Democrats in 1932 were able to build a coalition of Northern workers and unions with Southern and Western farmers and African Americans to redistribute wealth a bit. In 1980 the Republicans drew Southern and Western white voters away from the Democrats and transformed their party around Ronald Reagan's conservative response to the 1960s cultural turmoil and his promise to limit government. Election 2008 could win recognition as a transformative election around ideals of national rejuvenation, racial realignment, and a "New Deal" for the twenty-first century.

The two major parties bring together disparate and often conflicting political and attitudinal views. While parties tend to reflect social transformation, individual party member's views – often activists – do not alter as rapidly. In 2006, Senator Joe Lieberman, despite being the incumbent, lost the endorsement of the Connecticut Democratic Party, as many party activists felt he had too avidly supported President Bush and the War in Iraq. Lieberman ran as an Independent Democrat and won, demonstrating perhaps that the Democratic Party – and not Lieberman – had moved away from the majority of public opinion. In 2009, moderate Republican Senator Arlen Specter of Pennsylvania supported the Obama administration's economic stimulus program, despite an outcry from Republicans. Two liberal New England Republicans, Olympia Snowe and Susan Collins followed suit, demonstrating that parties are not monolithic (Hulse, 2009). A month later Specter officially switches parties.

Dominant groups within the Democrat Party include socially liberal and economically statist leftist-leaning party activists like Cleveland congressman Dennis Kucinich, social conservatives like Nebraskan senator Ben Nelson, and center-rightist reformers like Bill Clinton. The War in Iraq and Barack Obama's journey from being an Illinois Senator to winning the Presidency encouraged more radical and youthful voters to join the party – even as Obama himself sought to maintain a pragmatic, centrist profile. The Republican Party is just as composite, and contains remnants of the liberal eastern Republicans who once dominated the party, fiscal conservatives, libertarians, the religious right, and neo/radical Conservatives. Free market or interventionist economic philosophies, religious or secular cultural values, individualistic or communitarian social ideas, engaged or disengaged attitudes towards the rest of the globe, and regional preferences and traditions all mix to produce a blindingly diverse set of policy positions which force the parties to accept great internal compromise.

The 2001 terror attacks on the World Trade Center ultimately reinvigorated party differences. Neoconservatives (neocons) and radical conservatives, including George W. Bush and Dick Cheney, became the strongest element within the Republican Party. Well-funded neocon think-tanks such as the Heritage Foundation, the Project for the New American Century, and the American Enterprise Institute influenced policymaking and publicity outside the White House. Neocons aimed to alter public behavior towards self-reliance by diverting resources away from taxes and social welfare programs and back to people's pockets. Secondly, neocons supported the idea that societies abroad could be radically transformed by American military action. Democracy and self-determination were universal human urges which could be facilitated among people by a catalyst, such as the overthrow of dictatorial leaders like Saddam Hussein. Thirdly, neocons accepted the massive deficit spending required to finance military intervention in Iraq and Afghanistan and military spending across the board while reducing government income with lowered taxes. These ideas collectively moved the Republican Party away from traditional positions of balanced spending, patrician social welfare programs, and earlier conceptions of national self-interest.

Although initially weakened and constrained by patriotic surges extolling support for a president at war, the Democratic Party also became more radical and drew strength in the aftermath of 9/11. As the war in Iraq dragged on and casualties mounted, public opinion changed, abandoning most Democrats who genuinely believed in the war as a democratizing mission or as a necessity to guarantee national security. The faction of the party that had been skeptical of the war – supported increasingly by younger voters – drew strength and legitimacy from their opposition (Bai, 2007). Taboos against criticism of the war effort dissipated, strengthening those – like Obama – who had opposed the war from the start. Slow progress towards normalization in Iraq and Afghanistan also encouraged Democrats to seek international compromise in ending the conflict. Simultaneously, the vast spending on the war legitimized debates on how public money could best be spent, thereby signaling the end of two decades of cross party rhetorical restraint on government spending.

Analysts offer a "median" voter theory as an explanation for why the two-party system creates similar stances on issues, in spite of trends towards heightened polarization. Because there are more voters in the center than on the left or right, and because American elections are based on a winner-takes-all system – as opposed to proportional representation – politicians can expect to be elected only by attracting the middle-of-the-road voter who often switches between liberal and conservative issues. While other theories see economic, gender, North–South, rural–urban, cultural, or value-laden coastal–heartland divides as preeminent factors, median voter theory seems best – despite current political polarization – at explaining the variation in election outcomes from one year to the next, and between voters casting votes for different parties on election day; as candidate and party positions vary according to the national, state, or local character of the contest. Median voter theory also helps explain why candidates rush to embrace the center in campaigns. Table 4.1 indicates how Americans view themselves on a simple left-right spectrum, with "left" expressed as liberal and "right" as conservative. Most voters put themselves in the center, with the recent trend moving toward the poles. Whether centrist self-identification conforms with the position people actually take on specific issues is another matter, complicating strategy choices for politicians. Table 4.1 shows how ideological self-placement has moved over the last 16 years.

The Democratic and Republican parties navigate between three core American values: individuality (freedom), community (order) and fairness (equality). When asked whether they prefer absolute freedom or absolute equality, Americans by a three-to-one margin choose freedom; thus, they are choosing diversity and wide class differences over conformity, homogeneity, and social equality. Republican voters tend to stress the maintenance of order as the highest aim of government,

Table 4.1 Ideological Self-Placement and Party Identification

Ideology/party	*Year and Self-Placement Percentage*	
	1992	*2008*
All respondents		
Liberal	18	21
Moderate	40	36
Conservative	35	38
	2000	*2008*
Republicans		
Liberal	6	4
Moderate	28	25
Conservative	63	68
Democrats		
Liberal	27	34
Moderate	43	37
Conservative	24	25
Independents		
Liberal	20	20
Moderate	46	45
Conservative	28	30

Source: Pew (2008d).

with freedom second, and equality third. Democrats usually put equality issues first, freedom second, and order third – but even Democrats generally mean equality of opportunity, not equality of outcome. Conservatives favor less government intervention except in demanding harsher penalties for crimes, while liberals expect an activist government for minority and women's legal rights. Communitarians who want equality of outcome generally vote with the Democrats, while Libertarians who want the least possible government – except where necessary to protect life and property – vote on the Republican side. Democrats – victorious in Congress in 2006, and in the White House in 2008 – hoped that lower defense spending and modest tax rises for the wealthy could offer improved education, health care, and fund social security – in contrast with Republicans who valued lower taxes and strong defense. Equality thus won out over freedom. Ideological self-placement and party support obviously correspond. The voter's gender, race, education, religious fervor, and income also determine voting behavior, as is indicated in Table 4.2. Voting patterns are clearly more complex than socioeconomic left-right splits suggest.

Recent elections suggest that the Democrats have been more successful in adapting to social changes in the twenty-first century. In the

Table 4.2 Presidential Preference in 2008: Exit Polls

Voting Group	*Barack Obama*	*John McCain*
Males	49	48
Females	56	43
White	43	55
Black	95	4
Latino	67	31
High school or less	54	44
College degree	52	46
Income: lowest 6% (under $15,000)	73	25
Income: highest 6% (over $200,000)	52	46
Liberals	89	10
Moderates	60	39
Conservatives	20	78
First time voters	69	30
Party identification		
Democrat	89	10
Republican	9	90
Independents	52	44
Age		
18–29	66	32
30–39	54	44
40–49	49	49
50–64	50	49
65+	45	53
Religion		
Evangelical Protestant	26	73
Non-evangelical Protestants	44	55
Catholics	54	45
Jews	78	21
Others faiths	73	22
Unaffiliated	75	23

Sources: CNN (2008); Pew (2008c).

2006 midterm elections the Democrats won majorities in the House and the Senate. Democrats strengthened their grip in the 2008 general election, capturing the presidency for Barack Obama and reuniting all three elected branches of government. Both parties pragmatically change their platforms to conform to opinion polls as they compete for the support of median voters. Even though they vote less than their elders, the views of young people must be taken into account as they represent changing opinions and future concerns which parties must confront if they expect to maintain influence. No party wants to be seen as being unable to connect, or "out of new ideas." During the period 1964–2000, the numbers of Democrats declined and Republicans rose in almost all age groups; a development reversed since 2006. Until the new millennium, National Election Survey figures indicated shifts among voter self-identification which suggested that Americans had become increasingly individualistic.

The results recorded in Table 4.2 indicate that younger adults tend to favor Democrats more than their parents and grandparents in contemporary America. All age groups except those over 65 said they voted for Democrats in 2008, whereas the over-65s favored Republicans (CNN, 2008). The relative liberalism of younger Americans stems from concern over the ongoing war in Iraq, the state of the economy, and a perceived lack of leadership under George W. Bush. Underlying trends towards individualism may re-emerge once these current crises abate. Backed up by a generation of progress towards racial and gender equality, increasing living standards, falling crime rates, and geopolitical security, until 2001, Americans typically expressed beliefs in material, political, and spiritual progress; thus, younger Americans came to focus more on freedom and less on equality.

While in the 1960s and 1970s political behavior was unconventional – many citizens marched, burned draft cards, sat-in, and rioted to expand government responsibility toward equality – voters in the 1980s and 1990s often chose not to vote or they voted to dismantle social programs that demanded increased taxes. Analysts began to speculate that demographic developments favored Democratic core metropolitan constituencies – women, minorities, professionals, and seniors – over the white male, rural, and small business Republican core as early as 2002 (Judis and Teixeira, 2002). Other observers noted that many trends pointed in the opposite direction. America's growing outer-suburbs and "exurbs" (rural, outer suburbs) voted overwhelmingly Republican until 2006. Education and a better job may make a person more sympathetic to a Democratic ticket. However, getting ahead by getting away to the bigger houses, better schools, lower taxes and verdant environment in the outer suburbs pushes voters in the opposite direction.

Democrat Barack Obama won the 2008 presidential election on a ticket of national renewal and togetherness tied together in positive slogan promises – "Yes, we can" –to bring "change": change from politics as usual, change from war in the Middle East and elsewhere, change from the generational polarization of Clinton and Bush, and change which could bring more security for middle class Americans. Republican John McCain also ran as an outsider and a reformer, but embodied more achievements under the belt: quite naturally given McCain's age (72), longstanding role as bipartisan-leaning senate legislator, a man of conscience, and Vietnam prisoner of war. Obama's incredible media projection and his manifest slogan of belief in a better future enraptured Americans in a way that McCain's lifetime of service could not – despite the enduring presence of racial, ethnic, and gender preconceptions in politics.

Successful politicians must adapt their messages to different audiences, while taking care to avoid giving opportunities for television reporters to show obviously contradictory 15-second sound-bites on the national news. Because issues that hit home in Washington, DC, may not matter much elsewhere, candidates rely on a party's middle-of-the-road national platform for stability, devising specific strategies for local campaigns. Contemporary politicians are often more ideological than the voters to whom they cater, and their votes on specific issues sometimes contradict or go far beyond campaign promises. This ideological difference helps to explain why voters believe that politicians cannot be trusted to do what they say.

Historically, parties have not been good at mustering internal discipline for voting; this has been attributed to the need for ideological, ethnic, religious, and geographical compromise within a federal political system and a diverse nation. Lately however, with interest groups such as the Christian Coalition working feverishly to remove liberal candidates, and liberal Christian groups such as People for the American Way responding in kind, politicians have taken more rigid positions than usual. The 2000 and 2004 presidential contests increased partisanship, as the electorate split evenly and politicians clung tighter to party labels. Yet, while political parties may be increasingly important in the United States, the importance of candidate charisma resurfaced in the 2008 election.

Politics

Elections

Ordinary voters in the US are given the final say over which people should represent the parties in elections, unlike in many other Western democracies. Before the general election is held between one Republican and one Democrat – and a few Independents or others – a primary election is held to pick the party candidates. Although presidential primaries are most widely reported, primaries are held for almost all the country's elected offices. In a primary, voters elect one candidate from each party from a field of hopefuls who have simply announced that they are candidates for the particular office and wish to run as Republicans or Democrats. Some states allow for open primaries, whereby voters from either party can vote in either the Republican or Democratic primary. Other states hold closed primaries, restricting the vote in each primary to registered party members. The primary system increases democracy by giving the people the power to determine the official party candidates over the entire spectrum of political offices.

Presidential elections illustrate the complexity of the election process (Box 4.2), even though variations are of different scales for each public office. The visible process starts well over a year before the presidential

Box 4.2 The Path to the Presidency

1. Election day minus 4–8 years. A future president has usually first been elected as a state governor, US Senator, or Vice-President; sometimes a military hero will do.
2. Election day minus 2 years. Hopefuls fundraise the tens of millions of dollars needed to run a campaign. Contributors give money directly to the candidate and not to a political party.
3. Election day minus 18 months. Individuals announce that they are actively campaigning to be President of the United States. They begin to visit states with early primaries.
4. Election day minus 12 months. Opinion polls in state primaries have identified a field of two or three favorites in each party. Unpopular candidates begin to concede.
5. Election day minus 9 months. Results from the state primaries usually point to a clear frontrunner from each party, although this was not the case in 2008.
6. Election day minus 6 months. The winners are virtually assured the nominations of their parties.
7. Election day minus 3 months. Party conventions officially name their presidential candidates. The parties now begin to fund the nominee's campaign. Candidates announce their choices for vice-presidential running mates, visit states they can win, avoid those they will surely lose, and pour money into the toss-up states.
8. Election day minus 6 weeks. Hard campaigning and head-to-head television debates by which viewers/voters decide who performs best under the spotlights.
9. Election day. Voters nationwide cast ballots and electoral votes are tallied in a state-by-state fashion to name the winner.
10. Election day plus 6 weeks. The Electoral College officially declares the winner.
11. Election day plus 10 weeks. Inauguration of the President.

elections take place, when the states hold primary elections or closed political meetings called caucuses. Primaries and caucuses receive massive media coverage, and voters often turn out in significant numbers – as shown in the 2008 contests between Barack Obama and Hillary Clinton for the Democrats, and John McCain, Mike Huckabee, and Mitt Romney for the Republicans. Delegates are awarded according to a kaleidoscopic mix of criteria that guarantee only a rough overall form of proportionality in regard to population and some influence for senior party members – called "superdelegates."

Roughly three months before an election, the parties hold conventions where their presidential candidates are officially named and the campaigning accelerates. This long process of going from being a hopeful to becoming the party candidate helps to "personify" the political structure by focusing attention on the personal attributes of each candidate. Voters select candidates with whom they identify, or by habit of party affiliation. Overall, local interests and primaries put candidates in stronger positions towards their parties than in other countries where voters choose parties, not candidates. When casting ballots, voters weigh the personal qualities of the candidate as much as ideology; they are more likely to ask, "Is he like me, and do I like him?" than "Is he the best leader possible?" Emotional intelligence and empathy are seen as important assets (Westen, 2007). Table 4.3 shows that control of the White House has split fairly evenly between Democrats and Republicans since 1980 and how minor parties sometimes help determine the outcome of the elections – for instance in 1992 and 2000.

Because elections to the House of Representatives occur every two years, representatives must constantly be on the campaign trail. All 435 representatives pay closer attention to their home districts than to the wants of their parties, even though they tend to vote along party lines if the issue does not confront the interests of the people "back home." Those mavericks who support party interests over homefolks are usually defeated in the next election; one example of this was Senate Minority leader Tom Daschle (South Dakota) who lost his seat in 2004. Dakotans believed that Daschle had lost touch with the values of his home state and "gone native" in Washington, DC. The size of Congress has not changed since 1912, when the number was set at 435. Because of population growth, each representative represents an average of nearly 665,000 people, instead of the 60,000 people at the time of the Founders. In 2008, it cost well over a million dollars to run for a congressional seat, making fund-raising as important as legislative work (CFI, 2008).

The 100 US Senators are individually more powerful but are less-frequently connected to the people than are the representatives. Their

Table 4.3 Presidential Elections, 1980–2008

Year	*Candidate*	*Popular Votes (Millions)*	*%*	*Electoral College*
1980	Ronald Reagan (Rep)	43.9	50.8	489
	Jimmy Carter (Dem)	35.5	41.0	49
	John Anderson (NU)	5.7	6.6	0
	Ed Clark (Lib)	.9	1.1	0
1984	Ronald Reagan (Rep)	54.5	58.8	525
	Walter Mondale (Dem)	37.6	41.0	13
	David Berglund (Lib)	.2	.2	0
1988	George Bush (Rep)	48.9	53.4	426
	Michael Dukakis (Dem)	41.8	45.7	111
	Ron Paul (Lib)	.4	.5	0
1992	Bill Clinton (Dem)	44.9	43.0	370
	George Bush (Rep)	39.1	37.5	168
	Ross Perot (Ind)	19.7	18.9	0
	Andre Marrau (Lib)	.3	.3	0
1996	Bill Clinton (Dem)	47.4	49.2	379
	Bob Dole (Rep)	39.2	40.7	159
	Ross Perot (Reform)	8.1	8.4	0
	Ralph Nader (Green)	.7	.7	0
	Harry Browne (Lib)	.5	.5	0
2000	George W. Bush (Rep)	50.5	47.9	271
	Al Gore (Dem)	51.0	48.4	266
	Ralph Nader (Green)	2.9	2.7	0
	Pat Buchanan (Reform)	.4	.4	0
	Harry Browne (Lib)	.4	.4	0
2004	George W. Bush (Rep)	62.0	50.8	286
	John Kerry (Dem)	59.0	48.3	251
	Ralph Nader (Ind)	.5	.4	0
	Michael Badnarik (Lib)	.4	.3	0
2008	Barack Obama (Dem)	69.5	52.9	365
	John McCain (Rep)	59.9	45.6	173
	Ralph Nader (Ind)	.7	.6	0
	Bob Barr (Lib)	.5	.4	0

Note: Rep = Republican; Dem = Democrat; Lib = Libertarian; Ind. = Independent; NU = National Union.

Source: Leip (2008).

six-year-cycles insulate them from constant electioneering, and reduce the immediacy and necessity of courting interests for votes and contributions. Additionally, each senator has a large and changing statewide electorate. The states have vast differences in population with the result that California's senators represent 37 million people, while Wyoming's only represent 530,000. Until 1913, senators were appointed by state legislatures rather than being elected by the voters, emphasizing the point that senators were intended to be ambassadors for sovereign states, rather than representatives of the people. Moreover, senatorial election campaigns are far more expensive than House elections – for example, in the 2008 Minnesota contest, Republican incumbent Norm Coleman and Democrat challenger Al Franken raised $42 million between them (CRP, 2008a). Overall, winners in 2008 senate races raised over $5 million each in the 2007–8 election cycle (CFI, 2008).

However serious, elections are often more of a spectator sport than participatory activity in the United States, which has lower voter participation rates than most other Western democracies. In 2008, turnout rose to the highest level for over a generation – with nearly 62 percent of eligible voters and 57 percent of the voting age population, in contrast to the 2006 midterm election where 41 percent of eligible voters and 37 percent of voting age voters cast ballots (USEP, 2008). Statistically, voters tend to be older, whiter, wealthier, and better educated than non-voters. Americans have been concerned about this and have changed state and federal laws in order to ease registration rules and provide more locations to make it easier to enroll voters. The Motor Voter Bill of 1996 lets people register to vote whenever they renew their driver's licenses – something done every four years in most states and required when relocating from state to state. Federal marshals and legal groups ensure that anyone eligible to vote can vote. There are no longer discriminatory impediments to voting, such as existed up to the mid-1960s before the African American Civil Rights Movement forced legislation in the form of the Civil Rights Act of 1964 and the Voting Rights Act of 1965. In recent years, voting has become more convenient via the mail-in ballot.

Yet voting rates remain comparatively low. Although critics see poor turnout as hugely important, many political scientists point to the alternative access points that tie Americans to political institutions through interest groups, unconventional political behavior, and the courts. With a history of weak class-consciousness, with most politicians and parties navigating a middle road, and with a federal system enforcing the claim that "all politics are local," Americans seem to be more satisfied with – than jaded by – the system.

Media

The frequency of democratic elections and the spectacle of politics help knit civil society together. The media exert a powerful influence and offer a conduit for communications between the people and their politicians. Sometimes the media are most influenced by the profit motive and offer questionable stories to titillate and attract viewers, instead of informing them on the issues. At other times, the media can act too much like a government mouthpiece or, contrarily, can serve as a populist megaphone where ordinary people call for conventional or unconventional actions to change a political situation. Whether sitting on the government's lap or snapping at its heels, the media's role in politics cannot be ignored.

In the year between the first presidential primaries and the final election, journalists are relentless in exposing the lives of the likely winners. Primaries are both "beauty contests" and marathons, with every deviant feature of the candidate's lives and family backgrounds scarring them a bit until the unrelenting exposure of personal details finally convinces some candidates to quit the race. Many people do not enter political life simply because their private lives cannot bear the scrutiny from professional reporters or talk show pundits. For the American public, this is all great entertainment and more people closely follow the campaigns than actually vote.

Most media companies in the US are privately owned; thus newsworthiness must be balanced against market forces to provide profits. The First Amendment protects free speech and freedom of the press but also gives comfort to gossip pages that stretch the truth to sell papers or attract viewers. Mostly, though, the media take pride in the truthfulness and trustworthiness of their stories and are quick to retract or correct a falsehood.

There can be no doubt that the media are essential and convenient tools for politicians, all of whom develop press strategies to connect with potential voters. Franklin Roosevelt showed the power of radio in the 1930s, John Kennedy proved the effectiveness of television in the 1960s, and Barack Obama demonstrated the importance of the Internet and mobile phones. In 1992 Bill Clinton pioneered infotainment campaigning by playing a saxophone on the Arsenio Hall show and MTV; in 2008 the major candidates visited the sets of media royalty Jon Stewart, Jay Leno, David Letterman, Oprah Winfrey, and Larry King, to garner policy support and screen likability for their campaigns. Winfrey endorsed Obama early on, providing momentum to his nomination quest. Hillary Clinton and Sarah Palin appeared on Saturday Night Live alongside comedienne impersonators. Uncontrolled but free prime-time exposure is risky for candidates, but to decline an invitation to join one of these shows can be disastrous if the host makes a point of it. Generally, appearing on comedy and talk shows let the candidates show a more personal side and give them an upward bump in the polls.

Today, all high-level politicians spend a lot of money and time molding media moments to attract voters in the first place, stay in the public eye via a TV "photo opportunity," or by spinning – interpreting favorably – a negative story to diminish its impact. The terms "photo-op" and "spin-city" became common during the presidencies of Ronald Reagan and Bill Clinton, respectively. George W. Bush also showed great aptitude in using photo ops, such as the "Mission Accomplished" picture from 2004 (Illustration 4.3). This particular photo-op indicates the inherent danger of the genre, and has subsequently become one of the most analyzed, praised, and ridiculed releases in American history.

The national and local scope of the media presents an ambiguous picture. The connection of media to politics is complicated by

Illustration 4.3 "Mission Accomplished"

President George Bush co-piloted a S-3 Viking jet onto the aircraft carrier *Abraham Lincoln* on 1 May 2003 and optimistically declared an end to major combat operations in Iraq. The "Mission Accomplished" banner in the background was purportedly hung by the sailors themselves, but some commentators have argued that presidential photo-ops are too important to be left to chance.

(J. Scott Applewhite/Polfoto)

localism as no printed newspaper successfully reaches a national audience, even though the *Wall Street Journal* and *USA Today* come close. Digital versions of major newspapers like the *Washington Post* and *New York Times* have also become increasingly popular, while regional papers have struggled. On the other hand, television, radio, and newspapers are increasingly owned by large conglomerates, such as CNN-Time/America-On-Line. This monopolization of news outlets has been blamed for the centrism of political candidates who are wary not to offend media owners if they want favorable airtime or in-depth columns in any or all markets. Many critics have claimed that the media have acted the role of gatekeeper, controlling the flow of information and determining its spin. Conversely, the internet, mobile phones, weblogs, fax systems, satellite television and radio channels, segmentation of FM and medium-wave radio by ideology and religious views, and the growth of cable TV news complicate analyses of media influence. New technology and enhanced programming diversity allow individuals to personalize their viewing or listening by bypassing traditional media to create their own "liberal" or "conservative" media universes. The "instant" connectivity of the internet, messaging, and blogging, moreover, help balance the authoritative imbalance between journalist and reader – staggeringly demonstrated by the hundreds of written comments newspaper articles attract. The internet has overtaken the newspapers as a source of news, and vies with TV as the primary conduit of information for young people between 18 and 29 (PEW, 2008a).

Another recent problem is that competition has made the media both incredibly hungry for news and vicious in acquiring it. To keep viewers or subscribers, conglomerates feel that they must be the first to break the news. Thus, any citizen who runs for elective office risks being devoured by the press. Sarah Palin was initially seen as an inspired choice for vice president in John McCain's flagging 2008 campaign, but the media quickly focused on her lack of experience and she ended by being widely regarded as a liability. Palin had claimed foreign policy understanding based on her being Governor of Alaska – a state with two international borders – while interviewed by CBS Anchor Katie Couric (CBS News 2008). Palin, meanwhile, remained a darling of the religious right due to her stances on moral issues and her down-to-earth working mom-made-good representativeness. The media need the candidates' advertising money and headline-making ability and are thereby influenced by business considerations. However, because viewers decide what the media consider news by their "consumer votes" of tuning in to one station or out of another, or choosing between newspapers, the media is also a pipeline from the people, as public appetites shape political behavior and laws.

Exactly how great an influence the media have in voter education and political socialization – helping people determine how they should vote and where they fit into government – is debatable, yet the influence is clear. The Center for Responsive Politics estimated that Presidential, House, and senatorial candidates would spend $5.3 billion on election campaigns in the 2007–8 election cycle (CRP, 2008a). A huge slice of this $5.3 billion paid for media exposure. Obama alone raised $750 million dollars, fuelling charges that he had bought the presidency (Luo, 2008). Indeed, studies by the Project for Excellence in Journalism suggested that Barack Obama received less negative treatment from the media than McCain in 2008 (PEJ, 2008).

Campaign Finances

Election costs are paid by the candidates, the federal government, political parties, interest groups, and private contributors. The system favors the affluent because of the start-up money required to begin a campaign in the first place and the inadequacy of public funding to run an effective campaign. The idea – and sometimes reality – that the candidate who spends the most money for advertising can buy the election, rubs against long-standing myths that anyone can rise to be president, governor, or mayor. But the biggest concern among Americans is that private contributions to campaign coffers give the donor too much access and influence, thereby damaging the democratic process. In 1971 Congress passed the Federal Election Campaigns Act, and in 1974 created the Federal Election Commission to require candidates and donors to make full disclosures on contributions and spending. Under these laws, the government provides federal "matching funds" to help even the field between rich and poor candidates, and caps the amount of direct or "hard money" spending for each contest. The laws are clearly intended to limit the influence of wealthy donors, labor unions, and tax-exempt (religious or other interest groups) organizations from buying influence and increasing public cynicism about government. In 2008, the legal limit for hard money direct spending for each presidential candidate was approximately $82 million (FEC-PSL, 2008). That limit did not include public funding which roughly doubled the money available. Because he raised nearly ten times the limits, Obama declined public funding. McCain, meanwhile, opted for public funding. Prescribed limits do not apply to a candidate's personal money; for example, Republican primary candidate Mitt Romney personally paid over $40 million of the $100 million he spent in a failed attempt to win the nomination (CRP, 2008b).

Money was spent by parties, private individuals, and other organizations on indirect campaigns for voter education and voter registration drives, rather than by the candidates themselves. Called "soft money," this kind of spending was unregulated until the Bipartisan Campaign Reform Act of 2002. Vast soft-money spending – estimated at a quarter of a billion dollars in 2000 and 2002 elections – had been condemned by the press and some high-profile politicians. Many fretted that soft money bought access, and politicians' judgments could be clouded by too-cozy relationships with sponsors. The Bipartisan Campaign Reform Act (BCRA) attempted to tighten election finance laws, to control the use of soft money by parties and candidates, and to make financing more transparent. In return, hard money limits were raised. BCRA was immediately challenged as a restriction of free speech rights in the courts, but most of its provisions were upheld. Interpretation and implementation of the act is the responsibility of the Federal Election Commission, which in 2008 has still been unable to monitor adequately the flow of money.

Traditionally, Political Action Committees (PACs) have raised and distributed soft-money contributions for candidates from interest groups, religious organizations, and private citizens. PACs disbursed $580 million in 2000 (FEC, 2001). The BCRA aimed to replace soft money campaign contribution, but politicians still need money to campaign and individuals and groups have money and need to be heard by politicians. FEC rules change, but politicians and interests quickly learn to adapt to the new environment and to divert money so that it matches the rules and still keeps flowing. Since BCRA, the activities of nonprofit 501 charities and 527 nonprofit advocacy groups have become major pipelines of soft money. 501s can spend money on educational and voter registration guides, whereas 527s can also more openly advocate policy, and spend on advertising. 527 spending in 2006 and 2008 federal elections amounted to around $400 million, with large players including liberal America Votes and conservative RightChange (CRP 2008c).

One favorable finance development has been the growth of small donations over the internet, pioneered by Vermont Governor Howard Dean in 2004 and then tuned to perfection by the Obama campaign (Bai, 2007). Online donations cost so little to collect that small amounts quickly add up. Moreover, internet donations connected average citizens to the campaign directly, circumventing traditional media, and establishing a reserve army of donors Obama could repeatedly return to until they reached federally set limits of $2,300 a candidate. These popular donations replaced money regulated by BCRA and reinvigorated the political system. Obama's mastery of internet donations will be copied by political hopefuls in upcoming elections. Many people have argued the dangers of PACs, 527s and soft money's influence on elections, but, perhaps, these organizations give strength to civil society by allowing groups of people to gain access to a politician's office and ear. PACs and 527s help persuade candidates of the importance of issues by contributing volunteers and money to political campaigns. While Americans may be uneasy about the mix of money and politics, the 2008 campaign demonstrated that with sufficient enthusiasm, the fundraising power of the two main parties was well-matched, assuaging fears of enduring corruption.

Pluralistic Democracy

In America, where a winner-takes-all system determines election outcomes, the question of how to safeguard minority and class-based representation is difficult to resolve. In the 1980s, Congress encouraged states to redraw election districts to group minority voters together in such a way as to give a group a majority in a district. This gerrymandering of voters into "minority-majority" districts succeeded as minority representation in Congress rose by 50 percent. Sometimes this gerrymandering created election districts of snake-like dimensions, wriggling in and out of black neighborhoods, going down interstates to incorporate another community of African Americans until a majority could be ensured. When the media printed maps of these districts, many Americans were outraged by the obvious prejudice inherent in such a system and criticized the moves as favoring one group of citizens over another. Supporters argued that this was the only way to put more minorities into seats in the nation's capitol.

Congressional efforts to increase minority members were initially supported by the Supreme Court under the equal protection provisions of the 14th Amendment. But in the case of *Shaw* v. *Reno* (1993), concerning "racial gerrymandering" in North Carolina, the Court ruled that creating minority districts amounted to political apartheid. In *Easley* v. *Cromartie* (2001), the Court modified its stance somewhat, allowing race as a factor, as long as it was not the "dominant and controlling one" (Greenhouse, 2001). The issue remains controversial, especially to those who prefer a proportional system of representative democracy. Whether or not people feel better represented by a candidate of their own ethnicity is a question that the election of 2008 has considered (see Table 4.2, p. 116). As long as politicians regardless of their race, ethnicity, or gender come from the upper portion of the middle class, middle-class interests are likely to be upheld. Some political observers have also argued that racial gerrymandering helps Republican interests because in creating minority districts, it removes minority voters from other districts where their votes would be needed to provide Democratic majorities. Gerrymandering has also had the effect of making "safe districts" for incumbents who can rely on war chests, name recognition, and ideological conformity to win re-election campaigns. Even in the 2008 "landslide" congressional election only five of the 33 Senators up for reelection lost their seats, and just 19 incumbent Congressmen failed to secure mandates.

One way to dampen the advantages which incumbents have over challengers is to impose term limits on the number of years any one person can hold a particular office. The obvious legal precedent for this is the constitutional two-term limit on American presidents. Theoretically, citizens in democracies should be able to vote for any politician of their choice. This has led some to argue that the whole concept of limiting terms is anti-democratic, and threatens to weaken government by removing the most competent leaders and replacing them with inexperienced newcomers or with candidates who have independent means. On the other hand, many argue that democracies require turnover to bring forward new ideas and to involve more people in politics. Critics believe that as politicians accrue power, they think too much about how they will be remembered by their colleagues for their political skills – and not enough about the concerns of ordinary people back home.

Calling for "accountability" and promoting the idea that politics should not be a career-in-itself but should be open to citizen-politicians who do something else first and are legislators second, many states have now introduced term limits for public offices. In 2009, term limits for state legislators had been approved and enacted in 15 states, and approved but rejected by state supreme courts in four others (NCSL, 2009). Some states also have placed term limits on US Senators and Representatives. Although the Supreme Court ruled in 1995 that putting term limits on federal offices was unconstitutional, a number of representatives have declared that they will follow the will of the people by refusing to run for re-election when they reach the limit set by state law.

Overall, the American political system is a blend of direct democratic, plural, and elite interests. The more savvy, influential, or determined an individual or interest group is, the more the system bends to accommodate the pressure. A single dissenter or a mass movement can still bring about change through the court system or by taking to the streets. Dissent is an integral part of American political culture, from the throwing of tea into Boston harbor in 1773 to marching on Washington against the Vietnam War or for civil rights in the 1960s, blockading abortion clinics in the 1980s, protesting against globalization by vandalizing a McDonald's in 2000, or marching for immigrant rights in 2006. With a brief upsurge after the 9/11 attacks, Americans' belief in the federal government has remained consistently low since the early 1970s. In 2008, a little more than a third (37 percent) of Americans viewed the federal government favorably – a reflection of George W. Bush's unpopularity (PEW, 2008b; PEW, 2008e). A successful Obama administration may dispel this dissatisfaction; however, dissent and skepticism remain crucial to the American political system. Early 2009 opinion polls showed approval ratings for Obama's administration at close to two-thirds, while congressional approval rates remined at well under one-third.

Americans vote or have the opportunity to vote more times and for a wider range of officials than anyone else in the world. Some commentators claim that it is just this overabundance of democracy that explains apathy and reduces voting rates. Politics that seeks the center also dampens voter interest, as does the belief that big money controls politicians no matter what the voter does. The apparently narrow ideological spread within party constituencies may mean that some people feel unrepresented and doubt if their votes make any difference. Ralph Nader once argued that people saw Democratic and Republican candidates as "twiddle-dum, twiddle-dee" (FDCH, 2000): so similar that you could hardly tell them apart. An opposite argument is that the widespread use of polling may convince many voters that their views are already known and that candidates will obey the dictates of that public opinion.

American social behavior tempers American voting behavior as the majority of contemporary Americans pursue middle-class lifestyles centered on office work, secure suburban and increasingly "gated community," long commutes and the good life which double-incomes provide (Low, 2003). School and work-based activities crowd out available free time and life may actually be too full and too comfortable for the middle class to bother with political activities, especially when some believe the government is unresponsive to their needs anyway. On the other hand, the election of 2008 actually presented stark choices – between the past as represented by the Bush administration, and two versions of the future. The choices between Obama and McCain brought relatively large numbers of voters into the political arena.

So, the lack of civic involvement may be changing. The closeness of the 2000 election emphasized that votes do count and encouraged millions more Americans to vote in the 2004 election. The primary elections of 2008 attracted massive attention – especially the nail-bitingly close contest between Hillary Clinton and Barack Obama. This helped expand the Democratic Party and renewed it with the passions and commitment of a youth army – an example Republicans will learn from in upcoming campaigns. This policy-interested generation may well remain politically engaged – if they feel that political interest is time well spent.

The election of 2008 testified to the seriousness of the concepts of diversity, fairness, and opportunity that permeate the American self-understanding. The election of visibly different Barack Obama showed that America had moved on from prejudging a candidate because of his color – even if a fraction of voters still considered race a factor. Hillary Clinton's monumental primary campaign demonstrated that a woman could aspire to the highest office in the land. John McCain's valiant – if failed – bid for the presidency emphasized that age need not prohibit a candidate from seeking the presidency. McCain and Obama won their nominations over the "preferred" candidates of party leaders, testifying to the opportunity that exists within American democracy. In his concession speech, John McCain hushed the boos of his supporters who could not accept the result, stressed the historic nature of Obama's election for the black community and for Americans in general, and urged Americans to come together in support of Obama: "The American people have spoken, and they have spoken clearly" (McCain, 2008).

5

Society

Class

For most Americans, the opportunity for a better life is far more important than having a society where everyone is equal. Americans can see that there are rich and poor people, but they usually play down the reality of social classes. The Marxian concept that class division and inequality automatically gives rise to class consciousness and conflict does not ring true in the American experience. There is no particular envy of or deference to the rich and the enduring myths of equal opportunity, individual responsibility, and the abundant examples of those who have gone from "rags to riches," deflect class tensions which do arise. Most people are optimistic about their lives and think they can succeed with education, hard work and by their own efforts. Some cannot. Researchers are showing that social mobility has declined over the past thirty years as American society becomes increasingly unequal. A rising percentage of Americans are "working poor": in poverty in spite of working 40-hour-a-week jobs. Even before the economic crisis of 2008–9, economist Paul Krugman explained: "The myth of income mobility has always exceeded the reality" even though "America was once a place of substantial intergenerational mobility" (Krugman, 2004b). In 2009, with America more unequal than at any time since World War II, poor children have limited opportunities to move up the social ladder; middle-class kids still have a fighting chance.

The Middle Class

As George W. Bush turned over his stewardship of domestic society to Barack Obama in 2009, Americans hoped the new president could reestablish the economic progress on which its fabled middle-class ideology and lifestyle depends: the belief that the next generation would do better than the preceding one. In every decade of the twentieth century – except for the 1930s – the middle class improved its living standards in terms of material goods, property ownership, and discretionary income. Despite wide disparities in income, the vast majority of Americans self-define themselves as middle-class. At no time during the last 40 years has any poll had more than 20 percent of the total population defining themselves as anything else. In 2008 50 percent of African Americans, 54 percent of Hispanics and 53 percent of whites said they were middle class even though some of them made less than $20,000 a year, and others made over $150,000 (Pew, 2008b). One problem in grasping what it is to be middle-class is that having $150,000 a year while living in Manhattan and having $55,000 in rural Iowa amount to similar material rewards and quality of life – certainly the house would be much bigger in Iowa.

It might be easier to think of the middle class as being composed of those people who have at least a high-school education – and more likely a college degree – some real choice as to where to live and work, and who can live without government aid. The middle class is the working class, divided into white collar "desk" and blue collar "sweat" jobs. Most Americans feel that they are at least middle class and have achieved the American Dream if they own their own homes. With 130 million total housing units available, of the 112 million housing units occupied in September 2008, the homeownership rate was 68 percent, the rental rate 32 percent (US Census, 2008b). Still, since 2007 there has been a growing anxiety, a crisis in confidence, and a real loss of home equity as one in six mortgage holders watched their house values plummet and left them owing more than the houses were worth. Without home equity, Americans feel less rich and more anxious about their future. And most analysts say that prices will continue to fall as unemployment numbers rise and lower wages add to the number of foreclosures. Whether or not the trends of the last sixty years for suburban and exurban housing will be replaced as Americans return to the conveniences of urban living is a matter of dispute (Leinberger, 2008).

Political theorist Michael Lind identifies part of the middle class as an "Overclass": the professional class of bourgeois managers and politicians who make between $60,000 and $200,000 a year in salaries and stock options and who have achieved their status through education, hard work, and luck. They seem to be running the country – and they are. Members of this Overclass are not among the capitalist elite or those who have inherited wealth – a further class of super-rich people above these managers (Lind, 1995). David Brooks has explained that there is a culture war within the Overclass, divided between the "aristocracy of money" and the "aristocracy of the mind" – divisions of the educated class between those managers who work in business and those professionals (teachers, academics, journalists, artists, therapists) who focus on the distribution of knowledge (Brooks, 2004a).

In America, race informs class. Lind sees class conflict dampened by the inclusion of minority members of the Overclass into the upper echelons of university faculties, professional sports, law firms, religious organizations, and government. African–American, Hispanic, and other minority Overclass leaders provide examples of the American Dream by their own successes. The election of Barack Obama is a clear example of how the national conversation about race and discrimination can be changed and a celebration of "post-racial" America can be used to confront those who use statistics to show that most non-whites still make less, live shorter lives, are poorer, face daily discrimination and have fewer opportunities than white males.

Rural and Urban America

While many commentators construct an America divided between haves and have nots, others argue that economic differences do not explain much about the divide. The real divisions are between conceptions of self and in where people live. Americans outside the megalopolises often criticize the transformations wrought by the 1960s countercultural, multicultural, and feminist movements. They favor a return to traditional, disciplined, strictly moral, patriotic, and religious family values. Urban Americans, in contrast, are more likely to support real equality between men and women in families, to have a more flexible moral code, to be uneasy with too many open displays of patriotism, and to describe themselves as "non-religious." Rural Americans do not read the *New York Times,* but their radio stations are saturated with information about local fundraising activities, lodge meetings, and church services. Rural white Americans tend to vote Republican. A majority of urban Americans, especially in the metropolises along the East and West coasts, vote Democratic. Unlike urban Americans who see themselves as special, rural Americans conceive the self differently: "I am normal. Nobody is better, nobody is worse. I am humble before God" (Brooks, 2001: 63).

Basically, Americans seem to want to be left alone and do not bother themselves with the lives constructed or believed in by other

Americans, so long as the others do not get too loud or begin to infringe on their own lives. Most people live in communities or form social groups made up of family, friends, and co-workers that make them comfortable; they neither really care about nor try to reform other groups. One writer has noted that in America, "every place becomes more like itself" as people relocate into areas based upon cultural affinity and a "cafeteria choice" of options (Brooks, 2004b: 7). But a middle-class withdrawal syndrome can lead to a loss of community as Americans go "bowling alone," eschewing traditional big-membership organizations and spending their free time within a small circle of friends and family (Putnam, 2000). Many others argue that it is precisely the freedom of selecting a different lifestyle that binds the community and nation together. When confronted with a meaningful threat, such as 11 September, Americans quickly unite behind the myths of one nation, one people.

Poverty and Affluence

Poverty has been omnipresent in American history with slaves, poor whites, single mothers, and successive waves of low-paid immigrant workers working at whatever jobs they could find. During the last half century there has been a steady decrease in the percentages of citizens in poverty as the rising economy lifted wages and, more importantly, as wives entered the labor force and created two-income families. In America, in 2007, 37.3 million people were officially listed as poor (US Census, 2008). The 2008 US Conference of Mayors reported increases in hunger and homelessness were "particularly notable among working families" as requests for food and shelter rose 18 percent and 12 percent, respectively, increases attributed to a weakening economy and home foreclosures (US Mayors, 2008).

The disparity between rich and poor has widened in the last thirty years, increasing dramatically in the past fifteen years as the economic boom helped the richest group get astonishingly richer, the middle class get a little richer, and the poor get significantly poorer. In fact, some analysts point to a growing class divide as social barriers and economic inequality create the largest divide since the Great Depression. Much of this gap between rich and poor is due to the changing nature of work, the loss of industrial jobs to countries with cheaper labor costs, the unequal distribution of personal income, the growing number of single income families and an increasing emphasis on a well-educated workforce. Social mobility, while still there, has flattened out and possibly declined (Hacker, 2006). The poor are concentrated into inner-city neighborhoods, mobile home parks throughout the South and West, Indian reservations, rented farmhouses across the Midwest, or wander from here to there while they struggle quietly to make ends meet, keep families together, and live their lives to the fullest degree possible in sometimes desperate circumstances.

By 2007, with an official poverty line at $21,100 a year for a family of four and $10,400 for an individual, 12.5 percent of all Americans were poor and the proportion is much higher if the definition includes all families below $30,000 a year (HHS, 2008a). Polls show that even though they walk an economic tightrope with fears of job losses and inflation, most low wage workers retain their belief in the American Dream and its promise of advancement by hard work and admonition that while the government bears some responsibility for the welfare of the people, individuals are responsible for their domestic economies (Fletcher and Cohen, 2008). Low-wage workers are generally younger, female and less educated than others and they work without safety nets of health insurance or retirement benefits. The key factor seems to be the education level of the primary wage earner. Table 5.1 indicates the link between degree level and pay.

The richest one percent of all Americans have more wealth than the bottom 90 percent combined, with the latter group comprising not only everyone in the lower and middle classes, but also half of those in the upper class. The richest live in plush apartments atop Manhattan and have large houses worldwide. Just under them, many families of the super-rich and Overclass have moved into "gated communities" (Illustration 5.1) where high fences, security guards, and houses beyond the economic reach of all but a few people keep them isolated in luxury. Many other people are moving beyond

Table 5.1 Mean Earnings for Americans 18 Years and Older, 2006

Degree level	*Mean earnings*
No degree	$20,873
High School diploma	$31,071
Some college, no degree	$32,289
Associate (2-year) degree	$39,724
Bachelor's	$56,788
Master's	$70,358
Professional	$116,514
PhD	$103,944

Source: US Census (2009b) Statistical Abstract. Table 224.

Illustration 5.1 Gated Community near Atlanta, Georgia

The gated community of "Tara" near Atlanta, Georgia, offers privacy, security, and fine homes for upper-middle-class home buyers. The guardhouse and high fences keep out all visitors not specifically named on an access list. The house in the background serves as a club, with swimming pool and party rooms for residents and guests.

(Russell Duncan)

suburbia, into areas that – while not quite rural – invoke the powerful ideas of reinvention and frontier community. The philosopher George Santayana observed that Americans don't solve problems (such as traffic, crime, poverty), they just leave them behind, moving to a new city or into the countryside. In 2007, the average American held property and financial assets totalling $144,000.

To address the problem of the rising inequality of wealth, President Obama proposed programs to increase educational outcomes, create jobs, raise wages, and provide better housing for everyone. Obviously, a redistribution of income could be accomplished to make the country a comfortable and relatively middle-class nation from top to bottom. Setting a maximum and a minimum income could do this, but, overwhelmingly, Americans would fight such an effort tooth and claw, calling it immoral, un-American, socialistic and, possibly, Satanic. Critics of redistribution point to figures showing the poor growing as tall, living as long, and surfing as many cable channels as the rich, whether or not they live in gated-suburbs or in inner cities. And the

American secular myths of worth and merit combine with Christian admonitions of salvation to produce an egalitarian creed that is central to the fabric of society. While Americans overwhelmingly support an equality of opportunity, some propose that the focus should be more upon an equality of outcome.

The American Family

Family dynamics (Tables 5.2 and 5.3) have changed over the past few decades due to increasing life spans and the shift from three- to four-generation families in which children have long relationships with their great-grandparents. Maternal health and childcare have improved significantly, helping infants survive into adulthood. Adults are living longer and enjoy "decades of life after children," as some realists put it. Divorces are more common as people live longer and are unwilling to spend additional years in an unhappy marriage – and also because women have more independence as a result of earning higher wages. Additionally, the mobility of the American workforce, with people willing to travel across the nation or around the world to go where the jobs are, affects kinship cohesion and caregiving as adult children sometimes live thousands of miles from their aging parents.

Table 5.2 US Population by Age and Sex, 2008 (millions)

Age Group	*Males*	*Females*	*% of Total*
Under 15	31.3	29.9	20.1
15–64	101.8	102.2	67.1
Over 65	16.3	21.4	12.7
Total	149.4	153.5	100.0

Source: CIA, (2008).

Table 5.3 Life Expectancy

US Life Expectancy, 2008	
Male	75.3
Female	81.1
Overall	78.1

Source: CIA (2008).

In 2007, there were 116 million households, of which 59 million were composed of married couples with or without children present (US Census, 2008: Table 60). Americans are marrying later and having fewer children. The median age at first marriage continues to rise: 27.5 years for men and 25.6 for women, and the average size is 3.2 people (US Census 2008). Since the liberal revolutions of the 1960s, the number of American families with both husband and wife present has continued to shrink. The number of single-parent households has skyrocketed, and this, together with rising divorce rates, has put more women with children into poverty as two incomes are increasingly essential to middle-class lives. This, in turn, has caused anxiety over the future of the family and many have proclaimed a crisis situation. There is a nostalgia for the mythical good old days when women stayed home, men went to work, children were manageable and "above average," and two cars were in every driveway. A return to that model would require women to give up the gains of the past 30 years and return to patriarchal models, something most are not willing to consider.

Americans are torn between traditional and modern family models and are deeply ambivalent about the one they should construct for themselves. There is a culture war inside most individuals between traditional family values and contemporary liberalism. Tradition calls for limiting divorce, living near other family members, children obeying their parents, women focusing on domestic duties and motherhood, and everyone believing in God. But the reality of contemporary families promotes an absence of strict rules, puts both spouses as free agents in the labor market, nurtures children who are not the biological offspring of the adults they live with, and exists in a culture dominated by entertainment and emphasizing rights and sexual freedoms (Wolfe, 1998: 110). Affluence, too, contributes to the breakup of families as many young people grow up faster with cell phones, automobiles, and disposable incomes. But while parents are frustrated with the modern family, few seem willing to return to the 1950s.

The issue of homosexuality and family life continues to be debated. Stressing traditional values, since 1996, Republican party candidates and the Religious Right promoted one type of officially sanctioned marriage: One "born-that-way" man and one "born-that-way" woman. The evangelical wing of Christianity argued that God created the family consisting of Adam and Eve, not Adam and Adam, or Eve and Eve. In the past few years, Congress's 1996 Defense of Marriage Act defined a legal marriage as a union between one man and one woman. Since then the debate over who and who cannot be married has been brought to court or to the voters in many states. For example, in 2008, the California Supreme Court ruled that prohibitions against same-sex marriages were discriminatory; nevertheless, in November 2008, California voters rejected a ballot initiative allowing gay marriage. In 2008, only Massachusetts and Connecticut gave homosexual marriages the same rights and privileges as heterosexual unions. Vermont and New Jersey allow civil unions with benefits and responsibilities without labeling them "marriage" and New York recognizes gay and lesbian rights for couples who were legally married outside the state.

The 4,265,555 recorded births and a birthrate of 14.2 per 1,000 population in 2006 were the highest rates in four decades, increasing in virtually every age, race and ethnic group. 1.6 million births were to unwed mothers and, among teenagers, the increase reversed a fifteen-year decline (CDC, 2009). The rising birthrate is at odds with the usual explanation that in modern America, parents do not get an economic boon from having children, and are more likely to see the high costs of support and education as a drain on resources. In 2007, for families with an annual income above $45,000, the average cost of raising a child to 18 years old was estimated at $251,370 (USDA, 2008b). Costs can double if the child pursues a university education. About one in three American children is living only with its mother; but that can be said another way: nearly seven in ten American kids live with both parents.

For the vast majority of American teenagers, life outside the family revolves around school, part-time jobs, shopping, worrying about getting into college, athletics, and friends. The majority of teens have the philosophy of their own potential drilled into them by parents and teachers – an achievement ethos that makes them anxious about failing. Most teens get driver's licenses when they are 16 and, quickly thereafter, a car of their own. This is especially the case for suburbanites with both parents working. Middle-class teenagers have many social engagements in after-school athletics, clubs, volunteer organizations, music or dance lessons, and work. School days begin at or before 8 a.m. and end at 3 p.m. With stress increasing among America's youth, girls aged 12–17 surpass boys in tobacco and prescription drug abuse and equal boys in alcohol use and automobile accidents (Aratani, 2008). Similar to young adults in their twenties and thirties, teenagers are dating less but having more casual sexual encounters – "hooking up" – with a friend. Young people used to date a few times before deciding to have sex; but, in contemporary America, many hook up a few times before they decide to date (Blow, 2008b). While nearly half of all teenagers have had intercourse, it has become common in parts of the

South and West for teens to voluntarily agree to an abstinence pledge – popularly called a "Virginity Oath" – abstaining from vaginal sex until they enter college or get married. A religious-based organization called "The Silver Ring Thing" has thousands of teens wearing a silver ring and promising that upon marrying, they will present the ring – and their virginity – to their husband or wife (SilverRingThing.com, 2008). The continuing threat of AIDS and the general conservative climate have also been influential. Still, in 2006, there were over 400,000 births to females aged 10–19 (CDC, 2009).

Financial matters continue to be the biggest concerns for Americans, even more than terrorism, war or education. In 2007 only 50 percent said that the present was better than the past; in 2008 even that woeful percentage fell to 41 percent – something the Pew polling organization calls "the most downbeat short-term assessment of personal progress in nearly half a century of polling" (Pew, 2008b) – and this was before the bank failings and stock market crashes came. Most people have high expectations and seemingly unlimited sources of material goods from which to choose. Those with higher incomes come to expect more, and so many Americans in the highest income brackets either spend everything they make to live the most materially comfortable life available, or want things even more costly – a bigger house, newer car, designer clothes, and exotic vacations. From a world perspective, Americans as a group have been rich for a long time. The median yearly income for an American family of three in 2006 was $63,955 (Pew, 2008b).

Calling Americans "overworked" and "overspent," sociologist Judith Schor examined contemporary family life in the United States and concluded that Americans are caught in a work-and-spend cycle that weakens family and community ties. Certainly, Americans have chosen more time on the job and less with family than most Europeans. The last two decades witnessed an increase in competitive acquisition and conspicuous consumption and reinforcement of the long-standing American notion that "more and newer" is better. Schor pointed out that American materialism is central to personal identity as a marker of success or failure, and has evolved from comparisons to the next door neighbor's property to a "new consumerism" marked by "upscale spending" (Schor, 1998: 4). By trying to emulate the rich and famous lifestyles seen on television or among their professional coworkers and bosses, a family can put its household economy and personal well-being at risk.

It might be understandable that parents want their children to "keep up" with the children in fancy private schools or in wearing the latest fashion or flashing the latest product innovation. But to do this, parents must work longer hours to make the additional disposable income necessary to fund their own and their children's new gizmo addictions. The United States has always been a competitive society that wants to believe that the next generation will have life better than the previous one. Parents might want to downsize their own lifestyles but cannot and will not, because to do so would threaten the status and opportunities of their children. There is a culture of desire, but the concept of "need" has changed as the "must have" items now include blackberries, laptop computers, and iPods. Most American families have neither adhered to a family budget nor saved money for the future; instead, they spend their entire salaries between paychecks and further their acquisitiveness by buying on credit or using the equity in their homes to take second mortgages. This seems to be changing as recent national and global economic disasters have convinced or forced many to cut back on consumption, save a little and cut up their credit cards.

This growing debt burden weighs most heavily on poor families who overcharge credit cards and do not make the incomes to pay more than the monthly minimums, therefore staying perpetually in debt. The middle class, too, feels overextended, with single women and minorities leading the categories of those who owe much more than they can afford to pay. Two-income families with children and DINKS (double income no kids) have two salaries to help pay the bills, but their expectations and upscale spending patterns often leads to debt. Personal income and indebtedness affect the way people see the economy in general. It is therefore not surprising that poorer Americans are less optimistic about the future as prices rose faster than the incomes from 1996 to 2008. In the longest period of non-adjustment in its history, 1997–2007, the US government failed to raise the minimum wage from $5.15 an hour. In mid-2009, the minimum wage was $7.25 an hour.

Women

For at least two centuries, American women have been a majority within the nation's population, but, until the last two decades, they have faced limited choices in the job market. Moreover, the divisions of race, class, marital status, political philosophy, and immigration divide women as much as they do men. One thing is certain: women in contemporary America have come a long way since the 1960s in every field of private and public life. In contemporary America, women have risen to near-equality in access to jobs, education, and aspirations; and yet, "near-equality" is not equality and the struggle continues on how to create a more just society.

The rise of paid labor and industrialization in the early nineteenth century simultaneously gave women avenues to self-sufficiency outside the marriage and circumscribed their choices by funneling them into "women's work" and lesser salaries. Women were seen as helpmates to men, secondary wage-earners, and, primarily, as homemakers. This "separate sphere" philosophy held out the roles of piety, purity, submissiveness, and domesticity as the realm of true womanhood. Feminists from the 1830s and 1840s protested this inequality, but it would take until 1920 for women to push through the Nineteenth Amendment to win women's suffrage in national elections. Most of the gains focused on white women, with minority women stigmatized by race.

Women had long been seen as "weaker vessels" whose physical frailty needed protection. Even though the government had called for "Womanpower" to fill industrial jobs during World War II, until the 1960s court decisions and social convention limited work hours to keep women safe and healthy – of course, these provided rationalizations for paying women less, limiting their occupational choices, and maintaining their dependence upon men. As early as 1923, feminists believed that to change things, the country needed to adopt an Equal Rights Amendment (ERA): "Equality of rights under law shall not be denied or abridged by the United States or by any State on account of sex." Efforts to get Congress to consider such an amendment fell flat until it was resurrected in 1972, with Congress quickly passing the ERA and sending it to the states for ratification. It was not ratified, falling three states short of those required for amending the Constitution.

Partly, the ERA failed because conservative women fought vehemently against it, afraid that it would change conventions on child custody, which favored mothers, or that it would make females available for a wartime draft into the military. Highly-religious women clung to biblical readings that taught that a woman should support her husband and be subordinate to him. Big businesses fought the ERA because of the costs of higher salaries. Many liberals argued that the amendment was unnecessary because the 1964 Civil Rights Act had explicitly banned discrimination based on sex or race, that Affirmative Action programs were having a positive effect, and that the "equal protection" clause of the Fourteenth Amendment was increasingly being interpreted by the Supreme Court to overturn discriminatory laws and practices.

Laws have made workplace environments better by penalizing employers who allow or proffer unwanted sexual advances against women employees. Sexual harassment lawsuits against employers for making women uncomfortable in their jobs and for withholding promotions and pay raises if a woman refuses sex, have overwhelmingly been settled in favor of the woman filing the claim, although some high-profile exceptions exist. In televised hearings in 1991, law professor Anita Hill accused the nominee for the Supreme Court, Clarence Thomas, of past sexual harassment. Nationwide, more women began to file lawsuits alleging similar misconduct by male employers.

By the 1990s, overt signs of gender discrimination had decreased and women were found in increasing numbers in every profession. The gains have been made across racial and ethnic lines. Madeleine K. Albright was the first woman to serve as Secretary of State (1998–2000) and Condoleezza Rice became the first woman to hold the post of National Security Advisor (2001–5). In 2005, Rice became the first African American woman to be appointed to head the US Department of State and she was followed by former Senator Hillary Clinton in 2009. Since the early 1980s, women have surpassed men in the numbers of bachelor's and master's degrees, and in 2006 earned 49 percent of all doctoral degrees (NCES 2008) – educations that enabled them to enter the workforce on a higher pay scale. Women have reached historic highs in elected positions and those numbers are increasing with each election. In 2009, 17 women held US Senate seats; 78 had seats in the House of Representatives including the powerful position of Speaker of the House held by Nancy Pelosi; there were hundreds of female judges; a black woman, Shirley Franklin, was mayor of Atlanta; and at least one woman served on the US Supreme Court.

Glass ceilings for promotion still exist as do "pink collar" jobs where women are predominant, such as secretarial work, nursing, elementary-school teaching, waitressing, and in libraries. This keeps the issue of equal pay and ideas of "comparable worth" rightfully in the headlines. Women are also forced to choose between career and family because of the widely practiced idea of "equality without protective oversight." While there have been significant gains in the number of child-daycare facilities, these are costly privately-owned businesses. Many working mothers are forced to leave their children with grandparents, or home alone. Congress passed the Family and Medical Leave Act in 1993 to mandate maternity leave for pregnant and new mothers. However, as no provisions were made to make the leave paid, most women in single or poor circumstances cannot afford to take unpaid absences for very long.

The abortion controversy is a volatile issue in American politics, dividing conservatives from liberals (Illustration 5.2). The Supreme Court often hears cases to decide between the constitutional rights of women to control their own bodies and the rights of society to protect human lives. Even though most of its rulings are by 5–4 votes, the Court has continued to rule in favor of a woman's right to choose to give birth or have an abortion, a rule it established in the *Roe* v. *Wade* (1973) decision. In 2005, the number of reported abortions declined to 1.2 million, its lowest level since 1974. One in five pregnancies ended in abortion and there were 19.4 abortions for every 1,000 women aged 15–44 (Guttmacher, 2008). Part of this decline is explained by the ever-increasing use of an abortion pill, RU-486, which has been available since 2000, and which makes abortion more private and less statistical.

Illustration 5.2 Anti-Abortion Billboard

This anti-abortion billboard stands on the property of the Greater Pentecostal Temple near Pritchardville, South Carolina. The automobile junkyard provides graveyard imagery that echoes the message of death and thrown away parts.

(Russell Duncan)

In the past few decades Americans have done much to level the field for women; but there remains much to be done. The rising numbers of women in politics and universities – particularly the 47 percent female enrollment among law students – portends well for future gains. Still, in 2009, when all the numbers were added up, women earned 77 cents for every dollar earned by men, were twice as likely to live in poverty, and were less visible at the highest levels of corporate life.

Race

America is a society deeply conscious of color, most obviously in terms of black and white. It is certainly easy enough to focus on the African American inner-city poor, black criminals, police injustice, neo-Nazis and militant anti-immigrant groups. There are prejudices that need to be overcome and true equality remains a dream deferred. On the other hand, the successes of Barack Obama, Colin Powell, Condoleezza Rice, Will Smith, Oprah Winfrey, Denzel Washington, prominent African-American mayors, over 600 black state legislators, and thousands of others point to a society that respects equal opportunity and merit. While racial preferences are still all too common in hiring and promoting, in loaning money for new homes, in buying homes in certain neighborhoods, and in myths about intelligence and criminality, an oft-cited study concluded: "Racial progress is a train that left the station fifty years ago, and has been chugging along ever since" (Thernstrom, 1999: 12). African Americans alive in the 1950s could not have imagined the successes they would achieve, even while those gains are not evenly distributed across class or rural lines.

Americans have generally expected an individual to succeed or fail on his or her own merits; in fact, the American Dream revolves around the simple idea that within each individual human being is the capacity to do extraordinary things. Individuals, such as Barack Obama, have risen. But it is when a group claims rights that most Americans hesitate, because giving members of one group priority smacks of discrimination against individuals who are not in that group, current or historical circumstances notwithstanding. The tough question is whether or not to discriminate against single individuals for the benefit of a group. The answer is even harder to reconcile with the Constitution, especially when even the lowest group is not nearly as low as it once was and when racial and ethnic multiculturalism has been protected and encouraged. The extent of American racial diversity is shown in Table 5.4.

Table 5.4 American Population Diversity, 2000, 2008 and 2050 (in millions)

Group	*2000*		*2008*		*2050*	
	No	*%*	*No*	*%*	*No*	*%*
Non-Hispanic White	211.5	75	199.8	66	203.3	46
Hispanic/Latino (any race)	35.3	13	46.7	15	132.8	30
African American	34.0	12	41.1	14	65.7	15
Asian American	10.1	3	15.5	5	40.6	9
American Indian and Inuit	2.1	0.7	4.9	2	8.6	2
Native Hawaiian/Samoan	0.8	0.3	1.1	0.3	2.6	0.4

Note: Since 2000 the US Census Bureau has allowed individuals to mark more than one category for race. Most of the double markings are Non-Hispanic White plus one other category. The figures for 2008 and 2050 are estimates. Numbers are rounded.

Source: US Census (2008d).

Before World War II about 87 percent of the black population was mired in poverty and uneducated. In contemporary America, 74 percent are above the poverty line, 93 percent of those who are active in the labor force (working or looking for work) have found jobs, 83 percent of those above 25 years old have graduated from high school, 3 million have earned bachelor's degrees, one million have their Master's, 113,000 have Doctorates, and 166,000 hold medical, dental, or law degrees. 1.4 million African-American students are currently enrolled in college (NCES, 2007). Undoubtedly, things have changed for the better.

But the racial divide has not disappeared and the economic outcome is not equal. The poverty rate for blacks is three times that of whites, the unemployment rate is double, and black workers make on average 79 cents (males) and 67 cents (females) for every dollar white males make (BLS, 2008a). The number of black families headed by single women is triple the white rate and there are more than a million African-American men in prison or on parole. This situation increases poverty among single, uneducated, and underemployed women with children. Even if these women work – and most of them take part-time employment – they remain in poverty. Additionally, in 2008, only two states allowed voting by prisoners. 41 other states disfranchised voters who were in jail or on parole and seven had laws that permanently disfranchised people who committed felonies – a removal of voting rights for 4.7 million Americans, one in 43, further alienating people already on the fringe of society (NCFE, 2008).

Glass ceilings also exist for upwardly-mobile individuals who suddenly find their occupational advance within companies stopped before the big promotion to the topmost level of management. The court system often hears cases alleging discrimination because of skin color. In November 2000, in the largest racial discrimination lawsuit in American history, the Coca-Cola company was compelled to pay $192 million to African-American workers who had been "passed over" for promotions. In 2007, Federal Express paid out $54.9 million to 20,000 black and Latino employees for similar practices (Lieff, 2008). Clearly, the American legal system is unwilling to sanction further discrimination when it comes to opportunity.

Critics complain about whites "here" and blacks "there," but even if neighborhoods were integrated proportionally, only 12 of every 100 households would be black. When African Americans speak of integration, they refer to a mix of 50–50; when whites speak of integration, they mean the proportional representation reflecting American society (Thernstrom, 1999: 227). Not wanting to break up the culture of black communities, black families continue to buy houses near other black families and – as whites do the same – this form of self-segregation continues. While it is misleading to claim, as some do, that the United States has residential racial apartheid, America does have a society heavily divided by class, skin color, and a choice of subcultures.

In contemporary America, one-third of all African Americans live in the suburbs, sometimes completely integrated with whites, but more often in a checkerboard pattern of black street, white street, reflecting strong preferences to live in cultures within cultures. For example, in the working-class town of Vallejo, California, population 116,760, the 2001 population was 30.4 percent white, 24 percent black, 26.1 percent Asian, and 16 percent Latino – making it one of the nation's most racially-balanced cities. Yet, there was little interaction between groups, except for children playing together in the streets. Once teenagers get to high school, they separate themselves along racial lines and have fewer and fewer friendships with other groups. Still, great tolerance and little hostility existed as Vallejo residents go about their daily lives in a diverse and generally quiet coexistence (Holmes, 2001). Nationwide, racial attitudes have changed for the better, even though liberals often refer to racism as if it is still the era of segregation and conservatives act as if the American Dream is equally available for anyone who will work, marry, and lead a moral life. The daily experiences for African Americans lie somewhere in-between.

Latinos and Asians have an easier time integrating, even though it was not always so. Both groups have a long history of mistreatment by white racists. But during the last two decades, Asian Americans and Hispanic Americans have leapt over African Americans: in 2008, Asian Americans have been seen as a "model minority" and have commanded the highest education levels and salaries in America – surpassing the median weekly income for whites, $960 to $816 for men, and $723 to $649 for women (BLS, 2008a). Hispanics secured their place as the largest minority group, increasingly made their weight felt in politics and will have an enormous impact by 2050 when they will make up an estimated 30 percent of the American population (see Table 5.4).

Crime and Punishment

Americans rely on legal remedies to maintain order, equality, and freedom in a multicultural society. With more lawyers than any other nation in the world, Americans use the court system to settle disputes, large and small, and put real faith in the ability of the judges to ensure that constitutional guarantees overcome unfair actions by individuals, groups, the government, or even the law itself. The courts follow federal and state law, the Constitution and decisions from similar cases, called precedents, to establish verdicts and set sentencing.

The Constitution has much to say about the legal rights of Americans charged with crimes. Particularly, Amendments 4–8 provide the basics of due process of law, speedy and public jury trials, no cruel or unusual punishments, an adversary system, the right to remain silent, the right to a lawyer, the right to call and confront witnesses, no second trial for the same offense, no excessive bail, and no police coercion of witnesses. The Supreme Court has further ruled that police must advise people of these rights if they are to be questioned about committing a crime. Typically, a police officer must say:

> You have the right to remain silent. If you give up the right to remain silent, anything you say can and will be used against you in a court of law. You have the right to an attorney and to have an attorney present during questioning. If you cannot afford an attorney, one will be appointed for you without charge. Do you understand these rights as I have explained them to you?

If the arresting officer fails to advise the prisoner of these rights or does not follow the exact procedure in searching for and finding evidence, the courts will free the accused person, even if the evidence points to guilt.

During a lifetime, most Americans are involved in at least one court case, either criminal or civil in nature. The legal system is adversarial, pitting defendant(s) against accusor(s), while a judge and jury listen to evidence presented according to formal rules. Civil law accounts for the bulk of legal actions as individuals sue each other for financial compensation arising from accidental destruction of property, divorce and child custody, psychological "pain and suffering," accidental physical injury, breach of contract, or discriminatory acts of a racial or sexual nature. Civil cases have included suing McDonald's for selling dangerously hot coffee, class action suits against makers of faulty breast implants, and claims for general reparations to contemporary African Americans who suffer "post-slavery stress syndrome." Most cases involve the minor irritations neighbors cause each other with too loud music, dogs that bite, or too high fences. Civil courts often award compensation above the actual loss in property or medical costs, including punitive financial damages against companies for "negligence." For the most part, civil cases do not involve prison time – although failure to pay child support or follow court judgments can land the offender in jail.

Criminal cases are brought against those who are charged with committing a crime against individuals and, by extension, society. Murder, rape, assault, burglary, use of illegal drugs, theft, insider-trading, embezzlement, child molestation, kidnapping, and arson are a few of the most common charges (see Figure 3.3). For the most part, these cases are kept within the state court system, with appeals available through the US Court of Appeals and Supreme Court. Criminal cases are usually settled with a trial by a jury of 12 citizens, who, after listening to the evidence, must unanimously agree that the person is guilty beyond a reasonable doubt. If even one juror dissents, the prisoner is released. Defendants can skip the jury trial by agreeing to a "plea bargain" agreement with the prosecutor, typically agreeing to plead guilty to a lesser charge in exchange for a shorter prison term and/or financial penalty in lieu of a long trial and an undetermined verdict. If the defendant is too poor to hire an attorney, the state is required to appoint and pay the costs for a "public defender." These lawyers have enormous caseloads, are the poorest trained, youngest, and the least paid of all trial lawyers. Because about 80 percent of all people accused of felonies are poor, and thus defended by appointed counsel, the United States clearly has a wealth-based justice system favoring the middle and upper classes. Additionally, most juries are drawn from lists of registered voters on which the poor are under-represented, a practice which keeps the middle class and elderly in charge of deciding verdicts.

The United States has a notoriously high crime rate and the vitality of the legal system makes most observers believe that America has even more crime than it really does. Nearly every Hollywood movie revolves around a crime or includes a crime in the plot; newspapers and television news shows attract viewers with the news of one misfortune after another, knowing that horror sells better than feel-good stories; and television ratings continue to show that viewers want to see dramas which let them watch the courts and police in action. There is a love affair for violent spectacle.

America has nearly 18,000 separate state and local police departments with over 730,000 full-time police officers; there are also nearly 250,000 civilians involved in law enforcement (see Table 5.5). And it is expensive, costing at least $200 billion for courts, police, and prisons. These numbers are striking, even if we acknowledge the large population and economy of the country. The United States also has a greater percentage of people in prison than any country in the world, with more people incarcerated in contemporary America than at any time in American history and a number equal to almost one-quarter of all prisoners worldwide (Liptak, 2008). Part of the reason for this is the length of sentences given by American courts – double and triple the sentences for similar offenses in the rest of the developed world. In 2007, there were 2.3 million people behind bars in the United States: 780,000 in local jails, 1.4 million in state prisons, and 200,000 in federal penitentiaries (DOJ, 2008a). Six million more are on probation or parole. The prisons are marked by overcrowding, hundreds are now run by private corporations which contract services to federal and state governments, and most function mainly to detain people and to exact retribution, instead of rehabilitating them.

Table 5.5 US Law Enforcement Agencies

Type Agency	*Number of Agencies*	*Full-time Officers*
All State and Local	17,876	731,903
Federal	513	104,884
Total	18,389	836,787

Note: Numbers do not include US military, state national guard, or support staffs.

Source: DOJ (2008b).

The United States has had highly-structured criminal gangs since the early nineteenth century, as the movie *Gangs of New York* (2003) effectively demonstrated. An immigrant society of diverse ethnic groups almost institutionalizes such affiliations. In 2005, after defining a gang as "a group of three or more people whose binding reason for being is repeated criminal activity," the Department of Justice acknowledged 21,500 different gangs with 731,500 members nationwide (DOJ, 2005). If the economy worsens the number of gangs will rise significantly. Organized primarily by race, ethnicity, or language, these gangs commit most of the drive-by target-of-opportunity crimes and a significant portion of the 15,000+ annual murders in contemporary America. Additionally, Mexican, Asian and Russian gangs are part of the organized crime network responsible for most of the drug trafficking in the United States. The most violent gang is the notorious, highly-organized Mara Salvatrucha 13 (MS-13), a Los Angeles gang that began in the 1980s and by 2004 had approximately 10,000 members in 33 states and maintained very strong links to El Salvador. MS-13 offers for-hire services including drug distribution, gun running, people smuggling, murder, theft, strong-arm intimidation – you name it (FBI, 2005).

The vast numbers of guns available throughout society probably increases the number of violent crimes and undoubtedly increases the number of accidental shootings by children, although opinions range widely concerning the former. The pro-gun lobby, led by the National Rifle Association (NRA), continues to use snappy slogans such as "Guns don't kill people; people kill people!" and "If guns were outlawed, only outlaws would have guns!" to lobby for individual, not government, responsibility.

In 1994 Clinton pledged to "get tough on crime" and Congress mandated a five-day waiting period on the purchase of handguns so that the FBI can run background checks on the customer; banned most assault weapons; required the registration of all handguns; increased prison terms for criminals using guns to commit crimes; and restricted former criminals from being able to purchase guns. Over 87 million background checks were made between 1994 and 2007, with about 1.6 million rejections (DOJ, 2008b). There have been "buy back" programs offered by communities willing to pay for any and all handguns turned in voluntarily. It is debatable whether or not these measures made any difference in the falling rates of violent crime in the 1990s.

As recent as June 2008 in a 5–4 decision, the US Supreme Court interpreted the 2nd Amendment as giving individuals the constitutional right to own a gun for personal use and to keep loaded handguns at home for self-defense (Greenhouse, 2008a). Americans grew up with weaponry, killed the French, Spanish, British, Native Indians, Mexicans, and each other, as they shot their way westward. There are presently so many weapons in the US that they could never be collected and seem certain to remain a fixed feature in American life. In the aftermath of 11 September, Americans purchased handguns and ammunition in record numbers, with 1,029,691 new guns bought in the single month of October 2001 (Baker, 2001). The issue of gun ownership is highly contentious, even at the highest levels. In February 2008, President Bush and the Department of Justice supported a favorable court ruling for a strict control over handguns and assault weapons in the nation's capital. Vice President Dick Cheney and a majority in Congress put forward a brief disagreeing with the president and saying that any ban was unconstitutional. The US Supreme Court agreed with Cheney and overturned the District of Columbia's attempt to control weapons on its streets (Greenhouse, 2008b).

The 1994 Crime Act earmarked $30 billion to the states to put 100,000 more police officers on the streets. It also provided for tougher penalties for drug offenders. Not only are more people going to jail, but they are staying longer. Part of this move to incarcerate is due to society's fatigue with criminals and the political situation of judges who hammer down longer sentences as they campaign for reelection to the bench. The effect of the Crime Act has been a steady decrease in the number of criminal cases, as the total number of criminal offenses fell from 14 million in 1994 to 11.3 million in 2007, with the number of homicides dropping from 23,330 to 16,929 during the same period (FBI, 2008).

In 1999, at Columbine High School in Colorado and Heritage High School in Georgia, "average" white students shocked the nation by killing teachers and other white students. It is worth observing that if the killers had been black and the victims white, the response would have been quite different, with talk of criminality of young blacks rather than of the individual tragedies of both perpetrators and victims. It is a continuing feature of American society that whites are treated as individuals without blaming all whites, but blacks bear the onus of being blamed as a group for failures or crimes perpetrated by individuals. The court system continues to hand out harsher penalties to black men than to whites who commit similar crimes as plea bargains and higher qualified lawyers reduce sentences for whites.

In 2007, 4.6 percent of all African American males, 1.7 percent of Hispanic males and 0.7 percent of white males were in prison. One-third of all black men will spend time in jail at some point in their lives; in 2007, 36 percent percent of all prisoners were black (DOJ, 2008b). The ultimate penalty of capital punishment is disproportionately invoked against African Americans convicted of murder than against other groups. The United Nations Commission on Human Rights has charged that "race, ethnic origin and economic status appear to be key determinants of who will, and who will not, receive a sentence of death" in the United States (Olson, 1998). Blacks are not the only ones executed. Since its founding, America has used the death penalty to punish those found guilty of particularly gruesome murders. Timothy McVeigh was executed in 2001 for the deaths of 168 persons when he used a truck bomb to level a federal building in Oklahoma City. Karla Faye Tucker, who made headlines worldwide for becoming a born-again Christian while on death row and received an outpouring of support from the Pope and American Protestant leaders – who asked then-Texas Governor George W. Bush to pardon her – was executed in 1998 for an especially brutal double-murder with a pickaxe. State governors have the authority to pardon anyone for any crime, but they rarely use the power to overturn judicial decisions supported by the electorate.

In only one instance, *Furman* v. *Georgia* (1972), did the Supreme Court outlaw the death penalty by judging it "cruel and unusual punishment" prohibited by the 8th Amendment. At that time, because of a moratorium ordered by the courts, there had been no execution in the US for five years. In 1976, the high court reversed itself and the states began executing people again. By 31 December 2008, 1,136 people had been put to death and there were 3,309 people on death row awaiting lethal injection or electrocution (Table 5.6). The average time spent awaiting execution averages twelve years. The morality of

Table 5.6 Executions and Death Row Inmates, 1 January 1976–31 December 2008

Category	*Executed (2008)*	*Executed Since 1976*	*On Death Row*
Non-Hispanic White	18	642	1,489
African American	17	391	1,390
Hispanic/Latino	2	79	364
Other	0	24	66
Male	36	1,125	3,258
Female	1	11	51
Totals	37	1,136	3,309

Source: DPIC (2009).

Illustration 5.3 Death Penalty Protester

For more than two years, this individual protestor stood in front of the US Supreme Court. She quietly held her sign, "Jesus was a Victim of Capital Punishment. End the Death Penalty NOW," to ask the Justices to change their interpretation of the United States Constitution and thereby make the execution of humans unlawful. As of 2009, the death penalty was still constitutional.

(Russell Duncan)

capital punishment continues to be the subject of debate in contemporary America. Fourteen states and the District of Columbia do not have a death penalty and two states with the death penalty have not executed anyone since 1976. Recent polls report a decreasing support for capital punishment from 69 percent in 2007 to 64 percent in 2008 (DPIC, 2008). Illustration 5.3 shows a lone death penalty protester picketing the US Supreme Court.

To describe American society, the cohesion or culture wars in its midst, and the speed of change due to large-scale continuing immigration is a difficult proposition. Inequities in race, gender, and class abound – the first two categories moving rapidly toward more equal treatment and the latter category widening the distance between the richest and the poorest citizens. New immigrant groups continue to arrive and in their transition to American society, force compromises and new understandings that reinvigorate contemporary generations. The institutions of education and religion are highly significant portions of the story, as are the social programs put in place by government to provide for the general welfare of the citizenry. And, of course, any real understandings of the workings of society depend upon acknowledgement of the power of the overarching culture. These discussions continue in the following chapters.

6

Religion, Education, and Social Policy

The American experience displays an uneasy tension between individual advancement and a belief in equality. Religion, education and government services are marked by this tension, and each of these institutions helps to reconcile personal success and failure with ideas of the work ethic. In the United States, secular and religious faith remains strong and the election of Barack Obama and a Democratic majority in the Congress have strengthened the feeling that the nation will continue to progress through religion, education and a program of general welfare for those who "deserve" it. Religion, education and social policy provide avenues by which Americans maintain their faith in uplift, advancement, individualism and equality.

Religion

Religious Freedom

The United States is both remarkably religious and remarkably secular. The country's semi-official motto "In God We Trust" is located on every piece of currency, and the Pledge of Allegiance has long included the words "One Nation, Under God." The United States military employs chaplains and builds churches on military bases. Religious groups are supported by having tax exempt status. All of this seems clearly contradictory to the historical American rejection of an established religion as does the continuing tradition of lighting a Christmas tree on the White House lawn even though Congress cannot sanction any religious holiday. Presidents are often photographed praying or attending church services, as Barack Obama did on

Illustration 6.1 Inaugural Prayer Service

On 21 January 2009, newly-inaugurated President Barack Obama attended a religious-yet-secular service in the official religious building of the United States. The National Cathedral in Washington, DC, is best known as a venue for funeral services given high-ranking government leaders, such as for Ronald Reagan (11 June 2004) or Gerald Ford (4 January 2007). The cathedral also serves as a place of national mourning and rallying point for the president and nation after catastrophic events, such as the attacks of the World Trade Center (11 September 2001) and the natural disaster of Hurricane Katrina (29 August 2005). Pictured from left to right: First Lady Michelle Obama, President Barack Obama, Vice-President Joe Biden, Jill Biden, former President Bill Clinton, and Secretary of State Hillary Clinton.

(Jae C. Hong/AP/Press Association Images, 2009)

21 January 2009, the day after he was sworn in as President of the United States (see Illustration 6.1).

Religion has always found fertile soil in the United States, from Native American shamanism to Euro-American myths of providential foundings in a New Eden and manifest destinies to subdue the earth. The concurrent timing of the Protestant Reformation and the discovery of the New World compounded matters. While the Puritans and Pilgrims in Massachusetts, Anglicans in Virginia and Georgia, Jesuits in California, Mormons in Utah, and others, experimented at different times with official government-established religions, American history is punctuated by religious freedom. The mixture of large numbers of believers of different faiths has demanded tolerance and helped persuade the Founders to state in the First Amendment: "Congress shall make no law respecting an establishment of religion, or prohibiting the free exercise thereof."

This provision dampens ethno-religious conflicts even if it has caused a two-centuries-long struggle over the use of the Bible in public institutions. In fact, the First Amendment seems to want it both ways, allowing neither the establishment of nor interference with religion. This ambivalence has proven successful in that both government and religion have prospered by being independent of each other. After all, the political views of religious people widely vary. To establish a religion in a country of immigrants would endanger the survival of the nation while simultaneously making for "bad religion" – too formal, authoritarian and undemocratic. Americans associate churches with community spirit and they want to keep them free from the European associations with oppressive, established classes or governments.

Religious infighting still occurs within the United States. The arrival of each group of immigrants whose faith is new to the towns or regions in which they settle, often results in fear and hostility in the pre-existing population. Catholics, Jews, Transcendentalists, Amish, Shakers, Quakers, Muslims, Black Muslims, Buddhists, Mormons, Jehovah's Witnesses, Pentecostals, Fundamentalists, Moonies, Christian Scientists, Scientologists, Branch Davidians and others have been treated with suspicion, ridicule and violence. Recently, theologians are noting the extraordinary rise of what they call the New Religious Movement, which is a creation of faiths even more diverse than before (Lester, 2002). With more than 2,000 denominations active in the United States, it might be difficult to imagine more diversity.

Generally, Americans practice a "quiet faith," are non-judgmental and acknowledge the fundamental right of all individuals to believe in the god of their choice, as long as they abide by the law (Wolfe,

1998: 39). This is a classic Enlightenment view of tolerance and non-interference in the lifestyles of other people. Open religious prejudice is rare as Americans have faith in faith, and believe that regardless of doctrine, good people are rewarded and do not go to hell. In a December 2008 poll, half of all respondents said that belief in any religion could lead to eternal life and that even atheists could go to heaven (Blow, 2008a). Religion is *laissez-faire* and is discussed in everyday conversation, in greater or lesser amounts according to the community and region in which a person resides. Writer David Brooks says that Americans seek a "flexidoxy," which he defines as "the hybrid mixture of freedom and flexibility on the one hand and the longing for rigor and orthodoxy on the other" (Dionne, 2008: 5). When polled, 80 percent of those asked say that they believe in God and 59 percent believe in the devil and hell. 73 percent believe in heaven, 75 percent in miracles, and 71 percent in angels (Harris Poll, 2008). This is clearly a part of American optimism. About one-third of all Americans are "unchurched" and practice their faiths in private. Atheists and agnostics are not discriminated against.

Most Americans believe in a personal God who performs daily miracles. More Americans believe in the virgin birth of Jesus (61 percent) than believe in Darwin's theory of evolution (47 percent). Three-in-ten attend church at least once a week (Harris, 2008). One-third of all Americans say that God speaks directly to them and half pray at least once a day, with one out of five Christians uttering unintelligible language – called "speaking in tongues" – while praying for miracles (Pew, 2008e). Often prayers ask for good grades, a higher salary, a pretty girlfriend, or a victory in the football game. For most Americans, God is an affirming, not a demanding, entity and prayers are secular wishes not high worship.

Main Religious Groups

In 2008 Protestant denominations had been in a two-decades long decline, fragmented into thousands of congregations and barely holding a majority status at 51.3 percent (see Table. 6.1) (Pew, 2008i: 5). With approximately 69 million adult members, the Catholic church is the largest single religious group and its membership is relatively stable as Latinos lead the immigration lists. Christopher Columbus brought Catholicism with him to the New World in 1492 and Jesuits soon worked across the continent. The colony of Maryland was established as a refuge for French Catholics and large numbers of Irish Catholics poured into east coast cities after the Irish potato famine in

Table 6.1 American Religiosity (2008)

Affiliation		*% of American Adults*
Protestant		51.3
Baptist	17.2	
Methodist	6.2	
Protestant (unspecified)	5.2	
Lutheran	4.6	
Non-denominational	4.5	
Pentecostal	4.4	
Presbyterian	2.7	
Restorationist	2.1	
Episcopal/Anglican	1.5	
Holiness	1.2	
Other groups	1.7	
Catholic		23.9
Unaffiliated/Atheist		16.1
Jewish		1.7
Mormon		1.7
Jehovah's Witness		0.7
Buddhist		0.7
Muslim		0.6
Orthodox		0.6
Hindu		0.4
Others		2.3

Source: Pew Forum on Religion & Public Life, "US Religious Landscape Survey," 13 December 2008c: 5.

the 1840s. A larger, and different, group came during the massive influx of the 1880s–1920s. Some Protestants formed into xenophobic, nativist groups and used mob violence and rioting to protest against the culture of the newcomers and cheap labor. These conflicts between Catholics and Protestants largely disappeared from America after World War II, and certainly stopped after the election of John F. Kennedy to the presidency in 1960. In part this is because American Catholics, however much they admire the Pope, do not strictly follow his decrees. The overwhelming majority of American Catholics practice birth control, half get divorced, and some churches have asked that priests be allowed to marry and that women be elevated to the priesthood. As of early 2009, the Vatican has denied both requests.

One hundred million adult Americans are Protestants who divide themselves between at least 220 denominations and thousands of self-identified congregations. The two largest groups, Baptists and Methodists, spread rapidly among the lower and middle classes during the Great Revival of the 1830s. The evangelical message of appealing directly to an all-powerful God was soon translated into an anti-authoritarian individualism that bypassed clergy, government officials and the upper classes. In modern America, Baptists and Methodists are split into approximately 250,000 local congregations worshipping in various ways according to history, ethnicity, race, class or particular preacher. Even with the gains in equality and societal acceptance by minority groups, American churches are, with a few exceptions, not multiracial. In 1963, Martin Luther King, Jr. said that eleven o'clock Sunday morning is the most segregated hour in America; in 2009, this is still overwhelmingly true.

There are approximately five million American Jews divided into Orthodox, Conservative or Reform groups, with most feeling a solidarity with Israel and a common history of persecution both within and without the United States. Most Jews came to America from Germany (1820–80) and Russia or Poland (around 1900). Jewish scientists and intellectuals, including Albert Einstein in 1933, immigrated in the 1930s and 1940s. Supporting one another and pursuing education as the way to success, American Jews have risen economically and politically to become the most influential Jewish group in the world. They enter the professions in large numbers and are leaders in obtaining doctorates and teaching positions in American universities. Additionally, in rural areas where evangelism is strongest, the population is strongly pro-Israel and a large number of Protestant ministers have made pilgrimages to Jerusalem. Intermarriage by Reform Jews to Christians is widespread and well-funded political action committees affect foreign policy – as do the 30 US Congressional seats and the 13 Senate seats occupied by Jews in 2009. As way of comparison, the 2009 Senate includes 25 Catholics, 14 Presbyterians, 13 Jews, 9 Methodists, 7 Episcopalians, 7 Baptists, 6 Mormons, 3 Congregationalists, 3 Lutheran and 13 other Protestants.

Islam has grown from having 52 mosques in 1945 to approximately 3,000 mosques and Islamic centers and 200 schools in 2001 located throughout the 50 states (Haddad, 1998: 37; Mujahid, 2001). By 2008, the total Muslim population in the United States approached five million people. Even though nearly two-thirds of adult Muslims are first generation immigrants, they are highly assimilated and support integration into the larger society, rather than to separate themselves (Pew, 2007: 2). Forty-seven percent say they are Muslims first while 27 percent assert that they are Americans first (Pew, 2007: 31). The majority of Muslims are Sunnis and nearly 9-in-10 Muslims are traditionalists: 96 percent believe in "One God, Allah"; 91 percent think there will be a Day of Judgment; and 87 percent believe in angels (Pew, 2007: 23). While a majority of Muslims say that since 9/11 it has been more difficult for them because of prejudices, being seen as part of Al Qaeda, general ignorance about Islam, stereotyping, and increased religious profiling by government agencies, three out of four people say they "never experienced discrimination while living in this country" (Pew 2007: 4). In 2009, the 111th Congress has two elected Muslims in the House of Representatives.

Founded in 1830, the Church of Jesus Christ of Latter Day Saints – commonly called the Mormon Church – is the largest indigenous religious group in America. Its early attempts to establish a religious government in Utah, as well as the widespread practice of polygamy, confronted the First Amendment's ideas of religious pluralism, separation of church and state, and the common belief in sanctity of the family, defined as one husband, one wife. The result was long years of religious persecution with Congressional and Constitutional insistence that Utah be free of church control. By 1890, Mormon leaders agreed officially to stop polygamy, even though unsanctioned plural weddings continue in contemporary America. By 2007, there were 5.7 million Mormons in the United States. The 2002 Winter Olympic Games in Salt Lake City confirmed the acceptance of Mormonism into the diverse religious fabric of the United States, and in 2008, Governor Mitt Romney made a strong, if unsuccessful, run for the Republican presidential nomination.

Another indigenous religion, the Native American Church, has about 250,000 members in 100 branches. This church blends Christianity with the use of peyote cactus – which contains the hallucinogen mescaline – in worship services. In 1990 the Supreme Court ruled that states could prohibit the use of peyote, but 28 states have allowed the practice to continue, in private. In 1978 Congress passed the Religious Freedom Act to allow Indians to use sacred tribal places on public land. Most American Indians are Christians wholly, or have combined Jesus with traditional spiritualism of prayers, dancing and singing.

Revivalism

Periodically, America has experienced widespread evangelical movements which turn people back to God. Grounded in the core claim of Christianity that God sent his only Son to redeem the sins of the world, these "liberation" revivals occur during times of large scale immigration, fears of war or economic uncertainties. The First Great Awakening in the 1730s witnessed the arrival of Methodist

Reverend George Whitefield who preached up and down the colonies. His oratorical power made hell so vivid that some listeners searched for it on an atlas. Whitefield helped bind the colonists together and his message of salvation made a substantial contribution to inciting the American Revolution. The Second Great Awakening of the 1830s lit a religious fire that thrust thousands into Baptist and Methodist churches and formed others into groups to end slavery, set up communes, or join Mormon, Shaker, or 7th Day Adventist churches. A third great revival of the 1920s pitted the traditional agricultural and white nineteenth-century values of creationism against the industrial, urban, multicultural twentieth century and its embrace of the theory of evolution. This debate between fundamentalism and modernity played out spectacularly in the 1925 Scopes Monkey Trial, when a young teacher was jailed for teaching the scientific theories of Charles Darwin.

As the twenty-first century began, America was in the midst of a fourth great revival, which arose from the anxiety over contemporary themes of multiculturalism, feminism, post-modernism, terrorist threats, nationalist movements and globalization (Fogel, 2000; Jenkins, 2002). Some of the thrust for the revival is explained through generational theory, which maintains that children of the 1960s generation rebel against their parents by becoming more conservative (Leland, 2004). The new revival also benefits from the ending of the Cold War, when the six-decade-long archenemy of the United States disappeared suddenly, leaving Americans to renew their focus on an older enemy, Satan. George W. Bush's evangelical division of the world into good and evil fueled his political support and was an important aspect of his domestic and foreign policy agendas – something which led prominent analyst Garry Wills to point out that the Bush administration pushed forward "a faith-based war, faith-based law enforcement, faith-based education, faith-based medicine, and faith-based science" (Wills, 2006).

Religion has long been a part of American pop culture, placed prominently on display in a century of Hollywood film and literature. Glossy, media-savvy Christianity in the form of Mel Gibson's blockbuster film *The Passion of Christ* (2004) and the top-selling adult fiction book of 2003 and 2004 – and second in 2005 – Dan Brown's *The Da Vinci Code,* reached a wide audience and raised interest in the death and life of Jesus. Fundamentalist apocalyptic novels, such as the sixteen installments in Tim LaHaye and Jerry Jenkins's *Left Behind* series, topped the *New York Times* bestseller list, selling more books (75 million copies by December 2008) than John Grisham's legal novels and ranking second worldwide to the ultra-popular *Harry Potter* series – books which also focus on the mystical, magical world (see Table 7.1, p. 202). LaHaye and Jenkins fictionalize the scripture, deriving plotlines from the biblical chapter *Revelations,* when the Antichrist is on the earth and is engaged in a final battle with God. In a speech that conservative Christian readers can only find "sinister," the Antichrist tries to convince Americans of a one-world economy and one-world government: "We must disarm, we must empower the United Nations" (quoted in Didion, 2003). Like Gibson's film, the *Left Behind* books are militant, violent interpretations of the Scriptures.

On the softer side, Hollywood films like *The Devil's Advocate* (1997) play into the general belief that the Satan walks the earth and continues to seduce humans, offering wealth and sex in exchange for human souls. The film concludes that through the power of grace and free will, humans can thwart Lucifer's designs. In the past two decades, Max Lucado's fifty books have sold more than 40 million copies. Mitch Albom's inspirational *For One More Day* was the top-selling book in the fiction category in 2006, and *The Five People You Meet in Heaven* took the second spot in 2005. But the real winner has been evangelical pastor Rick Warren's *A Purpose-Driven Life: What on Earth Am I Here For?* (2003) – a self-help textbook asking readers to find the meaning of life through a surrender to God's will. In December 2004, Warren's book was in the top position on the *New York Times* bestseller list, where it had been for 100 weeks; in December 2006 the book still sold well at number 11. The success of the book is due to its adoption by Sunday School classes nationwide, where attendees read and discuss a chapter a week. In fact, many evangelical churches held a "40 Weeks of Purpose" program, culminating the Sunday of the 2004 presidential election. Warren added to his pre-election influence by sending an e-mail to 138,000 pastors with the message that the "non-negotiable" issues in the election (favoring Bush) were no abortions, no stem cell research, no cloning, no euthanasia and no homosexual marriages (Donadio, 2004). In 2008, "Pastor Rick" showed his power by holding the only non-media sponsored "debate" between Barack Obama and John McCain (see Illustration 6.2). He gained further notoriety after Obama named him to give the invocation at the inaugural ceremony on 20 January 2009, a move that set off a firestorm of criticism by feminists, gays, and liberals who vehemently disagreed with his judgmental stance.

The Fourth Awakening is led by dedicated evangelical Protestants who put God up front in their lives, sometimes wearing T-shirts

Illustration 6.2 "Pastor Rick" and the Presidential Hopefuls, 2008

On 16 August 2008, the most powerful evangelical preacher in the United States, "Pastor Rick" Warren, hosted the Republican and Democratic presidential nominees to a question-and-answer session at Saddleback (mega) Church in Lake Forest, California. The candidates did not debate, but sat, by turns, with Warren who asked questions on moral and domestic issues of concern to Christians, including the hot button issues of abortion and gay marriage.

(Richard Vogel/AP/Press Association Images, 2008)

boasting "Jesus is My Homeboy" or wristbands engraved with WWJD which they can rub and contemplate "What Would Jesus Do?" when confronted with everyday choices. In 2008, 52 percent of all Protestants (26 percent of the American population) defined themselves as evangelicals (Pew, 2008i: 5). Revivals have been held in America since the 1730s to bring sinners back to Christ. In one of the biggest revivals in 2004, the Reverend Billy Graham led a four-day preaching crusade to about 312,500 people in the Rose Bowl football stadium in Los Angeles (CBS News, 2004). It must be noted that fundamentalists – those who believe in the literal truth of the Bible – are not in the majority among evangelical groups, who run the gamut between extreme liberalism and radical conservatism. Pentecostal groups, formerly known as "holy rollers" for their habit of speaking in tongues and belief that some people are blessed by God with the ability to heal, are gaining adherents (Jenkins, 2002). Pentecostals are famous for tent revivals in which the lame are made to walk again through faith healings.

Perhaps the greatest gap between the US and other nations of the industrialized world is over American faith in an active God. In the aftermath of 11 September, religion is one of the main ways by which Americans are seeking to regain their balance. Many Christian groups are promoting a return to Ten Commandment morality and are exploiting the war on terrorism to push their conservative agendas of putting prayer back into the schools and expanding the role of religion in the public sphere. As various court decisions and government programs continue to blur the line separating church and state, liberals hope that the nation's secular faith in the Constitution will ultimately overcome.

Religion's foray into the political realm is the most controversial contemporary aspect of religion. This is not new, even if it has been discouraged by the constitutional separation of church and state and by the common assent of most Americans. Martin Luther King, Jr., liked to say, "God isn't going to do all of it by Himself" (quoted in Dionne and DiIulio, 2000: 6). King understood the complex balance of individual and collective responsibilities in a liberal society. Since the election of Jimmy Carter in 1976, presidents have increasingly invoked religious sentiments, thereby setting aside the taboo of keeping religion out of politics. Bill Clinton repeatedly employed biblical language and George W. Bush often spontaneously referred to his deep religious beliefs.

The present controversy is over conservative usurpation of liberal methods. Conservative Christians, reacting to the social upheavals of the 1960s and the anxiety of a globalizing post-Cold War world – increased by the terrorist attacks – have created an interfaith cooperative under the general idea of social action by a Christian Right. These conservatives have joined with fundamentalists to elect politicians more favorable to their beliefs to ban abortion, to allow prayer and the teaching of creationism in public schools, to make it unconstitutional to burn the American flag, to return power to the states by reducing federal taxes, and to get the government out of the welfare business. Jerry Falwell's Moral Majority helped elect Ronald Reagan, and the Christian Coalition linked evangelicals to politics by distributing 70 million "Voter Guides" and organizing churches nationwide to get out the vote for Republican Party candidates in the 2000 and 2004 elections. They provided the necessary votes in key states in 2000 and 2004 to put Bush in the White House and keep him there. In 2008 this technique failed as Obama was able to cut into the religious vote. His campaign theme of "Hope" and slogan "Yes, We Can!" appealed to a coalition of young voters, African–Americans, Hispanics and Asian–Americans who, while not exactly liberal, refuse to demonize evangelical fundamentalists as ignorant fanatics from "Jesusland" (Dionne, 2008: 15). Obama was also aided by a continuing trend toward separation of church and state; whereas 51 percent of Americans in 2000 and 2004 believed that churches should make political statements, in 2008, 52 percent said churches should "keep out" of elections (Pew 2008f).

A Portable Civil Society

The United States has both a highly-educated citizenry and a heavy emphasis on religion. Usually, the more technologically advanced a country becomes, the more religion is downgraded. This secularization thesis argues that religion fades as modernization and globalization expand. In contemporary America, religion is a growth industry, adapting, crossing denominational boundaries and expanding. The country oozes religion. In physical structures, there are nearly 500,000 churches, temples, mosques or gathering sites. Billboards and church locations along major interstates, street corner preachers, handbills attached to trees, and radio/television programs daily broadcast the good news or apocalyptic prophecy to anyone who tunes in (Illustration 6.3).

The megachurches, where from 2,000 to 40,000 members convene every weekend and thousands more are actively involved during the week, has grown from 700 congregations in 2003 to more than 1,200 in 2008 (James, 2003; Hartford, 2008). Some megachurches offer radio and television ministries. The churches encourage religion, rootedness and convenience where people live lives around church activities on a "24/7" basis – open all day, every day. These fellowships vary between evangelical denominational and independent, entrepreneurial, market-driven non-denominational entities. They are

Illustration 6.3 Religion Writ Large

Even though most Americans practice a "quiet faith" in their everyday dealings with others, religion has gotten "louder" with the expansion of the television, radio, and internet missions. Billboards along major highways often ask sinners to "repent" and the physicality of church buildings are ubiquitous across the American landscape. Just south of Lexington, Kentucky, the congregants of this evangelical megachurch erected an enormous aluminum crucifix to advertise themselves and Jesus Christ to the passing motorists along Interstate 75, one of the busiest highways in the United States.

(Russell Duncan)

mostly made up of middle-class Protestants and while teenagers might still wear wristbands embroidered with WWJD, some kid with the meaning: We Want Jack Daniels! Southeast Christian Church in Louisville, Kentucky, has 22,000 members in a church with 403 toilets in a sprawling compound where members shop, eat, bank, attend school, pray and work out in a gym. The Community Church of Joy in Glendale, Arizona, runs a school, mortuary, water-slide park, hotel, convention center and bookstore for its 12,000 members. Other megachurches offer up to 80 different activities each evening, including groups involved in bible study, legal clinics, basketball games, financial planning, marriage counseling, drug recovery support groups and teenage dance parties. Conveniences include on-property or in-church McDonalds, credit unions, schools, day care, AIDS clinics, language courses, sports fields, fitness centers, food courts, movie theatres – basically self-contained small towns. While convenient, scholar Wade Roof warns that the megachurch is "the religious version of the gated community" with "like-minded people" who "lose the dialogue with the larger culture" (quoted in Brown, 2003).

Instead of holding to dogmatic beliefs, Americans often change denominations, explaining this faith hopping as a spiritual journey toward individual fulfillment. One-quarter of all Americans have changed faiths – and in 2008, 44 percent of all Protestants had switched to another denomination in the course of their lives (Pew, 2008a). This is populist, not hierarchical, and is marked by privatism. Religion provides a portable civil society for a mobile nation. Because there is little direct state support for US churches, except for the benefit of tax breaks for non-profit groups, money for school books to church-sponsored schools and some funding to "faith-based initiatives" aimed at welfare support for the poor, religion is supported via private donations. Churches need a competitive product and they have to advertise it successfully to attract money. Many churches and individual preachers have expanded their congregations by television ministries or online cyber-sites which appeal to those who are sick or find it too difficult to travel or who want to "attend" more services every week. When Americans change residences, they seek out new churches, explore the market, and make choices based upon convenience, class, race, preaching style, beauty of the church structure, child-care, sports leagues, and position on conservative or liberal issues. This helps explain religious pluralism in America, the ever-expanding numbers of churches and the competitive business of American religion.

Polls consistently find that churches are as social and secular as they are religious. Churches succeed in getting half of all Americans to work two to three hours every week in volunteer service to the community and, in a nation that believes in private – not public – sector responsibility, they are vitally important institutions distributing free food and clothing services to the poor, housing the homeless, caring for the sick, and setting up day-care facilities for children of working mothers. So while many academics have seen religion as irrational, primitive, or superstitious, Americans continue to join churches for both spiritual and social reasons.

Education

Colleges and Universities

In 1944, Swedish sociologist Gunnar Myrdal identified the essence of the American belief in advancement: "Education has in America's whole history been the major hope for improving the individual and society" (Blanck, 2002: 138). It is a fundamental part of the American Dream and a part of the social compact idea that democracies require educated citizens. American education developed from European traditions, centered originally in families, and entered the public sphere when Puritans established the first community and church-related schools just after arriving in the New World. By the American Revolution, every colony had public and private schools and there were nine universities with a total of 731 students: Harvard (Puritan Congregational, 1636), William and Mary (Anglican, 1693), Yale (Puritan Congregational, 1701), Princeton (Presbyterian, 1746), University of Pennsylvania (nonsectarian, 1751), Columbia (Anglican, 1754), Brown (Baptist, 1764), Rutgers (Dutch Reformed, 1766), and Dartmouth (Congregational, 1769). America's university system is one of its greatest achievements.

After the Revolution, Americans developed a more nationalistic syllabus for students – this was done privately and was neither sanctioned by law nor mandatory – with texts emphasizing constitutional freedoms and the sacrifices of heroes such as George Washington, Thomas Jefferson and Benjamin Franklin. Students continued to study Greek and Latin and primarily read British literature. Noah Webster compiled an American dictionary to stress differences in spelling and pronunciations from British English. He sold his product with a promotion that "NOW is the time, and *this* the country. . . . Let us then seize the moment and establish a national language, as well as a national government" (Webster, 1789: 379). American leaders insisted that girls receive a thorough primary education so that they could fulfill their roles as "republican mothers" to the new nation. It was widely hoped that education would ease social tensions, provide upward mobility and equal opportunities for all free, white Americans in the marketplace.

Teaching expanded quickly in the North, but public schools in the South and West were not generally available until around 1900. African Americans and American Indians were widely deprived of anything beyond elementary education apart from a few missionary schools. With large-scale immigration around 1900, public schools expanded as a way to rid immigrants of foreign influences and to assimilate and Americanize them. The number of universities grew remarkably from 119 in 1850 to 356 in 1876, the year Johns Hopkins University became the first college to insist that research and graduate classes take precedence over undergraduate teaching. In contrast to all other nations, America was educating the masses. This unparalleled commitment to education gave rise to American power and has provided a gigantic global lead in favor of the United States. Today, many worry that the source of American greatness is in danger as its school system declines.

Contemporary America has roughly 2,600 universities which grant bachelor or higher degrees. There are 18 million enrolled students, 1.3 million faculty members, and an aggregate expenditure of $373 billion (NCES, 2007). State-supported colleges were established immediately after the Revolution, with the University of Georgia (1785) and the University of North Carolina (1789) leading the way. Today, every state has at least one central four-year university and most states have a university system with many campuses. The states also operate 1,195 two-year public community colleges, often called "junior colleges" whose average annual tuition fee in 2007 was $2,361 (AACC, 2008). These colleges provide education for the 11.5 million students who cannot afford the higher costs of four-year institutions, who are generally older (the average age in 2007 was 29), who have responsibilities of children or work, or who seek to improve their academic credentials in hopes of being admitted to a university. Students successfully completing the requirements at community colleges are granted an Associate degree. Additionally, since the 1960s, vocational-training colleges have been established to provide skills to students in specific occupations, or to provide English language classes to immigrants. This public system operates alongside and in competition with the large number of private universities and colleges.

Overall the system is market-driven, decentralized and pluralistic, providing opportunities for students of different abilities, income levels, family responsibilities, and goals. Enrollment has skyrocketed from 3 percent of college-age students attending in 1890, to 25 percent in 1950, to 67 percent in 2007. The largest increase came after World War II, when the US government's G. I. Bill (1944) offered subsidies to veterans who wanted to get college degrees. The Cold War increased the need for scientists and specialists and Congress passed the National Defense Education Act of 1958, which linked the nation's security to the mental resources and skills of university

Figure 6.1 Education, Unemployment, and Salaries

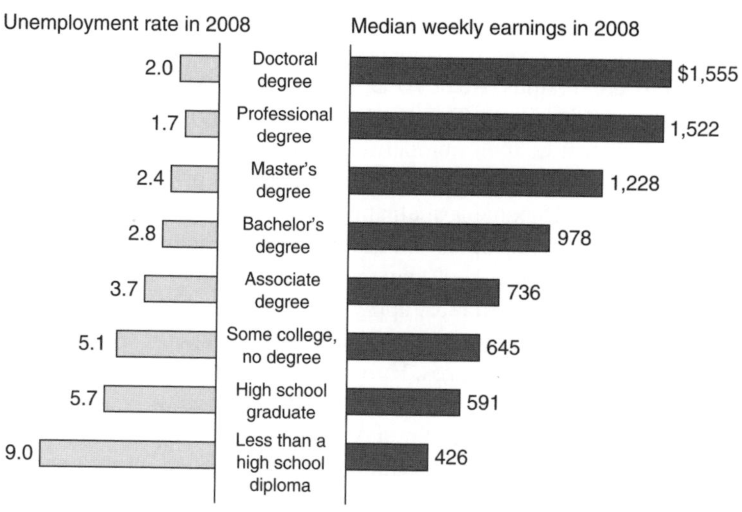

Note: Data includes all persons 25 years old and older with full time jobs.

Source: BLS (2009a), Current Population Survey, 6 March.

students. Federal grants to the nation's research universities exceeded $30 billion in 2006 (SSTI, 2007).

With globalization and the compelling need to absorb, process and combine information in the twenty-first century – something David Brooks calls "the cognitive age" – universities are the gatekeepers to the most lucrative jobs and occupational mobility (Brooks, 2008). Much of the class division in America stems from how much or how little education an individual has obtained (Figure 6.1). In the 1960s, college attendance doubled as the Baby Boom generation reached 18. The African American, Chicano, and American Indian Civil Rights Movements, the Feminist Movement, and the deferment granted from Vietnam for active students, further expanded enrollments. As more students experienced equal access to universities, the attitude toward higher education changed from being seen as a privilege to being claimed as an equal right. By the start of the twenty-first century, over one-half of all Americans over 18 had attended college at some point in their lives (Menand, 2001). The student population in 2005 consisted of 57 percent women, 31 percent minorities and 3.3 percent foreign (NCES 2006). In 2007, nearly 29 percent of all Americans over age 25 had at least a bachelor's degree – for Asian Americans in this category, an astonishing 51 percent had university degrees as compared with whites 32 percent, blacks 19 percent and Hispanics 13 percent (US Census, 2009a).

Universities compete for students and students compete for acceptance into universities. Most American students take a standardized Scholastic Achievement Test (SAT) and/or American College Test (ACT) to determine their competitiveness against all students graduating from high school in a given year. Prestigious private universities accept as few as 15 percent of all applicants, while some state and private colleges have an open admissions policy. Even at most public four-year universities, less than 50 percent of the applicants are admitted. Those rejected must apply elsewhere or go directly into the labor market, mostly at minimum wage. About two-thirds of all students enroll in public colleges. Universities since the 1960s have been sensitive to past discrimination, diversity, and minority needs and have selected students based upon Affirmative Action policies in relation to race, gender and class. Supposedly fairness to minorities and academic achievement determines placement, but, increasingly, the upper class has the advantage as Ross Douthat found, "Meritocracy is the ideological veneer, but social and economic stratification is the reality" (Hacker, 2005). So-called "need-blind" admissions principles are quickly dropped when the economy falters (Delbanco, 2007). With the economic crisis of 2008 causing loss of investments and tax revenues which resulted in immediate budget cuts, halting construction projects, hiring freezes, the firings of all but tenured faculty, and the drying up of financial aid packages in many universities, admissions offices have increasingly accepted applicants who can fully pay the costs rising tuitions without financial aid over those who have higher academic credentials but need financial assistance for tuition and expenses (Karmin and Hechinger, 2008).

An undergraduate degree takes a minimum of four years to complete and consists typically of 36–40 different courses. American colleges are uniform in requiring that one-third of a student's curriculum be in general classes in science, philosophy, history, literature, math and language so that students will be broadly-informed democratic citizens. After completing these required courses, students select a major and take 9–12 specialized courses. The remaining classes needed for graduation are electives which students choose to supplement other areas of interest or to concentrate on a minor field which strengthens the major. Lately, the trend is away from traditional disciplinary study in the arts and humanities toward business administration. For 2008, as ranked by the respected London *Times Educational Supplement,* the United States placed thirteen universities among the

Table 6.2 Foreign Students Studying in US Colleges/Universities in 2007–8

1 India	94,563
2 China	81,127
3 South Korea	69,124
4 Japan	33,974
5 Canada	29,051
6 Taiwan	29,001
7 Mexico	14,837
8 Turkey	12,030
9 Saudi Arabia	9,873
10 Thailand	9,004
11 Nepal	8,936
12 Germany	8,907
13 Vietnam	8,769
14 UK	8,367
15 Hong Kong	8,286
World total	623,805

Source: Institute for International Education (2008)

world's top twenty, including Harvard(1), Yale(2), Cal Tech(5), Chicago(8), MIT(9), Columbia(10), Pennsylvania(11), Princeton(12), Duke(13), Johns Hopkins(14), Cornell(15), Stanford(17), and Michigan (18). Those rankings, as well as high rankings in science and social sciences, pull thousands of foreign students to American classrooms. In a surprising reversal from the downturn caused by visa restrictions and anti-Americanism in the wake of 9/11/2001, 623,805 foreign students matriculated to US universities in 2007–8, surpassing all previous records and contributing about $15.5 billion to the US economy. Table 6.2 lists the top fifteen countries with students studying in the United States (IIE, 2008). Complementing these numbers, the number of American students studying abroad also reached record numbers, topping 241,000.

If a student wants to go on to graduate school, he or she first takes a standardized test, the Graduate Record Exam (GRE), which does what the SAT did at the undergraduate level. The competition for placement begins again. A Master's degree usually means an additional 6–18 courses plus a thesis, and a PhD could add another 6–18 courses plus a dissertation, depending upon the specific program and whether or not classes are on the quarter or semester system.

Most state universities charge moderate to high fees to residents of their states, while surcharges on students from other states are very expensive. The most recent trends indicate the steepest tuition hikes in

Table 6.3 Estimated Annual Costs for 4-year College/University Students for 2008–9

	Public (In State)	*Public (Out of State)*	*Private*
Tuition & Fees	$6,585	$17,452	$25,143
Room & Board	7,748	7,748	8,989
Books	1,077	1,077	1,054
Personal Expenses	1,720	1,720	1,720
Transportation	1,010	1,010	807
Other Expenses	1,906	1,906	1,397
TOTAL	$20,046	$30,913	$39,110

Note: The actual costs vary widely according to which of the 6,500 institutions a student attends, individual student economies, and scholarship grants. For the 2007–8 academic year, tax credits and grants to each student at private universities reduced costs by $10,200; students at public universities (in state) averaged $3,700 in reductions.

Source: College Board, Annual Survey of Colleges (2008)

a decade for both public and private institutions. In fact, the rising costs, which rose by 439 percent in the last twenty-five years, threatens the ability of families to pay for a university education (NCPPHE, 2008: 8). Eighty percent of American students attend public universities partly because a university education is overwhelmingly paid for by students and their parents. Average university costs for the 2008–9 academic year are compared in Table 6.3.

Nationwide, there are US government "need-based" scholarships for poorer students. In 2007–8, the maximum grant was $4,310 per student; 5.4 million students received an average $2,649 each for a total grant of $14.3 billion (College Board, 2008). Top athletes are given scholarships to matriculate while they compete in intercollegiate sporting contests. Both public and private "merit-based" scholarships are given by every university to attract the most academically-gifted students. Additionally, thousands of private foundations or individual donations promote education. The Bill and Melinda Gates Foundation has earmarked $21 million to support curriculum reform in Chicago schools and $1.5 billion for the United Negro College Fund, including the financing of full scholarships for 20 years (1999–2019) for 1,000 African American students a year (Gates, 2008). In 1999, the Lilly Endowment donated $30 million to the American Indian College Fund to help improve tribal community colleges – in 2008 there were some 30,000 students in 36 tribal colleges in 14 states – and African American television star Bill Cosby gave $20 million to Spelman College in Atlanta. At present, even though more than half of all students fail to finish their degrees, American universities are annually awarding nearly 555,000 Associate (two-year) degrees, 1.2 million Bachelor (four-year) degrees, 400,000 Master's, 76,000 professional (law, medicine, etc), and 45,000 doctorates. Many of the graduate degrees are to foreign students.

A State Responsibility

The United States does not have a national system of primary and secondary education even if the government sometimes makes land available, provides funding for special projects, and ensures that all citizens have equal access to schools. While the US Department of Education (DOE) has very limited supervisory powers, it does research, makes suggestions for national standards and directs money toward programs deemed essential to national interests. In 2008 the DOE appropriated $68.6 billion to these programs (DOE, 2008a).

The states have constitutional authority over education. This gives them the flexibility to meet the demands of a variety of citizens and ways of life. State Boards of Education set minimum requirements for teacher qualifications, student attendance and course offerings, but real control devolves to more local levels. The day-to-day management of 56 million students in the 97,000 public and 28,000 private schools and 3.7 million teachers is delegated to 14,600 independent school districts (DOE, 2008a). The private schools, divided between religious and class-based college-preparatory schools, are outside of state control – except that they are required to meet minimum guidelines for course offerings. They receive little state, federal, or local funding, and must raise money from endowments, donations, churches and tuition. The structure of education in the US is summarized in Figure 6.2

School Districts and School Boards

School districts are administered by school boards elected or appointed from the local communities or counties. School boards decide what will be taught in their schools and administer the funding. Generally, half the money to operate schools comes from the state and the remaining half is raised through local property and sales taxes, as decided by each community. Those communities which have high property values or a willingness to increase their taxes can provide high quality facilities, the newest software and the best teachers for

Figure 6.2 The American Educational System

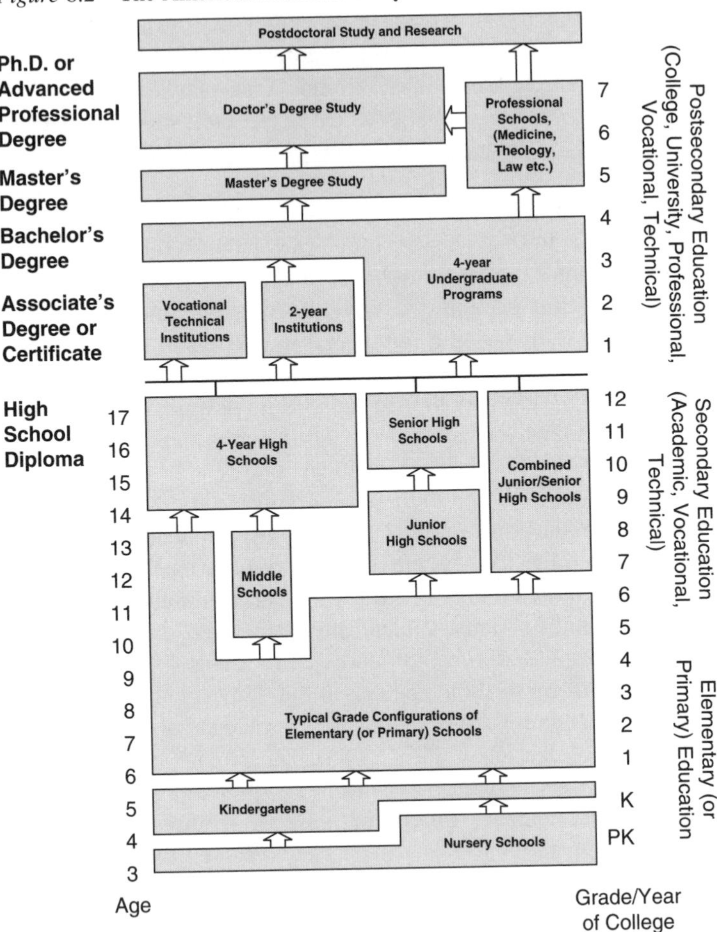

Note: Adult education programs, while not separately delineated above, may provide instruction at the elementary, secondary, or higher education level. Chart reflects typical patterns of progression rather than all possible variations.

Source: (NCES, 2009).

their schools. Poorer districts find it difficult to fund the basics and are marked by inadequate supplies, burned-out teachers, absent students, old computers and older physical structures. Under the Elementary and Secondary Education Act of 1965, the federal government offers financial assistance to these under-funded public schools. Additionally, since the 1960s, an Upward Bound program aids poor high-school students and Project Head Start provides pre-school education to help disadvantaged children improve their basic skills.

School boards decide which textbooks to buy and which courses to mandate – choices made with community needs in mind. Agricultural communities, African American communities, urban areas, Muslim groups, fundamentalist Christian communities, immigrant communities, liberal and conservative communities all have differing ideas of appropriate textbooks and courses. In 2006, 43 percent of students in public primary and secondary schools were from racial/ethnic minorities (NCES, 2008). Selection of texts and courses can be a daunting task in urban areas, especially, where the variety of students often consist of those speaking 80–90 first languages at home, while concentrating on English at school. From 1979 to 2006, in the age range of 5–17 years old, the numbers jumped from 3.8 to 10.8 million pupils who spoke a language other than English at home – fully 20 percent of all the students in this age group (NCES, 2008).

Studies indicate that while suburban areas have good schools, inner-city urban areas and the country's rural districts produce less well-prepared students. Americans research the differences among schools when they make decisions on home purchases or job relocation, often making the final decision exclusively on the school district their children will enter. Of course many poorer Americans have no chance to choose. Middle and upper-class Americans can pay to place their children in private schools if the public schools do not meet their expectations for discipline, safety and intensive education.

Americans expect their high schools to give comprehensive educations, wide-ranging and unspecialized. The educational philosophy is that everyone should receive twelve years of schooling, whether or not the student is motivated to study or is academically qualified for the task. This philosophy of not selecting among students aims at providing equal opportunity for everyone, to provide literate workers, and to make the complex variety of ethnic, racial, and cultural peoples into Americans. This inclusion of students of varying abilities in the same school and same courses can hold back the academic potential of individual students as teachers face the challenge of trying to teach everyone. Most schools have tried a "tracking" system that places students in classes by ability, still teaching everyone but often at vastly different levels. Tracking is controversial for those who want fairness over academic challenge. The most exclusive private "college preparatory" schools select only students with certain IQ scores and/or proven ability, as well as those whose parents stand high in the community or who will donate sizeable monetary gifts to the school. Whether educated

Figure 6.3 Educational Attainment, 2008

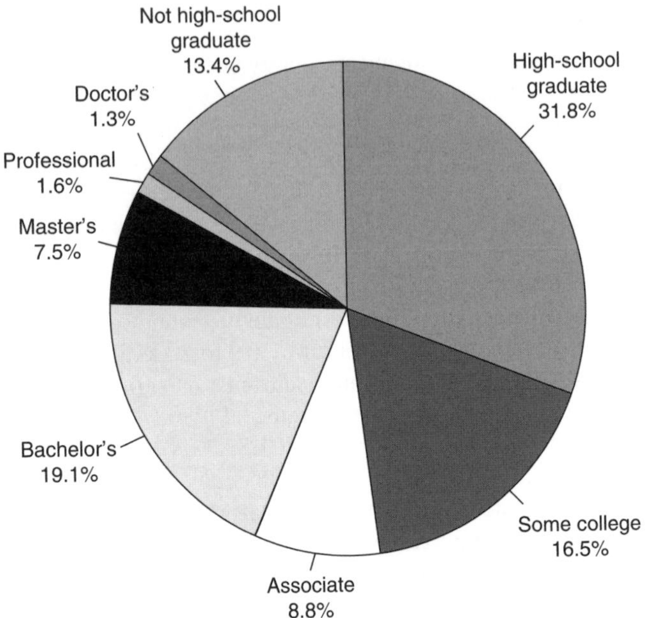

Note: Percentages are for the 194.3 million Americans age 25 and older. Numbers have been rounded.

Source: NCES (2009).

publicly or privately, by 2007, 86 percent of whites, 82 percent of blacks, and 60 percent of Hispanics in the total population had completed high school (US Census, 2009a). Figure 6.3 shows the level of highest educational attainment of Americans aged over 25 in 2008.

American schools are professionally run by administrators and teachers, who generally hold college degrees. It is not uncommon to find primary and secondary teachers with Master's degrees, and a few have gained PhDs. Prospective teachers must pass state written examinations to be certified to teach in the public schools; certification in one state does not necessarily transfer to another. Overall, Americans have built a system that is decentralized, comprehensive, universal and professional. And with all these students, faculties and administrators engaged on a full-time basis – representing around 25 percent of the American population – education is big business.

Debates over what happens in the schools and the quality of education are constant. Americans are competitive and dislike reports that students in other countries, states or school districts are achieving more. In recent years there has been much concern over the declining scores in 3rd- and 8th-grade achievement tests and on SAT/ACT examinations. Comparisons with student scores worldwide indicate that the US is in the lower half for most industrial nations in science and math (OECD, 2008b). Fingerpointing occurs as parents hold teachers and administrators responsible; teachers respond with studies which indicate that the presence or absence of family support and issues of poverty are key determinants to test scores. Teachers argue that the top 50 percent of American students compare with any students anywhere. Most suburban parents are content with their schools and say that it is the inner-city numbers or new immigrants who reduce the national scores; their own children are achieving. Asian Americans are held up as the model minority, receiving much support at home, excelling in testing and comprising up to 25 percent of the student population at prestigious universities nationwide. Some reformers want to see the implementation of a national curriculum, but most parents hold firmly to decentralized schools run by local citizens. Americans accept the role of government in providing monetary support and in intervening, sometimes, to uphold minority rights.

Integration and Affirmative Action

In the landmark case of *Brown* v. *Board of Education* (1954), the US Supreme Court ruled that separate schools for different races were "inherently unequal" and that the states had to desegregate all educational facilities. The struggle to integrate schools met with strong local resistance and sporadic violence, but schools were integrated. The government persuaded universities to use Affirmative Action guidelines to bring in minority students even when their test scores were below those of white students who were being denied admission. The government provided money to those universities which showed progress in integration; federal marshalls – and private organizations such as the NAACP – brought lawsuits against universities which discriminated against minority students. These actions were highly successful in integrating institutions of higher education, even while there have been setbacks.

The *Bakke* (1978) decision ruled that it is "reverse discrimination" and unconstitutional to set quotas for minorities at the expense of qualified white students. This of course begs the ironic question: does the Equal Protection Clause of the 14th Amendment perpetuate racial supremacy when it is used to stop Affirmative Action? The Court ruled that diversity could be taken into account in admissions decisions, but quotas could not be mentioned. In 1991, Congress outlawed the practice of "race-norming" where universities compared only black student scores to each other before adjusting them upward to match white student scores for admissions decisions; the Supreme Court agrees that race-norming hurts white students. With the white backlash in the 1990s against the claims of "preferential treatment" for minority students, President Clinton reiterated his support for Affirmative Action, saying, "Mend it, don't end it." This encapsulates the majority view that history requires some strategy favoring minority uplift, but that previous discrimination against one group does not warrant present discrimination against another. In 2003, in spite of President Bush asking the US Supreme Court to declare the policy unconstitutional, the Justices ruled 5–4 that the University of Michigan Law School policy of making race a factor in selecting students was appropriate (Greenhouse, 2003). Clearly, it is difficult to balance equal protection and equal opportunity with a history of disadvantage and discrimination in a multicultural society.

Another problem is that community schools are located in suburbs and cities, reflecting the race, ethnicity and class of the homeowners. In the 1960s the Supreme Court tried to solve this residential segregation dilemma by ordering school districts to use "busing" to transport inner-city children to suburban schools, and vice versa. Because public schools are funded primarily by property taxes, the middle class resisted this practice of taking students from well-financed school environments and placing them in schools in adjacent school districts which lacked the basics. African Americans protested that busing destroyed their inner-city neighborhoods and asked instead for more monetary assistance to keep their children in local schools. Whites increasingly put their children in private schools or fled further into the suburbs. Finally, in 1974, the Court reversed itself and decided that local control of the schools should be upheld and that busing between school districts must stop. But that was not the end to questions concerning *Brown*. In 2007, the Roberts Court ruled that the school boards were not to make decisions assigning students living *within* individual school districts to schools based upon the race of the student (Bazelon, 2008). As Americans of all races continue to segregate themselves socially by class, race, and increasingly by language as Hispanic immigration rises, schools are increasingly segregated in ways not seen since the 1950s. Activist Gary Orfield states frankly: "The biggest metro areas are the epicenters of segregation. It's getting worse for both blacks and Latinos, and nothing is being done about it" (Paulsen, 2008).

Prayers and NCLB

Just as controversial and long lasting has been the debate over the 1962 Supreme Court ruling that prayer has no place in public schools because it violates the separation of church and state and abridges the rights of non-believers or non-Christians. States responded with "moments of silence" to allow students to sit quietly in their own thoughts, or prayers. The Court has ruled against prayers to open football games and prayers at commencement ceremonies, even though groups of people often protest the order by simply reciting the Lord's Prayer aloud (Duggan, 2000). Since 1925 the courts have consistently ruled out the teaching of creationism as an alternative or complement to the teaching of Darwin. In 1987 the US Supreme Court ruled that the inclusion of religious materials in science classes was unconstitutional. But the controversy continues, as creationism has been dubbed "the theory of intelligent design" as a way to make it seem equivalent to the theory of evolution. From 2002 to 2008, nine states (CA, FL, GA, KS, KY, OH, PA, TX, VA) tried to modify or remove evolutionary theory from the curriculum and replace or complement it with "creation science." State boards of education and the courts ruled this unacceptable, again, and for now, the supporters of Darwin have maintained an upper hand.

In 2002, Bush signed the No Child Left Behind (NCLB) Act to advance federal goals to improve primary and secondary education by making the states more accountable when accepting federal funding, a program Bush initiated. The aim was lofty, asking all US schools to meet 100 percent proficiency standards in reading and math for all students by 2014, thus reducing the achievement gap between rich and poor students and promoting models that work over those that fail. Under NCLB, the states are required to give annual tests to show progress, something known as outcome-based or standards-based education. Even while it can withhold funding from states which do not develop assessment plans or progress, the Tenth Amendment prevents the NCLB from establishing national standards and so each state set its own goals. Despite that, the National Education Association (NEA) found that the program has been a disaster, with at least 80 percent of the states failing to meet their goals and the results for 2014 will be a 75–99 percent failure rate overall (NEA, 2008a). Because the DOE withdraws funding to states based on how many schools fail to achieve the goals, the NEA calls NCLB a "test-and-punish" approach to education that is counterproductive and leads to diminished achievement (NEA, 2008a). The DOE completed its own study in 2008 and likewise concluded that the NCLB effort had been "ineffective" (DOE, 2008a). Ignoring these studies, in 2009 Bush touted NCLB as one of his greatest domestic achievements. Obama criticizes the program as underfunded, inflexible, and punitive; he pledges to work with the NEA and Congress to strengthen NCLB and advance achievement for all students (McKinnon, 2009). As in the debates over religion, the education debates will continue to define the American experience.

Social Services

Seen from a global perspective – if not necessarily a Western one – the United States is a welfare state with an infrastructure designed to distribute services to those who qualify and to the poor, sick, aged and unemployed. That the aid is neither equal nor completely adequate does not diminish the fact of its existence. The expenditure for social programs is only exceeded by the money spent for defense. Over the last 50 years, government has played a big role in increasing incomes and life spans, primarily through subsidies for education, pensions and public health. This redistribution of tax money is highly controversial in a nation that promotes individual and family self-reliance, has a diversity of racial and ethnic groups and 50 states governed by elected politicians of varying conservative or liberal philosophies. Mostly, the government's social services attempt to alleviate suffering and to provide a minimum living standard for the poor and disabled.

In addition to public assistance, there are private organizations and charities which offer services outside the public framework. Moreover, many Americans feel the need to insure themselves privately, buying health care and contributing to pension plans over and above government provision, religious handouts or employer-employee benefit packages. These programs overlap. Americans dislike the idea of a dependency culture and therefore expect individuals to take care of themselves within the market economy. There is a clear understanding of who makes up the deserving or undeserving poor. Children, the elderly, war veterans and disabled persons are seen to "deserve" assistance and are fairly well-provided for, but people who consistently lose their jobs, drop out of high school, have children outside of marriage, or rely on assistance too often are dismissed as "undeserving" and part of a dependency culture that must be put to work (Harris Poll, 2000).

Government Assistance

From 1789 until the 1930s, the United States did not provide public assistance. Most of the government aid programs available in contemporary America are rooted in the social policies of Franklin Delano Roosevelt's New Deal (1933–9) and the 40 percent unemployment rate of 1932. About one-half of all American families had someone employed by a New Deal agency. Roosevelt announced that poverty was not a moral failure but arose from social and economic conditions not always in a person's control. He promoted the understanding that given the opportunity, any American would take a job instead of a handout. In the end, the New Deal changed *laissez-faire* welfare policies by taking the responsibility for aiding the poor and placing assistance squarely into federal government regulatory and social agencies. The Wagner Act protected labor's right to collective bargaining, the Works Progress Administration put hundreds of thousands of people to work in government programs, and the Fair Labor Standards Act mandated a minimum wage and restricted the hours of allowable work.

But the most important program proved to be the Social Security Act, which established the pension system, unemployment insurance, and a forerunner to what became, in 1962, Aid to Families With Dependent Children (AFDC). The old-age pension portion of the Social Security Act is compulsory and is raised by taxes paid into a trust fund by employers and employees during working years of the employee; it does not come from general tax revenues and it is not distributed equally to the elderly. The more an employee and employer pay in – usually corresponding to higher incomes – the bigger the individual's retirement pension. Social Security is a "pay-as-you-go" system whereby present-day workers pay present-day retirees' pensions; in 2006, 49 million retirees or their dependents received an average monthly check of just over $1,000 for total of $55.3 billion (US Census, 2009b: Table 527). As the number of retirees grows, more workers are required to cover the costs, the pensions could be lowered, or taxes could be raised to fund programs.

With the New Deal, the government committed itself to supporting those who were down on their luck. This helped to change attitudes toward the unemployed. Since the New Deal, various groups of workers, consumers and minorities have been able to press for government intervention, something formerly only available to big business interests. This transformed the nation into a "broker state" adjudicating claims among various interest groups in society and giving rise to "rights talk" – the notion that social programs are "entitlements" that all Americans are guaranteed under the Constitution.

President Lyndon Johnson announced a "War on Poverty" in the 1960s and rewrote New Deal programs to include the creation of the US Department of Housing and Urban Development, Department of Transportation, Corporation for Public Broadcasting, Office of Economic Opportunity, and two education acts to fund school districts and to provide college funding for poor students. All of these programs are still in force. A federal program of food stamps, whose name changed in 2008 to the Supplemental Nutrition Assistance Program (SNAP), provides an electronic debit card that works like an ATM card and can be used in grocery stores nationwide (USDA, 2008a). Even though students, people convicted of drug felonies and married couples without children are generally excluded, most households with a monthly gross income below 130 percent ($2,297) of the national monthly poverty line ($1,767) for a family of four in 2008–9 are eligible . In 2007, 26.5 million Americans used the program each month. In 2009 the maximum monthly aid for a family of four is $588 (USDA, 2008b). Further food support is provided by a School Breakfast and Lunch Program which serves free or reduced-cost meals for poor children (with family incomes below 185 percent of the poverty line) in public schools to 40.6 million students daily in 2007 (USDA, 2008b).

In 1965, the federal government established Medicare to fund health care costs for the disabled and for everyone over 65 years old, regardless of need; the next year, Medicaid expanded those health benefits to anyone living under the poverty line. Medicaid is administered by each state, has wide variations in the quality of service, and is funded by a combination of federal and state monies, with 50 million beneficiaries receiving a total $399 billion in 2007. In 2008 the expense equaled fully 8 percent of the federal budget and approximately 20 percent of the states' budgets. By 2017 the costs are expected to balloon to an astronomical figure: $5 trillion (Bankhead, 2008).

The contemporary United States is virtually alone among industrialized nations in not having a comprehensive health care system for its citizens. Clinton came into office in 1993 with health care reform as his key issue. Big businesses and labor unions supported the plan, but small businesses, insurance companies, the American Medical Association and the majority of the American people rejected it, the latter group because of higher taxes and loss of choice. Having failed to achieve wholesale reform, Clinton had to settle for a more modest change. In 1996 he managed to sign into law three bills which guaranteed that health coverage would continue even if an employee changed jobs; extended the hospital stay to 48 hours after childbirth; and forced companies to insure patients with preexisting medical problems. In 2007, 46 million Americans did not have health insurance (US Census, 2008g). The old, disabled and poor had Medicare and Medicaid to fall back on, and the middle and upper classes generally had employer-funded health insurance, but those workers above the poverty line in minimum wage jobs are uninsured and remain vulnerable. The majority of the population has very good health care plans (some critics say that Americans are overmedicated and overtreated) which give them a choice of doctors, hospitals, and medical providers, paying from 80–100 percent of the costs for themselves, a spouse and children. About half of all Americans have dental care plans to pay for regular checkups, braces for children and tooth repair.

Another significant factor in the high costs of health care for young and old is obesity. Nothing has changed in the decade since the Harris Poll frankly stated: "Americans are the fattest people on Earth and are getting fatter every year" (Harris Poll, 1999). Over one-third of all US adults, 72 million people, weighed in at over 20 percent of their recommended weight in 2006 (CDC, 2008). The fast food culture and sheer abundance of products supersize everything. Politicians cannot even address the issue for fear of alienating constituents. Government departments of health and private advocacy groups spend millions of dollars on advertisements trying to convince Americans to exercise more and eat less. It has been a losing battle. Health care problems – particularly the explosive increase in dementia, diabetes, colon, AIDS-HIV, and heart diseases – puts further stress on the health care system.

The federal government subsidizes the whole economy by being the nation's single biggest employer with 17 million workers in jobs such as the military, immigration, foreign service, post-office departments, federal law enforcement and janitorial staffs. The United States Postal Service alone employs over 800,000 workers and the government is responsible for 12 percent of the total workforce. Additionally, tax money in the form of housing and education loans, business bailouts and tax breaks to start up businesses help the middle and upper classes. The women and men who select careers in the armed services receive the most comprehensive packages. Military personnel receive free medical and dental care, housing, high-tech training, and shopping benefits for themselves, their spouses and children. If stationed overseas, they receive income supplements, cheap insurance rates and tax breaks on most purchases. For those who decide to quit the military after their enlistment period is up – usually three to six years – the government provides money to help underwrite a college education and offers low cost housing loans. Personnel who serve at least 20 years can retire at half of their normal salaries; if they serve 30 years, they get two-thirds – and both groups of retirees retain all the special benefits, except housing, which they had on active duty. Because people join the military when they are 18–22 years old, retirement comes at ages 38–52. There is plenty of time for a second career, and most retirees take full-time jobs while continuing to receive monthly military retirement checks.

Social Security, Medicare and Medicaid are presently the costliest programs in the social insurance system, consuming 25 percent of the entire federal budget. Until recently, politicians rarely dared to support changes because of the political strength of the elderly who claim the programs as entitlements. The "graying of America" – the aging Baby Boom generation combined with higher life expectancies – threatens the entire system as there are too many retirees in relation to the number of workers required to support them. In 2007, 10.2 million Americans were over 80 years old and 31 million others were between 60 and 79 years old. By 2017, 40 million more people will join this over-60 group (HHS, 2008b). Longer lifespans combine with the usual retirement age of 65 to increase demand on the pension and health care systems. Additionally, advances in biotechnology seem close to matching drugs to individual genotypes, thereby saving lives and extending lifespans, but at greater costs. The rising costs of health care are troubling. President Bush wanted to overturn much of the welfare state as a way to cut the budget and in line with his conservative philosophy of work, thrift, prudence, self-reliance and a faith in private markets. In 2003, his plan to reform Medicare by reducing costs of prescription drugs while increasing the amounts patients had to pay before they received funding, eventually cost the government, and thus the taxpayers, dearly – as much as $1 trillion over 10 years. In 2004 he suggested a privatization of the Social Security system, making each person responsible for saving their own pension money; this privatization of Social Security did not pass Congress.

Workfare

Americans continue to debate the issue of what should be done to help the poor. Many argue that private-sector economic growth will eradicate poverty; others want higher taxes coupled with a redistribution of income and job training. Some claim that the poor lack the will to rise, while others argue that all societies are marked by class inequalities. Critics claim that government has never had the will to invoke real programs that will work and has simply done the minimum to control the poor. Conservatives say that government programs have been adequate but that poverty and dependency are tenacious among various groups. There are strong historical attitudes toward giving or taking "handouts" from a government, a clear attachment to the work ethic, and strong ethnic, religious and racial prejudices in the way.

For nearly thirty years conservatives have blamed welfare programs for creating a cycle of dependency and a culture of poverty that would keep new generations on welfare. The New Deal's program of Aid to Families with Dependent Children (AFDC) had been formulated in the 1930s, when families were more traditional, and it was designed to help widowed or divorced mothers who were raising children alone. From the 1960s onward the number of divorces and single mothers had expanded claimants to 4 million adults and 9 million children. Since Ronald Reagan, presidents have been taking government out of the welfare business by implementing a "New Federalism," a program returning authority to the states. In line with his emphasis on economic freedom not economic equality, Reagan pushed through substantial cuts in food stamps, housing assistance and job-training programs. These were some of the first efforts to move the poor from welfare to "workfare." In 1996 Clinton agreed with the Republican Congress "to end welfare as we know it," by signing the Personal Responsibility and Work Opportunity Act, which created a program of Temporary Assistance for Needy Families (TANF). TANF ended AFDC, set time limits on welfare recipients, set up strong work requirements, and devolved power over welfare monies to the states, territories and Indian tribes, each with a different program.

In 2006 TANF was placed under the Office of Family Assistance. In 2008, TANF funds sent to the states amounted to $16.5 billion; in June 2008 there were 1.6 million families receiving various amounts as determined by individual states, territories or tribes. The Act requires recipients to be employed within two years after welfare starts and it makes the states responsible for finding the jobs. Each recipient, unless disabled, is limited to lifetime benefits of five years. New immigrants to the US were made ineligible for any benefits under the law, but the states stepped in to support jobless immigrants under the same general conditions provided by TANF.

Across the United States, once taxpayers see the poor as deserving workers who are temporarily unemployed, instead of as undeserving "welfare cheats," they have become more generous. With everybody willing to work, everybody is willing to help. The flood of single women into the labor market has been a solid achievement; but TANF has neither created more two-parent families nor reduced births to teenage mothers as supporters had hoped. With the press watching closely, there have been no reports of people starving, yet. Critics worry about what will happen as the economy slips into recession or when people reach the five-year lifetime deadline, the safety net falls away, and they still will not or cannot find work.

In the United States there is as much to condemn as to praise. The country has not been able or willing to eradicate poverty or to move closer to an equality of outcome for all its citizens. Cries of hypocrisy abound as critics point out that the nation says one thing and does another. There are layers and layers of objections and problems when it comes to equalizing treatment for an increasingly diverse population of citizens. The so-called "classless society" has failed to eradicate class, race, gender and age divisions. Debates over the role of science versus the belief in God, or religion, continue at a strong pace. Whereas Bush was skeptical, even suspicious, of science – from global warming, to contraception, to stem-cell research to the theory of evolution – Obama says that while he is a man of faith, his administration will "guarantee scientific integrity" in government by making "scientific decisions based on facts, not ideology" (Stolberg, 2009a). Whereas Bush often suppressed scientific information that did not support a conservative agenda, Obama's belief in "the centrality of science to every issue of modern life," attests to his support for university research and strengthened social programs. The long history of being remarkably religious and remarkably secular continues to teach the lessons of contemporary America.

7

Culture

Diversity

American culture, like America itself, can be all things to all people. Culture varies widely by locale, region, ethnicity, and race in a nation with 50 states as diverse in historical particulars as the French Quarter in New Orleans, Pine Ridge Sioux Reservation in South Dakota, Muslim Detroit, casino-rich Las Vegas, Japanese Honolulu, Irish Boston, African American Atlanta, Blues-bound Chicago, Chinatown in San Francisco, Inuit Alaska, Jewish Colorado, Elvis-afflicted Memphis, Mormon Utah, Cuban Miami, Protestant Indiana, Chicana Texas, Quaker Philadelphia, Scandinavian Minnesota, Puerto-Rican New Jersey, Navajo Arizona, Madison Avenue New York City, Amish Pennsylvania, Hollywood-starred Los Angeles, corn-fed Iowa, monument-crushed Washington, and Rock-‘n’-Roll Cleveland.

There has never been an official national language sanctioned by the US government, even though 30 states and 19 cities mandate English for governmental correspondence and Americans speak English first and foremost outside the homes (Brown, 2009). There has never been an official national religion, even though the country is known for its evangelical Protestants. There are no bans on flying the flags of other nations alongside, or instead of, the national banner. In America there is a compromise among languages, faiths, and nations. Nearly a century ago, novelist Willa Cather spoke of American diversity when she wrote of her own life growing up in the state of Nebraska in the American “heartland”:

> The county in which I grew up, in the south-central part of the State, was typical. On Sunday we could drive to a Norwegian

> church and listen to a sermon in that language, or to a Danish or a Swedish church. We could go to the French Catholic settlement in the next county and hear a sermon in French, or into the Bohemian township and hear one in Czech, or we could go to church with the German Lutherans. (Quoted in Bell, 2000: 3)

Striking in Cather's description is the agrarian world of Christianity in which she lived and the many European cultures existing in that rural environment. Because American cities dominate the news, we are more familiar with the view of cultural pluralism and melting pots existing in the urban metropolises.

The United States is a nation of immigrants whose personal histories diverge as they reach back into national histories and ethnic rivalries on every continent, each with different cultural memories. Longstanding notions of individualism, self-reliance, and freedom of action further divide people from a common community. America in its chaotic blend of multiculturalism is the world in its postmodern diversity. This isn't new. Cultural conflict has always been a part of the culture of discontent that is America and the current round of culture wars has long roots in American society.

E Pluribus Unum

And yet, it is possible to locate a single, dominant American culture. Were this not so, we would hardly hear the multitude of fearful voices arguing that American cultural imperialism is neocolonialism, making all the world's languages subservient to the linguistic-debasement of American English and all the world's people conform to cheap and transient American tastes. Perhaps the 1960s slogan advocated by Dr. Timothy Leary could be remade to express world fears about American dominance: "Tune in! [to the American idea], Turn on! [to Hollywood movies], Drop out! [of your own culture]." To many, America is a dangerous mind-altering drug. Critics complain that America has become a modern-day Babylon, spreading moral decay and diseased style, fashion, food, films and other iniquities outside its borders. American popular culture is blamed for everything from global warming to childhood obesity. Ironically, in the midst of all this resentment is the movement to copy and imitate. One thing that is clear about American culture is that it doesn't stay "American" very long. It is soon cozy in the farthest corners of the world. Even at the heights of anti-Americanism in the Middle East and elsewhere, American popular culture gained adherents. After all, as one of the directors of Warner Brothers Studios says "Batman is Batman, regardless of if Bush is in the White House or not" (Arango, 2008).

American culture is loud and American culture is fast. Critics sometimes dissolve the whole into a McCulture, boring in its homogeneity, cheapness, and ubiquity in shopping mall after shopping mall, another one just down the interstate at the next turnoff or around the next corner, past the traffic signal on both sides of the road. Some see America as a "fast food nation," eating out as much as four nights a week, eager for immediate service, and demanding cheap food prices, while paying scant attention to how the burgers got to the drive-thru window in the first place (Schlosser, 2001).

America is an "idea state" held together as much by a promise as by geography and law. The idea not only shaped the culture, it is older than the government and thus provides the impetus for nationalism. In 2001, President George W. Bush expressed this understanding in his first inaugural address: "America has never been united by blood or birth or soil. We are bound by ideals that move us beyond our backgrounds, lift us above our interests and teach us what it means to be citizens." In his farewell address on January 15, 2009, Bush spoke of the "proud moment of hope and pride" for America that would come on January 20th when "standing on the steps of the Capitol will be a man whose history reflects the enduring promise of our land." The election of Obama was partially due to the changes in the pop culture of the 1990s, when, in the words of Jeff Chang, "American culture became colorized" (Hsu, 2009). Tiger Woods exemplified an ethnic/racial ambiguity; Will Smith became one of Hollywood's leading men; the victory of hip-hop culture and the ethic of diversity in network and cable television shows helped many Americans recognize that a post-racial society might one day overcome. Even with this recognition, identity politics persist.

Lifestyle choices, race, ethnicity, class, gender, political persuasion and religious variations fit into subcultures, but do not destroy the umbrella idea culture. There is much debate and concern over culture wars that involve a separatism, maybe a balkanization, of African Americans, Latinos, Native Americans, Asian Americans, Whites, and women, into six competing tribes. Certainly multiculturalism and deep divisions exist, but the claim that it is tearing the country apart, making not only "two nations" black and white, but six – or more – nations misses an obvious point. Americans are divided but they are equally united. In his inaugural address, Barack Obama explained that difference is unity: "our patchwork heritage is a strength, not a weakness.

We are a nation of Christians and Muslims, Jews and Hindus – and non-believers. We are shaped by every language and culture, drawn from every end of this Earth." Diversity itself is a necessary component of the culture with its emphasis on boundary crossings, mergings, newness and co-existence. Diversity is expressed in the national motto, *E Pluribus Unum* (out of many, one), in the promise of equal opportunity that is the American creed, and in the overriding belief in freedom. Chaotic heterogeneity is the American cultural norm. America-the-dream is the self-conscious invention that has molded a huge population with varying, local folkways into a national culture.

The Rise of American Culture

Culture before the American Revolution was a hodge-podge of local customs, each town or rural area adhering to different laws, languages, and folkways. These local cultures began to change with the consciousness-raising efforts of nationalists who wanted to wrench power over American affairs from England. At the Continental Congress in 1775, patriot Patrick Henry declared an end to differences between the colonies and declared famously: "I am not a Virginian but an American."

Borrowing heavily on European masters, portraitists John Singleton Copley, Gilbert Stuart, Benjamin West, John Trumbull, and Charles Wilson Peale painted and repainted the heroes of the Revolution. Their efforts made myth, helped tie the nation together, and elevated George Washington into a symbol of the new America. Patriots wanted to assimilate Indians and immigrants into an Anglo-American culture praying in Protestant churches and learning the English language, efforts which persisted into the residential schools of the twentieth century. In the early decades of the nineteenth century, painters like Thomas Cole located the American difference in the sublime landscape stretching westward across the continent. In the twentieth century, the "hero" became the machines, industry and city life that gave rise to a superpower; even later, abstract expressionists located the "frontier" within the individual, pop artists celebrated consumerism and trash artists protested the masculinity, materialism and nationalism of the dominant culture.

For two hundred years, Americans have sought to develop an art, literature, and music that meets their idea and sense of being "American." Historian Michael Kammen has noted the rise in national pride in the face of critics who "did not believe that a democracy was capable of 'genuine' culture and that the United States, in particular, had a population too heterogeneous to produce a distinctive culture or identity in any case" (Kammen, 1999: 63).

American popular culture has been marked by nationalistic signifiers and innovation. From the middle of the nineteenth century, American literary expression was filled with clear American dialects in the works of Cooper, Thoreau, Emerson, Dickinson, and Twain. Herman Melville's complex precursor to the modernist novel, *Moby Dick* (1851), is the story of Captain Ahab's obsession with killing the great white whale which had bitten off his leg in a previous encounter. Melville shows the futility of assuming any single explanation of the truth and offers multiple meanings of the whale and of Ahab's desperation. Nathaniel Hawthorne's *The Scarlet Letter* (1850) is another characteristic example of American dissent against authority. Hawthorne spun the witches and judges of Salem on their heads, offering several suggestions for Hester Prynne's seduction of the Puritan cleric. Opposition to institutional power and conspiracies have remained at the heart of American literature for over 150 years.

American literature also followed the trends of urbanization, industrialization, and westward expansion. Mark Twain's *Adventures of Huckleberry Finn* (1885) is filled with the tension between nature and civilization, Stephen Crane's *Maggie: A Girl of the Streets* (1893) looks at poverty and sexuality in immigrant America, and Kate Chopin's *The Awakening* (1899) explores issues of sex and gender in middle-class life. These themes would continue to fill the great American novels of the twentieth century.

Advertising

Manufacturers and marketers capitalized on the differences inherent among immigrant groups and the period between 1885–1935 was a battleground for the transition of the Anglo-American model of assimilating everyone into a melting-pot American or of a new Euro-American model of cultural pluralism or mosaic (see Chapter 2). Corporations fostered a consumer culture of "100 percent Americanism" to shut out foreign competition and encourage common buying patterns and lifestyles revolving around standardization of packaging.

Yet in the midst of building a national culture, regional patterns of popular culture endured. There was a notable growth in leisure time, a commercialization of organized entertainment, innovations in transportation and technology, and a change in attitudes that allowed the rich to join the lower classes at movie theaters and elsewhere. Popular culture manifested itself in burlesque shows, vaudeville, the Buffalo Bill Wild West Show, and the Phineas T. Barnum Circus as well as in the several huge expositions – Chicago (1892) and Atlanta (1895) being the most famous. These extravaganzas were hyped by banner advertising and newspaper spots. European visitors often remarked contradictorily on the leveling of American society and the vulgarity of democratic cultural forms.

The ubiquity of advertising and the rubbing of shoulders with different classes shocked visitors more used to the ethnic homogeneity and hierarchies of their own societies. American advertising wizard Frances Alice Keller saw the potential of using advertising to assimilate people in the face of subcultural pluralisms: "National advertising is the great Americanizer. American ideals and institutions, law, order, and prosperity, have not yet been sold to all our immigrants" (quoted in Kammen, 1999: 66). Novelist F. Scott Fitzgerald's novels, particularly *The Great Gatsby* (1922), showed how the automobile and advertising changed the American way of life. The man who became known as the father of advertising, Bruce Barton, explained how to win friends and influence people. In *The Man Nobody Knows* (1925), Barton described a poor carpenter from Galilee, who, though born in a manger, assembled twelve believers from the lowest rungs of society and turned them into ad men who understood the principle that "reputation is repetition." Jesus built an empire of faith – and expressed an American Dream sensibility – based upon simple slogans and unsophisticated arguments, selling the same story over and over, and providing an example for ad men everywhere.

Advertising made newspapers and magazines affordable, but the flowering of consumer culture came in the 1920s when radio and billboard ads, the rise of household appliances, and an era of rising wages mixed commerce and culture together irrevocably. In 1929 Robert and Helen Lynd's *Middletown* concluded, "The American citizen's first importance to his country is no longer that of citizen but that of consumer. Consumption is a new necessity" (Lynd, 1929: 88). The absolute commercialization of American culture came with the Second World War and the shift of the consumer marketplace from city centers to suburban shopping centers to malls. Regional cultural gave way to national conformity in the realm of materialism. Television and advertising have been "pervasive, aggressive, repetitive, and intrusive" in flooding contemporary America – and the world – with mass culture (Kammen, 1999: 193).

Leisure Time

Americans are not good at relaxing, even if they currently spend over a trillion dollars a year trying to do so. Laziness confronts the work ethic and in a society rife with traditional homilies like "time is money," "don't leave for tomorrow what you can do today," "the early bird gets the worm," and "a rolling stone gathers no moss," Americans weigh the costs of leisure against the rewards of work. In the seventeenth century, Puritan clerics warned that "idleness is the devil's workshop" and preached a gospel of "work as its own reward." This attitude filters into all aspects of American life and combines democracy, Christianity and capitalism into a belief that "God helps those who help themselves." Seeking fun, Americans spent more about 8.7 percent of their total expenditures – $2,551 each – on entertainment in 2005 (Sherk, 2007).

The notions of equality of opportunity and of a constantly rising living standard based on merit and "by the sweat of one's brow" have long marked the American character. Americans are uneasy with leisure as they find themselves in a work-and-spend cycle of increasing wants, needs, and debts. In a he-who-dies-with-the-most-toys-wins mentality (consumption as utopia), the more he works, the more money he has to buy the newest item, the more he owes, the more he wants, the more he works, the more he makes, and so on. Additionally, the "winner take all" ethic of the American workplace whereby the most successful workers gets the highest salaries and the unequal distribution of rewards makes most workers struggle harder so as not to fall.

Part of the American Dream involves home ownership and so, when they have free time, most Americans work at domestic chores associated with maintaining and improving their property. Even with the loss of equity during the mortgage and financial crisis that began in 2007, the basic belief that one should strive to own a home of one's own is strongly rooted. The average selling price for existing family homes in 2007 was $266,200, the median selling price was $217,900 and the number of foreclosures rose to a record high of 1.3 million (RealtyTrac, 2008). In 2008, foreclosures increased, the number of new houses being built drastically diminished, and, in the midst of bank failures and government bailouts (see Chapter 8), potential borrowers were unable to secure loans to buy new homes, even if their credit was good. Many families had supersized their homes and it is commonplace to find a middle class family of three living in a house with over 3,500 square feet and five bathrooms. Many of the new homes have three-car garages, which American families use as a storage center for overflow purchases. Internet connections in the home pull Americans more toward work than relaxation. Whether lounging or working, home life has become more private as mass culture is experienced less in community and more in solitude or with a few relationships.

Americans believe that "all work and no play makes Jack a dull boy." When they are not at home with families and friends, Americans tend to go to the mall. In 2005, in addition to the stores in town centers and internet shopping groups, there were approximately 50,000 shopping centers and malls in the US (Statemaster, 2008). Standard stores, regular products and similar consumer environments link them all, even as bargain hunters look for that special item to mark their "good taste." Nationwide, the Super Wal-Mart stores serve up an array of products stretching down aisles as far as the eye can see. American life is marked by a psychology of abundance that turns aristocratic dreams into democratic consumption as all classes can afford to purchase from the same stores. Americans also depend on credit cards to buy what they need when they do not have enough cash on hand. Unfortunately, Americans overuse their cards and in contemporary America are drowning in debt as income did not keep up with costs of housing, education and material desires. In 2004, overconsumption had created an average debt of 108 percent of total income and Americans used 18 percent of their total income to pay interest on their debts (Weller, 2006). These dismal figures got worse from 2004 to 2008 and stand in stark contrast to earlier generations of thrifty Americans.

American workers generally take between one week (business and manufacturing firms) and four weeks (teachers and government workers) of paid vacation a year. Nationwide, companies have downsized free time to an average of only 8.1 days off after one-year employment period, and 10.2 days after three years on the job. Additionally, 13 percent of US companies allow leave, but without pay (Robinson, 2003). There are also growing numbers of people trapped in the work-and-spend cycle or have not just a work ethic – but an overwork ethic – and so opt for nothing longer than a weekend getaway now and then (Illustration 7.1). Longer vacations are coordinated with the period when schools are out for the summer. Many people use their private camping vans to cut costs and enjoy the "nature" of crowded campgrounds or try to find a serene spot in busy national parks. Commercial enterprises have their own camping facilities; Disney World in Florida, for example, even provides direct transportation from the campsite to the "Magic Kingdom." In addition to the vacation periods, most Americans have days off work on national holidays (Box 7.1), most of which have been placed to give three-day weekends.

Illustration 7.1 Times Square

New York City is a favorite three-day holiday destination for Americans. This photograph of Times Square is illustrative of urban America's pulsating blend of consumption, transportation, commercial advertising, and entertainment industries. Pedestrians shop for souvenirs, dance and eat in Planet Hollywood, watch a movie at Loews' Theatres, or turn left to take in a Broadway show. Some walk straight ahead to Central Park and its museums, or turn around for shopping along Fifth Avenue or to dip into the collections of the New York Public Library – all within a short walk. The famous yellow cabs drive others to the Statue of Liberty ferry, United Nations, Yankee Stadium, the Museum of Modern Art, Columbia University, Harlem, the Empire State Building, or other attractions.

(Russell Duncan)

Box 7.1 Official US Holidays

New Year's Day	January 1st
Martin Luther King, Jr. Birthday	3rd Monday in January
Presidents' Day (Washington & Lincoln)	3rd Monday in February
Memorial Day	last Monday in May
Independence Day	July 4th
Labor Day	1st Monday in September
Columbus Day	2nd Monday in October
Veterans' Day	November 11th
Thanksgiving Day	4th Thursday in November
Christmas Day	December 25th

Print Media

Americans have always had a trust-distrust relationship with government and the American media have been watchdogs, alerting the public to missteps by elected officials. The founding of the United States corresponded closely with the rise of newspapers. In 1775, the English colonies published 37 papers, which were important political organs carrying the debate over revolutionary ideas. A hundred years later, in 1880, America had 971 daily papers and 8,633 weeklies. Urban dwellers had a wide choice of local papers; New Yorkers, for example, picked among 29 and Chicagoans had 18. With the advent of radio and television news programs, many newspapers went out of business while others consolidated to survive. Since 2008, printed newspapers have the blues as advertisers and readers prefer online news sources (Mindlin, 2009).

The five papers with the largest daily print circulation in 2008 were the popular lowbrow *USA Today,* the business-oriented *Wall Street Journal*, the nation's best news source *New York Times*, the respected regional *Los Angeles Times*, and the politically-astute *Washington Post*. Because many Americans buy and read only the Sunday papers with their extravagant entertainment, sports, book, magazines, job, automobile, and home sections, the Sunday circulation is higher. In 2008, with precipitous declines in readership, the 500 biggest US papers had a daily circulation of only 38 million copies.

Magazines and periodicals are widely popular. Consumers have a choice among the current issues of nearly 11,000 magazines and periodicals. The 50 leading magazines enjoy a total circulation of nearly 200 million copies per issue. The top two, *American Association of*

Retired Persons (AARP) and *Modern Maturity,* are bought up by older persons at the rate of 21 million copies per issue. *Reader's Digest, TV Guide, Better Homes and Gardens, National Geographic, Good Housekeeping, Family Circle, Woman's Day,* and *Time* are perennial favorites.

Americans are avid readers. A paperback revolution, starting in 1939 when Pocket Books made cheap editions available, helped democratize culture. Believing that literacy and reflection are essential to a democracy, some analysts worry over the downward trend in book consumption, even though Americans are purchasing around 2.2 billion new books per year. In 2007, the number of new titles or new editions published in the United States increased to 276,649 – 758 books per day; 50,701 of these were in the fiction category (Bowker, 2008). If we add the number of "short run" books, or books published "on demand" via internet, the total becomes 411,422. Because consumers often feel overwhelmed at the long wall of "just released" books displayed in the big chain stores, like Borders Books or Barnes & Noble, most people rely on bestseller lists and familiar authors when they want something to read. The worry is that everyone ends up reading the same books and thereby diminishes the diversity of viewpoints necessary for nuanced contributions to democracy. Novels centering on the legal system and books in the self-help and spiritual/religious categories continue to be among the top sellers, as Table 7.1 shows.

Americans are also great book borrowers and, there are 16,592 lending libraries among the 123,129 total libraries. Every town has a public library and each of the nation's schools and universities have at least one library. The Bureau of Indian Affairs operates 106 reservation libraries and the US Military has 296 collections on bases worldwide (ALA, 2009). Overall, the two biggest collections are in the Boston Public Library (14.9 million books) which is the world's largest city library and Harvard University (15.8 million books plus 10 million microforms) which is the world's largest university library. There are also hundreds of private collections available to researchers and readers nationwide, among them the Henry H. Huntington Library in San Marino, California, and the world's best financially-endowed library, the J. Paul Getty Museum in Malibu, California. There are state and local archives with books and papers relating to regional affairs. The federal government maintains two of the biggest libraries in the world in the Library of Congress (LC) and National Archives (NA). Established in 1800 but secured in 1814 when Congress purchased 10,000 volumes from the private collection of Thomas Jefferson, the LC is the largest library in the United States, with more than 29.5 million

Table 7.1 What America Is Reading, 1998–2007

Fiction	*Year*	*Nonfiction*
The Street Lawyer, John Grisham	1998	*The 9 Steps to Financial Freedom*, Suze Orman
The Testament, John Grisham	1999	*Tuesdays with Morrie*, Mitch Albom
The Brethren, John Grisham	2000	*Who Moved My Cheese?* Spencer Johnson
Desecration, Jerry B. Jenkins and Tim LaHaye	2001	*The Prayer of Jabez*, Bruce Wilkinson
The Summons, John Grisham	2002	*Self Matters*, Phillip C. McGraw
The Da Vinci Code, Dan Brown	2003	*The Purpose-Driven Life*, Rick Warren
The Da Vinci Code, Dan Brown	2004	*The Purpose-Driven Life*, Rick Warren
The Broker, John Grisham	2005	*Natural Cures "They" Don't Want You to Know About*, Kevin Trudeau
The Innocent Man, John Grisham	2006	*For One More Day*, Mitch Albom
A Thousand Splendid Suns, Khalid Hosseini	2007	*The Secret*, Rhonda Byrne

Note: Bestseller lists exclude books sold by Church and Religious bookstores, a practice that would most likely lift the books by Tim LaHaye and Jerry B. Jenkins to the top spot in the fiction categories for the past fifteen years.
Source: *Publishers Weekly* (2008)

books and over a billion items of all types. The NA houses the documents of government agencies and includes such items as the original copies of the Declaration of Independence and the Constitution, soldiers' records, photographs, Indian treaties, and most of the official correspondence between government officials. Former presidents since Herbert Hoover (1929–33) also have a federally-funded presidential library in their home state.

Mass Entertainment

The Movies

Hollywood is American culture writ large. While its worldwide box office revenue for American film studios was $35.5 billion in 2007 – a fortune which excludes the market tie-ins such as clothing, posters, music, games and dolls – Hollywood provides a soft power approach that complements US educational power to further foreign policy goals. The scenes flickering on movie screens and the accents reaching the ears with wrap-around Dolby sound systems worldwide are Hollywood's. US culture reaches into the world's living rooms, not only through the VCR and DVD systems, but in the made-for-TV sitcoms (situation comedies), dramas, mini-series, and movies that are standard fare wherever television sets are turned on in the West, and increasingly worldwide. Conversely, globalization has had its effects on movie-making, as high US production costs encourage filmmakers increasingly to film scenes outside the United States. This shooting of movies overseas boosts sales and interest, as does the casting of non-American superstars like Gong Li, Kate Winslet, Viggo Mortensen, Charlize Theron, Djimon Hounsou, Nicole Kidman, Penelope Cruz, and Jude Law. Hollywood producers keep the international market in mind and play to global tastes for action movies while they release films simultaneously worldwide.

In many ways, entertainment has conquered reality (Gabler, 2000). Hollywood used to be associated primarily with leisure and entertainment, but since the 1960s, the broadcast images have increasingly mixed fiction with documentary and informational material – "infotainment" – to the point that people refer to movies as if they were real history. For years, the Sunday night primetime *Wonderful World of Disney* opened with the soundtrack: "When you wish upon a star, makes no difference who you are. When you wish upon a star, your dreams come true." Hollywood gives life to the American Dream and, particularly, to the viewers dreaming to recreate and reinvent life as seen in the movies. This can be a capitalist dream, a romantic dream, a religious redemption dream, or a democratic egalitarian dream.

Hollywood films have always functioned to help ethnic Americans assimilate. Today this assimilation is played out increasingly on a world scale whether or not viewers immigrate into the US or live in McWorld. Fantasy America has been a country that could teach the rich humility, the poor to rise, the ignorant to study, the doubters to believe, and the foreigner to assimilate. Disney Studios expressed these themes in films including *Pinocchio* (1940), *Bambi* (1942), *Lion King* (1994), *Finding Nemo* (2003), and *Wall-E* (2008) where young humans, animals or robots face homelessness, lose parents, and become heroes as they save themselves, adults, the community or the world in the process. Hollywood has always contrasted themes of wealth versus democracy and individualism versus community, but with its own very distinctive "Hollywood style" in terms of themes and happy endings. The superheroes never tire the audiences, even though Superman, Catwoman, Spiderman, Iron Man, and the Hulk have recently shown darker personalities, as did Batman in *The Dark Knight* (2008).

The movie industry was created in 1908 when Jewish-Americans moved production studios from NYC to a suburb of Los Angeles. Hollywood had its first studio by 1911 and its first prominent company, Universal City Studios, in 1917. Hollywood companies had advantages that led to dominance at home and abroad. The major companies forged monopolies during the 1920s, allowing them to minimize costs while maximizing profits, including showing their films in company-owned theaters. The dominance over an exceptionally large US domestic market allowed companies an economy of scale matched by no other country. By 2007, the rest of the world was catching up as the US made only half as many feature films as India, only 50 more feature films than China and 564 of the 5,039 total films worldwide (Screen Digest, 2008). And yet numbers of films do not reflect box office dominance, worldwide distribution, or soft power influence. In 2007, US filmmakers held a 41 percent revenue share of the global market, with Japan second at 9 percent and Britain third at 7.5 percent – India (12th) had 2.2 percent and China (17th) took 0.7 percent (UK Film Council, 2008). Even so, with the rising costs of production, Hollywood is only profitable because of home video sales and the "tie-in" products. Teenagers comprise the largest market because of their tendency to see movies over and over again. This results in great success for action films and romantic comedies. For example, all-time global box office leader *Titanic* (1997), with income over $600 million – excluding videos and tie-ins – combined history, myth, action and romance, even if most girls paid primarily to swoon over heartthrob Leonardo DiCaprio and most boys hoped to see more of Kate Winslet.

Radio

Radio was first broadcast commercially in the 1920s and, by 1935, almost every American family owned a receiver. The radio helped immigrants learn English, the language of the airwaves, and unified the population. Perhaps the most famous use of the radio was by President Franklin Roosevelt, whose "fireside chats" in the Depression and World War II helped the nation through hard times. Two other highlights include the live broadcast of the arrival and "on-air" explosion of the German airship *Hindenburg* in New Jersey in 1937 and the 1938 transmission, without explanation, of the H. G. Wells's novel, *The War of the Worlds* – a broadcast that caused panic and hysteria in listeners who thought the earth was actually under attack by spacemen from Mars.

In contemporary America, there are over 10,000 radio stations operating nationwide and every major city has dozens of stations. There are many public radio stations, operated mostly on college campuses or by National Public Radio (NPR), an association funded primarily by private subscriptions. NPR presents high quality programming and news specials similar to those presented by its television counterpart, the Public Broadcasting System (PBS). "Talk radio" began in 1970 and has continued to proliferate. Americans like to listen to the radio while they work in the yard, sit by the pool, or ride in the car – that is anytime they are away from the television. Radio has expanded its range via the internet and with satellite stations providing around 200 highly-focused channels from which listeners can personalize choices. In local areas, those who tune in to talk shows make the radio an interactive medium simply by calling the host or sending an e-mail to express an opinion – the more outrageous the opinion, the more likely to get it aired. Table 7.2 reflects the most popular formats and number of stations.

Radio targets partisan audiences, spanning the range from libertarian to fascist – with the conservative right dominating the AM-radio stations. Syndicated nationwide, Rush Limbaugh has built a weekly following of an estimated 15–20 million listeners for his three-hour-long politically-oriented program. Limbaugh consistently attacks liberal politicians and

Table 7.2 What America Is Listening To: Top 10 Radio Formats.

Ranking	*Primary Format*	*Number of Stations*
1	News/Talk	2,064
2	Country Music	2,024
3	Religion	1,290
4	Contemporary Christian	945
5	Spanish Variety	942
6	Oldies (Music)	745
7	Variety	687
8	Adult Contemporary Music	671
9	Sports	610
10	Classic Hits	569

Source: Econsultant.com "Top 31 Most Popular Radio Station Formats," November 2008.

welfare-state supporters. He has enormous influence with Republican Party voters who believe in flag, country, low taxes, pro-life, anti-gay and other "traditional" values. In 2008, Limbaugh thought John McCain too liberal, rallied behind Sarah Palin, and encouraged all Republican voters to join "Operation Chaos" – the plan that if Republicans would "cross over" to vote in Democrat primaries for whomever was behind, Hillary Clinton or Barack Obama, they would create chaos within the Democrat Party, and, maybe, a violent convention. After Obama won the nomination, Limbaugh aired a highly-controversial song, "Obama, the Magic Negro" – to the tune of "Puff the Magic Dragon" – to ridicule the nominee.

In March 2009, Obama's White House Chief of Staff Rahm Emanuel elevated – some say mocked – Limbaugh as "the voice and the intellectual force and energy behind the Republican Party" (Hamby, 2009). The media fixated on the "feud" between the president and Limbaugh only to shift focus when Republican National Chairman Michael Steele tried to assert his own leadership of the party and said that Limbaugh was "an entertainer" who often used "incendiary" and "ugly" rhetoric (Egan, 2009). Limbaugh retaliated that Steele was mismanaging the Republican Party and chided: "You do your job and I'll do mine." Recognizing the talk show host's standing with the Republican base, Steele quickly acknowledged the pundit's power and offered the apology: "There was no attempt on my part to diminish his voice or his leadership" (Amato, 2009). Undoubtedly, Limbaugh and conservative talk radio have become prominent players in Republican Party politics.

FM-radio stations tend towards different audiences. Many channels – like Washington, DC's WAMU (American University) are linked into the more liberal PBS networks which often garner local support (transmit) and facilities from universities., Here, the talk format is more traditional: involving various stakeholders and experts in informal debates and with news coverage often drawn from international organizations like the BBC. Religiously informed radio, meanwhile, also airs extensively on FM. Satelite radio – the newest innovation – is a fully-subscription based service picked up at home or in cars, and contains a dazzling diverse range of programming and positions which can satiate virtually any taste, all at the push of a button.

Television

France experimented with television in the early 1900s but the phenomenon grew fastest in the US, with 23 stations broadcasting in 1940 and 98 in 1950. In 1951, experimental broadcasts in color began and the first simultaneous coast-to-coast broadcast marked the rise of mass culture with its everyone-knows-this-at-the-same-moment phenomenon. By 1960, nine out of ten American families owned a TV set. Mass culture was reinforced by the dominance of three national channels: CBS, NBC, and ABC.

Ted Turner pioneered cable TV in the mid-1970s and within 10 years operated nationwide; in 1980, Turner presented Cable News Network (CNN), bringing continuous news simultaneously to a worldwide audience. Music Television (MTV) also arrived in 1980 and appealed to youth culture in style and structure, Other channels proliferated as television became even more popular with programs aimed at specific interests. In contemporary America, television newscasts are becoming increasingly partisan and viewers select between what they believe to be conservative or liberal viewpoints. Fox News advertises itself as a "fair and balanced" alternative to biased liberal media, when, in fact, Fox is a political force that openly pushes a conservative, even neo-conservative, agenda. In 2002, Fox took over the number one position among cable news channels, with an audience twice as big as CNN's. But with Mr. Bush's decline in national opinion polls, CNN rebounded and in 2008 had virtually tied Fox for the top spot (NYT blog, 2008).

In the twenty-first century, 99 percent of American households have at least one television set and many have three or more. The "on-demand" nature of cable, satellite, internet TV, and mobile phones diversifies programs and democratizes viewing styles. Watching television is participatory and interactive as the remote control and DVD's empower people. Viewers record and delete at will and gain flexibility in "time-shifting" schedules of work and play, becoming less dependent on broadcast schedules. American adults watch an average of four hours of television daily, for a total two months of non-stop viewing per year. The most popular primetime shows are listed in Table 7.3.

Government Activities

Generally, Americans are content to leave the media to private businesses because they view government ownership as unacceptable to freedom of speech and freedom in general. The nearly 1,200 commercial television stations are paid for by advertisers or by cable subscriptions. Much commercial broadcasting is "trash TV" because the profit motive makes it focus on the lowest common denominator in order to maximize audience appeal and because of the sheer number of hours of broadcast time to fill. There are also high-quality programs and a

Table 7.3 What America is Watching: Most Popular Primetime TV, 1984–2008

1984	Dallas (soap opera, drama)
1985	Dynasty (soap opera, drama)
1986–1990	The Cosby Show (situational comedy)
1991	Cheers (situational comedy)
1992–1993	60 Minutes (news)
1994	Home Improvement (situational comedy)
1995	Seinfeld (situational comedy)
1996–1997	ER [Emergency Room] (medical drama)
1998	Seinfeld (situational comedy)
1999	ER [Emergency Room](medical drama)
2000	Who Wants To Be A Millionaire? (reality game show)
2001	Survivor: The Australian Outback (reality TV)
2002	Friends (situational comedy)
2003–2004	CSI [Crime Scene Investigation] (crime drama)
2005–2008	American Idol (reality TV)

Source: A.C. Nielsen (2008).

wide range of more specialized channels, like Discovery, which concentrates on nature and scientific phenomena. Americans also support nearly 350 public television stations, broadcasting locally or regionally. The Public Broadcasting Service, founded in 1967, is nonprofit and educational, has no advertising, and is funded by small contributions from thousands of viewers, big foundation grants, and government support.

Even while believing in private ownership and freedom of speech, most Americans want the government to safeguard children from the programming of a violent, dirty language or sexual content. From the beginning Hollywood created controversy; in 1915, the US Supreme Court refused to ban the showing of *The Birth of a Nation* (1915), a film upholding the virtues of the Ku Klux Klan while stereotyping African Americans as brutish. In the 1930s Hollywood introduced a production code to self-censor its films, but films became bland and ridiculous, to the extent of only showing married couples sleeping in twin beds in the same room. In 1947, during the apex of the Red Scare, the House Un-American Activities Committee (HUAC) investigated Hollywood for films that might influence people toward communism. The Federal Communications Commission (FCC), an independent regulatory agency created by Congress in 1934, has five members appointed by the president to grant station licenses, maintain an acceptable – non-pornographic broadcast – and regulate media ownership. The Telecommunications Act of 1996 relaxed restrictions on media ownership, a measure that reduced diversity and brought more homogeneity to mass media.

Americans still debate the effects of television on behavior and generally believe that some impressionable viewers mimic what they see on TV, mostly of a sexual nature. Technology allows parents to block certain channels or shows and the violence-chip (V chip) lets parents eliminate the reception of all programs with a rating inappropriate for children. Americans also worry over racial and gender stereotyping. While Americans debate matters, the entertainment industry has been allowed to police itself, providing programs and instituting a rating system to safeguard minors and to provide information to adults on film contents. In 1996 President Clinton supported a communications decency act and warned Hollywood that it would have to clean up its practices of advertising and making violent movies aimed at an audience of children. For example, labeling programs as unsuitable for children under 15 (R-rated) or 18 (X-rated) does not help much if R- and X-rated advertisements are interspersed with regular programming on MTV. The Bush administration pursued public broadcasts that it viewed as "indecent" – as it did after Justin Timberlake ripped off Janet Jackson's shirt to expose a bare breast during the live broadcast of the Super Bowl football game in 2004. In fact, that incident led to the Broadcast Decency Enforcement Act of 2005, which increased penalties up to $325,000 for each broadcast incident of "indecency." Of course the trouble comes when trying to define what is indecent and by the fact that the act only applies to public broadcasting, not cable or internet.

In the past decade, cable television has pushed the boundaries with successful shows like *Sex and the City,* focusing on the sexual appetites of four successful single women in New York; *Will and Grace,* presenting a sanitized relationship between a gay man and a straight woman; *The Sopranos,* depicting a Mafia family leading a middle-class life in New Jersey; *Queer as Folk,* showing candor about the sexual behavior of five gay men; and *Desperate Housewives*, exploring the interconnected erotic lives and desires of families in one suburban neighborhood. Cable television can broadcast nearly anything its private corporations put forward, with the exception of child pornography.

The World Wide Web

The internet was born in 1969 as a Department of Defense project linking research universities. In 1993 only 50 websites existed worldwide; just five years later there were millions of sites and billions of users as the internet became the world's largest communications network. Among Americans, the demographics of internet use shows higher percentages among those in suburban/urban areas, who are younger, white, educated, and in the middle and upper classes (Pew, 2009). Ninety-five percent of the nation's public schools have been connected and two-thirds of all teachers incorporate net sources into their teaching. But with the United States slipping to 15th place in global interconnectiveness, President Obama has committed his administration to expanding or bettering internet broadband coverage.

The internet has spread American culture faster than ever, raising protests that while international, the internet feels stereotypically American: informal, consumer-oriented, competitive, individualistic, disrespectful, decentralized and diverse. The internet can help to democratize information, knocking down the walls of class, caste, and nationalism. The World Bank suggests an "end of geography" as information technology (IT) brings economic progress to isolated countries (Knowlton, 1999). That is a bold prediction especially in the face of the real danger of a growing technological gap between the "wired world" and the third world, unwired; for example, in Africa, only Egypt and South Africa have enough phone lines to take advantage of IT. Many commentators express fears about a digital divide and a widening income gap at home too, as the rich have access and the poor do not.

The US government has been quick to place its services on the web. In September 2000, www.firstgov.gov provided a single source site to access 20,000 separate government sites with 27 million federal agency web pages and a half-billion particular documents. Users can access federal trial transcripts, post messages to the president, reserve a campground in a national park, file tax returns, apply for citizenship or a green card, or check Social Security benefits. The web has made the government more responsive. The FCC also facilitates internet access through its Link-Up America and Lifeline Assistance programs which pays up to 100 percent of the costs for low income users.

Newspapers and radio stations have successfully moved on-line and now have the ability to deliver timely news nearly as fast as, and sometimes faster than, television. Additionally, newspaper search engines allow readers to dip backward into electronic archives for previous stories – a boon to students and researchers and a money-maker for the papers. The internet proved its power during and after the massive disaster of 26 December 2004, when an earthquake and tidal wave (tsunami) swept across south Asia, killing perhaps 250,000 people and leaving millions homeless or orphaned. People worldwide used the net to post notices, look for loved ones, offer assistance, and get information on the crisis. In 2008 and 2009 the internet showed its boundary-breaking effectiveness in the election campaign of Barack Obama, the undermining of information censorship by China, and the delivery of news during the Gaza-Israeli crisis when Israel refused to allow reporters into the war zone.

Yet, the internet continues to cause much controversy among Americans primarily due to the proliferation of "hate" and pornography sites and their accessibility to children. The Ku Klux Klan and affiliates have many pages on the web, chatrooms proliferate with racial and ethnic slurs, revolutionary groups are placing video clips showing the beheading of hostages, and sex sites present "unnatural" and tempting combinations. There have been many legal challenges to these sites but the courts have generally upheld the First Amendment's free speech and right to privacy guarantees. In 2008, the US Supreme Court overturned several communications indecency acts by ruling that the federal government could not limit the internet with legislation that it felt was "harmful to minors (EPIC, 2008). Many recognize that the internet is a positive force for multiculturalism and post-racialism. It helps establish what sociologist Dalton Conley describes as a "network nation" empowering people to create flexible identities and "crosscutting social groups" via Facebook, Twitter, YouTube, MySpace, and thousands of web logs (Hsu, 2009).

Sports

Americans love sports and have actively participated in organized games since the middle of the nineteenth century. The world's foremost yachting race, the America's Cup, began in 1851 and baseball, which can be traced to the English game of rounders, rose to prominence during the American Civil War. For the most part, Americans play the games of the world – winning the 1996, 2004 and 2008 Olympic Gold Medals for the US Women's Soccer Team, for example. In 2008, in Beijing, the United States finished first in the total count with 110 medals, although China was first in gold medals with 51. In the domestic arena, there are a number of sports particularly associated with America, such as baseball, basketball, and American football, whose final games – the World Series, National Basketball Association Championships, and Super Bowl – are broadcast worldwide.

With sporting figures and teams achieving hero status in the minds of many people and with salaries often reaching astronomical figures, each serious incident of drug abuse, cheating, or lawbreaking is reported and discussed. Americans want their athletes to compete fairly, while they also want them to win at any cost. This ambivalence is clearly seen in the ongoing debate over the use of performance-enhancing steroids and other drugs in professional sports, including cycling, sprinting, football and baseball. Over the past few years, America's "national pastime," baseball, has widely alleged to have entered a "steroid era" with as many as seven percent of all players using drugs to give them a competitive edge.

In an effort to put the sport back into its mythical and heroic narrative, former Senator George Mitchell led a wide-ranging independent investigation to find the guilty, while exonerating the game itself. The Mitchell Report alleged that 89 players were guilty of substance abuse, including the all-time home run king, Barry Bonds, the greatest pitcher of all-time, Roger Clemens, and the highest paid player ever, Alex Rodriguez (see Illustration 7.2) (Mitchell, 2007). Most players denied the charges, and their fans lined up to support them. But after 20 players admitted their guilt – including Rodriguez in 2009 – many fans supported criminal prosecutions or, at least, a removal of their batting and pitching records and a bar from future induction in the Baseball Hall of Fame. Team owners and players have vowed to comply with more rigorous testing procedures, but with the enormity of compensation packages for the best athletes – Rodriguez signed a 10-year deal for $305 million with the New York Yankees in 2007 and received untold millions for companies that make baseball products – the challenge will be a difficult one (Roberts and Epstein, 2009).

Baseball pits one man with a bat in his hand against a team of men ready to put him out. It represents the individual in competition against other men in one-on-one situations where no one can interfere to help the player succeed or fail. The game is highly-nuanced and every play has a winner and a loser. The man who "wins" hits the home run, strikes out the batter, steals second base, or makes the game-winning catch near the wall in left field; the loser swings and misses, fails to catch the ball, shows bad judgment by throwing the wrong pitch or being caught off base. One team wins and one team loses, but the credit is given to a "hero" and failure is blamed on a "goat." The size of the player is irrelevant but the skill of the player is all important. Time is not a factor and game length depends on how long it takes to play nine innings, as measured by the success or failure of individuals to get base hits or to make outs. Baseball is orderly and appeals to the American legal sense as an umpire rules on every

Illustration 7.2 Baseball Players, American Heroes

The fabled New York Yankees baseball team has been blessed with more records and heroes than any team in professional sport: Babe Ruth, Lou Gehrig, Mickey Mantle, Reggie Jackson and many others. But baseball in contemporary America has entered "the Steroid Era" with players such as Alex Rodriguez and Roger Clemens (above) being accused of taking performance-enhancing drugs to gain a competitive edge – and enormous contracts.

(Julie Jacobsen/AP/Press Association Images, 2007)

single action of the game. Baseball is played on grass and the generally slow speed of the action reflects the pre-industrial pace of life and offers a respite from the hurried world of urban living. Softball has basically the same rules and feel of baseball and is played by women as well as men.

Basketball is more chaotic and represents a Rock-'n'-Roll society in the movement of players, constantly in motion, racing up and down the court at extremely high speed. Time matters and is highlighted on the scoreboard, with stopwatch precision down to hundredths of seconds. Unlike baseball, physical size matters. Basketball began as a way to Americanize immigrants by organizing boys and girls into teams. It was invented in 1891 by James Naismith at a Young Men's Christian Association (YMCA) meeting in Springfield, Massachusetts, and quickly spread to Settlement Houses where immigrants lived.

American football is played by precise rules on a field laid out in grids. Each play has been completely rehearsed in long days of practice and is activated in particular situations and against the opposing team's specific alignment and personnel. Football is violent and the game depends on the gain and loss of territory (Schrank, 1995). As in basketball, size matters. There is a certain lawlessness to the game with 22 players all in motion, pushing and shoving, and trying to gain advantage by breaking the rules – something almost impossible to do in baseball. The corporate mentality of the team counts more, and individuals must submerge their own glory so that the group can penetrate most deeply into the opposing group's side of the field in order to score the most points and win the game. Movement is characterized in military terms as in "throwing the bomb," "the ground attack," and "shredding the defense" (Kanfer, 1995: 382).

Baseball, basketball, and football are games played by a wide variety of Americans at many levels. To Americans, success in sports represents the faith that individuals and teams have an equal opportunity to win, but that hard work and merit lifts some above others. Sometimes the underdog can beat the champion – even the greatest athletes lose about half the time. The games are highly-institutionalized rituals which combine Christianity, capitalism, and politics. Every American school has weekly physical education classes organized around these, and other, sports – such as volleyball, tennis, swimming, field hockey, and soccer. Every town of any size has organized baseball and basketball leagues where people from six to sixty years old can compete. The Friday-night high-school or Saturday-afternoon college football games, with their ferocious emphasis on winning, bring communities, social classes, and ethnic groups together to worship the home team at a level approaching religious belief in nearly all parts of the country. Teams and heroes in each sport become mythical, legendary, and historical. Writers often use sports in their novels and Hollywood produces movies highlighting a particular team, league, and player, including a scene of a game or ballpark. On the individual and team levels, sports act as rallying points for civic pride, provide mass culture and Americanization, and fill television airways. And players' salaries make sports one of the most lucrative occupations in the world; for example, in 2007, 32-year-old golfer Tiger Woods earned $112 million in earnings and endorsements (Freedman, 2008).

Sports has been central to definitions of American masculinity and has long been seen as crucial to the development of manliness. Until very recently, sporting women were stereotyped as unfeminine or lesbian. Women and men are still generally segregated by teams and leagues. Race has also been an issue, with African Americans and Native Americans historically excluded from participation and spectatorship at university and professional levels. For to include them – and to have them excel – questioned the rules of racial hierarchy and theories of manhood which long dominated American society.

Sports has advanced equality in recent years as college and professional teams have been integrated or opened to women. Minority groups and women have increasingly participated in even the most class-based sports of golf and tennis, as is evidenced by the rise of Tiger Woods and Michelle Wie in golf and the Williams sisters (Venus and Serena) in tennis. Recent studies show that the chance to compete for status and income in sporting venues has kept many children focused on finishing high school. Additionally, American sports spectatorship strengthens family by its orientation of adults attending games with children. This may help explain the lack of fan violence that punctuates games in other countries.

The Arts

Few, if any, cities contain more art museums than New York City. The Museum of Modern Art, Metropolitan Museum of Art, Henry Frick Collection, Guggenheim Museum, J. P. Morgan Library, Brooklyn Museum of Art, Whitney Museum of Modern Art, and Museum of the American Indian are just a few of the better known, world-class collections. While these museums reflect New York's tastes in high culture, the city by no means has a monopoly in that area. Every American city of medium size has its own list of high culture sites.

American painting originally patterned itself after European models in the romantic landscape renderings of the Hudson River School. Most prominent American artists were traditionalists, such as Winslow Homer, Thomas Eakins, and James McNeil Whistler, who studied abroad and learned to combine portraiture with landscape. In the 1930s, the Ashcan School, realistically painted the crowded streets and confusion of urban America. Later on, Edward Hopper's depictions of the solitude of city life and the loss of community reflected modernizing trends. American art came into its own in the 1940s with public recognition and influence worldwide when Jackson Pollock began to drip paint over canvases and Andy Warhol depicted celebrities and consumer products. Pollock and others in the "New York School" who let their unconscious direct their creations came to be known as abstract expressionists. Shunning all legible symbolism, Pollock explained, "I am not aware of what is taking place. . . . It is only after [I have painted] that I see what I have done" (quoted in Tallack, 2000: 261). Warhol's depictions of soup cans, Elvis Presley, and Marilyn Monroe, exploited popular culture icons and was dubbed "pop art." Robert Rauschenberg used recognizable items, including tires and toy animals and pictures of John Kennedy to construct collages mocking abstract expressionism but still asking for interpretation of a chaotic culture.

American arts are primarily self-sufficient, supported more by private donations than by the federal government. States and cities also offer funding for various projects. Americans have long been resistant to the use of public funding for the arts, with the notable exception of the Federal Programs for the Arts under President Franklin Roosevelt's New Deal and the National Endowment for the Arts (NEA) which was established in 1965. From 1935–43, federal funding supported thousands of artists who created hundreds of thousands of public art projects – most of them focusing on the themes of strong family and the heroic worker. With a 2008 budget of $145 million, the NEA continues to support "excellence in arts" and since 1966 has provided over 120,000 monetary awards in music, theater, dance, literature, education and the visual arts (NEA, 2009). Because visual and performing arts can be so contentious during periods of conservative ascendancy, since 1996 there has been no direct funding to individual artists, but supports them indirectly through organizations.

Overall, Americans insist that individual or corporate patrons support their own causes. Contributions by philanthropic groups such as the Pew Charitable Trust, the John T. and Catherine D. MacArthur, John D. Rockefeller, Andrew Carnegie, George Soros, Bill and Melinda Gates, and Henry Ford foundations plus individual donations raise most of the money needed to build theaters and museums and to fund cultural programs in the United States. The Lincoln Center for Performing Arts in New York, which is home to the Metropolitan Opera and New York Philharmonic Orchestra receives all but five percent of its funding from private gifts, advertising revenues and ticket sales. In 2007, the total charitable giving – to all causes, including the arts – topped $306 billion, an amount equal to 2.2 percent of the GDP. In 2008, chemical engineer David Koch gave $100 million to New York's Lincoln Center theater and, in 2007, the MacArthur Foundation handed out nearly $50 million of its $267 million total charitable grants to various cultural centers (Pogrebin, 2008; MacFound, 2008).

Even the museums and libraries in Washington, DC, which receive initial funding from the federal government, such as the American History Museum, National Air and Space Museum, Holocaust Museum, Natural History Museum, Library of Congress, and the National Portrait Gallery are supported primarily by private donations, backed up with sales of articles in their museum gift shops and restaurants. In 2003 President Bush signed an Act to create a National Museum of African–American History and Culture to cost $300 million and to be built with funding of half by federal tax money and half by private donations (Clemetson, 2003). The general rule is that after museums are built, private donations are to support them with little help from federal funds.

One of the reasons Americans distrust government funding of museums is because visual arts offer the irresistible temptation by politicians to censor art for personal reasons and political gains. In the 1990s, Robert Mapplethorpe, an NEA-funded artist, brought attention to how tax dollars were spent on the NEA when his photographs of naked children, gays and a particularly "appalling" picture of a man urinating in another man's mouth caused public outcry (Lewis, 2008). In February 2001, New York City Mayor Rudolph Giuliani announced that he was freezing the city's annual multi-million dollar subsidy to the Brooklyn Museum of Art because a photography exhibit contained a picture offensive to his tastes. The exhibit showcased the work of 94 contemporary African American artists, but the picture Giuliani focused on was Renee Cox's "Yo Mama's Last Supper" which depicts Jesus as a naked woman surrounded by 12 black apostles. The picture highlights the Catholic Church's refusal to recognize women and minorities. "Why can't a woman be Christ?" Cox asked (AP, 2001c). Giuliani tried the same maneuver in 1999 to prevent the display of a picture showing an elephant-dung covered Virgin Mary.

As usual, when these cases reached federal courts, the judges upheld the First Amendment protection of freedom of speech to overrule censorship and restore funding. The courts uphold the maxim that the people can and must choose for themselves.

Concert halls and major orchestras began with the New York Philharmonic (1842). By the beginning of the twentieth century, every major city had its own orchestra, dominated by European compositions and conductors. Today the US has some 1,500 orchestras, including at least 40 world-class symphonies and nearly as many Americans go to hear the orchestras as attend professional baseball games. There are also more than 400 ballet and 100 opera companies.

Popular Music

American popular music is a leading agent of globalization and cultural imperialism as the world is tuned in to American rhythms. The music industry is perfect capitalism, creating a market and supplying the product. The pop music craze exploded in the 1950s and 1960s as television brought stardom to musicians and bands and as technology produced affordable record players for the adolescents of the Baby Boom era.

There had always been Native American music, slave songs in the fields, and political tunes to help the country through the various wars, but mostly, music was confined to religious observances or played at large community gatherings. With the rise of American imperialism in the late-nineteenth century, military music and marching bands played the nationalistic music of John Philip Sousa. Black marching bands in New Orleans took up this movement, mixed in the Blues of slave songs and developed not only Jazz, but a music with a special "ragged" beat, Ragtime – two forms that emphasized both the modern and the exotic. Jazz spread quickly to Europe after World War I, developing from instrumental creations to the vocal patterns of Billie Holiday, Charlie Parker, Louis Armstrong and, a little later, B. B. King. The Depression and World War II brought in Swing, with the big band sound of Glenn Miller, Benny Goodman, and Duke Ellington. Patriotic folk ballads of hard work, heroism, and sacrifice were also popularized by the likes of Woodie Guthrie.

Country music arose during the Depression in the poorest white sections of rural America in the Appalachian Mountain region of Tennessee and Kentucky. Tales of coal miners, cheating hearts, and "poor-white-but-proud" lyrics expressed the reality many lived. After

Roy Acuff and his Smoky Mountain Boys became the preeminent live music radio show in America, the genre spread. Hank Williams, Sr., became the first true star with his songs about hard drinking and hard loving; his death at age 29 from a mixture of alcohol and pills increased the fame of Country music (HOF, 2002). Loretta Lynn, Willie Nelson, Johnny Cash, Dolly Parton, Garth Brooks, and the Dixie Chicks have so popularized the form that it remains the number-one music format for radio stations in twenty-first-century America.

A momentous change came when African-American Blues patterns merged with white Country music's lead guitar to produce Rock-'n'-Roll. This emerged from the larger social prosperity, northward migration of southern blacks, rapid expansion of the automobile culture, and revolutionary movements toward equality. The youth rebellion was on as Chuck Berry, Jerry Lee Lewis, Bill Haley, and Elvis Presley mixed sexual innuendo with a fast pace which crossed the Atlantic to inspire the Beatles and the Rolling Stones. Young people began to live for the music, an addiction that is still obvious. Rock-'n'-Roll helped provide the vehicle for the youth culture protesting the Vietnam War and the conformity of the older generation. Rock-'n'-Roll, and later Rock, became as much an attitude as an art form. Since the advent of the form, many adults criticized the beat and lyrics as immoral, depraved, and way too loud. Cultural critic Allan Bloom has lambasted Rock as a "barbaric appeal to sexual desire" which destroys the hearer's ability to reason due to its drug-like effects (Bloom, 1988: 73).

At the same time, James Brown, Aretha Franklin, and Wilson Pickett sang the lyrics in a slower, deeper manner called Soul. Folk singers such as Bob Dylan, Joan Baez, Pete Seeger and Jimi Hendrix mixed ballads, spirituals and Rock into protest music. George Clinton and others mixed Soul with Jazz to produce an urban syncopation called Funk. In the 1970s and 1980s, Michael Jackson became the "King of Pop" with his dance steps, adolescent voice, and tender lyrics. In the 1980s and 1990s, Madonna – with more number-one hits than anyone ever – criticized the materialism, racism, sexual prudery, and religious hypocrisies of American culture while hooking the world on that culture.

The influence of Rap, or Hip-Hop, on American culture has been truly significant. Music critic Hua Hsu cites Rap's influence on the post-racial landscape and the rise in the international imagination as "hip-hop – the sound of the post-civil-rights, post-soul generation – found a global audience on its own terms" (Hsu, 2009: 49). Springing out of street culture in the 1970s and 1980s, and promoted by producer

Russell Simmons, Rap expanded the vocabulary of the inner city anti-hero, becoming a philosophy among American youth, and young people worldwide. Quickly, middle-class African Americans who had never been in gangs, such as Niggaz4Life, Run-DMC, and Public Enemy took over. Rap's biggest audience is white suburban teenagers who seek the runaway thrills of gangbanging, drugs, guns, and crime without any risk to themselves. These fans particularly admire white rapper Eminem, who through his use of misogynist, raunchy, homophobic and violent lyrics, has given them a way to express adolescent rage and confusion (Harris, 2000). Even though Eminem confuses the issue, basically rappers and record producers use an escalating image of violent and defiant black males to increase their white audience, who use these images of blackness to define their difference, their whiteness (Samuels, 1991: 284–8). Another view explains Rap as cultural expression whereby black musicians explode the racial stereotypes by exaggerating them into parody (Gates, 1990: 295).

Of course, it is easy to argue that the rise of Rap is the newest generation's youthful rebellion against the music of their parents. But is Rap obscene? The Supreme Court has defined "obscenity" as something undeniably offensive to the average person and which contains no serious artistic value. Courts and juries are left to decide matters on a case-by-case basis. Generally the courts have found rappers "not guilty" because of the First Amendment's protection of free speech. In 1997 the Supreme Court declared the Federal Communications Decency Act (1996), which made it a crime to put "indecent" material on the internet, unconstitutional. Rappers have used this decision to be "As Nasty As They Wanna Be" – as the highly controversial 2 Live Crew album did.

With the surge of Latino immigrants during the past decade, American music is making another change to the electric pulses and rhythms of Christina Aguilera and Jennifer Lopez, singing in English and Spanish. There is a growing market for Spanish-language releases and some worry how this might affect assimilation within national borders even though no one argues against the power English-language music has had in globalization. American culture is a created culture which relies on newness and change for vibrancy. That vibrancy continues the expansion of American culture around the world.

8

The Economy

In 2009 the world was increasingly anxious about the most dangerous economic crisis since the Great Depression of the 1930s. Banks failed, global stocks tumbled, whole nations defaulted, worker disturbances accelerated and the worldwide job loss was forecast to include 50 million people by the end of the year. Global instability and rising nationalism threatened security and peace. One month into his presidency and standing before a joint session of Congress and a nationwide television audience, Barack Obama optimistically but urgently told his countrymen that there was "promise amid peril," "we are not quitters," and the "day of reckoning has arrived" (Obama, 2009b). It was time for national ambition, not surrender: "While our economy may be weakened and our confidence shaken, though we are living through difficult and uncertain times, tonight I want every American to know this: We will rebuild, we will recover, and the United States of America will emerge stronger than before" (Obama, 2009b). The president praised the passage of the American Recovery and Reinvestment Act, a $787 billion stimulus package, which, he said, would save 3.5 million jobs, mostly in the private sector, provide a tax cut for 95 percent of working Americans, and create new jobs by a heavy investment in education, health care, clean energy and technology.

Insisting that the "weight of this crisis will not determine the destiny of this nation," Obama asked for a budget of $3.6 trillion – a massive amount equal to one-fourth of the US's total gross domestic product. Many leading economists hoped for even more spending as the government dealt with crises in the automobile industry, the housing market, and the financial sector. Of the four oft-cited engines of economic growth: consumer spending, exports, business investment and government spending, only government spending was still fully functioning, and it was slowing as state government revenues fell and legislatures cut programs. Only the federal government could mobilize the necessary resources to encourage a recovery; but with years of massive deficits and debt caused by enormous imbalances of trade and wars – something Obama called "an era of profound irresponsibility," many worried that the cure might be worse than the illness.

Obama inherited the crises from the Bush administration and from the deregulatory practices that began in the Reagan administration in the 1980s which accelerated in the 1990s and 2000s. In 2007, the losses that began to mount in the mortgage lending market were early warning signs that turned into such shocking bank failures in 2008 that "the financial system actually melted down" – as financier George Soros put it (Soros, 2008). Economist Joseph Stiglitz agreed, linking the crises to what engineers call a "system failure" (Stiglitz, 2009).

And yet, in the midst of these depressing economic scenarios, the United States remains the capital of capitalism with the largest and most powerful economy in the world, a gross domestic product (GDP) of $13.8 trillion, and a per capita GDP of $45,500 for 2007 (BEA, 2009a; OECD, 2008b). The US economy benefits from the country's favorable geographical location, which provides an abundance of agricultural products to the internal market, as well as makes the United States the world's largest exporter of food and foodstuffs. Additionally, the nation's geological reserves, timberlands, river systems, ocean harbors, and one of the world's largest fishing fleets strengthen its economic power. The US has one-quarter (27 percent) of the world's known coal reserves and three percent of the world's known oil reserves – but with a production of 8.5 million barrels of oil a day against a daily consumption of over 20 million barrels, the nation is vulnerable to disruptions in supplies and cost increases (CIA, 2009).

The US population enjoys one of the highest living standards in the world in relation to property and income; in 2006, US citizens reported a total taxable income of $8 trillion (IRS, 2008a). This wealth combines with the sheer numbers of citizens to create a huge economy based on mass production and mass consumption. Americans have voracious appetites for all products domestic and foreign and the enormity of their purchasing power and rates of spending can cause a surge in the world economy or a recession, as occurred almost overnight in 2008. The total official labor pool consists of 154 million people and a continued strong immigration of legal (and illegal) workers provides a range of highly skilled and unskilled labor (BLS, 2009a).

The economy has benefited by the historical circumstances of a nation born in modern times, being physically removed from the arenas of two world wars, enjoying the expansion of English as the global language, and through the technological inventiveness of thousands of immigrants. For example, in the last two decades, scientists from India and China, especially, immigrated to the US and advanced science, technology and their personal fortunes. Other factors forming the American philosophy of the market, include the Protestant or Puritan work ethic, a strong belief in education and research, 220 years of basically stable government – the Civil War notwithstanding – and the creative tension between individual freedom and state responsibility. Historically, the government has generally followed *laissez-faire* and free-market principles of Scottish economist Adam Smith, whose 1776 book *The Wealth of Nations* shared the natural law philosophy in Thomas Jefferson's Declaration of Independence. Except in the most extraordinary times of protest or widespread, systemic economic distress, the American population has agreed with Smith that individual self-interest would promote the general welfare, not regulation, intervention and the required high taxes to support bigger government.

The US Domestic Economy

The American Work Force

A higher percentage of working-age Americans are employed than in virtually all other major industrial nations (BLS, 2006). In early 2009, nearly 144 million Americans, age 16 and over, were employed in the labor force, 11.6 million were unemployed, and 81 million were "not looking for work"; the number of unemployed represented a 7.6 percent unemployment rate – a one-year increase from 7.5 million and 4.9 percent in 2008, respectively (BLS, 2009b). Most economists expect these numbers to worsen significantly throughout 2009 and 2010 (see Table 8.1).

In 2008, women held 46 percent of the jobs and men 54 percent (BLS, 2009c); but with the economic downturn causing employers in manufacturing and construction industries to fire more men than women, by 2009 women held more wage and salary jobs than men for the first time in American history. The difference in layoffs is partly explained by the fact that women are paid less than men overall, employed in education, health care and service jobs, with many in part

Table 8.1 Unemployment Rates, July 2008–February 2009

Category	*UNEMPLOYMENT RATES (%)*					
	Quarterly averages		*Monthly data*			
	III 2008	*IV 2008*	*Nov. 2008*	*Dec. 2008*	*Jan. 2009*	*Feb. 2009*
All workers	6.0	6.9	6.8	7.2	7.6	8.1
Adult men	5.8	6.8	6.7	7.2	7.6	8.1
Adult women	5.0	5.6	5.6	5.9	6.2	6.7
Teenagers	19.7	20.7	20.4	20.8	20.8	21.6
White	5.4	6.3	6.2	6.6	6.9	7.3
Black or African American	10.7	11.5	11.3	11.9	12.6	13.4
Hispanic or Latino ethnicity	7.8	8.9	8.6	9.2	9.7	10.9

Source: BLS (2009a), Table A.

time jobs without health and unemployment insurance – all of these factors make it cheaper for employers to retain women and fire men (Rampell, 2009). As the very first Act of his administration, Barack Obama signed the Equal Pay Act into law (see Illustration 8.1).

Wages differ substantially by education level. Those with less than a high-school degree averaged $428 a week; those with a high-school diploma $604; and those with a bachelor's degree $987 (BLS, 2008a). During a working career, a college graduate earns around $800,000 more than a high-school graduate; a PhD or professional degree adds another one million dollars. A gender gap exists as women average $35,102 to men's $45,113, or about $780 for every $1,000 (US Census, 2008a). Part-time versus full-time employment, pink-collar jobs, and historical factors of discrimination and less education account for this difference. Strikingly, the pay for "never married" women with full-time jobs is equal to that made by men. For American families, the median annual household income was $50,233 – $966 a week before taxes; but there are many differences as Table 8.2 indicates (US Census, 2008a). Nearly two-thirds of all families had both husband and wife working.

The United States has an unemployment insurance program paid for in combination by employers, federal and state governments. The program does not apply to temporary, part-time and self-employed workers and it requires that workers are unemployed through no fault

Illustration 8.1 Obama Signs Fair Pay Act

On January 28, 2009, just days after taking office, President Obama signed his first Bill into law. Named after an Alabama women who, for 19 years, was paid less than the men she worked with, just because she was a woman, the Lily Ledbetter Fair Pay Act had been opposed by the Bush administration. Obama remembered his own grandmother, "who worked in a bank all her life, and even after she hit that glass ceiling, kept getting up again." He invoked his daughters: "I want them to grow up in a nation that values their contributions, where there are no limits to their dreams." He praised the new law, by referring to the Declaration of Independence: "we are upholding one of this nation's first principles: that we are all created equal and each deserve a chance to pursue our own version of happiness." The law expands the rights of aggrieved worker to sue an employer for discriminatory treatment. Ms Ledbetter is fourth from the left; Speaker of the House Nancy Pelosi is seen applauding the law (Stolberg, 2009b).

(Ron Edmonds/AP/Press Association Images, 2009)

of their own. The changes in welfare provisions from AFDC to TANF (see pp. 189–90) make the states primarily responsible for deciding how much money should be paid to individual recipients. In March 2009, the total number of unemployment claims nationwide totaled 6.2 million, a rapid increase from the 3.3 million total claims for 2007 and the total annual amount per receipt, while varying from state to state, was nearly $4,500 (DOL, 2009).

Table 8.2 Yearly Median Household (Family) Income by Selected Characteristics (117,000,000 households, 2007)

Group	*Median Yearly Income*
All Groups	$50,233
African American	$33,916
American Indian	$35,343
Latino/Hispanic	$38,679
White (non Hispanic)	$54,920
Asian American	$66,103
Native-Born	$50,946
Foreign-Born	$37,637
Large cities	$57,444
Metropolitan areas	$51,831
Non-metropolitan areas	$40,615

Note: Race/Ethnicity as reported by principal income earner.

Source: US Census (2008a, 2008c).

Laws prevent employers from discriminating in hiring on the basis of age, sex, race, religion, physical handicaps or national origin. There are laws to maintain safe working conditions and to allow release time for childbirth, adoption, or to care for sick relatives. The United States has had a federally-mandated work week and minimum wage since 1938, when the maximum hours an individual can be required to work was set at 40 hours and the base wages put at $0.25 an hour. In 2009, all full-time workers over 18 years old were guaranteed at least $6.55 an hour (rising to $7.25 on July 24); those under 18, or those in jobs where tips made up a large part of their salaries or worked for small companies, might receive less. At minimum wage, a full-time (40-hours-a-week) worker would make $290 a week before taxes. Moreover, 23 states and the District of Columbia have laws putting minimum wages above the national requirement. Washington sets it at $8.55, Oregon at $8.40; Connecticut and California at $8.00, for example. In fact, most businesses pay higher wages than are required by law, usually about $9 an hour for beginners. In January 2009 the average hourly pay for all US wage and salaried workers was $18.46 an hour (BLS, 2009b). Any work done beyond the 40-hour maximum is subject to overtime pay at a higher rate of 1.5 to 2 times the hourly rate. High wages increase pressure on the workers, as employers push them to be even more productive, a trade-off that most workers accept.

Four in five American workers say they are satisfied with their jobs, three in five say they were "well paid," and four in five either prefer to maintain their work and pay levels or have the chance to work more for even more pay (Harris Poll, 2007). Not only is the intensity of work increasing, the average work week is 46 hours for most Americans. Technological advances increase the speed on assembly lines, and companies "downsize" the number of workers while asking them to work faster and longer. Part of the problem has been that personal consumption – with high home mortgages and transportation costs – and the fears of an economic slowdown make workers work harder to prove their worth. Those who have worked long hours hope to be among those retained if and when downsizing comes. Beyond the office, technology is affecting work hours as the internet and mobile phones allow the job to spill over into home life. Additionally, the average two-way commute nationwide adds 48 minutes to the workday. For those working in big cities like New York and living in the suburbs, commutes can often total 1.5 hours each way.

Historically, about 15 percent of the labor force is in motion in any given year, offering their skills in the marketplace to the highest bidder as they change employers and geographical locations. These moves stimulate the economy but also increase stress as most workers expect to sell a house in order to buy a house in the new location. Most workers sign yearly or long-term contracts and expect annual pay increases based upon inflation and merit promotions. The notion of merit, not inheritance, is a long-standing tenet of faith as Americans accept that there will be winners and losers. The father of the Constitution, James Madison, called the unequal distribution of property a natural truth arising from disparities in human talent. That idea continues to resonate. Usually, Americans display more anger at welfare payments to poor families than to the extreme wealth of the privileged class. But in times of economic recession, the bankers are vilified as "banksters" – part banker, part gangster – and the CEOs of major companies that contributed to the economic recession are pilloried for high salaries, bonuses and corporate privileges that seem to mock the working class and notions of fair play. This is especially true when companies fail and the government steps in to use taxpayer money to bail them out. In 2008–9 populist anger rose against the CEOs of institutions that broke the public trust, such as bankers, automobile executives, insurance officers and stock brokers (see Illustration 8.2).

In the world of white-collar jobs, a winner-take-all market has been the rule for a quarter century. A "star system" exists where the top performers accumulate pay and prestige through lavishly high salaries and stock options that skew the distribution of wealth. A company's

Illustration 8.2 Bank CEOs Testifying Before Congress

On 11 February 2009 the CEOs of eight powerful US banks struggled through a seven-hour nationally-televised, tongue-lashing congressional inquiry into their financial operations. Congress and the public were especially interested in how the so-called "Masters of the Universe" had used the bailout money supplied to them by the Bush administration's TARP loans. Was the bailout working, would they ask for more money, and were they spending the money wisely? Among American taxpayers a growing, populist anger threatened any further expenditures to bankers, businesses and others whose greed had created the economic crisis. From right to left are the CEOS of banking giants Wells Fargo, Citigroup, Morgan Stanley, State Street Corporation, Bank of America, Mellon Bank of New York, and J. P. Morgan Chase.

(Doug Mills/New York Times, 2009)

chief executive officer can make 500 times what the average worker makes. For much of American history, land was the essential source of wealth. In contemporary America it is human capital in knowledge, skill, and starpower. There are lesser stars, too, making double or triple the salaries of their colleagues in similar jobs. College professors, for example, who win awards or whose books gain popular fame turn that recognition into hard cash as universities compete to get them for their faculties. Stars attract money, so to pay high salaries for their talent does not dismay most Americans, even if it leads to a smaller pot to divide among the others. Since the 1990s, real disparities in the star system meant that the weaker or unacknowledged workers got only cost-of-living increases that kept pace – or failed to keep up – with inflation.

Table 8.3 Individual Income Tax Rates for Year 2008

Single	*Pay*	*plus %*	*Married (filing jointly)*	*Pay*	*plus %*
0–$8,025	0	10	0–$16,050	0	10
$8,025–$32,550	$803	15	$16,050– $65,100	$1,605	15
$32,550–$78,850	$4,481	25	$65,100–$131,450	$8,963	25
$78,850–$164,550	$16,056	28	$131,450–$200,300	$25,550	28
$164,550–$357,700	$40,052	33	$200,300–$357,700	$44,828	33
$357,700 and over	$103,792	35	$357,700 and over	$96,770	35

Note: dollar amounts have been rounded.

Example: If a married couple filed a return on a combined income of $210,000, they would owe $1,605 for the first $16,050; 15 percent ($7,358) for the amount between $16,050–$65,100; 25 percent ($16,587) for the amount between $65,100–$131,450; and 28 percent ($19,278) for the amount between $131,450–$200,300; and 33 percent ($3,201) for the rest. Their tax owed *before deductions* would be $48,029, or about 23 percent of their combined income.

Source: IRS (2008b).

Taxes

Most Americans detest the idea of high taxes. "No taxation without representation" was a rallying cry that helped bring on the American Revolution. Since then, except in times of national economic distress, Americans have decided to keep as much of their income as possible and to accept fewer government services. Historically, excise tariffs funded the government until federal income taxes came into being with the 16th Amendment (1913). Those first taxes were set progressively at one percent for incomes over $3,000, rose to seven percent for those over $500,000, and created an ongoing debate over the fairness of a progressive tax system. So far, Americans have chosen to reform, but retain, the progressive system, with variations according to the political composition of Congress (Table 8.3). In addition to the national tax, the states – excepting Alaska, Florida, Nevada, South Dakota, Texas, Washington and Wyoming, which do not have income taxes – levy state income tax at varying levies between 4 and 11 percent. Cities and counties also tax residents, usually at rates below 2 percent. Consumers pay sales taxes on everything – up to 9.4 percent in Tennessee – and excise taxes on purchases of gasoline, alcohol, and cigarettes. Vermont leads the way with per capita state and city taxes equaling 14.1 percent of total income (RLIC, 2009).

President Reagan's Tax Reform Act of 1986 cut taxes on the highest income groups in line with his belief that high taxes and government regulations limited economic enterprise. Believing that deficit spending could stimulate the economy, Reagan paid little attention to the rising federal debt as he lavishly supported the defense industry. Whether his plan was correct or not is difficult to assess, but through "Reaganomics," the United States enjoyed a huge business expansion from 1983–9. The country also had a greater national debt after eight years under Reagan than had been accumulated in its entire history. George H. W. Bush continued Reagan's policies, but when the economy hit a small recession as the Cold War ended and markets adjusted, Bush approved a tax increase that ultimately led to voter disapproval and his re-election defeat.

Bill Clinton's presidency coincided with the longest period of continuous growth in US history. Some analysts credit this to Reaganomics and see the Clinton boom as part of a 17-year-long expansion (1983–2000). From 1998 to 2000, a booming economy provided huge tax revenues and a three straight years of budget surpluses, totaling $456.2 billion (Aversa, 2000). The 1990s – a period bracketed by the fall of the Berlin Wall, the end of the Cold War in November 1989 and the onset of the "Age of Terrorism" in September 2001 – have been described in books as *The Fabulous Decade* and *The Roaring Nineties.* The collapse of the Soviet Union raised American faith in free market capitalism to new heights. Some analysts spoke of an end of ideology as the market economy triumphed; others put forward ideas that economic recessions would fade into obscurity as globalization opened all markets to increased prosperity for all nations (Stiglitz, 2003: 278). While the Nineties was a decade of massive technological change and productivity gains, it was also an age of deceptive corporate mega-deals and market manipulation, including insider trading, overvalued stocks and investor spending exuberance.

Upon taking office in 2001, George W. Bush's overriding concern was to return the budget surplus to the people through a tax cut and to win support from Americans who like to get a check in the mail. Bush proposed $1.6 trillion, but Congress cut it to – and it is worth putting in all the zeros – $1,350,000,000,000. In addition to sending each American taxpayer a refund averaging $300, the Tax Relief Act of 2001 further reduced rates on the top and middle-income brackets. Five additional tax cuts in 2002 and 2003 benefited the wealthiest Americans and, proportionately, put more of the burden on the middle class.

The changes in the tax rates, higher oil prices and the costs of the war in Iraq ($4 billion a month) have had a massive impact on the total tax revenues and spending, turning the budget surpluses into record deficits as the government experienced its most dramatic revenue drop since 1946 (Jehl, 2003). The 2008 budget deficit reached $455 billion for that year alone, the 2009 shortfall was estimated at between $1.2 and $2 trillion, and the forecast for similar scenarios extended into the foreseeable future (Stout and Andrews, 2009). Economists who favored the tax cuts insisted that after a few years of deficit spending, revenues would catch up with expenses; other economists, like Nobel Prize winners Joseph Stiglitz and Paul Krugman, argued that Bush economic policies would seriously injure the world economy (Stiglitz, 2003: 9).

Labor Unions

Unless a person is self-employed there is a built-in tension between management and labor over levels of production, work hours, benefits and pay. Nearly 90 percent of American workers negotiate individually with management without trade union representation as membership in the nation's 67 unions increased slightly to 16.1 million members (12.4 percent of all workers) (BLS, 2009d). 80 percent of the unionists work in industrial, construction or manufacturing plants and were members of 58 unions affiliated with the American Federation of Labor-Congress of Industrial Organizations (AFL-CIO). The rest were divided among nine independent unions, mostly composed of teachers, police officers, university professors, and government employees (BLS, 2009d).

Local craft unions existed before the American Civil War but the first major nationwide group was the Knights of Labor (KOL) which reached its zenith in the 1880s by accepting all workers into one organization. But because the KOL wanted to improve the immediate situation of pay inequities through strikes and violence, without a long-range program of reform, many craft workers founded a rival group, the American Federation of Labor (1886). The AFL represented skilled trade unionism and represented all groups that organized themselves and asked to join the federation. The AFL never enrolled more than 15 percent of all American workers because of the widespread fear of socialism and a view of unions as anarchistic or un-American. Federal and state government police forces supported corporations against strikers. Additionally, the AFL suffered from a lack of cooperation from a heterogeneous labor pool of varying ethnicities, races, the sheer number of available workers and a free-market ideology of individual responsibility. In 1890, Congress passed the Sherman Anti-Trust Act to stop big business from forming "conspiracies in restraint of trade" and to provide mechanisms for breaking apart monopolies. Later, this act was turned against labor unions, which, when they went on strike, were seen as "conspiracies in restraint of trade."

From the 1870s to the 1930s, union members used strikes and violence to demand changes in safety conditions, benefits and pay. Given the general level of violence in the country, it is not surprising that the United States has had one of the bloodiest labor histories among industrialized nations. Strikes were accompanied by the destruction of private property or even assault and murder of replacement – often immigrant – workers who dared cross the picket lines. Companies employed private detectives, state governors sent in police, and, sometimes, the president deployed federal troops to break up strikes. This era generally witnessed business expansion under *laissez-faire* rules of free-market capitalism. President Calvin Coolidge summed up the majority opinion that "The man who builds a factory, builds a temple. The man who works there, worships there" (quoted in Bittinger, 2009). Hundreds of these "worshippers" died or were arrested trying to change conditions for the working man and woman.

During the Great Depression, workers unhappy with the AFL, or not skilled enough to qualify for membership, created the Congress of Industrial Organizations (CIO). The New Deal's National Labor Relations Act of 1935 (Wagner Act) gave workers the right to collective bargaining, an action prompting 35 percent of the workforce – 12 million workers – to join unions by 1945 (Peck, 1991). Worried that labor would get too powerful, Congress passed the Taft-Hartley Act in 1947 to outlaw any "closed-shop" agreement which required employers to hire only labor union members. The act also forbade agreements requiring workers to join or be represented by unions after they were hired. In 1955, the two biggest unions merged into the AFL-CIO. Collective bargaining tripled hourly wages between 1945 and 1970 and forced both unions and companies to accept the full enrollment of African American and women workers, who had been excluded by closed-shop conventions favoring a white, male workforce.

In the 1980s the union movement foundered under deregulation, foreign imports, a recession, newer technology, downsizing and hostile national administrations. Reagan was openly anti-union and effectively used executive power to stop strikes, keep wages low and stunt union growth. Most Americans believe that big labor has been co-opted as management improved conditions in the workplace and made workers "part owners" by issuing stock to employees in a profit-sharing system in return for increased production rates. In 2008, union members were in the middle class and while median weekly earnings for full-time non-union workers averaged $691, union members got $886 (BLS, 2009d).

Business and Industry

Foreign investment has been essential to the rise of American business since colonial times. For 150 years, British joint-stock companies, with the support of the Royal Navy and under the rules of mercantilism, poured money into the shipbuilding firms in the free-labor North and the plantation agriculture of the slave-labor South. By the time of the American Revolution in 1776, the United States possessed one of the world's largest merchant fleets and maintained ties with nearly every European nation along the North Atlantic rim. Except for the embargoes during the Napoleonic Wars and the War of 1812, trade continued uninterrupted as the European desire for American food products, cotton and tobacco soared and the money-making possibilities for investment capital in America's westward expansion surged.

Beginning in the 1830s, European investment capital made the transportation revolution possible as American companies built hundreds of canals and new harbors and thousands of miles of roads and railroad lines. Railroad companies, entirely private, were the nation's first big businesses and, during the Gilded Age, were the keys to the expansion of steel and oil industries, the building of western cities, the moving of crops quickly from coast to coast to establish an integrated internal marketplace, and the rapid rise of a superpower.

The first factory in the United States was a textile mill built in Pawtucket, Rhode Island, in 1793. The gathering of workers together into one building increased production as did the development of a system of interchangeable parts in the handgun and market industry around 1800. The system was demonstrated to President Jefferson by bringing in 10 markets, dismantling them, mixing the parts, reassembling and firing each one. This mass production – called "the American System" by Europeans – revolutionized products, brought prices down, and all but eliminated the need for master craftsmen who built things one product at a time. About mid-century the growing need for machine tools that were used to make, package, or harvest other products spurred a whole new industry which made mechanical reapers, spinning and weaving machines, and precision tools.

By 1890 the value of the nation's manufactured goods exceeded agricultural production for the first time and, already the world's leading agricultural nation, America became the leading industrial nation as the number of urban dwellers and industrial workers surpassed the rural population for the first time. In 2009, fewer than 3 million Americans lived off farming; most of the nation's crops are produced by giant agribusinesses which feed the internal and external marketplaces.

In World War I, factories in the United States were turning out fully one-third of all industrial products produced worldwide and were implementing Henry Ford's idea of improving efficiency and lowering automobile costs by using continuously moving assembly lines. Ford's innovations and ideas of "scientific management" began to be taught in another American innovation, the Business School. By World War II, American universities were turning out professional managers who had taken advanced courses in accounting, economics, finance, marketing and management. These managers quickly increased production to half of the world's total and from World War II to the late 1970s, the US dominated export markets. In 2009, the country still produced about one-quarter of the world's industrial goods by value.

During the Gilded Age, businessmen formed corporations, monopolies and oligopolies and set up trusts and holding companies to control prices, production, and competition. When government regulation limited their size with the Clayton Anti-Trust Act (1914) and demanded that competition be fair and open as supervised by the Federal Trade Commission (1914), businesses increased research and development and expanded advertising and packaging of standard "name brands." Huge economies of scale meant lower costs per item. In contemporary America there are nearly 4 million corporations and an uncounted number of unincorporated businesses. Even with the advantages held by large corporations, the United States is perhaps the most accommodating "start-up" place for entrepreneurs who want a business of their own. Each year, over 100,000 Americans take a shot at owning their own shops – a few hundred of these enterprises grow into large corporations.

The United States continues to lead the world in the development of high-technology products, especially in the aerospace and IT arenas. This is hardly surprising given the head start the country had with automobile, computing and space shuttle industries. The US also puts great emphasis on targeting international scientists for US universities and companies through immigration-friendly rules, a practice that mitigates the lead of China and India in graduating nearly one million new engineers a year, compared with 70,000 in the United States. The World Economic Forum ranks the US first in technology, first in innovation, first in spending for research, first in research universities, and first in technological readiness. Americans have won the lion's share of Nobel prizes for physics, chemistry and medicine (Zakaria, 2006). Furthermore, the continued upgrading of weapons systems demands high-tech inventions to maintain military superiority.

The American space program is important to innovations and furthers America's scientific and military preeminence. Most of the real gains have been made in unmanned flights such as those putting the Hubble Telescope in position to explore the outer rim of the galaxy or via the five successful missions to Mars – such as in May 2008 when the landing craft "Phoenix" began to move about the Martian landscape analyzing the ice fields for signs of life (Chang, 2008). The funding for military or national security space programs, which operates more satellites than all other countries combined, is double the funding for NASA's scientific programs.

And yet, it is the manned missions, with their promises of future colonies, that gain the most attention and prestige. By 2009, the National Aeronautics and Space Administration (NASA) had launched 118 space shuttle flights and made over 100 spacewalks (Illustration 8.3). Disaster struck the program in 2003 with the loss of the shuttle *Columbia* and seven astronauts during the reentry stage of the mission. The fleet was grounded and retooled before flights recommenced in 2006 in support of the international space station – a joint venture by the US, Russia, China, Europe and Japan. The shuttle program is scheduled for retirement in 2010 and is to be replaced by 2015 with a newer generation of machines capable of carrying people and equipment to the moon and beyond. This is part of the competitive exploration, exploitation and commercial globalizing of space; in 2008 competition increased after Chinese astronauts made a spacewalk and India announced an ambitious program of manned flights, while launching a rocket that put a record ten satellites in orbit on one mission.

Government and Business

Regulation and Deregulation

Government and business cooperate and the government has often intervened to promote or protect economic growth even if its leaders

Illustration 8.3 Launch of the Space Shuttle *Discovery*

The US Space program furthers America's economic and military preeminence even while it cooperates with other nations in the exploration of the galaxy. On 9 March 2009, the Shuttle *Discovery* made a night launch from NASA's Kennedy Space Center at Cape Canaveral, Florida. Its mission was to install new solar panels on the orbiting International Space Station (ISS). *Discovery*'s crew consisted of seven members, including Japanese Astronaut Koichi Wakada, who remained to work in the laboratory of the ISS.

(Chris O'Meara/AP/Press Association Images, 2009)

prefer free-market capitalism. From the Reagan administration (1981–9) through the presidency of George W. Bush (2001–9), deregulation replaced the strong interventionist and regulatory role played by the government from the Great Depression of the 1930s to the 1970s. For most of American history, private interests have had a relative freedom to control themselves. Even such necessities as telephone services, railroads, airlines, hospitals and electric power have remained in private, not public, hands. The government buys goods and services for the public from the private sector. While operating under a philosophy of *laissez-faire* and applying a Darwinian logic that systems which adapt best to changing conditions will survive and multiply, the American government uses taxes on imported goods (tariffs), subsidies, tax breaks and a federal reserve bank to protect domestic enterprises. The American economy combines individual self-interest with a communitarian approach that serves the national interest. The idea that a liberal nation must be a limited nation with low levels of government direction has long held sway among the American populace. Whenever the government steps in to aid businesses, banks or individuals, many critics complain that public money is being spent to rescue those who have been too greedy, imprudent and dumb at the expense of those who have sought reasonable profits and lived within their means.

And yet, big industry and the industrial workforce have always been the strongest advocates for protectionism at home. They generally ask the government to put tariffs on foreign imports so that their domestic products will cost less. The real fear is that if the market is flooded with cheaper imported goods, domestic wages will suffer and businesses will collapse. But because American consumers want cheaper prices brought by open markets and lower tariffs, the United States has vacillated between periods of protectionism and free trade. Since international trade demands good will and trust, tariff issues can damage relationships or lead to retaliatory tariffs and quotas by trading partners. Some nations are favored and some pay more. In 2007, the United States collected $26 billion in tariffs on imported goods worth $2 trillion, with Cambodia charged at 17 percent, China 3, Brazil 1.8, Japan 1.7, Germany 1.4, Russia 0.3, South Africa 0.1 and Saudi Arabia 0.1, for example (PPI, 2008).

The government also regulates business through acts designed to ensure that all products are safe. In 1906, the Pure Food and Drug Act put standards and restrictions on food processing and meat packing and created the Food and Drug Administration (FDA) to test the safety of all prescription drugs. Today, the Center for Disease Control (CDC) issues warnings and guidelines for what may be imported and exported. The Occupational Safety and Health Administration (OSHA) oversees workplace safety and health environments to reduce injuries and illnesses (4 million in 2007) and fatalities (5,488 in 2007) (BLS, 2008b and c). The National Safety Council, a non-governmental agency with close ties to the government, inspects the construction and flammability of all toys to increase children's safety; it also tests all electrical inventions to reduce the risks to the consumer (NSC, 2002). Additionally, the government requires that all products are labelled with a list of ingredients or material composition and requires that all sellers mark prices clearly and advertise honestly. Any product claims that cannot be substantiated by government inspectors are illegal. Consumers have access to reimbursement through the legal system but also by making complaints to state and local offices of the Consumer Protection Agency or Better Business Bureau. Usually, companies show goodwill and business savvy by quickly refunding money or offering items in exchange.

Historically, the government helped settle the west by offering large acreages of public land to individuals who would "homestead" it and companies that would build railroads. In contemporary America, state governments continue this facilitator role by granting tax breaks and time-limited pollution exemptions to encourage companies to relocate to their states. The federal government also stands ready to intervene to prop up businesses which it holds vital to the national economy. In the 1980s the government saved the Chrysler Corporation from bankruptcy and, in 2001, it supported airlines hurt in the aftermath of the terrorist attacks. In 2008 and 2009, the government rushed money to companies deemed "too big to fail" – meaning that the loss in jobs and products would have a ripple effect throughout the system, causing other companies to fail and unemployment to rise, as is evident in the automobile industry, for example. Even while opposing the principle of government intervention, Bush told the nation that "the risk of not acting would be far higher" and supported a Troubled Asset Relief Program (TARP) of $700 billion (Bush, 2008). All in all, Bush approved a total $868 billion in bailout packages to save the gigantic insurance company American International Group (AIG), the essential bank J. P. Morgan, and the two biggest government-backed mortgage companies Federal National Mortgage Association (Fanny Mae) and Federal Home Loan Mortgage Corporation (Freddie Mac), among others. Since taking office, Obama has consistently supported the use of taxpayer money to prop up corporations that are essential – "too big to fail."

The Banking System

The central bank for the United States is the Federal Reserve (Fed), which consists of a board of seven governors who set policy, and 12 regional banks located around the country to handle the day-to-day operation of printing and circulating money to the 5,000 different banks that are members of the system. The Fed was established in 1913 and expanded its influence during the New Deal, when member banks were required to keep a certain amount of their total deposits on reserve in one of the 12 regional banks to cover sudden credit needs and stave off financial panics that could lead to another great depression. The chairman of the Fed is appointed by the president to serve for four years. The primary function of the Federal Reserve is to establish a monetary policy which will enhance confidence and trust, encourage economic stability, reduce or increase inflation as needed, and limit unemployment by stimulating the market (Fed, 2009).

The US economy experiences the boom-and-bust cycles that are common to all market economies as business expands or contracts. Congressional fiscal policy – taxation and spending programs – also affects the economy as does any change in consumer spending patterns. Any disruption in the supply of oil, major terrorist assault, or natural disaster – forest fire, hurricane, a bad harvest – alters the economy in unpredictable ways. The Federal Reserve can moderate these fluctuations by adjusting the national interest rates for borrowing money: a high rate discourages borrowing and consumer spending while a low rate does the opposite. Between September 11, 2001, and June 2003, with pressure from the Bush administration, the Fed lowered interest rates from 6.5 to 1.0 percent to stimulate consumer confidence and spending, especially in the housing market – an errant move that led to overconfidence and overspending out of sync with the Fed's manifest duty to protect the economy. By the end of 2004, the rate had rebounded to 2.25 percent, but was sliced to near zero in 2008 in the face of the credit crunch. There are 5,000 private banks that are not members of the Federal Reserve and are capitalized by other means. Whether or not a bank is part of the Fed, the Federal Deposit Insurance Corporation (FDIC) protects individual deposits up to a maximum, usually $100,000, in the event the bank collapses.

The Fed was not designed to fix speculation, fraud and bad management by the nation's financial institutions and bankers, even though it has acted as a last resort to avert disasters. In the 1980s, the Fed funded the nation's Savings and Loans (S & L) banks by granting $150 billion over and above FDIC guarantees for individual depositors. The bailout reimbursed the millions of average citizens who had put their life's savings into institutions that failed, a necessary action to restore trust among consumers and to prevent a financial panic leading to a run on bank deposits. In late 2008, Bush ordered the FDIC to calm public fears by increasing guarantees from $100,000 to $250,000 for individual deposits (FDIC, 2009).

Wall Street, the Banks and the Crisis of 2008/9

The New York Stock Exchange (NYSE) is located on Wall Street in New York City (NYC) and is the world's leading organized market for the trading of stocks and bonds. The NYSE is the oldest and best-known stock market in the United States (established 1792), even though the American Stock Exchange (AMEX) and the Chicago

Commodities Exchange handle nearly 25 percent of all transactions. The National Association of Securities Dealers Automated Quotations (NASDAQ) is an electronic stock market located in Times Square in NYC with internet links to over one million brokerage firms worldwide.

Major corporations rely on investments to supply the capital required to develop their businesses. The stock market serves to encourage that investment and to provide a solid measure of a company's present and anticipated performance as stocks rise and fall. Famously, the stock market crash of 1929 signaled the beginning of the Great Depression and, in 1934, Congress established a regulatory agency, the Securities and Exchange Commission (SEC), to monitor the trading of stocks so that wildly inflated profit claims and speculative financing could be controlled to prevent future crashes. The NYSE and other markets are privately run, but publicly supervised. In contemporary America, it is obvious that the failure of the SEC to provide adequate oversight was a major reason for the financial speculation and scandals that led to the crash of 2008.

The SEC is responsible for monitoring traders by ensuring that real assets such as property or cash reserves are adequate to back purchases while it regulates stock mergers and sets rules to disqualify persons from making profits from dumping or buying stocks before public announcements have been made – a practice known as insider trading. The SEC also requires businesses to present standardized and accurate profit-and-loss disclosures to accounting firms who check the accuracy of their claims, both protecting investors and providing confidence in the American way of business.

At least it is supposed to operate that way. Capitalism works well when the players can trust one another and when companies act not only for their own benefit but for the benefit of the economy at large, as Adam Smith argued. Ethical standards are fundamental to the American – and global – economic system. Any loss of confidence triggers a removal of capital into more trusted markets, thereby discouraging foreign investors – who own some 15 percent of US stocks. In December 2008, the biggest known fraud in market history became public: former NASDAQ chairman Bernard Madoff used his inside knowledge of the system and his personal acquaintances to cheat clients. Using a classic pyramid ("ponzi") scheme to provide fake profits to old investors by using money gained from new investors, Madoff avoided the scrutiny of the SEC, even though the regulatory body was warned several times that Madoff was up to no good. By the time the SEC realized its mistake and brought charges of federal security fraud against Madoff, the losses topped 50 billion dollars (Efrati, *et al.* 2008).

As precursor to the crash of 2008, the 2001 Enron scandal lowered international confidence in the SEC and led to a devaluation of the dollar. Listed as the seventh-largest company in America and as the leading provider and trader of energy commodities, such as electricity and oil, Enron collapsed into bankruptcy during a six-month period in mid-to-late 2001, losing $60 billion in stocks, $2 billion in employee pension funds and thousands of jobs. Its financial tentacles reached into thousands of companies, its monetary contributions to the Republican Party and the close business and political ties of Enron founder Ken Lay to President Bush, Vice-President Dick Cheney, and Secretary of the Army Thomas White, and its use of its employees' retirement funds to speculate in stocks exposed the problems of under-regulated capitalism (Stiglitz, 2003: 251). Millions of individual Americans lost substantial amounts of retirement income when the company's real assets were divided among its creditors.

Companies rise and fall, but Enron's collapse exposed what economist Paul Krugman calls "Crony Capitalism, USA." (Krugman, 2002). Conflicts of interest soar as accounting firms do lucrative consulting work for companies whose accounts they audit and as regulators are appointed by and tangled up with politicians whose campaign funding depends on business contributions. Public and private interests are further tangled as economists run the Fed and SEC, government agencies have a stake in promoting optimistic figures, and the business press and financial news spread the message that the best investments are, for example, Enron. The Enron scandal is the story of deliberately concealed and misrepresented financial statements, of complicity by one of the nation's most respected accounting firms, Arthur Andersen Associates, and charges of special favors by the Bush administration in opening up oil reserves in protected wilderness areas in return for campaign contributions. Enron's activities in weakening pollution controls and storing nuclear waste in Nevada and failures by the Federal Reserve, SEC and Congress to oversee the wrongdoings pointed out the abuses possible in an under-regulated economy. Fears mounted among investors, that if Enron had gotten away with such misdeeds, then other companies had done the same. Even while expecting further revelations of mismanagement, the American government did nothing to increase regulation. In a 2003 poll, 65 percent of Republicans and 49 percent of Democrats agreed with the statement: "Government regulation of business usually does more harm than good" (Pew, 2004).

By 2008 it was crystal clear that the system had broken down. In analyzing the causes behind the current financial crisis, economists point first to the mortgage lending system. The 1990s and early twenty-first century provided boom times for many people as the economic scheme of Reaganomics with its emphasis on deregulation, tax cuts, free markets and deficit spending became a "religion" under George W. Bush. Speculation and crony capitalism increased and filtered through the system to middle class citizens who did not want to be left behind in the good times. The American Dream of homeownership combined with the almost universally-acknowledged belief that a house was a family's biggest investment/biggest asset to encourage a surge in real estate purchases. Banks offered so-called "sub-prime" loans at astonishing low rates to people who did not have enough resources to afford the payments. As mortgage standards declined and as foreign capital invested heavily in the US stocks and bonds markets – especially in bundles of mortgage-backed securities – even cheaper money flooded in. Financial institutions got caught up in the bonanza of profits as bank directors, board members and mortgage specialists worldwide placed their corporations at risk by overreliance on mortgages and mortgage-backed stocks.

When the rapid surge in house prices declined in late 2007 and suddenly collapsed in mid-2008, banks reduced the availability of loans and the credit system failed, bringing on a global calamity. Americans could not afford to pay their more expensive, adjustable rate mortgages and thousands lost their dreams of homeownership to foreclosure – a bank action that affected 10 percent of US families in 2009, and rising. Investors withdrew more money, banks filed for bankruptcy or approached it, and the stock markets tumbled dramatically. The collapsing financial structure put the world in a position unknown since the Great Depression. Many analysts believe that the best way out of such an economic crisis is not via the isolated actions of national states, but in the multinational institutions of the global marketplace.

The Global Marketplace

World Trade Organization

From the time of the first explorers to the New World, Americans have been involved in the web of commercial relations that stretched from Asia to Europe and beyond. What we call globalization began about 500 years ago with the advent of capitalism and has been expanding ever since even if the immense worldwide economic changes brought about by the end of the Cold War and the rise of the internet represent a significant acceleration. Issues concerning trade agreements, tariffs, subsidies, and agreements are central to US foreign policy. And even in its most isolationist periods, America has been strongly interventionist in promoting business interests and pursuing a "dollar diplomacy" of rewarding nations with monetary help in return for a favorable trade policy and inflicting punitive economic sanctions on such "undesirables" as Cuba, Iran, and North Korea.

The US-dominated International Monetary Fund (IMF) and World Bank set requirements on nations that borrow money. This intervention into the internal affairs of other nations causes extreme controversy as these nations need the money to bail out their economies or for development of new resources but do not necessarily want the greater movement of jobs, goods, capital, and democracy across national borders that is the price of the loans. Globalization can be seen as a destructive, exploitative system, especially when operated by the old colonial/imperial powers of the West who have proven untrustworthy in the past. Supporters of IMF and World Bank policies say that they will help close the gap between the wealthy Northern hemisphere and the under-industrialized Southern hemisphere. Former UN Secretary General Kofi Annan, from Ghana, acknowledged that "arguing against globalization is like arguing against gravity" (quoted in Crossette, 2000) and added that "The poor are not poor because of too much globalization, but because of too little" (quoted in DOHA, 2002: 11). Domestic critics of globalization complain that it hurts American workers by creating a global labor market which keeps wages down.

The United States has an 8.4 percent share of total world exports and a 19.1 percent share of total world imports (CIA, 2009). American trade averages over one billion dollars a day with each of four partners: Canada, Mexico, China and the European Union. The World Trade Organization (WTO), established in 1995, is an international forum designed to open markets and expand free trade in general, but particularly among developing countries. The WTO is designed as the UN of the global economy and tries to resolve disputes and monitor fair trade among the 153 member nations (WTO, 2008). The Seattle round of meetings in 1999 was marked by the street violence of anti-free trade groups and failed because of disputes between the US and EU. The Doha, Qatar, session, which began in 2001, saw real progress as developing nations and the industrial world seemed more prepared to reduce tariffs and quotas on industrial goods. But with the Bush administration pushing a strict free trade line, by mid-2008 the negotiations continued to stall as the US opposed India's efforts to allow developing nations to use high tariffs without reprisal from developed nations. Obama has the opportunity to reestablish the momentum needed to compromise, but, with the recent excesses of capitalism, the world is less sure of the advantages of free trade than ever before.

The WTO replaced the older General Agreement on Tariffs and Trade (GATT) conferences with a more permanent body of negotiators and grew much stronger in late 2001 when China and Taiwan joined – this was possible after the US Congress in 2000 voted to normalize trade relations, overturning a policy aimed at punishing mainland China for alleged human rights abuses. The WTO regulates trade, encourages fair competition, discourages domestic support to national businesses that distort trade, debates fair use of intellectual property, and promotes environmental standards. The WTO adjudicates complaints of unfair practices, such as the US complaint against the average 62 percent tariff on agricultural imports worldwide – as opposed to the average 4 percent for industrial imports – or the dispute with the EU over hormone-treated beef (DOHA, 2002). In 2002, the WTO prohibited the long-running practice of "offshore tax havens" such as Guam and the Virgin Islands, which saved US companies about $4 billion a year in export taxes, thus lowering the final costs of US goods, particularly aircraft, in foreign countries and thereby giving them an unfair market advantage (Rosenbaum and Olson, 2002). The US responded that state-run airlines in Europe had an extreme advantage over private US carriers. Tariffs on iron and steel constantly threaten a trans-Atlantic trade war. In 2009, when the US government agreed to bailout its failing automobile industry, some charged that this was an illegal subsidy prohibited by the WTO under international trade laws (Bacchus, 2008).

The United States is the world's leading developer and exporter of technology. Its manufacturing base is extensive but is mainly geared to internal consumption. Leading industries include steel, aerospace, textiles, automobiles, chemicals, telecommunications, semiconductors, biotechnology, and computers. Changes in technology and industrial organization continue to flow from US sources and the US dominates in the export of movies, DVDs and CDs. But Americans still make most of their money in the domestic market as total exports make up only 10 percent of the GDP, compared to the EU's nearly 30 percent.

Table 8.4 Top 20 US Trade Partners, Exports and Imports, 2008 (in billions of dollars: 597.0 = $597, 000, 000, 000)

Country	*Exports*	*Imports*	*Total Trade*
1 Canada	261.4	335.6	597.0
2 China	71.5	337.8	409.3
3 Mexico	151.5	215.9	367.8
4 Japan	66.6	139.3	205.9
5 Germany	54.7	97.6	152.3
6 UK	53.8	58.6	112.4
7 South Korea	34.8	48.1	82.9
8 France	29.2	44.0	73.2
9 Saudi Arabia	12.5	54.8	67.3
10 Venezuela	12.6	51.4	64.0
11 Brazil	32.9	30.5	63.4
12 Taiwan	25.3	36.3	61.6
13 Netherlands	40.2	21.1	61.3
14 Italy	15.5	36.1	51.6
15 Belgium	29.0	17.4	46.4
16 Singapore	28.8	15.9	44.7
17 India	18.7	25.8	44.5
18 Malaysia	13.0	30.7	43.7
19 Ireland	9.0	31.6	40.6
20 Switzerland	22.0	17.8	39.8

Source: ITA. International Trade Administration (2009).

The United States is also the leading importer of world products, both in terms of raw materials to fuel factories and in goods aimed at the consumer market. Since American imports far exceed its exports – $2.5 trillion to $1.8 trillion in 2008 – the country has a serious balance of trade problem. The trade deficit widened from $362.7 billion in 2001 to $677.1 billion in 2008 (BEA, 2009b). While the US imbalance in trade is spread among the majority of the world's nations, the deficit is largest with China at $266 billion, a debt equaling what the US owed to the European Union ($93 billion) and OPEC ($176 billion) combined (BEA, 2009b). Over the past decade, the connection of American consumers to Chinese producers has created a symbiotic economic relationship dubbed "Chimerica" which includes one-fourth of the world's population and one-third of its GDP. The importance of Chimerica to the US well being and as the engine of the global economy is apparent in Table 8.4 (Ferguson, 2008b).

NAFTA

The North American Free Trade Agreement (NAFTA) was established in 1994 among the United States, Canada and Mexico as the largest free trade bloc in the world. NAFTA agreements began removing the investment and agricultural tariff barriers that restricted trade, with the final restrictions eliminated on January 1, 2008. Originally, Congress strongly opposed the deal because of Mexico's failure to enforce environmental laws and from concerns that its cheap labor market would hurt American workers. Fearing that manufacturers might relocate to Mexico, labor unions especially opposed NAFTA. Clinton used his position as president – "lobbyist-in-chief" – as well as the lobbying support of ex-presidents Ford, Carter and Bush, to get enough votes for the agreement. In 1995, when the collapse of the Mexican peso threatened the trading block, Clinton sidestepped Congressional disapproval of a bailout and quickly transferred $25 billion to the Mexican government. The infusion worked and NAFTA grew stronger as Mexico repaid the loan, plus $1 billion in interest (Sanger, 2000).

Trade inside NAFTA benefits its members, even though China–US trade provides intense competition, as Table 8.4 indicates. Former Mexican President Vicente Fox credited NAFTA's growth not only to "an economic partnership, based on shared goals and shared responsibilities," but to the fact that "democracy has been brought about in Mexico," and to the social "trust" existing between Mexicans and Americans (Fox, 2001). NAFTA reflects a growing regionalism marked by the April 2001 agreement in which leaders of 34 countries in the Western Hemisphere met in "The Summit of the Americas" in Quebec City, Canada, proposing to replace NAFTA with a massive Free Trade Area of the Americas to include the whole of the Western hemisphere and its 800 million people (Milbank and Blustein, 2001). But, since 11 September 2001, the US focus on securing its borders and the ideological tension between the US and Venezuela have stifled these discussions (see Illustration 10.1).

The Dollar, the Trade Deficit, and the Crash of 2008

In 2005, the United States began to feel the results of a three-decade-long imbalance in trade – where imports exceeded exports – as the nation's international debt climbed to nearly 30 percent of its GDP. From 1944 to 1971, world currencies were tied to the dollar, with the dollar convertible to gold at a fixed rate ($35 per ounce). That established the greenback as the global currency for trade. The Fed's strong dollar policy encouraged the foreign investment capital upon which the American superpower depends for the expansion of its market dominance. From 1980–5, the dollar rose 40 percent in value against all major currencies and that appreciation caused the US trade deficit to balloon. After the terrorist attacks in 2001, the Bush administration decided on a *laissez faire* approach: it would not prop up the dollar and would watch it fall against world currencies to a level determined by the market.

By late 2004, the dollar was in such a rapid freefall against the European Euro, British Pound and Japanese Yen, that investors wondered about a crisis in capitalism. Bush and Fed Chairman Alan Greenspan insisted that the dollar had been kept artificially high, a condition which unfairly hurt US exports and favored foreign imports – and responsible for the massive imbalance in trade and US debt. With a weaker dollar and stronger foreign currencies, the market corrected a bit in the US's favor by dropping the price of US goods and increasing those of foreign producers. But China did not play Bush's game and kept a strong position by keeping its currency, the Yuan, pegged to the dollar – thus maintaining a price advantage for Chinese goods with the American consumer. Thus, China holds the biggest share of the $3.3 trillion US debt and US–China policy is highly nuanced. China's modernization has advanced without political liberalization, as the size of its middle class and domestic consumption increases. Favoring trade first and foremost and afraid of starting a retaliatory trade war, the Bush administration exerted only minor, and ineffective, pressure to get the Chinese to de-couple the Yuan from the dollar and let it float in a free market.

In the end, Bush's *laissez faire* approach to the global economy failed. One Nobel laureate explained: "Economies can suffer from an overintrusive government, but so too can they suffer from a government that does not do what needs to be done – that does not regulate the financial sector adequately, that does not promote competition, that does not protect the environment, that does not provide a (social) safety net" (Stiglitz, 2003: 318). Bush's policies of deregulation, lack of oversight and belief that markets were self-correcting contributed mightily to the financial recession in 2008 and beyond. America's massive national debt had been financed by other countries through years of allowing the US a negative balance of trade and huge deficit spending.

Countries have been willing to lend America so much money because of the massive American consumer market and the acknowledgment that the US is the only "consumption superpower" in the world (Schwenninger, 2004). With the crisis of 2008 continuing, an overwhelming number of Americans began to feel poor, became more frugal, cut up credit cards, reduced buying to the minimum and began to increase their savings in ways not seen in fifty years (Uchitelle, *et al.*, 2008). This is having huge ramifications for the world's economy and, even with stimulus packages, the pullback in spending patterns could cause further business failures and job losses as consumers resist buying new cars, flying to expensive locations, eating in fancy restaurants and buying premium clothing brands. But with public fear that the banks and corporations are not making full disclosures of their balance sheets, with an expectation that if one Bernard Madoff is found, there are a hundred others hiding among investment firms, and with worries that Obama and government bureaucrats lack the skills and resources to coordinate a global economic rescue, American consumer patterns have changed.

While Ronald Reagan famously said that "government is not the solution to our problem; government is the problem," the Obama administration promotes a "new era of responsibility" that will use the power of the government in a complex program aimed at expanding social services and righting the economy. Focusing on a more equitable distribution of wealth, Obama asked for higher, progressive taxes on the wealthiest Americans, less taxes on the poor and middle classes, an end to subsidies to agribusiness and to private banks who profit from college loans. Far from being *laissez faire*, the US government took shares in private corporations, including banks, and even though politicians are averse to using the term "nationalization," the actions clearly indicate that the policy of "Reaganomics" is over. For example, in March 2009, the government owned 80 percent of AIG and 30 percent of Citigroup (Sorkin and Walsh, 2009).

Many critics think Obama has gone too far and suggest that the way forward is through even more tax cuts and less government. Talk radio superstar and highly-influential Republican activist Rush Limbaugh blames Obama for not doing enough and at the same time worries that the president's policies might end the hard times and expand the role of the federal government. Limbaugh openly says, "I hope Obama fails" (Limbaugh, 2009). Former Speaker of the House, Newt Gingrich, summed up the Republican disdain for Obama's new era as "the boldest effort to remake America since Lyndon Johnson's Great Society in 1965 [and] sets the stage for the biggest fight over the future of America since 1965" (Gingrich, 2009). And the fight is international, not just domestic. The American people will have to see results to support the expansion of an increasingly activist government; but so too will international markets and investors, particularly the Chinese, who must continue lending money and accruing American debt. Recognizing the wide-reaching matrix of capitalism, with unemployment and business health dependent on multilateral solutions not protectionism, British Prime Minister Gordon Brown met with Obama and supported: "a global new deal, whose impact can stretch from the villages of Africa to reforming the financial institutions of London and New York – and giving security to the hard-working families in every country" (Knowlton, 2009). Even while Obama seeks a cooperative multinational solution, the world still acknowledges the potential power of US consumption and looks to the US to lead. Obama is a transformational figure in American politics, whose early program promises a return to the expansive programs of Franklin Roosevelt's New Deal or Lyndon Johnson's Great Society. Whether he can save the world economy is another matter.

9

Foreign Policy

Foreign policy revolves around power relationships among nations and peoples. Hard power – sometimes called sharp power – refers to military forces deployed in wars, used as a threat to force others to do what you want them to do, or to take over their country if they refuse to yield. Soft power is the persuasion done subtly by advancing ideals and culture to get others to want what you have in terms of lifestyle, politics, freedom, material goods, education and so forth (Nye, 2002). Sticky power involves trade agreements, markets, globalization and the economic institutions and policies that connect nations and, ultimately, give power to the one who can control the flow of money. In the contemporary world, the United States maintains its hegemony through the combination of hard, soft and sticky power, controlled – and uncontrolled – by presidential agreements, treaties and the legal system (Mead, 2004).

"To Future Generations"

From the first president to the present one, American leaders have conducted an often ambivalent foreign policy marked by a consistent belief in New World exceptionalism and the central idea of freedom. Because America was founded in revolution against British imperialism and, in the twentieth century, reluctantly entered both world wars, Americans retain a widespread distrust of other nations as places inclined toward war, conspiracies, class-based privilege, a lack of order and, increasingly in recent years, breeding places for terrorism. Poet Ralph Waldo Emerson wrote that the American revolution was "the shot heard round the world" because it led to the establishment of the world's first democracy and advanced a national mission to help others toward freedom. In 1776, Thomas Paine's pamphlet *Common Sense* proclaimed: "We have it in our power to begin the world over again." In another pamphlet, *The Crisis*, Paine called on the patriots to stand firm through "the times that try men's souls." Paine expressed not only the distinction Americans make between themselves and others but also the notion of rebirth and reinvention that marks American ideology. In his inaugural address in 2009, President Obama (2009a) proved himself an heir to Paine: "Let it be said by our children's children that when we were tested we refused to let this journey end, that we did not turn back nor did we falter; and with eyes fixed on the horizon and God's grace upon us, we carried forth that great gift of freedom and delivered it safely to future generations."

The United States began its national life with the Declaration of Independence, a document formulated to ensure "a decent respect for the opinions of mankind" (see Box 1.1). American history is marked by ambivalent adherence to and deviation from that hallowed principle. From 2001 to 2009, the Bush administration did not use multilateral solutions to global problems. The president's unilateral actions and his rhetoric of freedom versus tyranny and of expanding democracy rang hollow and chauvinistic. For example, in his twenty-minute-long second inaugural address, while not once uttering the words "Iraq," "September 11," or "terrorism," Bush used the words "freedom," "free," and "liberty," a total of forty-nine times (Bush, 2005). He insisted that America would promote freedom everywhere and asked rhetorical questions revealing his sense of mission and place in history: "Did our generation advance the cause of freedom? And did our character bring credit to that cause?" Bush warned: "The rulers of outlaw regimes can know that we still believe as Abraham Lincoln did: Those who deny freedom to others deserve it not for themselves; and, under the rule of a just God, cannot long retain it" (Bush, 2005).

This vision was not universally welcomed as world commentators worried over who might be next: Iran or North Korea. Some predicted that the latest anti-democratic actions by Vladimir Putin, could lead to a revival of Cold War tensions with Russia. China and India have their own systems and will not be bullied by the United States. For many in the Arab world, America has long had a deaf ear, especially wherever the interests of Islam confronted the US–Israeli alliance. But there is also a deepening rift within the West, including many changes not connected to American policies. British historian Niall Ferguson cites three monumental changes that separate Europe from the United States: (1) the Soviet Union no longer exists as an imminent threat, (2) the creation of "Eurabia" as the present-day

15 million Muslims in Europe dramatically increase, and (3) increasing secularization and loss of religion among Europeans (Ferguson, 2005: 44). This chapter surveys American power and its ambivalent approach to foreign policy.

Separation of Powers and Foreign Policy

The United States operates under a federal system where states share power. This gives foreign interests multiple entry points to influence policy. Many nations have established lobbying groups in Washington and various state capitals to convince legislators to favor their proposals. Officially, the Constitution divides power over foreign policy between the executive and the legislative branches. But in practice, Congress had most of the power in the nineteenth century and the president has had it ever since. The president is commander-in-chief of the military, has the power to make treaties, appoint ambassadors, and is head of state in according diplomatic recognition to foreign heads of state. Only Congress can declare war, approve spending, raise an army, make rules regulating commerce and create international programs. The Senate alone approves ambassadorships and must ratify all treaties made by the executive before they are legally binding. Often, Congress makes laws to control executive prerogatives. For example, the 1973 War Powers Resolution limits the president's ability to wage war by requiring him to notify Congress within 48 hours of sending in troops and by providing a limit of 60 days on their deployment, unless Congress specifically approves an extension. The 1988 Arms Control Export Act restricts the president's ability to transfer arms approved for one nation to another nation.

Presidents chafe under these legislative controls and often sidestep Congressional wishes by using executive agreements, discretionary funds, undeclared wars and other devices. From 1974 to 1997, Congress authorized American presidents to make "fast track" trading agreements with foreign leaders. These agreements could be accepted or rejected by Congress, but not amended. The fast-track agreements helped presidents open foreign markets by making foreign leaders more confident that the president's agreement would not be changed to include Congressional restrictions. In 1997, in retaliation for Clinton's support of NAFTA, Congress ended fast-track agreements, then reversed course in 2002, giving Bush the power once again.

A president can also use an agreement between himself and a foreign head-of-state to make policy. The Supreme Court has ruled that these "executive agreements" are constitutional and the number of executive agreements outpace formal treaties by almost 25 to one. Executive agreements are only valid while the president is in office; a new president must renew, reject or make his own agreements. Discretionary funds provide the president with a large amount of money to use in a crisis situation or to pursue pet projects. For example, in 1995, Clinton directed a $25 billion loan to Mexico and, in 2004–9, Bush used billions in Iraq.

The Administration of Foreign Policy

The executive authority over war is strengthened by the Department of State, Department of Defense (DOD), Central Intelligence Agency (CIA), and National Security Council (NSC), all under the direction of the president. The Department of State has primary responsibility for foreign affairs and the secretary of state is the highest-ranking cabinet official, a key figure in formulating and implementing policy. Since 1997, presidents picked women and African Americans to represent US interests to the world: Madeleine Albright (1997–2001); Colin Powell (2001–5), Condoleezza Rice (2005–9), and Hillary Clinton (2009–). The secretary of state supervises all US ambassadors, who are political appointees, and the nearly 4,000 permanent foreign service officers.

The Department of Defense consists of the military forces of the United States and acts to coordinate the military under the control of a civilian, the secretary of defense. The army, navy, and air force also have civilian heads, known as the secretary of the army, etc. Next in command come professional military soldiers: the chairman of the Joint Chiefs of Staff (JCS) and the respective military commanders.

The Central Intelligence Agency is the official intelligence-gathering arm of the foreign policy establishment. Since 1947 the CIA has collected, analyzed and circulated information relating to national security to other agencies on a "need to know" basis. Most of the activities of the CIA are entirely mundane, collecting information from statistical reports and newspapers, but the agency is best-known for its covert activities such as assassinations, spying, destabilizing governments and wiretaps. Historically, the CIA plays the role of scapegoat when presidential decision-making goes awry (Powers, 2004). For example, the CIA took most of the blame for failing to stop the terrorist attacks and for its analyses that Iraq had or was building weapons of mass destruction. Because the CIA works at the direction of the president, there are flaws in intelligence reporting when an administration demands "proof" and analyses that support its own view of a particular situation – something that clearly happened in the case of Iraq.

The National Security Council consists of advisors who help the president shape a coherent foreign policy. Permanent members include the President, vice president, secretaries of state and defense, director of the Office of Homeland Security, and the national security advisor. Others, such as the JCS, CIA and FBI directors, and treasury secretary serve at the discretion of the president. The NSC discusses policy for foreign aid, military intervention, "best-guess" scenarios for political and military alliances around the globe, how to deal with threats as diverse as Iran, North Korea, and China, and all other issues deemed relevant to national security. The NSC often recommends a course of action and helps persuade Congress to pass funding bills or loans to foreign countries. For example, in 2000, Congress agreed with an NSC directive and authorized $1.3 billion, which included the purchase of 60 attack helicopters, to Colombia to help stop heroin and cocaine production by the powerful drug cartels.

During the Bush presidency, transatlantic tensions increased as the 60-year-old post-World War II community between Europeans and Americans came under stress. Many allies feared the unilateral militarism of the Bush administration as well as the traditional financial, technological, environmental and cultural threats. Historically, the US often got its way in foreign policy by either ignoring world opinion or by coercing nations into accepting its demands. American leaders sometimes increase fears by stressing that all they want is a free market. Foreign leaders worry that once the business interests expire, the US will ignore and abandon them or drag them into an unwanted military conflict. The United States has enormous power to reward nations who conform to American wishes. The government grants access to the unparalleled American consumer market, distributes foreign aid in many forms, sponsors entry into international organizations, ignores violations of human rights, forgives debts and lifts economic sanctions. All of these are understandable components of a nation's responsibility to its own well-being, but these actions create resentment in a competitive and nationalistic world. In 2009, the inauguration of Obama eased tensions overnight as the new president consistently upheld multilateral cooperation.

American policymakers are aware of the danger of "imperial overstretch" – the condition that brought down the empires of Greece, Rome, the Ottomans, Spain, Great Britain, and the Soviet Union by having too many properties and allies and too few armies, resources, or will to protect them all. The United States operates at least 737 military bases in 132 foreign countries, has a powerful navy in every ocean, and supports approximately 325,000 military personnel living overseas (Freedland, 2007). History eventually catches up with every empire, replacing each with a stronger one. Fareed Zakaria wrote that the future of American power is threatened by the "third great power shift of the modern era – the rise of the rest" (Zakaria, 2008b). He explained that the first great power shift was the rise of the West and modernity in the fifteenth–eighteenth centuries. The second shift was the rise of the United States to dominance in the twentieth century. The growth of powerful nations in South America, Asia and the Middle East represents the rise of the rest and an emerging international system that American leaders can still dominate by embracing the multipolar reality instead of trying to hold on to the unipolar moment that has existed since the breakup of the Soviet Union.

The world is closely connected via communications and transportation but is dangerously divided by nationalism and cultural differences. American presidents must balance the difficulties of conducting a war on terrorism when nations fear that information-sharing and military strikes endanger the relationship between each nation and the superpower. The United States has to balance a realistic, pragmatic and sometimes harsh foreign policy with a more cooperative multipolar participation that does not make American actions seem like "bossism." Anti-Americanism rose rapidly after the US invaded Iraq and the world press described Bush with such adjectives as dumb, violent, militaristic, imperialistic, arrogant, unilateral, unbound and lawless. Even while Obama is more temperate and respected in the global arena, presidential rhetoric of noble and ruthless kinds will coexist and the United States will continue both to attract and repel the international community.

History of Foreign Policy

Isolation and Expansion

In 1796, America's first president, George Washington, advised the nation to promote trade while being careful to avoid entangling political agreements: "'Tis our true policy to steer clear of permanent Alliances with any portion of the foreign world. . . . Our detached and distant situation invites and enables us to pursue a different course" (Washington, 1796). In his first inaugural address, America's third president, Thomas Jefferson, soothed fears stemming from the French Revolution and the competition between France and Britain by stating that America desired a policy of "peace, commerce, and honest friendship with all nations, entangling alliances with none." In common with many of his successors, even while Jefferson espoused isolationist sentiments, his actions were interventionist. In 1801, Jefferson used US marines to wage war against the Barbary Coast pirates who were raiding shipping lanes north of Algiers and, in 1803, he doubled the size of the nation by agreeing to purchase the Louisiana territory from Napoleon. Expansion westward held the symbolic and real function of withdrawing from the Old World toward a new frontier.

Americans have never seen themselves as imperialists, maintaining a great capacity for myopia to Indians and others who occupied land they desired for themselves. In 1821 future president John Quincy Adams said that while America everywhere opposes tyranny and supports new democracies, "she goes not abroad, in search of monsters to destroy" (quoted in Daalder and Lindsay, 2004: 3). As early as 1823, President James Monroe established a touchstone of American foreign policy by issuing the Monroe Doctrine to claim a sphere of influence and hegemony over the Americas, closing them to further European colonization. Rapidly, the nation extended its boundaries to the Pacific Ocean.

During the Civil War, Abraham Lincoln insisted that the fate of global liberty rested on the outcome of that war when "this nation, under God, shall have a new birth of freedom – and that government of the people, by the people, for the people, shall not perish from the earth." Lincoln's claim of American exceptionalism has long echoes in the American imagination with its "city upon a hill" mission to save the world. Lincoln's sentiment is often invoked by presidents, as George W. Bush did in his first inaugural address: "The stakes for America are never small. If our country does not lead the cause of freedom, it will not be led."

In the 1890s the US competed with Europe for overseas territories. The Reverend Josiah Strong preached that commerce always followed the missionary and Captain Alfred Thayer Mahan's book, *The Influence of Sea Power on History* (1890), convinced Congress to build a modern navy. In 1898, President William McKinley ordered a war to liberate Cuba from Spanish control after the US battleship *Maine* exploded in Havana harbor. Secretary of State John Hay lauded "that splendid little war" which lasted three months but made America a world power. With the peace, the United States established a protectorate over Cuba and gained Guam, Puerto Rico and, after a three-year land war with Filipino nationalists in which 2,000 Americans and 200,000 Filipinos died, the Philippines. McKinley used the US presence in Asia to force Japan, Russia and the European powers to allow free trade – the "Open Door" – in China.

The twentieth century witnessed the rise of America as both superpower and empire. President Theodore Roosevelt was an enthusiastic imperialist who intervened often in Latin America. His Corollary to the Monroe Doctrine made the United States an international police power which would maintain order in – and keep Europeans out of – the Western Hemisphere. Where the Monroe Doctrine had pledged American power to ensure sovereignty for American nations, the Roosevelt Corollary committed the United States to intervene in its neighbors' affairs. Roosevelt used gunboat and dollar diplomacy to establish an ambiguous policy combining imperialism and isolationism.

A World Power

When war erupted in Europe in August 1914, a deeply-divided American citizenry mostly insisted that the war was a foreign matter. President Woodrow Wilson declared US neutrality and campaigned for re-election on the slogan "He Kept US Out of War." But Germany's use of unrestricted submarine warfare and Wilson's massive propaganda effort "to make the world safe for democracy," put American soldiers in France in late 1917. The next year, at the Paris Peace Conference, Wilson's "Fourteen Points" offered a way to secure lasting peace and proposed the establishment of a League of Nations, the rights of national self-determination, free trade, arms reductions and open diplomacy.

But the American people rejected the entangling alliances of Wilsonianism and the Senate refused to ratify the peace treaty or to allow the United States to join the League of Nations. Clearly unprepared for global leadership, America defined its security interests narrowly, restricted them primarily to what a regional power could do, and removed itself as far as possible from European politics. Writer Ernest Hemingway captured the mood of the times: "We were fools to be sucked in once in a European war and we should never be sucked in again" (Hemingway, 1935). To Americans, it seemed that Europeans loved wars and rumors of wars. America was better off going it alone.

With the Great Depression of the 1930s and the supra-nationalist movements in Japan and Germany, Congress passed a series of Neutrality Acts. In 1939, as World War II began, American neutrality became one-sided as President Franklin Roosevelt made executive agreements to ensure that Britain had the necessary supplies to fight Nazi Germany. Roosevelt called the US "the arsenal of democracy" lending and leasing supplies and equipment to those fighting totalitarianism. Even so, America kept its small 185,000-man army at home and refused to sign military alliances with anyone. Suddenly, on 7 December 1941, Japan erased isolationist sentiment overnight by its successful carrier-borne airstrike against the US fleet at Pearl Harbor naval base in Hawaii. The United States fought a two-ocean war, helped its allies defeat Germany, and took the ultimate revenge against Japan by dropping two atomic bombs on Hiroshima and Nagasaki to end the war.

In 1945 two superpowers emerged and an exhausted Europe and divided Asia took the consequences. The United States clearly had the most power – it produced half the world's steel, had a nuclear monopoly, possessed 70 percent of the world's ships and aircraft, and manufactured 50 percent of the world's goods. As the Soviet Union expanded into Eastern Europe and Asia, the United States helped rebuild Japan and consolidated its influence in Western Europe by pumping in billions of dollars through the Marshall Plan. A new type of war developed, a Cold War marked by rivalry, ideological suspicion and military buildups.

The Cold War, 1945–90

For nearly five decades of Cold War, the United States had a well-defined enemy to confront on every issue, anywhere in the world. The contest was ritualized and rule-bound and every encounter became a crisis. Americans generally viewed communism as an evil ideology of godless, totalitarian, anti-democratic, and anti-capitalist actions – an ideology obstructing the spread of freedom, democracy and free trade. As the acknowledged leader of the free world, America not only acted with an arrogance of power, it created consensus to wage wars in distant countries, stifle debate, prop-up right-wing dictatorships, and enroll dozens of allies in the cause of anti-communism. As the Soviet Union countered each move, the superpowers practiced mutual restraint and maintained order in a bipolar world system.

Historian John Gaddis has bluntly stated that the Cold War established a "long peace" by which the industrialized West (including Japan) directed the trade and finances of the global political economy. In fact, the concept of the "West" rose up during the Cold War to define the bloc of nations confronting communism. Mutual security and dependence intertwined the domestic and international affairs of Western Europe and America so tightly that it became difficult to separate national from international interests.

In 1947 President Harry Truman contrasted two ways of life: one free and one enslaving. He stressed the need to contain Soviet expansion in a statement known now as the Truman Doctrine: "It must be the policy of the United States to support free peoples who are resisting attempted subjugation by armed minorities or by outside pressures." Truman enacted a policy of "containment" to stop Soviet expansionism. America thrust itself into the internal affairs of third world nations, a role that meant high defense expenditures and a large military financed by tax dollars. That same year, 1947, the National Security Act created the National Security Council (NSC), Central Intelligence Agency (CIA), and Department of Defense (DOD).

Events accelerated. In 1948 when the Soviets tried to seize Berlin by blockading all land routes, only a massive airlift by American and British cargo planes kept West Berlin in allied hands. Truman authorized the Marshall Plan, spending $15 billion in Europe over the next three years to provide humanitarian aid, tie the economies of the West into a common market, provide a market for American surpluses and dampen the appeal of communism. The General Agreement on Tariffs and Trade (GATT) helped stabilize currency rates, pushed free trade, and made the US the world's banker. In 1949, the Chinese Civil War ended with victory for Mao Zedong, the Soviets exploded an atomic bomb, and the 12 nations (Belgium, Canada, Denmark, France, Great Britain, Iceland, Italy, Luxembourg, Netherlands, Norway, Portugal, United States) of the North Atlantic Treaty Organization (NATO) promised that an attack against a member nation would be considered an attack against them all. The next year an internal memorandum, NSC-68, put American power at the core of the Western military coalition and asked Congress to quadruple military spending. That same year, an effort by North Koreans to reunite their country with South Korea sent UN – mostly US – troops into a hot war that cost 33,000 American lives and 103,000 wounded and a combined 2.5 million Korean and Chinese casualties. The entry of China on the side of North Korea escalated fears of communism and created a new urgency for a more powerful thermonuclear weapon, the hydrogen bomb.

In 1953, with an armistice in Korea, President Dwight D. Eisenhower decided that the Truman Doctrine did not go far enough. Liberation policy replaced containment and included "roll back," "massive retaliation" and "brinksmanship." The United States would help to liberate countries lost to communism. If any country attacked the US or its allies, it would be met with overwhelming military might, to include atomic weaponry, and the United States would accept the risk of taking enemies to the brink of nuclear war and beyond. In hindsight, all this was a change of rhetoric rather than reality. But the arms race was real. The politics of nuclear deterrence depended less on conventional armies – and potential casualties – and more on the fearsome technology of long-range rockets, bombers and submarine-based atomic weapons which provided "more bang for the buck."

The Soviet Union accelerated its own nuclear programs, created the Warsaw Pact (WP) in 1955, and launched a space satellite named Sputnik in 1957. Still, there were rules to the bipolar world, and when the USSR invaded Hungary in 1956 and Czechoslovakia in 1968, the US declined to intervene in what it saw as an internal WP matter. Nations outside WP and NATO, however, were legitimate objects of interference, including Iran, Guatemala, Taiwan, and Vietnam. In 1961 the Soviet Union built a wall in Berlin that became a visible symbol of the Cold War division of peoples and ideologies. The world shivered under threats of massive retaliation and mutual assured destruction (MAD) whereby any nuclear strike by one superpower against the other would result in a complete annihilation of both sides.

In October 1962, after the United States discovered Soviet missiles in Cuba, the superpowers raced to the brink of nuclear war, launching bombers and positioning navies with atomic weapons ready for firing. Clearly an international crisis, the Cuban Missile Crisis was also a domestic crisis challenging the American sense of security in North America and showing the nation's vulnerability. Having frightened the world and themselves before backing down, President John F. Kennedy and Soviet leader Nikita Khrushchev, and their successors, signed a series of test ban treaties and arms limitations agreements, even while they continued to build weapons of mass destruction. Military planners concluded that a more "flexible response" using conventional weapons and tactics was necessary.

Vietnam

After World War II, nationalist movements in developing countries wrested control away from colonial powers. American involvement in Vietnam began in the 1940s as a way to keep France in the Western coalition and away from the allure of communism. When the forces of Ho Chi Minh defeated the French army at Dienbienphu in 1954, the United States intervened, supported the division of Vietnam into North and South and financed the South. Politicians expounded a "domino theory" that if one nation fell to communism it would create a chain reaction as others fell in turn.

In his inaugural address in 1960, Kennedy declared: "Let every nation know, whether it wishes us well or ill, that we shall pay any price, bear any burden, meet any hardship, support any friend, oppose any foe, in order to assure the survival and the success of liberty." After the assassination of Kennedy in 1963, a more cautious Lyndon Johnson told the public, "We are not about to send American boys nine or ten thousand miles away from home to do what Asian boys ought to be doing for themselves" (quoted in Tindall and Shi, 1996: 1417). By 1965, Johnson reversed himself, took up Kennedy's challenge and sent the first US combat troops to Vietnam. In 1969, President Richard Nixon had 543,000 soldiers in country in a war in which 2.5 million Americans served and 58,000 died (Illustration 9.1). A peace treaty in 1973 allowed the US to withdraw, while Nixon claimed victory in achieving "peace with honor." Whether or not the US should have intervened in Vietnam remains contentious.

The impact of the Vietnam loss cannot be overstated. With the failure to win the war, the revelations that they had been misled, and skyrocketing inflation, Americans lost faith in their ability to control world events. Toward the end of the war, Nixon cited the loss of national consensus and the need for a new approach: "America cannot – and will not – conceive all the plans, design all the programs, execute all the decisions, and undertake all the defense of the free nations of the world" (quoted in Kegley and Wittkopf, 1996: 48).

Nixon and Secretary of State Henry Kissinger pursued detente and trade agreements with Russia, entering into an Anti-Ballistic Missile (ABM) Treaty, Strategic Arms Limitations Talks (SALT I), and initiating a joint space mission. Nixon explained the "friendship" as containment in that simultaneous overtures to China created a more stable world. Europeans, who had never liked the bipolar division of the world, now fretted over a bipolar cooperation by superpowers who made global decisions without consulting them.

A Crisis of Confidence

President Jimmy Carter (1976–80) rejected both containment and liberation, focusing instead on a liberal human rights policy and hoping

Illustration 9.1 Vietnam War Memorial, Washington, DC

Americans favor monuments to national sacrifice. The polished black marble wall with the names of over 58,000 American servicemen and women who died in the service of their country in Vietnam is among the most visited sites in the national capital, a city crowded with marble and bronze statues, gigantic memorial buildings – such as the Lincoln Memorial – and Arlington National Cemetery. The names tell a story of immigration diversity and the flowers and flag have been left behind in commemoration of personal loss.

(Russell Duncan)

to normalize relations with the Soviet Union by downplaying the threat of communist expansion, which he saw as illusory. The attention of the world focused on the continued violence between Israel and Egypt following their 1973 war, the quadrupling of energy prices, the Soviet invasion of Afghanistan in 1979 and the 1979 overthrow of the Shah of Iran by Islamic fundamentalists, who complicated matters by holding 50 Americans hostage in Tehran for over a year. Carter declared Middle Eastern oil vital to American security interests and issued his Carter Doctrine that the United States would intervene militarily to protect the region. His threat was coupled with his greatest triumph. Through private talks with Israel's Menachem Begin and Egypt's Anwar Sadat, Carter helped bring an end to the 30-year-long Egyptian–Israeli conflict.

But Carter's inability to free the hostages seemed to the public just the latest in the series of conspicuous failures by their leaders and played a large part in the election of his successor, the oldest man ever to be elected to the nation's highest office, the former actor, governor of California, and super-patriot who once testified that Hollywood was full of communists – Ronald Reagan. Reagan believed in the myth of America as "still a magnet for all who must have freedom, for all the pilgrims from all the lost places who are hurtling through the darkness towards home" (Reagan, 1989: 97). He held the Soviets personally responsible for the problems of the world, endorsed liberation, referred to the USSR as "the evil empire," promised to help "freedom fighters" everywhere and vowed never to compromise with terrorists. When the public later learned that the Reagan administration had approved a secret arms deal with Iran and that the money from the arms sale had been funneled – in direct violation of specific Congressional prohibition – to "Contras" in Nicaragua who were trying to overthrow the communist Sandinista government, Reagan denied knowing anything about that.

The End of the Cold War

Reagan frightened the world by acting unilaterally. He expanded presidential power in foreign policy and his "Reaganomics" economic policy created huge deficits and made the US the world's largest debtor nation. Reagan pressured NATO to deploy cruise missiles and sophisticated rocket delivery systems by threatening to decouple the US from Western Europe. He showcased American military muscle by doubling defense spending and promoting a "Star Wars" Strategic Defense Initiative (SDI) of putting nuclear weapons and lasers in space. He sent US marines into Beirut (1983), Grenada (1983), and launched an airstrike against Libya (1986). Reagan also stopped American payments to the United Nations and rejected World Court jurisdiction in the case of Nicaragua. After years of warming, the Cold War got colder.

Then in 1986, after Afghanistan proved to be the "Russian Vietnam" as the fight against Islamic fundamentalists bankrupted the Soviet Union, President Mikhail Gorbachev reached out to Reagan, who quickly reciprocated. Reagan claimed victory for his unilateral actions when, just after the election of George Bush in 1988, the Warsaw Pact disintegrated. Quickly, fantastically, the Berlin Wall fell, Germany reunited, Hungary and Poland threw off communism and the Soviet Union broke apart. The Cold War ended on 19 November 1990 when Gorbachev and Bush signed the Charter of Paris, and declared that the East and West would no longer be adversaries.

The New World Order

Throughout the 1990s, the United States was a superpower in search of a coherent foreign policy and a national interest to promote (Huntington, 1999). Many of America's closest European allies worried of the dual possibility of abandonment and dominance. NATO was established as the cornerstone of the Atlantic alliance when it seemed a permanent division of Europe was likely, but with the growing power of the European Union, and without the Cold War to unite them, Americans and Europeans have been described as fundamentally different in world views. Conservative analyst Robert Kagan explained: "Europeans see Americans as cowboys, belligerent and crude; Americans dismiss Europeans as decadent, spent and weak-willed" (Kagan quoted in Schmemann, 2003). Yet, the war on terror, the global economic crisis and the election of a new US president maintains the alliance known as the West.

In 2009, the United States maintained preeminence in every arena of power: military, economic, cultural, and technological. This primacy is likely to continue well into the twenty-first century; but primacy is not the same as hegemony. America cannot realize its ambitions without the tolerance or support of regional powers. Confronted with resurgent nationalism, ethnic conflict and religious fundamentalism, the US leadership role is problematic as any forceful action brings cries of "imperialism" and any inaction is condemned as indifference. Having jumped as it did during World War II from geographical isolation to superpower status, the United States has no real experience in dealing with equals. An inertia of power makes lesser roles difficult. The world also wonders about the wisdom of destroying American primacy because the balance of power approach did not work before or after the First World War. The two likeliest successors to American dominance, India and China, are so unlike the West that Europe prefers US primacy. Additionally, any balancing of power necessitates significant increases in military spending for nations that have historically placed emphases on other priorities while the US picked up the tab.

When the Cold War ended, President George Bush presented a globalist view: "We stand today at a unique and extraordinary moment. . . . A new world order can emerge . . . a world in which nations recognize the shared responsibility for freedom and justice, a world where the strong respect the weak" (quoted in McGrew, 2000a: 216). America would lead, Bush said, but in a multilateral way as a superpower with support from the leading regional powers of Germany and France in Europe, Japan, China, and India in Asia, and Brazil in South America. There is no regional power in Africa, although South Africa's mineral wealth and nuclear capability give it some authority. Russia and Britain remain key players on the world stage and, therefore, must be consulted by the United States in nearly every situation requiring military intervention.

In response to Iraq's expansionist thrust into Kuwait in 1990, Bush achieved a consensus – including Arab states and Russia – before sending the largest expeditionary force since World War II into the Gulf. "Operation Desert Storm" was a 100-day-long war fought primarily by United States troops and managed by the Chairman of the Joint Chiefs of Staff, General Colin Powell. The "Powell Doctrine" declared that any intervention by US troops be predicated on a threat to American strategic interests, that overwhelming force be used to accomplish results with the least risk to American lives, and that there be a clear timetable for the withdrawal of US soldiers. Iraq clearly lost the war but Saddam Hussein remained in power, committed atrocities in the killing of ethnic and religious minorities who disagreed with him, and put up roadblocks to UN inspectors trying to determine whether or not Iraq continued to research and build chemical, biological and nuclear weapons of mass destruction.

Enlargement and Engagement

In the 1990s, Americans hoped for a "peace dividend" and a safer, multilateral world with a mingling of cultures and without ideological conflicts (Kagan, 2007). President Clinton understood that economic policy is tied to national security and the increased meshing of international and domestic – "intermestic" – markets has created interdependence and interpenetration on a global scale. Clinton and the country were reluctant to spend American blood in conflicts where US interests were ill-defined. Called "zero casualty" or "Vietnam syndrome," this attitude surfaced during the 1990s in such flashpoints as Palestine, Somalia, Rwanda, Bosnia, Kosovo and Macedonia.

Americans often believe they are being used and complain that Europeans are not bearing the burden of a "New Europe," citing as proof the EU failures to check Russian power or the reluctance to send forces into peacekeeping or war situations. Europeans answer that the United States should pay the $2 billion it owes to the UN (Global Policy Forum, 2009). Defense spending is another contentious issue. The European unwillingness to expand defense budgets constrains their capacity for independent action and leaves them uncomfortably dependent on US forces to project power. In 2008, France and Britain spent half of all the defense expenditures among European NATO members, but most European nations kept spending levels at less than 2 percent of GDP. In 2009, predictions for US spending is $590 billion (4 percent of GDP) compared to Europe's collective $280 billion (Defense Update, 2009).

Clinton accepted the Powell Doctrine while articulating his own "enlargement and engagement" policy. In his first inaugural address Clinton rejected neo-isolationism while using the exceptionalist argument that "America must continue to lead the world we did so much to make. . . . Our mission is timeless." Stressing geo-economics, Clinton focused on the importance of the new technological and political trends of worldwide internet access, democratization, vast migration, and free markets implicit in the recasting of GATT into the World Trade Organization (WTO). The central tenets of Clinton's foreign policy involved American aid to nations transitioning to democracy and embracing free markets.

As for engagement, Clinton stressed humanitarian intervention to prevent genocide and other catastrophes even if no strategic interests exist: "Whether you live in Africa, or Central Europe, or any other place, if somebody comes after civilians and tries to kill them *en masse* because of their race, their ethnic background, or their religion, and it's within our power to stop it, we will stop it. We should not countenance genocide or ethnic cleansing anywhere in the world" (quoted in Korb, 2000). This stated policy lacked real commitment, even if the US did finally attempt to stop the ethnic cleansing in

Bosnia and Kosovo once it became clear that Europeans would not intervene. The United States remained in Bosnia until late 2004, when it ended its nine-year military peacekeeping role.

Clinton did nothing to stop the genocide of half a million Tutsis in Rwanda. Bush's earlier use of American troops in Somalia, with the televised footage of a pilot being dragged naked behind a jeep, prompted Americans to demand that the troops be withdrawn. With a glance at US opinion polls, Clinton backed away from any engagement that might lead to such an incident. Even though a major intervention in Rwanda would have presented massive logistical problems and costs, the fact is that US policy-makers have done very little to stop the slaughter because public support withers if no strategic interests or strong cultural ties exist. In 1999 the US did not respond to the civil war in East Timor, and the decade-long war in Sudan, which Secretary of State Powell called "a genocide" in 2002, continues.

Clinton acted primarily in the Middle East. In his first week in office in 1993, Clinton ordered a cruise missile attack against the palace and military centers in Baghdad in an effort to kill Saddam Hussein, who had been linked to an assassination attempt on former President Bush. For the next eight years, Clinton approved thousands of military flights into Iraqi airspace and hundreds of retaliatory strikes were made against "perceived threats." In 1996, Clinton sent a strike against Osama bin Laden's terrorist command center in Afghanistan. He also supported economic sanctions against Iraq, Libya, Cuba and Iran.

In 2000, Clinton went to North Korea and Vietnam to soothe long-term hostilities and advance business. The fact that Asian immigration and trade to the United States is at an all time high helps US interests in Asia, linking families and cultures in transnational ways. The Philippines, Malaysia, Singapore and Thailand are major trading partners. Japan and South Korea continue to be two of America's staunchest allies. The next superpower could be China, a country growing in economic prowess and accounting for one-fifth of the world's population. Cold War tensions linger, but appeasement has worked better than confrontation and economic punishment. China has increased military spending and manpower and has an ambitious space program with the stated goal of establishing a base on the moon. The Chinese nuclear arsenal of around 250 warheads – of which 20 could reach the United States – pales in comparison to America's 6,500 deployed warheads – or Russia's 5,600 (*NYT Almanac*, 2005: 494). Differences over Taiwan, Tibet, human rights, the selling of nuclear material to Pakistan, currency manipulation, and the ownership of intellectual property continue to be major issues as China's relationship with the United States is competitive and adversarial. At the same time, the two countries depend on each other for economic power. In 2000 Clinton signed a permanent trade and benefits agreement with China; the next year, the United States spent nearly $40 billion on Chinese imports. American corporate investment is active in the Chinese manufacturing sector and, as an example of American business – and cultural – influence, a Hong Kong Disneyland opened in 2006. And because China is firmly in favor of modernization over tradition, it is generally cooperative with other modern states, including the US, Russia, Japan, the EU, Brazil and the other great powers – even if national ambition and ideological differences make confrontations inevitable.

The Bush Administration

The world often depicts US political leaders as unsophisticated in international dealings. In the twenty-first century, many worried as much about a "rogue superpower" as they did about rogue nations or terrorists. For some, the Bush administration was marked by a unilateral and muscular approach and a rigidity that verged on hubris. Foreign policy realist Robert Kagan calls this a mirage whereby "Many prefer to believe the world is in turmoil not because it is in turmoil but because Bush made it so by destroying the new hopeful era. And when Bush leaves, it can return once again to the way it was" (Kagan, 2007).

On 16 February 2001, in just his third week in office, Bush authorized a strike against Iraqi air defense forces to keep the pressure on Saddam Hussein. The airstrike sent a message to the world that while he might be inexperienced in foreign affairs, he would not be timid. Bush reinforced the perception of toughness by picking an experienced set of advisors. He selected his father's secretary of defense, Dick Cheney, as his vice-president, took Ford's former secretary of defense, Donald Rumsfeld, as secretary of defense, and former General Colin Powell, as secretary of state. The world pondered the choices of hardliners Cheney and Rumsfeld, and, as if to demonstrate its fears by an action equal to a no-confidence vote, the United Nations in May 2001 removed the United States from its seat on the Human Rights Commission, a seat it had held since 1947. In part, Bush angered the world by his announcement that he would not support the Kyoto treaty on global warming and that the US would put its national interests above global compromises. The US Congress quickly voted to withhold $244 million of an already agreed upon monetary payment to the UN (Eilperin, 2001).

11 September 2001

By mid-2001, terrorism was recognized as a general threat to world peace and a particular threat to US interests. The number of anti-US attacks, most of them small-scale without casualties, rose from 169 in 1999 to 200 in 2000 (AP, 2001a). Incidents such as the first bombing of the World Trade Center in New York in 1993, the attacks on the US embassies in Kenya and Tanzania in 1998 and of the US destroyer *Cole* in Aden in 2000, were bold and frightening. Congress formed a National Commission on Terrorism which reported its findings in *Countering the Changing Threat of International Terrorism* (2000).

The report concluded that because of its superpower status, the US would be the target of an increasing number of attacks. While Iran, Afghanistan, Iraq, Libya and Syria continued to sponsor terrorism, the new threat consisted of individuals and groups who were "less dependent on state sponsorship and are instead, forming loose, transnational affiliations based on religious or ideological affinity and a common hatred of the United States" (US Congress, 2000: 3). Osama bin Laden's Al Qaeda network and the fundamentalist Islamic Taliban government in Afghanistan were highlighted. Bin Laden, a Saudi who had been trained and used by the CIA for an earlier role, turned into a radical jihadist, encouraging terrorism against Americans worldwide, hating Israel and determining to remove Western influences from the Middle East. The Commission called for immediate action and coordination of all sanctions and intelligence communities, recognizing that with over one million visitors legally entering the US daily and with thousands of foreign students enrolled in universities, the problem was enormous (AP, 2001a).

On 11 September 2001, a shockwave swept the world as Al Qaeda terrorists hijacked and crashed four commercial airliners into the twin towers of the World Trade Center in New York City, the Pentagon building in Washington, DC, and, a cornfield in Pennsylvania. People worldwide watched live coverage as planes hit the buildings, people jumped to their deaths, and the towers collapsed into the streets. 3,025 people from 80 countries died. Bush responded quickly by assembling a global coalition against terror, even while his rhetoric of a "crusade," and putting a "Wanted, dead or alive" bounty on Osama bin Laden alarmed many people (Knowlton, 2001). As part of his effort to calm

Americans, Bush called for the immediate establishment of a cabinet-level position, the Department of Homeland Security (DHS). The mission of the DHS would be "to develop and coordinate the implementation of a comprehensive national strategy to secure the United States from terrorist threats and attacks" (Bush, 2001).

The United States began a diplomatic attack on the Taliban, with the support of Pakistan, Russia, and Afghan warlords, before it began a military bombing and search-and-destroy mission in Afghanistan. At the same time, Bush authorized millions of tons of food and clothing to be distributed among Afghan civilians and increased economic aid to Pakistan and Russia. With overwhelming international support, US forces routed the Taliban and, quickly, a democratic election gave Afghanistan its first popularly-elected president. But the Taliban proved resilient and Osama bin Laden has not been located in his mountainous hiding place. By January 2009, with insurgency on the rise and 644 total US solders killed, Obama's national security team insisted that Afghanistan is "much tougher than Iraq." Commanding General David Petreaus said that the situation had "deteriorated" and warned: "Afghanistan has been known over the years as the graveyard of empires. . . . We cannot take that history lightly" (Whitlock, 2009). President Obama ordered more airstrikes, shifted troops and resources from Iraq, and pledged to double the number of US soldiers in country to 60,000 (Colvin, 2009). Many critics are warning of another Vietnam.

The War on Terror

Looking at the internal foreign policy debate on the day before 11 September, experts viewed the situation five ways, ranked here by order of support. Advocates for a "benign globalization" saw an increasingly secular, prosperous, liberal, and peaceful world. Second came the idea of a "power transition" which consolidated US and Western power by blocking the rise of the next likely superpower, China. Others pushed for American "unilateral preeminence," a go-it-alone approach of increasing power. The fourth position advanced a "clash of civilizations" thesis. The least-argued position warned of "domestic vulnerability" with terrorist threats to American cities (Bobrow, 2001).

On 11 September, the ranking was overturned and a fusion of positions three, four and five fueled US foreign policy. Huntington's "clash of civilizations" thesis that a modernizing world did not mean a Westernizing world and that culturally-conscious nationalism was rising, particularly in Asia, Africa and the Middle East, continues to have strong support among policymakers. Huntington dismissed notions of a New World Order or *Pax Americana* and predicted a religious and cultural conflict (Huntington, 1996). Since 2001, hiding somewhere in Afghanistan, probably, bin Laden continues his efforts to free the Middle East of Western influences. Overwhelmingly, Muslims do not support terrorism, but most are angry over the continuing Israeli occupation of Palestine (divided into the West Bank and Gaza Strip) – for which they blame the United States. Some analysts agree with Huntington that the Cold War was insignificant when compared to the centuries-long struggle between the West and Islam, or maybe, "the West against the Rest" (Kaplan, 2001).

Across the Islamic world, the Israeli-Palestinian conflict continues to rake the coals of anti-Americanism and strengthens Al Qaeda. The US is vulnerable to the charges that everything Israel does is right and everything Arabs do is wrong. The Bush administration points out that American soldiers were deployed (and died) in non-Israeli places like Bosnia, Somalia, and Afghanistan, proving that the US is not anti-Muslim. The tsunami relief effort of 2005, in an overwhelmingly Muslim area of the world in South Asia, had Secretary of State Colin Powell pleading for the Islamic world to see "American generosity" and "American values in action" and not to be so hostile toward the United States (Illustration 9.2) (quoted in Friedman, 2005). But the unfinished war in Iraq, the rising power of Iran, and continued grievances over Israel keep passions inflamed.

On the other hand, as historian Robert Lifton points out, with an attack on its homeland "the United States became an aggrieved superpower, a giant violated and made vulnerable, which no superpower can permit" (Lifton, 2003). President Bush declared that the conflict would go on indefinitely. In a war without end, the division of power and constitutional freedoms are jeopardized by concentrating political power in the executive branch. Vice President Richard Cheney, long a believer in enhanced presidential powers, used his influence with Bush to justify any response, legal and illegal, to oppose the dangers facing the United States. Bush was tough and aggressive, but he was more "the enabler" than the architect of what was immediately labeled the "war on terror" (Brinkley, 2008a). In wartime, the president, his advisors, the military, and the intelligence agencies operate with more secrecy and the people, fearing attacks, accept it. The American government continues to tighten domestic surveillance, profiles Muslims as potential terrorists, arrests thousands of people on

Illustration 9.2 Tsunami Relief Effort

On 26 December 2004, the biggest tsunami in a century devastated coastal towns, killed an estimated 250,000 people, and made millions homeless in Asian countries bordering the Indian Ocean. An American military task force took part in the international relief effort. This photograph shows US military helicopters leaving the deck of the USS *Abraham Lincoln* to ferry food and medicine to areas isolated by the destruction. In mid-January 2005, the US had $20 billion dollars of combat equipment (20 warships, 90 aircraft) and 13,000 soldiers on site, plus the $5.6 million daily costs of deployment (Shanker and Brooke, 2005).

(US Navy-AFP/Getty Images)

the flimsiest excuses of immigration violations, and seeks tighter coordination of security efforts.

Six weeks after the 11 September attacks, Cheney prodded a fearful and hurried Congress to pass the USA Patriot Act, which is short for the remarkably Orwellian title: "Uniting and Strengthening America by Providing Appropriate Tools Required to Intercept and Obstruct Terrorism Act of 2001." Renewed in 2006 with only minor changes, the Patriot Act revokes legal barriers to permit information sharing among federal and state agencies. More troubling, the Patriot Act gives wide latitude to law enforcement officers and military police for the arrest and treatment of suspected terrorists. The act sets aside long-standing legal protections of civil liberties to allow police officials to arrest suspects, snoop, secretly enter people's homes without notice, freeze bank assets, have access to which books a person borrows from a public library or buys from a bookstore, and compile dossiers of private individuals – indefinitely, in secret and without legal remedy. The government can open private letters, read e-mail, and request personal records from any source, including medical records, and it is a crime for the source to notify the person whose records have been investigated. Clearly, this is dangerous to a democratic society when the power of the government to keep secrets increases and private lives of the people are made more transparent. Along with the ubiquitous phrase "war on terror," the Patriot Act has promoted the emergence of a culture of fear that has been reinforced by the mass media and Hollywood depictions of Arab terrorists. Things might have been different. On the day after 9/11 when the French newspaper *Le Monde* summarized a global solidarity with the United States in its headline "We Are All Americans," there was a chance to form an international alliance, including Muslims, against extremism and terror. Instead, the Bush administration kept war and fear of another attack prominent, thus promoting hysteria and paranoia (Brzezinski, 2007).

Cheney and Bush approved some of the most disturbing and extraordinary tactics in the history of the United States, including a systematic and widespread use and defense of torture in secret prisons worldwide (Mayer, 2008). In Iraq, the abuse of Iraqi detainees by American soldiers inside Abu Ghraib prison was universally condemned as an abuse of power and a violation of the long-standing Geneva Convention rules on the treatment of prisoners of war. Photographs posted online of humiliating acts – including sadistic torture and pornographic poses – scandalized the world. Since the start of the war in Iraq, nearly 750 suspects have been jailed under secret and harsh conditions in the US military detention camp at Guantánamo Bay, Cuba, (Baldauf, 2008). Bush and Cheney denied violations of international law, snubbed the Supreme Court and world opinion, and ignored or silenced opponents in the CIA, FBI, Justice Department, Congress and the military. CIA interrogations were sometimes brutal, especially with the simulated-drowning of prisoners known as waterboarding, and in what is known as "extraordinary rendition" – the kidnapping of suspects who are then turned over to other governments, mostly in the Middle East, for questioning and torture (Mayer, 2008).

Citing the need for secrecy to ensure national security, the Bush administration denied the prisoners any access to the courts. This clearly violates the American Constitution, but, historically, the Judicial branch cedes power to the Executive branch when the issue is one of national security. Still, in June 2008, the US Supreme Court ruled that "the laws and Constitution are designed to survive, and remain in force, in extraordinary times" (Robinson, 2008). The Court ordered Bush to respect the law and to acknowledge the legal rights of the detainees, instead of claiming that enemy combatants have no legal rights. Bush ignored the ruling and order. When they are scared, Americans historically have demanded fewer checks on presidential power. Explaining this trend, Ignatieff said, "majorities care less about deprivations of liberty that harm minorities than they do about their own security" (quoted in Lewis, 2004). The US Constitution has never been adequately able to protect civil liberties against national security overzealousness in time of war.

Three days after his inauguration, Obama issued an executive order that "The United States will not torture." He began to reverse Bush administration detention and torture policies by ordering the closing of Guantánamo Bay prison within a year, banning many "enhanced" interrogation methods, transferring the 245 remaining prisoners to facilities within the United States, and promising speedy adjudication of their cases (Warrick and DeYoung, 2009).

Since 2004, foreign visitors entering the United States have been fingerprinted and photographed at the 115 airports and 14 seaports serving international passengers. This is in addition to the normal customs procedures of checking names of all arrivals against the FBI electronic database of former and at-large criminals and terrorists. Also, all passengers leaving the United States are confronted with inspectors, metal detectors and, sometimes, strip searches. While these procedures have increased the general European belief that the US is overreacting to the threat of terrorism, support for even tighter measures has come from large majorities in Britain, Russia and other countries (Pew, 2004).

In December 2004, Congress passed a law to reorganize and help unify the intelligence-gathering community under the direction of the Department of Homeland Security (DHS), a department created in November 2002 to coordinate federal and state resources against future attacks. The FBI, CIA, NSC and Defense Intelligence Agency (DIA) have pledged closer cooperation in analyzing information. Critics of the DHS warn that "Big Brother" will take away the rights of the people and create an atmosphere of distrust similar to the "Red Scares" which followed both world wars. To many civil libertarians, the calls for even more stringent vigilance threatens freedom of movement and speech. Other Americans bristle at this criticism of the government and respond with calls of "America, love it or leave it."

The courts will have to balance freedoms and security interests as excesses of the war on terror continue to confront the Constitution.

The War in Iraq

Insistent that the war in Iraq was part of the war on terror, the Bush administration overturned five decades of US foreign policy of multilateral cooperation with UN, NATO and international law. Bush set aside the doctrines of containment and deterrence to create a new strategic doctrine committing the United States to a unilateral use of military might – something analysts call "anticipatory self-defense" (Schlesinger, 2003) or "defensive imperialism" (Johnson, 2003). The Bush Doctrine of preventive war and pre-emption played into the psychological trauma many Americans felt after the 11 September attacks as the public accepted military actions striking a potential enemy before it could strike the US.

While Bush won the public's support for the war in Iraq, most Americans have always seen the use of the military abroad as a possible threat to domestic tranquility. As the US neutrality stances in both world wars shows – and with a clear memory of Vietnam – the reason to go to war has to be overwhelmingly in the national interest or to stop a clear and present danger. The attack of 11 September gave the administration the opportunity to present a case against an old enemy. Actually, two prominent members of the Bush team, Deputy Defense Secretary Paul Wolfowitz (a radical conservative) and Secretary of Defense Donald Rumsfeld (a patriotic nationalist), joined 16 others in a letter to President Clinton in 1998 "arguing that a regime change in Iraq 'needs to become the aim of American foreign policy' " (quoted in Schlesinger, 2003). With Saudi fundamentalists among the strongest supporters of Al Qaeda, a secular, democratic Iraq at peace with Israel seemed the most likely base for US power in the Middle East. But this reason would not "sell the war."

While the search for bin Laden and the war in Afghanistan continued, the Bush administration began to make the case for an invasion of Iraq and the deposal of a dictator: Iraq was a breeding ground for terrorists, Saddam Hussein was "certainly" connected with Al Qaeda, and Iraq had or soon would have weapons of massive destruction to use against its neighbors and the United States (Powers, 2003). Bush announced "a new policy: a forward strategy of freedom in the Middle East. . . . The advance of freedom is the calling of our time. It is the calling of our country" (Bush, 2003). Many analysts disagreed with Bush and in cities across America, protest demonstrations against the war held to the theme: "No War For Oil." Even those critics who acknowledged that Bush might be right about the reasons, questioned the rush to arms.

From the beginning, most of the world remained unconvinced of the necessity for war, opposing the intervention as a unilateral act of conquest that could further alienate Islamic public opinion and work as a recruiting tool for even more terrorist attacks. America became isolated as the Western alliance split, Russia and China opposed the actions, and a growing anti-Americanism accompanied the official protests by France and Germany and other traditional allies. Anti-war protests worldwide called on Bush to stop. In November 2002 Bush did convince the UN Security Council to vote 15-0 in favor of UN Resolution 1441, warning Iraq that it must comply with UN inspections or face the consequences. By 17 March 2003, unable to get the support of NATO or UN troops, Bush assembled what he called "a coalition of the willing," called the war "Operation Iraqi Freedom," and ordered the attack to begin. The coalition consisted "on paper" of 80 countries, but the US would do the heavy lifting, with Britain, Spain, Denmark, Poland and Japan in supporting roles.

Bush predicted that the Iraqis would welcome the American liberators and that the war could be won at a bargain $60 billion price. The speed of the US attack and the sophisticated weaponry impressed the world as almost everything went smoothly. Secretary Rumsfeld disregarded the advice of many military experts for more troops and armor. Instead, he emphasized what experts call the "theory of rapid dominance" whereby highly mobile, highly informed, flexible forces of "Network-Centric Warfare" bring apocalyptic firepower to bear on many places at once (Danner, 2003). The state-of-the-art American air and ground power quickly routed the Iraqi defenses and on 1 May, a jubilant President Bush landed in a jet fighter on the *USS Abraham Lincoln* under a banner declaring "Mission Accomplished" (see Illustration 4.3). Rumsfeld's plan spectacularly won the stand-up fight, but the postwar plans were woefully inadequate, partly because the US military is a war machine not readily adaptable for peacekeeping operations, partly because of the nature of the civil war, the chaos that followed deposed dictatorship, an insurgency that targeted Americans and the influx of terrorist groups from other countries.

The conflict escalated beyond the ability of US troops to control the situation, even with a constant force of 140,000 soldiers in country, a total deployment of nearly 1.6 million American troops, a cost estimated by some economists at upwards of $3 trillion (Stiglitz and

Bilmes, 2008) and an unprecedented growth in the defense budget, from $267 billion in 2000, to $651 billion in 2009. The capture, trials and deaths of Saddam Hussein and his henchmen, and the discovery of mass graves of hundreds of thousands of Kurdish and Shiite victims of Hussein's rule, did not stop the growing hatred and resistance by average Iraqis to the American occupation. Insurgents created spectacles by beheading foreign soldiers and civilians on the Internet and by setting off suicide bombs in town squares; but off-target US bombing and thousands of incidents between US occupiers, under stress, and the occupied increased tension. Additionally, old grudges among Kurds, Sunnis, and Shiites continue to be acted upon. By January 2009, the total number of Iraqi civilian deaths was estimated at between 100,000 and 1.3 million people while, officially, 4,327 Americans had been killed and 31,004 wounded (Griffis, 2009).

Insisting that the war was a worthy venture because an evil tyrant was removed and another democracy was added to the Middle East, the Bush administration blamed the intelligence community for assuring him that weapons of mass destruction existed. For him, the war was not about oil, revenge, Israel, or domestic politics. George Will analyzed Bush's actions as part of the "messianic impulse" ever-present in liberalism, "a constant of America's national character, and a component of American patriotism" (quoted in Kagan, 2006). Historian Arthur Schlesinger wrote that Bush "dreams of making his place in history by converting the Arab world to representative democracy" (Schlesinger, 2003). Certainly, the effort in Iraq has been the most massive effort at nation building since the days of the Marshall Plan. Describing Bush as a "hotblooded moralist," political scientist Michael Ignatieff added: "Bringing freedom to the Iraqis seems to matter to him, which is why, perhaps, he rushed to Baghdad not caring whether he had a coalition behind him or not (Ignatieff, 2003). Political analyst Michael Lind links the war to the surge and power of neoconservative think tanks like the Heritage Foundation, American Enterprise Institute and Center for Strategic and International Studies: "Neoconservative foreign policy does not reflect business interests in any direct way. The neo-cons are ideologues, not opportunists" (Lind, 2003). President Bush praised the chance to push a "freedom agenda;" his successor has taken a different path.

Responding to the policies of his predecessor, President Barack Obama began his term on January 20, 2009, by clearly stating: "We reject as false the choice between our safety and our ideals." He called on Americans to once again grasp the Jeffersonian respect for the opinions of mankind: "Recall that earlier generations faced down fascism and communism not just with missiles and tanks, but with sturdy alliances and enduring convictions. They understood that our power alone cannot protect us, nor does it entitle us to do as we please." Five weeks later, Obama announced: "By August 31, 2010, our combat mission in Iraq will end" even though 35,000 US "transitional" troops will remain for another year (Baker, 2009).

As his predecessors did, Obama will use both soft and hard power and the United States will continue to attract and repel – a natural phenomenon given the history of dominant and lesser power relationships. Analyst Roger Cohen explained: "That is America's lot, the poisoned fruit of its power. The world looks to it for peace, for prosperity. . . . The burden is an impossible one, and one complicated by all the ambivalence that great power inspires. Even as they look to Washington, countries resent the fact that they are obliged to do so" (Cohen, 2005).

Nationalism and globalization coexist uneasily. The ongoing technological revolutions in communications and transportation ensure that nations and individuals can easily penetrate the borders of other nations. At the same time, resurgent nationalism with its tendency towards cultural ethnocentrism threatens world peace. While modernization has increased secularism, religion and national cultures have proven resilient and dangerous. Interlocking world economies can be dangerous to national stability. Immigrants of vastly different cultures increasingly stand at the doors of industrialized nations, knock to enter, or climb over the walls without permission.

10

Prospects for the Twenty-First Century

The twenty-first century began with a curious presidential election that seemed first to elect Gore, then Bush, then Gore, then Bush. The world watched the spectacle of democracy in America that had jumped its tracks. In the end Bush was inaugurated and in the first months of his presidency announced his opposition to the Kyoto convention on climate change, denied the authority of the International Criminal Court, overthrew the Comprehensive Nuclear Test Ban Treaty and revoked the Anti-Ballistic Missile Treaty with Russia. The world widely agreed that Bush made decisions "based only on US interests" (Kagan, 2008). Then, suddenly, the surreal attacks of 11 September gave the US – and Bush – a narrower mission: national security as pursued by a war in Iraq, a war in Afghanistan, and a global war on terror. The world saw an angry Leviathan, a vengeful hyperpower that pursued its own interests and endangered the world. Seven years later, a bigger war appeared, scarier than all the others, as the global economy began to fail, threatening to eclipse the Great Depression of the 1930s and throw the world into chaos. When asked in early 2009 to list their biggest concerns, Americans skipped past national security, immigration reform, Al Qaeda, and global warming, to put the economic downturn in first place among their fears.

In 2009, the United States enjoyed a renaissance in world opinion by electing a man of mixed ethnicity and race to the world's most powerful office. Barack Obama seemed to defy gravity through his "yes, we can" optimism of renewing America's spirit and to reversing the global malaise. As he broke the ultimate racial barrier, he came to embody the American dream of equality, tolerance and inclusivity. Reporters outside the United States could agree with the exuberance of one of their colleagues: "From Paris to New Delhi to the beaches

Illustration 10.1 Barack Obama and Hugo Chavez

After taking office, President Barack Obama gave his first interview to TV network al-Arabiya. Obama defended this controversial choice by highlighting the importance of meaningful dialogue between the Muslim/Arab world over the Iraq war, Iranian arms procurement and the Palestinian-Israeli conflict. Three months later, Obama warmly greeted and shook hands with President Hugo Chavez of Venezuela, one of America's most vocal critics. Many conservative commentators condemned Obama's interview on *al-Arabiya* and his cordial encounter with Chavez, but Obama emphasized that the way forward was through compromise and mutual respect.

(Marianna Kambon/AP/Press Association Images, 2009)

of Brazil . . . America seemed suddenly more connected to the rest of the world." Nelson Mandela spoke of the "dare to dream of wanting to change the world" and Desmond Tutu said that the election of Obama tells "people of color that for them, the sky is the limit" (Sullivan, 2008). One *Der Spiegel* reporter praised the "self-cleansing" American democracy and celebrated the new president as "a beacon of hope in a crisis-ridden world" (Steingart, 2009). Others proclaimed the coming of the first truly global president, a welcome relief from the narrow nationalism of his predecessor, the man many have called "the most disastrous president in [US] history" (Brinkley, 2008b).

A Glance Backward

The presidency of George Walker Bush is behind us, just over our shoulder in the recent past and any full assessment awaits the passing of time and the verdict of historians. Nevertheless, some comment is unavoidable. As he departed, President Bush gave more exit interviews than any president ever, as he seemed determined to shape his own legacy. He admitted to "intelligence failures" in pursuing the war on terror and war in Iraq, but insisted: "I was a wartime president and war is very exhausting" (quoted in Rich, 2009). Presidents are usually narcissists, but Bush was always too secure in the hubris of his own judgment, proclaiming himself "the decider," and brushing past the reasoned opinions of those who disagreed with him. This often came across as swaggering and reckless, or worse. Given multiple opportunities to mend diplomatic fences or assemble a multilateral force, or compromise to conform to world opinion, Bush often opted for unilateralism and whatever was in America's best interests as he defined them. Generally supported – many say manipulated – by Vice President Richard Cheney, Bush was inflexible once he set a course of action. He was an "imperial" president in a country that believes in democracy and republican virtue.

In the 2008 presidential election his own party found Bush's record unusable and distanced itself from him. By the time the president left office, a January 2009 NBC News/Wall Street Journal poll found that 79 percent of the people had given up on Bush, disapproved of his job performance, and would "not miss him" after he is gone (Rich, 2009). Many applauded the Iraqi journalist who threw his shoes at the president during a press conference in Baghdad the month before he left office (see Illustration 1.4). Declaring that no one is above the law, Paul Krugman, the 2008 Nobel laureate in economics, called on Obama to launch "an investigation of possible crimes by the Bush administration" (Krugman, 2009). Krugman listed the issues of torture, illegal wiretapping, environmental policy, voting rights, "no-bid contracts to politically-connected companies," and the undermining of the Justice Department by illegal appointments as among the most egregious abuses of power. Obama was not inclined to support such an investigation.

A Leap Forward

Overnight, with the election of Obama, world opinion swung favorably to the United States as people around the world anxiously

Illustration 10.2 Secretary of State Hillary Clinton in China

On 21 February 2009, Chinese President Hu Jintao met with Secretary of State Hillary Clinton in the Great Hall of the People in Beijing. Hu stressed deeper and more developed Sino-American relationships. Clinton stressed the need for China and America (Chimerica) to work together to solve the economic crisis. While disagreeing on, but downplaying, the issue of human rights, China and America would work together on improving the three E's: energy, environment and economy.

(Oliver Weiken/AP/Press Association Images, 2009)

watched and waited for positive American leadership. Talk of a "rogue superpower" all but disappeared on the day Obama took office. China, Russia, Japan, Brazil, India, Britain, France, and Germany might seek more power for themselves, but they are also wary of each other and, with Obama as president, accepted the reality that the United States will maintain its relative position as superpower supported by several great powers. Former UN Secretary General Kofi Annan noted "the dramatic change of leadership in the United States of America which I am witnessing with great emotion. . . [is] rightly celebrated around the globe, from the villages of Africa to the chancelleries of Europe" (Annan, 2009). Many nations remain cautious and anti-Americanism will stay strong for some time, especially in the Middle East. But the idea of a non-white president with an African father, who went to school in a Muslim *madrassa* in Indonesia and opposed the war in Iraq from the beginning, works in favor of the United States and broader world community. In his inaugural address, Obama stood up for American values: "We will not apologize for our way of life." He offered to engage those who wanted to damage or destroy the United States: "We will extend a hand if you are willing to unclench your fist." After becoming president, Obama gave his first television interview to the Islamic network *al-Arabiya* and promised to give priority to restoring "respect and partnership" with the Arab/Muslim world by clearly saying: "Americans are not your enemy" (AP, 2009b). Two weeks later Obama dispatched Secretary of State Hillary Clinton to Indonesia, China, South Korea and Japan to emphasize the importance of these regions to his administration (Illustration 10.2).

Much of what Obama will or will not be able to accomplish is linked to the global economy and to whether or not the plethora of economic proposals offered in the first year of his administration can ultimately stave off a repeat of the 1930s Great Depression. His countrymen must not retreat into protectionism and isolation. Obama must keep the nation safe from terrorist attacks. His success as a world leader is also clearly linked to whether he can convince the Arab world to accept him as an honest broker, especially in disputes involving Israel. His success or failure is inherently bound up with the actions of the great powers. The world hopes for a transformative presidency, a new cycle of American history, and the redemption of a dream. As Kofi Annan put it, "Above all, his presidency demonstrates America's extraordinary capacity to renew itself and adapt to a changing world" (Annan, 2009). We await the outcome of such prophecy. Many things can go wrong. Many things can go right.

Appendix: Constitution of the United States

We the People of the United States, in Order to form a more perfect Union, establish Justice, insure domestic Tranquility, provide for the common defense, promote the general Welfare, and secure the Blessings of Liberty to ourselves and our Posterity, do ordain and establish this Constitution for the United States of America.

Article I

Section 1. All legislative Powers herein granted shall be vested in a Congress of the United States, which shall consist of a Senate and House of Representatives.

Section 2. The House of Representatives shall be composed of Members chosen every second Year by the People of the several States, and the Electors in each State shall have the Qualifications requisite for Electors of the most numerous Branch of the State Legislature.

No Person shall be a Representative who shall not have attained to the Age of twenty five Years, and been seven Years a Citizen of the United States, and who shall not, when elected, be an Inhabitant of that State in which he shall be chosen.

Representatives and direct Taxes shall be apportioned among the several States which may be included within this Union, according to their respective Numbers, which shall be determined by adding to the whole Number of free Persons, including those bound to Service for a Term of Years, and excluding Indians not taxed, three fifths of all other Persons. The actual Enumeration shall be made within three Years after the first Meeting of the Congress of the United States, and within every subsequent Term of ten Years, in such Manner as they shall by Law direct. The Number of Representatives shall not exceed one for every thirty Thousand, but each State shall have at Least one Representative; and until such enumeration shall be made, the State of New Hampshire shall be entitled to choose three, Massachusetts eight, Rhode Island and Providence Plantations one, Connecticut five, New-York six, New Jersey four, Pennsylvania eight, Delaware one, Maryland six, Virginia ten, North Carolina five, South Carolina five, and Georgia three.

When vacancies happen in the Representation from any State, the Executive Authority thereof shall issue Writs of Election to fill such Vacancies.

The House of Representatives shall choose their Speaker and other Officers; and shall have the sole Power of Impeachment.

Section 3. The Senate of the United States shall be composed of two Senators from each State, chosen by the Legislature thereof, for six Years; and each Senator shall have one Vote.

Immediately after they shall be assembled in Consequence of the first Election, they shall be divided as equally as may be into three Classes. The Seats of the Senators of the first Class shall be vacated at the Expiration of the second Year, of the second Class at the Expiration of the fourth Year, and of the third Class at the Expiration of the sixth Year, so that one third may be chosen every second Year; and if Vacancies happen by Resignation, or otherwise, during the Recess of the Legislature of any State, the Executive thereof may make temporary Appointments until the next Meeting of the Legislature, which shall then fill such Vacancies.

No Person shall be a Senator who shall not have attained to the Age of thirty Years, and been nine Years a Citizen of the United States, and who shall not, when elected, be an Inhabitant of that State for which he shall be chosen.

The Vice President of the United States shall be President of the Senate, but shall have no Vote, unless they be equally divided.

The Senate shall choose their other Officers, and also a President pro tempore, in the Absence of the Vice President, or when he shall exercise the Office of President of the United States.

The Senate shall have the sole Power to try all Impeachments. When sitting for that Purpose, they shall be on Oath or Affirmation. When the President of the United States is tried the Chief Justice shall preside: And no Person shall be convicted without the Concurrence of two thirds of the Members present.

Judgment in Cases of Impeachment shall not extend further than to removal from Office, and disqualification to hold and enjoy any Office of honor, Trust or Profit under the United States: but the Party convicted shall nevertheless be liable and subject to Indictment, Trial, Judgment and Punishment, according to Law.

Section 4. The Times, Places and Manner of holding Elections for Senators and Representatives, shall be prescribed in each State by the Legislature thereof; but the Congress may at any time by Law make or alter such Regulations, except as to the Places of choosing Senators.

The Congress shall assemble at least once in every Year, and such Meeting shall be on the first Monday in December, unless they shall by Law appoint a different Day.

Section 5. Each House shall be the Judge of the Elections, Returns and Qualifications of its own Members, and a Majority of each shall constitute a Quorum to do Business; but a smaller Number may adjourn from day to day, and may be authorized to compel the Attendance of absent Members, in such Manner, and under such Penalties as each House may provide.

Each House may determine the Rules of its Proceedings, punish its Members for disorderly Behavior, and, with the Concurrence of two thirds, expel a Member.

Each House shall keep a Journal of its Proceedings, and from time to time publish the same, excepting such Parts as may in their Judgment require Secrecy; and the Yeas and Nays of the Members of either House on any question shall, at the Desire of one fifth of those Present, be entered on the Journal.

Neither House, during the Session of Congress, shall, without the Consent of the other, adjourn for more than three days, nor to any other Place than that in which the two Houses shall be sitting.

Section 6. The Senators and Representatives shall receive a Compensation for their Services, to be ascertained by law, and paid out of the Treasury of the United States. They shall in all Cases, except Treason, Felony and Breach of the Peace, be privileged from Arrest during their Attendance at the Session of their respective Houses, and in going to and returning from the same; and for any Speech or Debate in either House, they shall not be questioned in any other Place.

No Senator or Representative shall, during the Time for which he was elected, be appointed to any civil Office under the Authority of the United States, which shall have been created, or the Emoluments whereof shall have been increased during such time; and no Person holding any Office under the United States, shall be a Member of either House during his Continuance in Office.

Section 7. All Bills for raising Revenue shall originate in the House of Representatives; but the Senate may propose or concur with amendments as on other Bills.

Every Bill which shall have passed the House of Representatives and the Senate, shall, before it become a Law, be presented to the President of the United States; If he approve he shall sign it, but if not he shall return it with his Objections to that House in which it shall have originated, who shall enter the Objections at large on their Journal, and proceed to reconsider it. If after such Reconsiderations two thirds of that House shall agree to pass the Bill, it shall be sent, together with the Objections, to the other House, by which it shall likewise be reconsidered, and if approved by two thirds of that House, it shall become a Law. But in all such Cases the Votes of both Houses shall be determined by Yeas and Nays, and the Names of the Persons voting for and against the Bill shall be entered on the Journal of each House respectively. If any Bill shall not be returned by the President within ten Days (Sunday excepted) after it shall have been presented to him, the Same shall be a Law, in like Manner as if he had signed it, unless the Congress by their Adjournment prevent its Return, in which Case it shall not be a Law.

Every Order, Resolution, or Vote to which the Concurrence of the Senate and House of Representatives may be necessary (except on a question of Adjournment) shall be presented to the President of the United States; and before the Same shall take Effect, shall be approved by him, or being disapproved by him, shall be repassed by two thirds of the Senate and House of Representatives, according to the Rules and Limitations prescribed in the Case of a Bill.

Section 8. The Congress shall have Power To lay and collect Taxes, Duties, Imposts and Excises, to pay the Debts and provide for the common Defense and general Welfare of the United States; but all Duties, Imposts and Excises shall be uniform throughout the United States;

To borrow Money on the credit of the United States;

To regulate Commerce with foreign Nations, and among the several States, and with the Indian Tribes;

To establish an uniform Rule of Naturalization, and uniform Laws on the subject of Bankruptcies throughout the United States;

To coin Money, regulate the Value thereof, and of foreign Coin, and fix the Standard of Weights and Measures;

To provide for the Punishment of counterfeiting the Securities and current Coin of the United States;

To establish Post Offices and post Roads;

To promote the Progress of Science and useful Arts, by securing for limited Times to Authors and Inventors the exclusive Right to their respective Writings and Discoveries;

To constitute Tribunals inferior to the supreme Court;

To define and punish Piracies and Felonies committed on the high Seas, and Offenses against the Law of Nations;

To declare War, grant Letters of Marque and Reprisal, and make Rules concerning Captures on Land and Water;

To raise and support Armies, but no Appropriation of Money to that Use shall be for a longer Term than two Years;

To provide and maintain a Navy;

To make Rules for the Government and Regulation of the land and naval Forces;

To provide for calling forth the Militia to execute the Laws of the Union, suppress Insurrections and repel Invasions;

To provide for organizing, arming, and disciplining, the Militia, and for governing such Part of them as may be employed in the Service of the United States, reserving to the States respectively, the Appointment of the Officers, and the Authority of training the Militia according to the discipline prescribed by Congress;

To exercise exclusive Legislation in all Cases whatsoever, over such District (not exceeding ten Miles square) as may, by Cession of particular States, and the Acceptance of Congress, become the Seat of the Government of the United States, and to exercise like Authority over all Places purchased by the Consent of the Legislature of the State in which the Same shall be, for the Erection of Forts, Magazines, Arsenals, dock-Yards, and other needful Buildings; – And

To make all Laws which shall be necessary and proper for carrying into Execution the foregoing Powers, and all other Powers vested by this Constitution in the Government of the United States, or in any Department or Officer thereof.

Section 9. The Migration or Importation of such Persons as any of the States now existing shall think proper to admit, shall not be prohibited by the Congress prior to the Year one thousand eight hundred and eight, but a Tax or duty may be imposed on such Importation, not exceeding ten dollars for each Person.

The Privilege of the Writ of Habeas Corpus shall not be suspended, unless when in Cases of Rebellion or Invasion the public Safety may require it.

No Bill of Attainder or ex post facto Law shall be passed.

No Capitation, or other direct, Tax shall be laid, unless in Proportion to the Census or Enumeration herein before directed to be taken.

No Tax or Duty shall be laid on Articles exported from any State.

No Preference shall be given by any Regulation of Commerce or Revenue to the Ports of one State over those of another; nor shall Vessels bound to, or from, one State, be obliged to enter, clear or pay Duties in another.

No Money shall be drawn from the Treasury, but in Consequence of Appropriations made by Law; and a regular Statement and Account of the Receipts and Expenditures of all public Money shall be published from time to time.

No Title of Nobility shall be granted by the United States: And no Person holding any Office or Trust under them, shall, without the Consent of the Congress, accept of any present, Emolument, Office, or Title, of any kind whatever, from any King, Prince or foreign State.

Section 10. No State shall enter into any Treaty, Alliance, or Confederation; grant Letters of Marque and Reprisal, coin Money; emit Bills of Credit, make any Thing but gold and silver Coin a Tender in Payment of Debts; pass any Bill of Attainder, ex post facto Law, or Law impairing the Obligation of Contracts, or grant any Title of Nobility.

No State shall, without the Consent of the Congress, lay any Imposts or Duties on Imports or Exports, except what may be absolutely necessary for executing its inspection Laws: and the net Produce of all Duties and Imposts, laid by any State on Imports or Exports, shall be for the Use of the Treasury of the United States; and all such Laws shall be subject to the Revision and Control of the Congress.

No State shall, without the Consent of Congress, lay any Duty of Tonnage, keep Troops, or Ships of War in time of Peace, enter into any Agreement or Compact with another State, or with a foreign Power, or engage in War, unless actually invaded, or in such imminent Danger as will not admit of delay.

Article II

Section 1. The executive Power shall be vested in a President of the United States of America. He shall hold his Office during the Term of four Years, and, together with the Vice President, chosen for the same Term, be elected, as follows

Each State shall appoint, In such Manner as the Legislature thereof may direct, a Number of Electors, equal to the whole Number of Senators and Representatives to which the State may be entitled in the Congress: but no Senator or Representative, or Person holding an Office of Trust or Profit under the United States, shall be appointed an Elector.

The Electors shall meet in their respective States, and vote by Ballot for two Persons, of whom one at least shall not be an Inhabitant of the same State with themselves. And they shall make a List of all the Persons voted for, and of the number of Votes for each; which List they shall sign and certify, and transmit sealed to the Seat of the Government of the United States, directed to the President of the Senate. The President of the Senate shall, in the Presence of the Senate and House of Representatives, open all the Certificates, and the Votes shall then be counted. The Person having the greatest number of Votes shall be the President, if such Number be a Majority of the whole Number of Electors appointed; and if there be more than one who have such Majority, and have an equal Number of Votes, then the House of Representatives shall immediately choose by Ballot one of them for President; and if no Person have a Majority, then from the five highest on the List the said House shall in like Manner choose the President. But in choosing the President, the Votes shall be taken by States, the Representation from each State having one Vote; a quorum for this Purpose shall consist of a Member or Members from two thirds of the States, and a Majority of all the States shall be necessary to a Choice. In every Case, after the Choice of the President, the Person having the greatest Number of Votes of the Electors shall be the Vice President. But if there should remain two or more who have equal Votes, the Senate shall choose from them by Ballot the Vice President.

The Congress may determine the Time of choosing the Electors, and the Day on which they shall give their Votes; which Day shall be the same throughout the United States. No Person except a natural born Citizen, or a Citizen of the United States at the time of the Adoption of this Constitution, shall be eligible to the Office of President; neither shall any Person be eligible to that Office who shall not have attained to the Age of thirty five Years, and been fourteen Years a Resident within the United States.

In Case of the Removal of the President from Office, or of his Death, Resignation, or Inability to discharge the Powers and Duties of the said Office, the Same shall devolve on the Vice President, and the Congress may by Law provide for the Case of Removal, Death, Resignation or Inability, both of the President and Vice President, declaring what Officer shall then act as President, and such Officer shall act accordingly, until the Disability be removed, or a President shall be elected.

The President shall, at stated Times, receive for his Services, a Compensation, which shall neither be increased nor diminished during the Period for which he shall have been elected, and he shall not receive within that Period any other emolument from the United States, or any of them.

Before he enter on the Execution of his Office, he shall take the following Oath or Affirmation: – "I do solemnly swear (or affirm) that I will faithfully execute the Office of President of the United States, and will to the best of my Ability, preserve, protect and defend the Constitution of the United States."

Section 2. The President shall be Commander in Chief of the Army and Navy of the United States, and of the Militia of the several States, when called into the actual Service of the United States; he may require the Opinion, in writing, of the principal Officer in each of the executive Departments, upon any Subject relating to the Duties of their respective Offices, and he shall have Power to grant Reprieves and Pardons for Offenses against the United States, except in Cases of Impeachment.

He shall have Power, by and with the Advice and Consent of the Senate, to make Treaties, provided two thirds of the Senators present concur; and he shall nominate, and by and with the Advice and Consent of the Senate, shall appoint Ambassadors, other public Ministers and Consuls, Judges of the supreme Court, and all other Officers of the United States, whose Appointments are not herein otherwise provided for, and which shall be established by Law: but the Congress may by Law vest the Appointment of such inferior Officers, as they think proper, in the President alone, in the Courts of Law, or in the Heads of Departments.

The President shall have Power to fill up all Vacancies that may happen during the Recess of the Senate, by granting Commissions which shall expire at the End of their next Session.

Section 3. He shall from time to time give to the Congress Information of the State of the Union, and recommend to their Consideration such Measures as he shall judge necessary and expedient; he may, on extraordinary Occasions, convene both Houses, or either of them, and in Case of Disagreements between them, with Respect to the Time of Adjournment, he may adjourn them to such Time as he shall think proper; he shall receive Ambassadors and other public Ministers; he shall take Care that the Laws be faithfully executed, and shall Commission all the Officers of the United States.

Section 4. The President, Vice President and all Civil Officers of the United States, shall be removed from Office on Impeachment for, and Conviction of, Treason, Bribery, or other high Crimes and Misdemeanors.

Article III

Section 1. The judicial Power of the United States, shall be vested in one supreme Court, and in such inferior Courts as the Congress may from time to time ordain and establish. The Judges, both of the supreme and inferior Courts, shall hold their Offices during good Behavior, and shall, at stated Times, receive for their Services, a Compensation, which shall not be diminished during their Continuance in Office.

Section 2. The judicial Power shall extend to all Cases, in Law and Equity, arising under this Constitution, the Laws of the United States, and Treaties made, or which shall be made, under their Authority; – to all Cases affecting Ambassadors, other public Ministers and Consuls; – to all Cases of admiralty and maritime Jurisdiction; – to Controversies to which the United States shall be a Party; – to Controversies between two or more States; – between a State and Citizens of another State; – between Citizens of different States; – between Citizens of the same State claiming Lands under Grants of different States, and between a State, or the Citizens thereof, and foreign States, Citizens or Subjects.

In all Cases affecting Ambassadors, other public Ministers and Consuls, and those in which a State shall be Party, the Supreme Court shall have original Jurisdiction. In all the other Cases before mentioned, the supreme Court shall have appellate Jurisdiction, both as to Law and Fact, with such Exceptions, and under such Regulations as the Congress shall make.

The Trial of all Crimes, except in Cases of Impeachment, shall be by Jury; and such Trial shall be held in the State where the said Crimes shall have been committed; but when not committed within any State, the Trial shall be at such Place or Places as the Congress may by Law have directed.

Section 3. Treason against the United States, shall consist only in levying War against them, or in adhering to their Enemies, giving them Aid and Comfort. No Person shall be convicted of Treason unless on the Testimony of two Witnesses to the same overt Act, or on Confession in open Court.

The Congress shall have Power to declare the Punishment of Treason, but no Attainder of Treason shall work Corruption of Blood, or Forfeiture except during the Life of the Person attainted.

Article IV

Section 1. Full Faith and Credit shall be given in each State to the public Acts, Records, and judicial proceedings of every other State. And the Congress may by general Laws prescribe the Manner in which such Acts, Records and Proceedings shall be proved, and the Effect thereof.

Section 2. The Citizens of each State shall be entitled to all Privileges and Immunities of Citizens in the several States.

A Person charged in any State with Treason, Felony, or other Crime, who shall flee from Justice, and be found in another State, shall on Demand of the executive Authority of the State from which he fled, be delivered up, to be removed to the State having Jurisdiction of the Crime.

No Person held to Service or Labor in one State, under the Laws thereof, escaping into another, shall, in Consequence of any Law or Regulation therein, be discharged from such Service or Labor, but shall be delivered up on Claim of the Party to whom such Service or Labor may be due.

Section 3. New States may be admitted by the Congress into this Union; but no new State shall be formed or erected within the Jurisdiction of any other State; nor any State be formed by the Junction of two or more States, or Parts of States, without the Consent of the Legislatures of the States concerned as well as of the Congress.

The Congress shall have Power to dispose of and make all needful Rules and Regulations respecting the Territory or other Property belonging to the United States; and nothing in this Constitution shall be so construed as to Prejudice any Claims of the United States, or of any particular State.

Section 4. The United States shall guarantee to every State in this Union a Republican Form of Government, and shall protect each of them against Invasion; and on Application of the Legislature, or of the Executive (when the Legislature cannot be convened) against domestic Violence.

Article V

The Congress, whenever two thirds of both Houses shall deem it necessary, shall propose Amendments to this Constitution, or, on the Application of the Legislatures of two thirds of the several States, shall call a Convention for proposing Amendments, which, in either Case, shall be valid to all Intents and Purposes, as Part of this Constitution, when ratified by the Legislatures of three fourths of the several States, or by Conventions in three fourths thereof, as the one or the other Mode of Ratification may be proposed by the Congress; provided that no Amendment which may be made prior to the Year One thousand eight hundred and eight shall in any Manner affect the first and fourth Clauses in the Ninth Section of the first Article; and that no State, without its Consent, shall be deprived of its equal Suffrage in the Senate.

Article VI

All Debts contracted and Engagements entered into, before the Adoption of this Constitution, shall be as valid against the United States under this Constitution, as under the Confederation.

This Constitution, and the Laws of the United States which shall be made in Pursuance thereof; and all Treaties made, or which shall be made, under the Authority of the United States, shall be the supreme Law of the Land; and the Judges in every State shall be bound thereby, any Thing in the Constitution or Laws of any State to the Contrary notwithstanding.

The Senators and Representatives before mentioned, and the Members of the several State Legislatures, and all executive and judicial Officers, both of the United States and of the several States, shall be bound by Oath or Affirmation, to support this Constitution; but no religious Test shall ever be required as a Qualification to any Office or public Trust under the United States.

Article VII

The Ratification of the Conventions of nine States, shall be sufficient for the Establishment of this Constitution between the States so ratifying the Same.

Done in Convention by the Unanimous Consent of the States present the Seventeenth Day of September in the Year of our Lord one thousand seven hundred and Eighty seven and of the Independence of the United States of America the Twelfth. In witness thereof We have hereunto subscribed our Names, Articles in Addition to, and Amendment of, the Constitution of the United States of America, Proposed by Congress, and Ratified by the Several States, Pursuant to the Fifth Article of the Original Constitution.

Amendment I

Congress shall make no law respecting an establishment of religion, or prohibiting the free exercise thereof; or abridging the freedom of speech, or of the press; or the right of the people peaceably to assemble, and to petition the Government for a redress of grievances.

Amendment II

A well regulated Militia, being necessary to the security of a free State, the right of the people to keep and bear Arms, shall not be infringed.

Amendment III

No Soldier shall, in time of peace be quartered in any house, without the consent of the Owner, nor in time of war, but in a manner to be prescribed by law.

Amendment IV

The right of the people to be secure in their persons, houses, papers, and effects, against unreasonable searches and seizures, shall not be violated, and no Warrants shall issue, but upon probable cause, supported by Oath or affirmation, and particularly describing the place to be searched, and the persons or things to be seized.

Amendment V

No Person shall be held to answer for a capital, or otherwise infamous crime, unless on a presentment or indictment of a Grand Jury, except in cases arising in the land or naval forces, or in the Militia, when in actual service in time of War or public danger; nor shall any person be subject for the same offence to be twice put in jeopardy of life or limb; nor shall be compelled in any criminal case to be a witness against himself, nor be deprived of life, liberty, or property, without due process of law; nor shall private property be taken for public use, without just compensation.

Amendment VI

In all criminal prosecutions, the accused shall enjoy the right to a speedy and public trial by an impartial jury of the State and district wherein the crime shall have been committed, which district shall have been previously ascertained by law, and to be informed of the nature and cause of the accusation; to be confronted with the witness against him; to have compulsory process for obtaining Witnesses in his favor, and to have the Assistance of Counsel for his defense.

Amendment VII

In Suits at common law, where the value in controversy shall exceed twenty dollars, the right of trial by jury shall be preserved, and no fact tried by a jury, shall be otherwise reexamined in any Court of the United States, than according to the rules of the common law.

Amendment VIII

Excessive bail shall not be required, nor excessive fines imposed, nor cruel and unusual punishments inflicted.

Amendment IX

The enumeration in the Constitution, of certain rights, shall not be construed to deny or disparage others retained by the people.

Amendment X

The powers not delegated to the United States by the Constitution, nor prohibited by it to the States, are reserved to the States respectively, or to the people. [The first ten amendments were ratified Dec. 15, 1791]

Amendment XI

The Judicial power of the United States shall not be construed to extend to any suit in law or equity, commenced or prosecuted against one of the United States by Citizens of another State, or by Citizens or Subjects of any Foreign State. [Jan. 8, 1798]

Amendment XII

The Electors shall meet in their respective states and vote by ballot for President and Vice-President, one of whom, at least, shall not be an inhabitant of the same state with themselves; they shall name in their ballots the person voted for as President, and in distinct ballots the person voted for as Vice-President, and they shall make distinct lists of all persons voted for as President, and of all persons voted for as Vice-President, and of the number of votes for each, which lists they shall sign and certify, and transmit sealed to the seat of the government of the United States, directed to the President of the Senate; – The President of the Senate shall, in the presence of the Senate and House of Representatives, open all the certificates and the votes shall then be counted; – The person having the greatest number of votes for President, shall be the President, if such number be a majority of the whole number of Electors appointed; and if no person have such majority, then from the persons having the highest numbers not exceeding three on the list of those voted for as President, the House of Representatives shall choose immediately, by ballot, the President. But in choosing the President, the votes shall be taken by states, the representation from each state having one vote; a quorum for this purpose shall consist of a member or members from two-thirds of the states, and a majority of all the states shall be necessary to a choice. And if the House of Representatives shall not choose a President whenever the right of choice shall devolve upon them, before the fourth day of March next following, then the Vice-President shall act as President, as in the case of the death or other constitutional disability of the President – The person having the greatest number of votes as Vice-President, shall be the Vice-President, if such number be a majority of the whole number of Electors appointed, and if no person have a majority, then from the two highest numbers on the list, the Senate shall choose the Vice-President; a quorum for the purpose shall consist of two-thirds of the whole number of Senators, and a majority of the whole number shall be necessary to a choice. But no person constitutionally ineligible to the office of President shall be eligible to that of Vice-President of the United States. [Sept. 25, 1804]

Amendment XIII

Section 1. Neither slavery nor involuntary servitude, except as a punishment for crime whereof the party shall have been duly convicted, shall exist within the United States, or any place subject to their jurisdiction.

Section 2. Congress shall have power to enforce this article by appropriate legislation. [Dec. 18, 1865]

Amendment XIV

Section 1. All persons born or naturalized in the United States and subject to the jurisdiction thereof, are citizens of the United States and of the State wherein they reside. No State shall make or enforce any law which shall abridge the privileges or immunities of citizens of the United States; nor shall any State deprive any person of life, liberty, or property, without due process of law; nor deny any person within its jurisdiction the equal protection of the laws.

Section 2. Representatives shall be apportioned among the several States according to their respective numbers, counting the whole number of persons in each State, excluding Indians not taxed. But when the right to vote at any election for the choice of electors for President and Vice President of the United States, Representatives in Congress, the Executive and Judicial officers of a State, or the members of the Legislature thereof, is denied to any of the male inhabitants of such State, being twenty-one years of age, and citizens of the United States, or in any way abridged, except for participation in rebellion, or other crime, the basis of representation therein shall be reduced in the proportion which the number of such male citizens shall bear to the whole number of male citizens twenty-one years of age in such State.

Section 3. No person shall be a Senator or Representative in Congress, or elector of President and Vice President, or hold any office, civil or military, under the United States, or under any State, who, having previously taken an oath, as a member of Congress, or as an officer of the United States, or as a member of any State legislature, or as an executive or judicial officer of any State, to support the Constitution of the United States, shall have engaged in insurrection or rebellion against the same, or given aid or comfort to the enemies thereof. But Congress may by a vote of two-thirds of each House, remove such disability.

Section 4. The validity of the public debt of the United States, authorized by law, including debts incurred for payment of pensions and bounties for services in suppressing insurrection or rebellion, shall not be questioned. But neither the United States nor any State shall assume or pay any debt or obligation incurred in aid of insurrection or rebellion against the United States, or any claim for the loss or emancipation of any slave; but all such debts, obligations and claims shall be held illegal and void.

Section 5. The Congress shall have power to enforce by appropriate legislation, the provisions of this article. [July 28, 1868]

Amendment XV

Section 1. The right of citizens of the United States to vote shall not be denied or abridged by the United States or by any State on account of race, color, or previous condition of servitude.

Section 2. The Congress shall have power to enforce this article by appropriate legislation. [March 30, 1870]

Amendment XVI

The Congress shall have power to lay and collect taxes on incomes, from whatever source derived, without apportionment among the several States, and without regard to any census or enumeration. [Feb. 25, 1913]

Amendment XVII

The Senate of the United States shall be composed of two Senators from each State, elected by the people thereof, for six years; and each Senator shall have one vote. The electors in each State shall have the qualifications requisite for electors of the most numerous branch of the State legislatures.

When vacancies happen in the representation of any State in the Senate, the executive authority of such State shall issue writs of election to fill such vacancies: Provided, That the legislature of any State may empower the executive thereof to make temporary appointments until the people fill the vacancies by election as the legislature may direct. This amendment shall not be so construed as to affect the election or term of any Senator chosen before it becomes valid as part of the Constitution. [May 31, 1913]

Amendment XVIII

Section 1. After one year from the ratification of this article the manufacture, sale, or transportation of intoxicating liquors within, the importation thereof into, or the exportation thereof from the United States and all territory subject to the jurisdiction thereof for beverage purposes is hereby prohibited.

Section 2. The Congress and the several States shall have concurrent power to enforce this article by appropriate legislation.

Section 3. This article shall be inoperative unless it shall have been ratified as an amendment to the Constitution by the legislatures of the several States, as provided in the Constitution, within seven years from the date of the submission hereof to the States by the Congress. [Jan. 29, 1919]

Amendment XIX

The right of citizens of the United States to vote shall not be denied or abridged by the United States or by any State on account of sex.

Congress shall have power to enforce this article by appropriate legislation. [Aug. 26, 1920]

Amendment XX

Section 1. The terms of the President and Vice President shall end at noon on the 20th day of January, and the terms of Senators and Representatives at noon on the 3d day of January, of the years in which such terms would have ended if this article had not been ratified; and the terms of their successors shall then begin.

Section 2. The Congress shall assemble at least once in every year, and such meeting shall begin at noon on the 3d day of January, unless they shall by law appoint a different day.

Section 3. If, at the time fixed for the beginning of the term of the President, the President elect shall have died, the Vice President elect shall become President. If a President shall not have been chosen before the time fixed for the beginning of his term, or if the President elect shall have failed to qualify, then the Vice President elect shall act as President until a President shall have qualified; and the Congress may by law provide for the case wherein neither a President elect nor a Vice President elect shall have qualified, declaring who shall then act as President, or the manner in which one who is to act shall be selected, and such person shall act accordingly until a President or Vice President shall have qualified.

Section 4. The Congress may by law provide for the case of the death of any of the persons for whom the House of Representatives may choose a President whenever the right of choice shall have devolved upon them, and for the case of the death of any of the persons from whom the Senate may choose a Vice President whenever the right of choice shall have devolved upon them.

Section 5. Sections 1 and 2 shall take effect on the 15th day of October following the ratification of this article.

Section 6. This article shall be inoperative unless it shall have been ratified as an amendment to the Constitution by the legislatures of three-fourths of the several States within seven years from the date of its submission. [Feb. 6, 1933]

Amendment XXI

Section 1. The eighteenth article of amendment to the Constitution of the United States is hereby repealed.

Section 2. The transportation or importation into any State, Territory, or possession of the United States for delivery or use therein of intoxicating liquors, in violation of the laws thereof, is hereby prohibited.

Section 3. This article shall be inoperative unless it shall have been ratified as an amendment to the Constitution by conventions in the several States, as provided in the

Constitution, within seven years from the date of the submission hereof to the States by the Congress. [Dec. 5, 1933]

Amendment XXII

Section 1. No person shall be elected to the office of the President more than twice, and no person who has held the office of President, or acted as President, for more than two years of a term to which some other person was elected President shall be elected to the office of the President more than once. But this Article shall not apply to any person holding the office of President when this Article was proposed by the Congress, and shall not prevent any person who may be holding the office of President, or acting as President, during the term within which this Article becomes operative from holding the office of President or acting as President during the remainder of such term.

Section 2. This article shall be inoperative unless it shall have been ratified as an amendment to the Constitution by the legislatures of three-fourths of the several States within seven years from the date of its submission to the States by the Congress. [Feb. 27, 1951]

Amendment XXIII

Section 1. The District constituting the seat of Government of the United States shall appoint in such manner as the Congress may direct:

A number of electors of President and Vice President equal to the whole number of Senators and Representatives in Congress to which the District would be entitled if it were a State, but in no event more than the least populous State; they shall be in addition to those appointed by the States, but they shall be considered, for the purposes of the election of President and Vice President, to be electors appointed by a State; and they shall meet in the District and perform such duties as provided by the twelfth article of amendment.

Section 2. The Congress shall have power to enforce this article by appropriate legislation. [Mar. 29, 1961]

Amendment XXIV

Section 1. The right of citizens of the United States to vote in any primary or other election for President or Vice President, for electors for President or Vice President, or for Senator or Representative in Congress, shall not be denied or abridged by the United States or any State by reason of failure to pay any poll tax or other tax.

Section 2. The Congress shall have power to enforce this article by appropriate legislation. [Jan. 23, 1964]

Amendment XXV

Section 1. In case of the removal of the President from office or of his death or resignation, the Vice President shall become President.

Section 2. Whenever there is a vacancy in the office of the Vice President, the President shall nominate a Vice President who shall take office upon confirmation by a majority vote of both Houses of Congress.

Section 3. Whenever the President transmits to the President pro tempore of the Senate and the Speaker of the House of Representatives his written declaration that he is unable to discharge the powers and duties of his office, and until he transmits to them a written declaration to the contrary, such powers and duties shall be discharged by the Vice President as Acting President.

Section 4. Whenever the Vice President and a majority of either the principal officers of the executive departments or of such other body as Congress may by law provide, transmit to the President pro tempore of the Senate and the Speaker of the House of Representatives their written declaration that the President is unable to discharge the powers and duties of his office, the Vice President shall immediately assume the powers and duties of the office as Acting President.

Thereafter, when the President transmits to the President pro tempore of the Senate and the Speaker of the House of Representatives his written declaration that no inability exists, he shall resume the powers and duties of his office unless the Vice President and a majority of either the principal officers of the executive department or of such other body as Congress may by law provide, transmit within four days to the President pro tempore of the Senate and the Speaker of the House of Representatives their written declaration that the President is unable to discharge the powers and duties of his office. Thereupon Congress shall decide the issue, assembling within forty-eight hours for that purpose if not in session. If the Congress, within twenty-one days after receipt of the latter written declaration, or, if Congress is not in session, within twenty-one days after Congress is required to assemble, determines by two-thirds vote of both Houses that the President is unable to discharge the powers and duties of his office, the Vice President shall continue to discharge the same as Acting President; otherwise, the President shall resume the powers and duties of his office. [Feb. 10, 1967]

Amendment XXVI

Section 1. The right of citizens of the United States, who are eighteen years of age or older, to vote shall not be denied or abridged by the United States or by any State on account of age.

Section 2. The Congress shall have power to enforce this article by appropriate legislation. [June 30, 1971]

Amendment XXVII

No law, varying the compensation for the services of the Senators and Representatives, shall take effect, until an election of Representatives shall have intervened. [May 7, 1992]

Recommended Reading

1 History

Among the many excellent history texts, the best short survey is Jenkins (2007) and the most comprehensive, single-authored text is Foner (2006). A unique text combining culture and foreign policy from 1945 to the present is Levine and Papasotiriou (2005). Lipset (1996) explains American exceptionalism and Foner (1999) is indispensable for understanding American freedom. On race, manifest destiny, and religion, see Horsman (1981) and Wood (1990). Schlesinger (1986), Williams (1966) and Wood (2008) explain the foundations of and cycles in American history from various viewpoints. Niebuhr (2008) is enjoying a revival and his understandings of the dangers of trying to control history speak volumes when applied to the contemporary era. Slotkin (1993) is excellent on the role of violence and frontier in American mythology. For a fine study on political thought and American culture see Wolfe (2009).

2 Land and People

The main issues concerning environmentalism and conservation are found in Merchant (ed.) (2005) and the film and book by Gore (2006). Friedman (2008) examines the dangerous convergence of global warming, global population, and global consumption. For immigration history and the changing ethnicities of immigrants, the publications of the Pew Research Center are superb as is Zolberg (2006). Gjerde (ed.) (1998) provides a good combination of primary sources and academic essays on immigration issues. See Suárez-Orozco and Páez (2002) for a thorough look at Latinos. The newest revision of Franklin and Higginbotham (2009) is the standard for African American history. On Native Americans, a sterling short survey is Rawls (1996) and the most comprehensive coverage is Ewen (2009).

3 Government

Janda, Berry, and Goldman (2008) provide a readable text on government. For discussions of the Presidency, see Schlesinger (1973), Neustadt (1990), Cronin and Genovese (1997), Dallek (2001), and Gregg (2005). Davidson, Oleszek, and Lee (2007) provide an overview of the workings of the modern Congress. Clayton and Giordano (1998) consider the role of judicial philosophy in

Supreme Court Decisions while Toobin (2007) delves into the complex dynamics of the Court. Bailey (1998) draws on research charting the changing nature of contemporary federalism, whereas Lind (1995) criticizes federalism for its inflexibility, based on an immutable constitution. Peele *et al.* (2006) assesses how government and politics have coped with the post 9/11 environment.

4 Politics

Judis and Teixeira (2002) argue for a realignment of American Politics based on social and demographic change, whereas Frank (2004) and Edsall (2006) explain the ascent of conservatism. Putnam (2000) sees growing individuality, and obliquely offers explanations for low rates of participation. Wolfe (1998) suggests that Americans maintain a basic consensus of ideas. Lind (2004) illustrates the polarization of American political culture through attacks on the Bush Administration from the center-left. Lipset (1996) and Hutton (2002) put American political attitudes into a comparative context. Flippin (2008) and Weisberg (2008) collect the best political journalism and cast light on discussions involving the meeting of government and politics in the public sphere. Westen (2007) argues the important of emotion in voter preferences. Ansolabehere, Behr, and Iyengar (1993) deal with the media's role in political communication, whereas Kurtz (1998), Klein (2002) and Moore and Slater (2003) concentrate on how politicians and their advisers use the media. Bai (2007) argues that the internet has become vital to the political process.

5 Society

The best overall primary source is the monthly updated material in the US Census Bureau of Labor Statistics. For classic views of American society, start with Riis (1901), Lynd (1929), Galbraith (1958) and Patterson (1981). On American values and culture wars see Hunter and Wolfe (2006). For suburbanization, see Jackson (1985) and for an analysis of the change from a geography of nowhere to liveable space, see Kunstler (1996). Wolfe (1998) is a superior study of American middle-class values and lifestyles, and contrasts with a more pessimistic view by Putnam (2000), who finds a loss of civic virtue in the American community. For a comprehensive look at the dramatic way in which women changed American culture and attitudes see Rosen (2006). Hacker (2003) shows how race and crime have split the country into two cultures. Schor (1993, 1998) presents a lively discussion of the contemporary realities of overwork and overspend. On this theme, also see Hochschild (1997).

6 Religion, Education, and Social Policy

Provocative links between religion and popular culture are Goff and Harvey (2004), Prothero (2004) and Marsden (2000). The best general introduction to religion is Morone (2004). A highly critical view of how Christianity merged with capitalism is Wood (1990). Studies praising the liberalism of American faiths are found in Dionne (2008), Wolfe (1998) and D'Souza (2002). Kozol (1991) indicts the American primary and secondary education system for its inequalities. Bloom (1988) laments the loss of intellectual desire among university students. For American education from a transnational comparison see Gutek (2005). A comprehensive overview of contemporary social policy can be found in Karger and Soetsz (2009).

7 Culture

Belton (2008) studies the cultural productions of Hollywood film. For a comparative view of how European and American culture diverged and united after World War II, see Pells (1997). Kammen (1999) is an excellent study of the contours of American culture during the twentieth century. Gitlin (1995) clearly explains the culture wars. Lears (1994) and Leach (1993) are must-reads for those interested in how companies advertise and promote desire. The drive-thru culture is examined by Schlosser (2001). Gabler (2000) turns the cameras on Hollywood to show how life imitates art. Good leftist studies of American sports mentalities and culture are Higgs (1995) and Morgan (1994). For an critical overview of American thought see Hollinger and Capper (2006) and for interconnections to the global intellectual tradition see Watson (2001). Highly illustrative and readable studies on the social history of American art are found in Pohl (2008), Updike (2005) and Strand (2007). Zukin (2005) shows how consumerism changes culture.

8 The Economy

Comprehensive treatments of the development of the American economy are particularly clear in Heilbroner and Singer (1999) and Dethloff (1997). Hutton and Giddens (eds) (2001) provide a useful debate from conflicting viewpoints on economic globalization. Two insiders in the Clinton administration, Reich (2001) and Stiglitz (2002) examine the downside of the domestic economy on national cohesion and the impact of globalization on emerging economies, respectively. Phillips (2008) spells out the failure of American capitalism, Krugman (2008) compares the 2008 recession with the Great Depression, and Ferguson (2008a) puts the 2008 crisis in perspective with an overview of the history of global finance.

9 Foreign Policy

Fukuyama (1992) predicted an end to history with the ending of the Cold War but Barber (1995) and Huntington (1996) indicate that Islam and the West are increasingly at odds. Kagan (2009) explores the return of history and global conflict. Gordon and Shapiro (2004) look at the growing discord in the Atlantic Alliance over what to do about the Middle East. Addington (2000) provides an excellent narrative history of the Vietnam War. Nye (2002) delivers a thoughtful comparative approach, Zakaria (2008a) explores the rise of the rest of the world, and Bacevich (2008) examines the end of American exceptionalism. Mead (2005) provides the best comprehensive history of American foreign policy, balancing praise with trenchant criticism – especially when dissecting the Bush administration. The best book on the US wars in Iraq and Afghanistan is Filkins (2008) and on the US practice of torture is Mayer (2008).

10 Prospects for the Twenty-First Century

The two autobiographies by Obama (2004, 2007) are important for understanding the rise and values of the president. Any predictions about future happenings are hazardous but some themes are useful to explore. For example, Hutton (2002) denounces American capitalism and calls for other capitalist models to prevail. While Stiglitz (2002) flails the West's policies of globalization, D'Souza (2002) comes to America's defense by looking at what is right with the country. Zakaria (2008a) and Ferguson (2008a) see a diminishing of American power, but not enough to take away the American Century for the foreseeable future. The rise of big government and a liberal welfare state are welcomed in Wolfe (2009) and Madrick (2008).

America on the Internet

US Government

Using the primary website (www.firstgov.gov), students can access all US government offices, departments, and agencies. Direct access to selected agencies include:

Department of the Interior:	www.doi.gov
White House:	www.whitehouse.gov
Department of State:	www.usinfo.state.gov
US Census Bureau:	www.census.gov

News Sources

Almost every US news source has its own website for current news and analyses. Many have searchable archives for past news, among them:

Newspapers

New York Times:	www.nytimes.com
Washington Post:	www.washingtonpost.com
Los Angeles Times:	www.latimes.com
Wall Street Journal:	www.wsj.com

Billboards

Arts and Letters Daily:	www.aldaily.com
The Drudge Report:	www.drudgereport.com

Magazines

Mother Jones:	www.motherjones.com
The Atlantic Monthly:	www.theatlantic.com
The Nation:	www.thenation.com
The Weekly Standard:	www.weeklystandard.com
The New York Review of Books:	www.nybooks.com
The National Review:	www.nationalreview.com

TV/Radio

Public Broadcasting:	www.pbs.org
CNN:	www.cnn.com
Fox Cable News:	www.foxnews.com

MicroSoft/NBC:	www.msnbc.com
CBS:	www.cbs.com
NBC:	www.nbc.com
ABC:	www.abc.com
National Public Radio:	www.npr.org

Journals

Most important American journals can be accessed through www.jstor.org with the caveat of a five-year quarantine on the most recent issues. Current journals are available online through most university libraries and some public libraries.

Libraries

University of North Carolina:	www.lib.unc.edu
National Archives:	www.nara.gov
Library of Congress:	www.loc.gov
Harvard Library:	www.lib.harvard.edu
New York Public Library:	www.nypl.org

Political Parties

Democratic National Committee:	www.democrats.org
Republican National Committee:	www.rnc.org
Libertarian Party:	www.lp.org
Green Party:	www.gp.org
Reform Party:	www.reformparty.org

Opinion and Attitudes

Gallup Organization	www.gallup.com
Pew Research Center	www.people-press.org
National Election Survey	www.umich.edu/~nes/

Think-Tanks

Institute for Policy Studies:	www.ips-dc.org
The Progressive Policy Institute:	www.ppionline.org
The Brookings Institution:	www.brookings.org
The Cato Institute:	www.cato.org
The Heritage Foundation:	www.heritage.org
The American Enterprise Institute:	www.aei.org
Project for the New American Century	www.newamericancentury.org

Bibliography

Abbreviations:
AJC = *Atlanta Journal-Constitution*
AMO = *Atlantic Monthly*
AP = *Associated Press*
CSM = *Christian Science Monitor*
ECON = *Economist*
IHT = *International Herald Tribune*
LA = *Los Angeles Times*
LRB = *London Review of Books*
NR = *New Republic*
NYRB = *New York Review of Books*
NYT = *New York Times*
TNR = *The New Republic*
WP = *Washington Post*
WSJ = *Wall Street Journal*

AACC. American Association of Community Colleges (2008) "About Community Colleges."

Abraham, H. (1993) *The Judicial Process: An Introductory Analysis of the Courts of the United States, England, and France,* 6th edn, New York: Oxford University Press.

A.C. Nielsen Media Research (2008) Homepage.

Addington, L. (2000) *America's War in Vietnam: A Short Narrative History,* Bloomington, Indiana: University of Indiana Press.

AFT. American Federation of Teachers (2008) "Weingarten Hails Obama Victory as Extraordinary Milestone for Country."

ALA. American Library Association (2009) "Number of Libraries in the United States." January.

Alba, R. and V. Nee (2003) *Remaking the American Mainstream: Assimilation and Contemporary Immigration*, Cambridge: Harvard University Press.

Alterman, E. (2003) *What Liberal Media? The Truth About Bias and the News*, New York: Basic Books.

Altman, D. (2003) "Some Lose, Some Win, Some Break Even," *NYT*, 20 May.

Amato, J. (2009) "Top of the Ticket: John Amato on Michael Steele and the GOP's Troubles," *Los Angeles Times*, 5 March.

Ambrose, S. and D. Brinkley (1997) *Rise to Globalism: American Foreign Policy Since 1938,* 8th edn, UK: Penguin.

Annan, K. (2009) "America Will Re-Engage with the World," *The Independent*, 21 January.

Ansolabehere, S. R. Behr and S. Iyengar (1993) *The Media Game: American Politics in the Television Age,* New York: Palgrave-Macmillan.

AP (2009a) "Iraqi Journalist Sentenced for Throwing Shoes at Bush," *WSJ*, 12 March 2009.

AP (2009b) "Obama on Arab TV: 'Americans Are Not Your Enemy,'" *USA Today*, 27 January.

AP (2002) "Bush Defends Pledge on 4th of July," *NYT,* 4 July.

AP (2001a) "Powell: Terrorists More Isolated," *NYT*, 1 May.

AP (2001b) "Guiliani Angered by Nude Female Exhibit," *AJC,* 16 February.

Arango, T. (2008) "World Falls for American Media, Even as It Sours on America," *NYT*, 1 December.

Aratani, L. (2008) "Catching Up to the Boys, in Good and Bad," *NYT*, 10 February.

Armstrong, J. and M. Zúniga (2006) *Crashing the Gate: Netroots, Grassroots, and the Rise of People-Powered Politics*, White River Junction, VT: Chelsea Green Publishing Company.

Aversa, J. (2000) "Clinton Announces Record $237B Surplus," *USA Today,* 25 October.

Bacchus, J. (2008) "After the Bailout, Tariffs?" *Forbes*, 19 December.

Bacevich, A. (2008) *The Limits of Power: The End of American Exceptionalism*, New York: Metropolitan Books.

Bai, Matt (2007) *The Argument: Billionaires, Bloggers, and the Battle to Remake Democratic Politics*, New York: Penguin.

Bailey, C. (1998) "The Changing Federal System," in G. Peele, C. Bailey, B. Cain and G. Peters (eds), 114–37.

Baker, A. (2001) "Steep Rise in Gun Sales Reflects Post-Attack Fears," *NYT*, 31 December.

Baker, P. (2009) "With Pledges to Troops and Iraqis, Obama Details Pullout," *NYT*, 28 February.

Baldauf. S. (2008) "Former Guantanamo Prisoner Asks US to Review Its Founding Ideals," *CSM*, 6 February.

Bankhead, C. (2008) "Medicaid Spending Expected to Outpace Economic Growth," *MedPageToday*, 17 October.

Banks, C and J. Blakeman (2008) "Chief Justice Roberts, Justice Alito, and New Federalism.Jurisprudence," *Publius: The Journal of Federalism*, April 2008. [http://publius.oxfordjournals.org].

Barber, B. (1995) *Jihad vs. McWorld: How Globalism and Tribalism are Reshaping the World,* New York: Times Books.

Bazelon, E. (2008) "The Next Kind of Integration," *NYT*, 20 July.

BEA. US Bureau of Economic Analysis (2009a) US Department of Commerce. "Gross Domestic Product, 4th Quarter 2008 (Preliminary)," 27 February.

BEA. US Bureau of Economic Analysis (2009b) US Department of Commerce. "U.S. International Trade in Goods and Services, December 2008," 11 February.

Bedau, H. (ed.) (2003) *Debating the Death Penalty: Should America Have Capital Punishment? The Experts on Both Sides Make Their Best Case*, Oxford: Oxford University Press.

Bell, I. (2000) "The Constructions of American Culture: An Overview," in R. Maidment and J. Mitchell (eds), 1–12.

Belton, J. (2008) *American Cinema, American Culture*, New York: McGraw-Hill.

BIA. Bureau of Indian Affairs (2008) Homepage.

Birt, J. and D. Frost [Producers] (2002) "The Nixon Tapes, Part 1," Discovery Communications.

Bittinger, C. (2009) "The Business of America is Business?" Calvin Coolidge Memorial Foundation.

Blanck, D. (2002) " 'We Have a Lot to Learn From America': The Myrdals and the Question of American Influences in Sweden," *Angles on the English Speaking World 2* (2002), 129–45.

Bloom, A. (1988) *The Closing of the American Mind,* New York: Touchstone.

Blow, C. (2008a) "Heaven for the Godless?" *NYT*, 27 December.

Blow, C. (2008b) "The Demise of Dating," *NYT*, 13 December.

BLS. US Bureau of Labor Statistics (2009a) "The Employment Situation, February 2009," 6 March.

BLS. US Bureau of Labor Statistics (2009b) "Table B.4. Hourly Average Earnings of Production and Non-Supervisory Workers" 6 February.

BLS. US Bureau of Labor Statistics (2009c) "Labor Force Statistics from the Current Population Survey," 28 January.

BLS. US Bureau of Labor Statistics (2009d) "Union Members in 2008," 28 January.

BLS. Bureau of Labor Statistics (2008a) US Department of Labor. "Earnings by Demographics: Highlights of Women's Earnings," April.

BLS. US Bureau of Labor Statistics (2008b) "Workplace Injury and Illness Summary," 23 October.

BLS. US Bureau of Labor Statistics (2008c) "Census of Fatal Occupational Injuries Summary," 20 August.

BLS. Bureau of Labor Statistics (2006) US Department of Labor. "Employment as a Percent of the Working-Age Population, 2004," April.

Bobrow, D. (2001) "Changing the US World Role," paper delivered at the 50th Anniversary of the Fulbright Program, Copenhagen, Denmark, 8 November.

Booth, W. (2001) "A Slow Start to an Environmental End-Run," *WP*, 13 January.

Bowker, R. (2008) "Bowker Reports US Book Production Flat in 2007," 28 May.

B-PAC. Bowling Proprietors' Association Political Action Committee (2008) "Bowling PAC's 2007–2008 Strategy."

Brenner, R. (2002) *The Boom and the Bubble: The U.S. Economy Today*, London: Verso.

Brinkley, A (2009) "Worse than Hoover," in *TNR*, 13 January.

Brinkley, A. (2008a) "Black Sites," *NYT*, 3 August.

Brinkley, A. (2008b) "In Search of Bush," *NYT*, 2 March.

Brooks, D. (2008) "The Cognitive Age," *NYT*, 2 May.

Brooks, D. (2004a) "Bitter at the Top," *NYT*, 15 June.

Brooks, D. (2004b) *On Paradise Drive: How We Live Now (And Always Have) in the Future Tense, New York: Simon & Schuster.*

Brooks, D. (2003a) "The National Creed," *NYT*, 30 December.

Brooks, D. (2003b) "Refuting the Critics," *NYT*, 25 November.

Brooks, D. (2002) "On the Playing Fields of Suburbia," *AMO*, January.

Brooks, D. (2001) "One Nation, Slightly Divisible," *AMO*, December.

Brooks, D. (2000) *Bobos in Paradise: The New Upper Class and How They Got There*, New York: Simon & Schuster.

Brown, P. (2003) "Megachurches as Minitowns," *NYT*, 9 May.

Brown, R. (2009) "Nashville Won't Make English Official Language," *NYT*, 23 January.

Brzezinski, Z. (2007) "Terrorized by 'War on Terror,'" *NYT*, 25 March.

Buchanan, P. (2001) *The Death of the West: How Dying Populations and Immigrant Invasions Imperil Our Country and Civilization*, New York: Thomas Dunne.

Bush, G. (2008) "George Bush's Speech on the Financial Crisis," Council on Foreign Relations, 19 September.

Bush, G. (2005) "Inaugural Address by George W. Bush," *NYT*, 20 January.

Bush, G. (2004a) "President Holds Press Conference," 4 November [www.whitehouse.gov].

Bush, G. (2004b) "State of the Union Address," 20 January.

Bush, G. (2004c) "Remarks by the President on Immigration Policy," 7 January. [www.whitehouse.gov].

Bush, G. (2003) "In Bush's Words: 'Iraqi Democracy Will Succeed,'" *NYT*, 6 November.

Bush, G. (2001) "Executive Order Establishing Office of Homeland Security," 8 October. [www.whitehouse.gov].

Camarota, S. (2007) "Immigrants in the United States, 2007," Center for Immigration Studies, 7 November.

Campbell, J. (1998) "Clinton: I Did Not Have Sex With Lewinsky," *Evening Standard* (London), 26 January.

Carter, J. (1979) "Address to the Nation," 20 July.

CBS News (2008) "Exclusive: Palin on Foreign Policy," 25 September.

CBS News (2004) "Graham Packs Rose Bowl," 22 November.

CC. Christian Coalition (2009) "About Us."

CDC. Center for Disease Control (2009) "National Vital Statistics Reports," 7 January.

CDC. Center for Disease Control (2008) "US Obesity Trends, 1985–2007," 24 July.

CFI. Campaign Finance Institute (2008) "A First Look at Money in the House and Senate Elections," 6 November.

Chang, K (2008) "NASA Spacecraft Lands on Mars," *NYT*, 26 May.

Childress, Marjorie (2008) "Desert Rock Fuels Debate Over Just How Clean Coal Should Be," *New Mexico Independent*, 18 September.

CIA. Central Intelligence Agency (2009) "The World Factbook: Rank Order Exports"

CIA. Central Intelligence Agency (2008) "The World Factbook."

Clarke, R. (2005) "Ten Years Later," *AMO*, January.

Clayton, C., and J. Giordano (1998) "The Supreme Court and the Constitution," in G. Peele, C. Bailey, B. Cain and G. Peters (eds), 71–97.

Clemetson, L. (2003) "Bush Authorizes a Black History Museum," *NYT*, 17 December.

Clinton, W. (1997) "Inaugural Address of President William J. Clinton," 20 January. National Archives and Records Service.

CNN.com (2008) "Election Center 2008: Exit Polls," 5 November.

CNN.com (2006) "Thousands March for Immigrants Rights," 2 May.

CNN.com (2004) "Court Dismisses Pledge Case," 15 June.

Cohen, R. (2005) "What the World Wants from America," *NYT*, 16 January.

College Board (2008) "Trends in College Pricing 2008."

Colvin, R. (2009) "Obama Says Most US Troops in Iraq Home Within a Year," *Boston Globe*, 1 February.

Congressional Quarterly (2008) "CQ Guide to the New Congress," 6 November.

Cronin, T. and M. Genovese (1997) *The Paradoxes of the American Presidency*, Oxford: Oxford University Press.

Crossette, B. (2000) "Globalization Tops Agenda for World Leaders at UN Summit," *NYT*, 3 September.

CRP. Center for Responsive Politics (2008a) "US Election Will Cost $5.3 Billion, Center for Responsive Politics Predicts," 22 October. [www.opensecrets.org]

CRP. Center for Responsive Politics (2008b) "Presidential Candidate Mitt Romney."

CRP. Center for Responsive Politics (2008c) "527s: Advocacy Spending in the 2008 Elections."

Daalder, I. and J. Lindsay (2004) *America Unbound: The Bush Revolution in Foreign Policy*, Washington: Brookings Institution Press.

Dallek, R. (2001) *Hail to the Chief: The Making and Unmaking of American Presidents*, New York: Oxford University Press.

Danner, M. (2004) *Torture and Truth: America, Abu Ghraib, and the War on Terror*, New York: NYRB.

Danner, M. (2003) "Iraq: The New War," *NYRB*, 25 September.

Dart, B. (2000) "Feds Open 'All-In-One' Website for Public," *NYT*, 23 September.

Davidson, R., W. Oleszek, and F. Lee (2007) *Congress and its Members*, Washington, DC: CQ Press
Defense Update (2009) "European Defense Spending Shrinks," February.
Delbanco, A. (2007) "Scandals of Higher Education," *NYRB*, 29 March.
DeNavas-Walt, C., B. Proctor, and R. Mills (2004) *Income, Poverty, and Health Insurance Coverage in the United States, 2003*, Washington: US Census Bureau.
Dethloff, H. (1997) *The United States and the Global Economy Since 1945*, New York: Harcourt Brace.
Devine, R. (2004) *Bush Versus the Environment*, New York: Anchor Books.
DHS. Department of Homeland Security (2009) "Budget in Brief, Fiscal Year 2009," October.
DHS. Department of Homeland Security (2008a) "Immigration Enforcement Actions, 2007," December.
DHS. Department of Homeland Security (2008b) "Yearbook of Immigration Statistics, 2007," September.
Didion, J. (2003) "Mr. Bush and the Divine," *NYRB*, 2 November.
Dionne, E. (2008) *Souled Out: Reclaiming Faith and Politics After the Religious Right,* Princeton: Princeton University Press.
Dionne, E., J. Elshtain, and K. Drogosz (2004) *One Electorate Under God? A Dialogue on Religion and American Politics*, Washington, DC: Brookings Institution Press.
Dionne, E. and J. DiIulio (2000) *What's God Got To Do With The American Experiment?* Washington, DC: Brookings Institution Press.
DOE. US Department of Education (2008a) *Digest of Education Statistics, 2007.*
DOE. US Department of Education (2008b) "Reading First Impact Study: Interim Report," April.
DOHA. Doha, Qatar, Conference of the WTO (2002) "Economic Perspectives: Trade in the Post-Doha Global Economy," *An Electronic Journal of the U.S. Department of State,* 7 January.
DOJ. Department of Justice (2008a) "Prisoners in 2007," 10 December.
DOJ. Department of Justice (2008b) "Law Enforcement Statistics," 25 September.
DOJ. Department of Justice (2008c) "Background Checks for Firearm Transfers, 2007," 16 July.
DOJ. Department of Justice (2008d) "Slower Growth in Nation's Prison and Jail Populations," 6 June.
DOJ. Department of Justice (2005) "2005 National Gang Threat Assessment."
DOJ. Department of Justice (2001) "2000 Year End Report in the Federal Judiciary," January.
DOL. US Department of Labor (2009) "Unemployment Insurance Weekly Claims Report," 5 March.
Donadio, R. (2004) "Faith-Based Publishing," *NYT*, 28 November.
DOS. US Department of State (2002) "Death Penalty Support Dropping in the US, Growing in Europe – Ambassador Minike's Remarks to the OSCE Permanent Council," 6 June.
Dos Passos, J. (1979) *The Big Money,* New York: New American Library.

DPIC. Death Penalty Information Center (2009) "The Death Penalty in 2008: Year End report," December.

DPIC. Death Penalty Information Center (2005) "Facts About the Death Penalty," 5 January.

D'Souza, D. (2002) "*What's So Great About America?*" New York: Regnery.

Duggan, P. (2000) "A Few Faithful Make Stand for Prayer," *WP,* 2 September.

Duncan, R. (2004) "Crossing Borders: Hispanic Atlanta, 1990–2004," in Duncan, R. and C. Juncker, *Transnational America: Contours of Modern US Culture*, Copenhagen: Museum Tusculanum Press.

Econsultant (2008) "Top 31 Most Popular Radio Selection Formats in USA, Nov. 2008," November.

Edsall, T. (2006) *Building Red America: the New Conservative Coalition and the Drive for Permanent Power*, New York: Basic books

Efrati, A., T. Lauricella and D. Searcey (2008) "Top Broker Accused of $50 Billion Fraud," *WSJ*, 12 December.

Egan, T. (2009) "Fears of a Clown," *NYT*, 4 March.

Eilperin, J. (2001) "House Votes to Block Payment of UN Dues," *WP*, 11 May.

EPIC. Electronic Privacy Information Center (2008) "ACLU v. Mukasey," 22 July.

Esping-Andersen, G. (1996) *Three Worlds of Welfare Capitalism,* Cambridge: Polity Press.

Ewen, A. (2009) *Encyclopedia of the American Indian in the Twentieth Century*, New York: Facts on File.

Faulkner, W. (1948) *Intruder in the Dust,* New York: Modern Library.

FBI. Federal Bureau of Investigation (2008) "Crime in the United States, 2007," 15 September.

FBI. Federal Bureau of Investigation (2005) "How We're Ganging Up on MS-13," 13 July.

FDCH. Federal Document Clearing House Political Transcripts (2000) "Ralph Nader Delivers Remarks at News Conference," Washington, DC, 6 November.

FDIC. Federal Deposit Insurance Corporation (2009) "Insuring Your Deposits."

FEC-BPAA. Federal Election Commission (2008) ID: C00079855: Bowling Proprietors Association of America PAC.

FEC-ACT. Federal Election Commission (2008) ID: C00028860: American Federation of Teachers, AFL-CIO Committee on Political Education.

FEC-PSL. Federal Election Commission (2008) Presidential Spending Limits for 2008.

FEC. Federal Election Commission (2001) "PAC Activity Increases in 2000 Election Cycle," Released 31 May.

Fed. Federal Reserve Bank (2009) "US Monetary Policy: An Introduction," 1 March.

Ferguson, N. (2008a) *The Ascent of Money: A Financial History of the World*, London: Penguin Press.

Ferguson, N. (2008b) "Rough Week, But America's Era Goes On," *WP*, 21 September.

Ferguson, N. (2005) "The Widening Atlantic," *AMO* (January), 40–2.
Ferguson, N. (2004) *Colossus: the Price of America's Empire*, London: Penguin.
Filkins, D. (2008) *The Forever War*, New York: Knopf.
Fletcher, M. and J. Cohen (2008) "Hovering Above Poverty, Grasping for Middle Class," *WP*, 3 August.
Flippin, R. (ed.) (2008) *Best American Political Writing 2008*, New York: Public Affairs Press.
Florida, R. (2002) *The Rise of the Creative Class*, New York: Basic Books.
Fogel, R. (2000) *The Fourth Great Awakening and the Future of Egalitarianism,* Chicago: University of Chicago Press.
Foner, E. (2006) *Give Me Liberty!: An American History*, New York: Norton.
Foner, E. (1999) *The Story of American Freedom*, New York: Norton.
Ford, G. (1974) "Gerald R. Ford's Remarks on Taking the Oath of Office as President," Gerald R. Ford Library and Museum.
Fox, V. (2001) "More Trust on Both Sides of the Border," *NYT,* 4 September.
Frank, T. (2004) *What's The Matter With America?: The Resistible Rise of the American Right*, London: Secker & Walburg.
Franklin, J. and E. Higginbotham (2009) *From Slavery to Freedom: A History of African Americans*, 9th ed., NewYork: McGraw-Hill.
Freedland, J. (2007) "Bush's Amazing Achievement," *NYRB*, 14 June.
Freedman, J. (2008) "The Fortunate 50," *Sports Illustrated*, December.
Friedman, T. (2008) *Hot, Flat, and Crowded: Why We Need a Green Revolution—and How It Can Renew America*, New York: Farrar, Straus and Giroux.
Friedman, T. (2005) "Pop Tarts or Freedom?" *NYT*, 16 January.
Fukuyama, F. (1992) *The End of History and the Last Man,* New York: Free Press.
FWS. US Fish and Wildlife Service (2008) "Threatened and Endangered Species," 26 September.
Gabler, N. (2000) *Life the Movie: How Entertainment Conquered Reality,* New York: Vintage.
Gaddis, J. (1998) *The Long Peace: Inquiries into the History of the Cold War,* New York: Oxford University Press.
Galbraith, J. (1958) *The Affluent Society,* Boston: Houghton Mifflin.
Gans, H. (2004) *Democracy and the News*, New York: Oxford University Press.
Gates Foundation. Bill and Melinda Gates (2008) "Fact Sheet."
Gates, H. (1990) "2 Live Crew, Decoded," *NYT,* 19 June.
Gingrich, N. (2009) "Washington Unplugged," 28 February [www.CBSNews.com].
Gitlin, T. (1995) *The Twilight of Common Dreams: Why America is Wracked by Culture Wars,* New York: Henry Holt.
Gjerde, J. (ed.) (1998) *Major Problems in American Immigration and Ethnic History*, Boston: Houghton Mifflin.
Global Policy Forum (2009) "US vs. Total Debt to the UN: 1996–2008."
Goff, P. and P. Harvey (eds) (2004) *Themes in Religion and American Culture*, Chapel Hill: University of North Carolina Press.

Gordon, P. and J. Shapiro (2004) *Allies at War: America, Europe and the Crisis Over Iraq*, New York: McGraw-Hill.

Gore, A. (2007) "Nobel Prize Acceptance Lecture," 10 December.

Gore, A. (2006) *An Inconvenient Truth: The Planetary Emergency of Global Warming and What We Can Do About It*, London: Earthscan Limited.

Greenhouse, L. (2008a) "Justices Rule for Individual Gun Rights," *WP*, 27 June.

Greenhouse, L. (2008b) "Gun Control Case Causes Bush Administration Rift," *NYT*, 17 March.

Greenhouse, L. (2003) "Justices Back Affirmative Action by 5 to 4," *NYT*, 23 June.

Greenhouse, L. (2001) "Justices Clarify Rule on Using Race in Redistricting," *NYT*, 19 April.

Gregg, G. (2005) *Thinking About the Presidency: Documents and Essays from the Founding to the Present*, Lanham, MD: Rowman and Littlefield.

Griffis, M. (2009) "Casualties in Iraq," Antiwar.com, 1 February.

Gutek, G. (2005) *American Education in a Global Society: International and Comparative Perspectives*, Long Grove, IL: Waveland Press.

Guttmacher Institute (2008) "US Abortion Rate Continues Long-Term Decline," 17 January.

Hacker, A. (2006) "The Rich and Everyone Else," *NYRB*, 25 May.

Hacker, A. (2005) "The Truth About Colleges," *NYRB*, 3 November.

Hacker, A. (2003) *Two Nations: Black and White, Separate, Hostile, Unequal,* New York: Scribner.

Hacker, A. (1997) *Money: Who Has How Much and Why,* New York: Scribner.

Haddad, Y. (1998) "Islam in the United States: Interview with Yvonne Haddad," *American Studies Journal*, 42 (Winter), 35-42.

Hamby, P. (2009) "Emanuel Says Limbaugh GOP Leader," *CNN.com*, 2 March.

Harris Poll (2008) "More Americans Believe in the Devil, Hell and Angels Than in Darwin's Theory of Evolution," 3 December.

Harris Poll (2007) "Six Nation Survey Finds Satisfaction with Current Job," 9 October.

Harris Poll (2004) "More Than Two-thirds of Americans Support the Death Penalty," 7 January.

Harris Poll (2000) "The Public Tends to Blame the Poor, the Unemployed and Those on Welfare for Their Problems," 3 May.

Harris Poll (1999) "Smoking, Obesity, and Not Using Seat Belts Much More Common Among People with the Least Education," 3 March.

Hartford Institute for Religion Research (2008) "Fast Facts: Largest 25 Denominations."

Heilbroner, R. and A. Singer (1999) *The Economic Transformation of America: 1600 to the Present*, New York: Harcourt Brace.

Hemingway, E. (1935) "Notes on the Next War," *Esquire*, September.

Herbert, B. (2002) "Fouling Our Own Nest," *NYT,* 4 July.

HHS. US Department of Health and Human Services (2008a) "The 2008 HHS Poverty Guideline," 23 January.

HHS. US Department of Health and Human Services (2008b) "Population of States by Five-Year Age Groups."

Higgs, R. (1995) *God in the Stadium: Sports and Religion in America*, Lexington, KY: University of Kentucky Press.

Ho, I. and A. Terrazas (2008) "Foreign-Born Veterans of the US Armed Forces," *Migration Policy Institute*.

Hobsbawm, E. (2003) "Only in America," *Chronicle of Higher Education*, 4 July.

Hochschild, A. (1997) *The Time Bind*, New York: Metropolitan Books.

HOF. Country Music Hall of Fame (2002) "The Rise of an Industry: Country Music Comes of Age."

Hollinger, D. and C. Capper (eds) (2006) *The American Intellectual Tradition*, 2 volumes, New York: Oxford University Press.

Holmes, S. (2001) "A Diverse City Exists Equal but Separate," *NYT*, 11 May.

Horsey, David (2007) "The (Tilting) Scales of Justice (Kennedy)," *The Seattle Post Intelligencer*.

Horsman, R. (1981) *Race and Manifest Destiny: The Origins of American Racial Anglo Saxonism*, Cambridge: Harvard University Press.

Hsu Hua (2009) "The End of White America," *AMO*, January.

Hulse, C (2009) "Maine Senators Break with Republican Party on Stimulus," *NYT*, 11 February.

Hunter, J. and A. Wolfe (2006) *Is There a Culture War?: A Dialogue on Values and American Public Life*, Washington, DC: Brookings Institution Press.

Huntington, S. (2004a) *Who Are We? America's Great Divide*, New York: Free Press.

Huntington, S. (2004b) "The Hispanic Challenge," *Foreign Policy*, April.

Huntington, S. (1999) "The Lonely Superpower," *Foreign Affairs*, April.

Huntington, S. (1996) *The Clash of Civilizations and the Remaking of the World Order*, New York: Simon & Schuster.

Hutton, W. (2002) *The World We're In*, London: Little, Brown.

Hutton, W. and A. Giddens (eds) (2001) *On the Edge: Living with Global Capitalism*, London: Vintage.

Ignatieff, M. (2003) "Why Are We in Iraq? And Liberia? And Afghanistan?" *NYT*, 7 September.

IIE. Institute for International Education (2008) "International Students in the US," 17 November.

INS. Immigration and Naturalization Service (2002).

IRS. Internal Revenue Service (2008a) "Individual Income Tax Returns. 2006."

IRS. Internal Revenue Service (2008b) "Tax Tables 2008."

ITA. International Trade Administration (2009) US Department of Commerce. "Top Trade Partners, December 2008."

Jackson, K. (1985) *Crabgrass Frontier: The Suburbanization of the United States*, New York: Oxford University Press.

Jacoby, T. (2006) "Immigration Nation," *Foreign Affairs*, December.

James, G. (2003) "Exurbia and God: Megachurches in New Jersey," *NYT*, 29 June.

Janda, K., J. Berry and J. Goldman (2008) *The Challenge of Democracy: Government in America,* 8th edn, Boston: Houghton Mifflin.

Jehl, D. (2003) "Washington Insiders' New Firm Consults on Contracts in Iraq," *NYT*, 30 September.

Jenkins, P. (2007) *A History of the United States*, London: Palgrave-Macmillan.

Jenkins, P. (2002) "The Next Christianity," *AMO* (October), 53–68.

Johnson, C. (2008) *Nemesis: The Last Days of the American Republic*, New York: Metropolitan.

Johnson, P. (2003) "America's New Empire for Liberty," *Hoover Digest* (4).

Judis, J. and R. Teixeira (2002) *The Emerging Democratic Majority*, New York: Scribner.

Judt, T. (2008) "What Have We Learned, If Anything?" *NYRB*, 1 May.

Kagan, R. (2009) *The Return of History and the End of Dreams*, New York, Vintage.

Kagan, R. (2008) "The Bush Era in Perspective," *Foreign Affairs*, October.

Kagan, R. (2007) "End of Dreams, Return of History," *Policy Review*, September.

Kagan, R. (2006) "Our Messianic Impulse," *WP*, 10 December.

Kagan, R. (2003) *Of Paradise and Power: America and Europe in the New World Order*, New York: Knopf.

Kammen, M. (1999) *American Culture, American Tastes: Social Change and the 20th Century,* New York: Knopf.

Kammen, M. (1987) *A Machine That Would Go Of Itself: The Constitution in American Culture*, New York: Knopf.

Kanfer, S. (1995) "The Greatest Game," in M. Petracca, and M. Sorapure (eds), 380–3.

Kaplan, R. (2001) "Looking the World in the Eye," *AMO*, December.

Karger, H. and D. Stoesz (2009) *American Social Welfare Policy: A Pluralistic Approach*, London: Allyn & Bacon.

Karmin, C. and J. Hechinger (2008) "Crisis Shakes the Foundations of the Ivory Tower," *WSJ*, 17 October.

Kegley, C. and E. Wittkopf (1996) *American Foreign Policy: Pattern and Process*, 5th edn, Boston: Houghton Mifflin.

King, M. (1963) *Why We Can't Wait,* New York: Mentor.

Klein, J. (2002) *The Natural: The Misunderstood Presidency of Bill Clinton,* New York: Doubleday.

Knowlton, B. (2009) "Brown Urges Bold Effort to Shape an Expansion," *NYT*, 4 March.

Knowlton, B. (2001) "Bush Says He Wants bin Laden Brought to Justice 'Dead or Alive,'" *IHT,* 18 September.

Knowlton, B. (1999) "Wired World Leaves Millions Out of Loop," *IHT*, 9 October.

Korb, L. (2000) "Defense," Council on Foreign Relations. [www.foreignpolicy2000.org/library/issuebriefs/IBDefense.html]

Kozol, J. (1991) *Savage Inequalities: Children in America's Schools*, New York: Harper Perennial.

Krugman, P. (2009) "Forgive and Forget?" *NYT*, 16 January.
Krugman, P.(2008) *The Return of Depression Economics and the Crisis of 2008*, New York: Norton.
Krugman, P. (2005) "America's Senior Moment," *NYRB*, 10 March.
Krugman, P. (2004a) *The Great Unraveling: From Boom to Bust in Three Scandalous Years*, London: Penguin.
Krugman, P. (2004b) "The Death of Horatio Alger," *The Nation*, 5 January.
Krugman, P. (2002) "Crony Capitalism, USA." *NYT*, 15 January.
Krugman, P. (1999) *The Return of Depression Era Economics*, New York: Norton.
Krugman, P. (1997) *The Age of Diminished Expectations*, Cambridge: MIT Press.
Kunstler, J. (1996) *The Geography of Nowhere: The Rise and Decline of America's Man-Made Landscape*, New York: Free Press.
Kurtz, H. (1998) *Spin Cycle: How the White House and the Media Manipulate the News*, New York: Simon & Schuster.
Lazo, A. (2008) "Mexicans Sending Less Money Home," *WP*, 31 July.
Leach, W. (1993) *Land of Desire: Merchants, Power, and the Rise of a New American Culture*, New York: Pantheon Books.
Lears, J. (1994) *Fables of Abundance: A Cultural History of Advertising in America*, New York: Basic Books.
Leinberger, C. (2008) "The Next Slum?" *AMO*, March.
Leip, D. (2008) *Atlas of U.S. Presidential Elections*.
Leland, J. (2004) "Christian Cool and the New Generation Gap," *NYT*, 16 May.
Lester, T. (2002) "Oh, Gods!" *AMO* Vol. 289 (February), 37–45.
Levine, P. and H. Papasotiriou (2005) *America Since 1945: The American Moment*, London: Palgrave-Macmillan.
Lewis, A. (2004) "Bush and the Lesser Evil," *NYRB*, 27 May.
Lewis, M. (2008) "After the Art Wars," *Commentary*, January.
Lieff Cabraser Heimann and Bernstein LLP (2008) "Fed Ex Employees Racial Discrimination Class Action" [www.lieffcabraser.com/fe-race-discrim.htm].
Lifton, R. (2003) "American Apocalypse," *The Nation*, 22 December.
Limbaugh, R. (2009) "Limbaugh: I Hope Obama Fails," *The Rush Limbaugh Show*, 16 January.
Lind, M. (2004) *Made in Texas: George W. Bush and the Southern Takeover of American Politics*, New York: Basic Books.
Lind, M. (2003) "The Weird Men Behind George W. Bush's War," *New Statesman*, 7 April.
Lind, M. (1999) *Vietnam, The Necessary War: A Reinterpretation of America's Most Disastrous Military Conflict*, New York: Free Press.
Lind, M. (1995) *The Next American Nation: The New Nationalism and the Fourth American Republic*, New York: Free Press.
Lipset, S. (1996) *American Exceptionalism: A Double-Edged Sword*, New York: Norton.
Liptak, A. (2008) "Inmate Count in U.S. Dwarfs Other Nations," *NYT*, 23 April.
Low, Setha (2003) *Behind the Gates: Life, Security, and the Pursuit of Happiness in Fortress America*, New York: Routledge.

Luo, M (2008) "Obama Hauls in Record $750 Million for Campaign," *NYT*, 5 December.

Lynd, R. and Lynd, H. (1929) *Middletown: A Study in American Culture,* New York: Harcourt, Brace.

MacFound. MacArthur Foundation (2008) "Homepage."

Madigan, N. (2002) "Tribe Prepares for Renewed Fight Over Gold Mine," *NYT,* 3 July.

Madrick, J. (2008) *The Case for Big Government*, Princeton: Princeton University Press.

Madrick, J. (2002) "Enron: Seduction and Betrayal" *NYRB,* 14 March.

Markheim, D. (2008) "The Future of the WTO Doha Round," Heritage Foundation WebMemo #2179, 22 December.

Marsden, G. (2000) *Religion and American Culture,* Belmont, CA: Wadsworth.

Mayer, J. (2008) *The Dark Side: The Inside Story of How the War on Terror Turned Into a War on American Ideals*, New York: Doubleday.

McCain, J. (2008) "John McCain's Concession Speech," *NYT*, 5 November.

McGrew, A. (2000a) "A Second American Century? The United States and the New World Order," in A. McGrew (ed.) 211–50.

McGrew, A. (ed.) (2000b) *The United States in the Twentieth Century,* London: Hodder & Stoughton.

McKinnnon, J. (2009) "Bush to Tout His 'No Child Left Behind' Initiative," *WSJ*, 7 January.

McPherson, J. (1982) *Ordeal by Fire: The Civil War and Reconstruction*, New York: Knopf.

Mead, W. (2005) *Power, Terror, Peace and War: America's Grand Strategy in a World at Risk*, New York: Vintage.

Mead, W. (2004) "America's Sticky Power," *Foreign Policy*, April.

Media Project, The. (2005) "Teens and Sex: Abstinence and Contraception," 14 January.

Menand, L. (2001) "College: The End of the Golden Age," in *NYRB,* 18 October.

Merchant, C. (ed.) (2005) *Major Problems in American Environmental History,* Boston: Houghton Mifflin.

Milbank, D. and P. Blustein (2001) "Leaders Affirm Free Trade Zone," *WP*, 23 April.

Mindlin, A. (2009) "Web Passes Papers as News Source," *NYT*, 5 January.

Mitchell, G. (2007) "Report to the Commissioner of Baseball of an Independent Investigation into the Illegal Use of Steroids and Other Performance Enhancing Substances by Players in Major League Baseball," 13 December.

Moore, J. and W. Slater (2003) *Bush's Brain: How Karl Rove Made George W. Bush Presidential*, New York: John Wiley & Sons.

Morgan, E. (1995) *American Slavery, American Freedom: The Ordeal of Colonial Virginia,* New York: Norton.

Morgan, W. (1994) *Leftist Theories of Sport: A Critique and Reconstruction*, Urbana: University of Illinois Press.

Morone, J. (2004) *Hellfire Nation: The Politics of Sin in American History*, New Haven: Yale University Press.

Moser, B. (2007) "Purple America," *The Nation*, 25 July.

MPI. Migration Policy Institute (2007) "Migration Facts, Stats and Maps."

Mujahid, A. (2001) "Muslims in America: Profile 2001," *Soundvision.com*.

Myers, S. and A. Rubin (2008) "Iraqi Journalist Hurls Shoes at Bush and Denounces Him on TV as a 'dog,' *NYT*, 14 December.

National Commission on Terrorism (2000) "Countering the Changing Threat of International Terrorism."

NCAI. National Congress of American Indians (2004) "NCAI Testimony on FY2005," 25 March.

NCES. National Center for Education Statistics (2009) US Department of Education, "Digest of Education Statistics 2009."

NCES. National Center for Education Statistics (2008) US Department of Education, "The Condition of Education 2008."

NCES. National Center for Education Statistics (2007) US Department of Education "Digest of Education Statistics 2007."

NCES. National Center for Education Statistics (2006) US Department of Education, "Digest of Education Statistics 2006."

NCFE. National Campaign for Fair Elections (2008).

NCHS. National Center for Health Statistics (2007) "NCHS Data Brief" [www.cdc.gov/nchs].

NCPPHE. National Center for Public Policy and Higher Education (2008) "Measuring Up 2008," 1 December.

NCSL: National Conference of State Legislatures (2009): "Legislative Term Limits."

NCSL. National Conference of State Legislatures (2008a) "Ballot Measures Preview 2008" 28 October.

NCSL. National Conference of State Legislatures (2008b) NCSL Backgrounder: Full and Part Time Legislatures, January.

NEA. National Education Association (2008a) "2008–09 Adequate Yearly Progress (AYP) Results: Many More Schools Fail in Most States," 20 October.

NEA. National Education Association (2008b) "No Child Left Behind Act" (NCLB)/ESEA.

NEA. National Endowment for the Arts (2009) "About Us."

Neustadt, R. (1990) *Presidential Power: The Politics of Leadership from Roosevelt to Reagan,* rev. edn, New York: Free Press.

Niebuhr, R. (2008) with an Introduction by A. Bacevich. *The Irony of American History*, Chicago: University of Chicago Press.

NYT. New York Times (2008) "Important Supreme Court Decisions, 2007–2008," *NYT*, June 29.

New York Times Almanac, 2009 (2008) New York: Penguin.

New York Times Almanac, 2006 (2005) New York: Penguin.

Niebuhr, R. (1952) *The Irony of American History,* New York: Charles Scribner's Sons.

9/11 Commission Report: Final Report of the National Commission on Terrorist Attacks Upon the United States (2004), New York: Norton.

NRLC. National Right to Life Committee (2004) "Abortion in the United States: Statistics and Trends," 20 October.

NSC. National Safety Council (2009) "About the National Safety Council."

NSC. National Safety Council (2002) "About the Council," 16 March.

Nye, J. (2002) *The Paradox of American Power: Why the World's Only Superpower Can't Go It Alone*, New York: Oxford University Press.

Obama, B. (2009a) "Address to Congress," 24 February.

Obama, B. (2009b) "Inaugural Address by Barack Obama," *NYT*, 20 January.

Obama, B (2008a) "Remarks to the National Governors Association," 2 December.

Obama, B (2008b) "Obama on Economic Crisis, Transition," *CBS News*, 16 November.

Obama, B. (2008c) "Remarks to NALEO," 28 June.

Obama, B. (2007) *The Audacity of Hope: Thoughts on Reclaiming the American Dream*, New York: Random House.

Obama, B. (2004) *Dreams of My Father: A Story of Race and Inheritance*, New York: Random House.

OECD. Organisation for Economic Co-operation and Development, (2008a) "Economy, Environmental, and Social Statistics," *OECD Factbook*.

OECD. Organisation for Economic Co-operation and Development (2008b) "OECD in Figures, 2008."

Olson, E. (1998) "UN Report Assails US Death Penalty," *IHT*, 8 April.

Oppel, R. (2002) "Bush Extols Military Service and Expedites Citizenship," *NYT*, 5 July.

OPS. Office of the Press Secretary (2004) "President Bush Meets with Michigan Judicial Nominees," 7 July.

Park, E. (2009) "How Will Obama Administration Impact Immigration?" *The National Law Journal*, 20 January.

Patterson, J. (1981) *America's Struggle Against Poverty in the Twentieth Century*, Cambridge: Harvard University Press.

Paulsen, A. (2008) "Resegregation of U. S. Schools Deepening," *CSM*, 25 January.

Peck, I. (1991) "Labor in America," Washington: US Information Agency.

Peele, G., C. Bailey, B. Cain and G. Peters (eds) (2006) *Developments in American Politics 5*, London: Palgrave Macmillan.

PEJ. Project for Excellence in Journalism (2008) "Winning the Media Campaign: How the Press Reported the 2008 Presidential Election," 22 October.

Pells, R. (1997) *Not Like Us: How Europeans Have Loved, Hated, and Transformed American Culture Since World War II*, New York: Basic Books.

Petracca, M. and M. Sorapure (eds) (1995) *Common Culture: Reading and Writing about American Popular Culture*, Englewood Cliffs, NJ: Prentice Hall.

Pew. Pew Research Center for the People and the Press (2009) "Internet and American Life Project," 6 January.

Pew. Pew Research Center for the People and the Press (2008a) "Internet Overtakes newspapers as news Source," 23 December.

Pew. Pew Research Center for the People and the Press (2008b) "Bush and Public Opinion," 18 December.

Pew. Pew Research Center for the People and the Press (2008c) "US Religious Landscape Survey," 13 December .

Pew. Pew Research Center for the People and the Press (2008d) "Some Final Thoughts on Campaign '08," 8 December.

Pew. Pew Research Center for the People and the Press (2008e) "Winds of Political Change Haven't Shifted Public's Ideology," 25 November.

Pew. Pew Research Center for the People and the Press (2008f) "More Americans Question Religion's Role in Politics," 21 August.

Pew. Pew Research Center for the People and the Press (2008g) "Federal Government's Ratings Slump," 14 May.

Pew. Pew Research Center for the People and the Press (2008h) "Inside the Middle Class: Bad Times Hit the Good Life," 9 April.

Pew. Pew Research Center for the People and the Press (2008i) "US Religious Landscape Survey," 23 February.

Pew. Pew Research Center for the People and the Press (2007) "Muslim Americans: Middle Class and Mostly Mainstream," 22 May.

Pew. Pew Research Center for the People and the Press (2005) "Public Divided on Origins of Life," 30 August.

Pew. Pew Research Center for the People and the Press (2004) "A Year After Iraq War," 16 March.

Pew. Pew Research Center for the People and the Press (2003) "2004 Political Landscape: Evenly Divided and Increasingly Polarized," 5 November.

Pew. Pew Research Center for the People and the Press (2001a) "Post September 11 Attitudes," 6 December.

Pew. Pew Research Center for the People and the Press (2001b) "Economic Inequality Seen as Rising: Boom Bypasses Poor," 21 June.

Phillips, K. (2008) *Bad Money: Reckless Finance, Failed Politics, and the Global Crisis of American Capitalism*, New York: Viking.

Pogrebin, R. (2008) "David H. Koch to Give $100 Million to Theater," *NYT*, 10 July.

Pohl, F. (2008) *Framing America: A Social History of American Art*, London: Thames and Hudson.

Powers, T. (2004) "Secret Intelligence and the 'War on Terror,'" *NYRB*, 16 December.

Powers, T. (2003) "The Vanishing Case for War," *NYRB*, 4 December.

PPI. Progressive Policy Institute (2008) "The United States Collects More Tariff Money from Cambodia than from Britain," 20 February.

Prothero, S. (2004) *American Jesus: How the Son of God Became a National Icon*, New York: Ferrar, Straus and Giroux.

Putnam, R. (2000) *Bowling Alone: The Collapse and Revival of American Community,* New York: Simon & Schuster.

PW. Publishers' Weekly (2008) "Bestselling Books of the Year, 1996–2007," 24 March.

Rampell, C. (2009) "As Layoffs Surge, Women May Pass Men in Job Force," *NYT*, 6 February.

Rawls, J. (1996) *Chief Red Fox Is Dead: A History of Native Americans Since 1945*, Ft. Worth, TX: Harcourt-Brace.

Reagan, R. (1989) "Farewell Address," *Congressional Quarterly Weekly Report*, 14 January, 95–7.

RealtyTrac (2008) "US Foreclosure Activity Increases 75 Percent in 2007," 29 January.

Reich, R. (2001) *The Future of Success*, London: Heinemann.

Reisman, D. (1950) *The Lonely Crowd: A Study of the Changing American Character*, New Haven, CT: Yale University Press.

Rich, F. (2009) "A President Forgotten but Not Gone," *NYT*, 4 January.

Riis, Jacob (1901) *How the Other Half Lives*, New York: Dover.

RLIC. Retirement Living Information Center (2009) "Tax Rates by State," January.

Roberts, S. and D. Epstein (2009) "Sources Tell SI Alex Rodriguez Tested Positive for Steroids in 2003," *Sports Illustrated*, 7 February.

Robinson, E. (2008) "A Victory for the Rule of Law," *WP*, 13 June.

Robinson, J. (2003) "Ahh, Free at La—Oops! Time's Up," *WP*, 27 July.

Rosen, R. (2006) *The World Split Open: How the Modern Women's Movement Changed America*, London: Penguin.

Rosenbaum, D. (2005) "Bush to Return to 'Ownership Society' Theme in Push for Social Security Changes," *NYT*, 16 January.

Rosenbaum, D. and E. Olson (2002) "US Loses Trade Case to Europeans on Offshore Tax Havens," *NYT*, 15 January.

Rothschild, E. (2004) "Real, Pretended or Imaginary Dangers," *NYRB*, 25 March.

Safire, W. (1978) *Safire's Political Dictionary*, New York: Random House.

Samuels, D. (1991) "The Rap on Rap," *NR*, 11 November.

Sanger, D. (2000) "Economic Engine for Foreign Policy," *NYT*, 28 December.

Schlesinger, A. (2003) "Eyeless in Iraq," *NYRB*, 23 October.

Schlesinger, A. (1986) *The Cycles of American History*, Boston: Houghton Mifflin.

Schlesinger, A. (1973) *The Imperial Presidency*, Boston: Houghton Miffllin.

Schlosser, E. (2001) *Fast-Food Nation: The Dark Side of the All-American Meal*, Houghton Mifflin.

Schmemann, S. (2003) "'Of Paradise and Power': The Divergence Thesis," *NYT*, 30 March.

Schor, J. (1998) *The Overspent American: Upscaling, Downshifting, and the New Consumer*, New York: HarperCollins.

Schor, J. (1993) *The Overworked American: The Unexpected Decline of Leisure*, New York: Basic Books.

Schrank, J. (1995) "Sport and the American Dream," in M. Petracca and M. Sorapure (eds), 358–61.

Schwenninger, S. (2004) "America's 'Suez Moment,'" *AMO* (January).

Screen Digest (2008) "Film Production and Distribution."

Shanker, T. and J. Brooke (2005) "Tsunami Tests U.S. Forces' Logistics," *NYT*, 9 January.

Sherk, J. (2007) "Upward Leisure Mobility? Americans Work Less and Have More Leisure Time Than Ever Before," HeritageWeb Memo, 31 August.

Sherman, M. (2007) "Supreme Court Rebukes Bush on Carbon Dioxide Policy," *Live Science*, 2 April.

SilverRingThing (2008) "Silver Ring Thing."

Skocpol, T. (1995) *Social Policy in the United States,* New Brunswick, NJ: Princeton University Press.

Slotkin, R. (1993) *Gunfighter Nation: The Myth of the Frontier in Twentieth-Century America,* New York: HarperCollins.

Sorkin, A. and M. Walsh (2009) "U.S. Is Said to Offer Another $30 billion in Funds to A.I.G." *NYT*, 2 March.

Soros, G. (2008) "The Crisis & What to Do About It," *NYRB*, 4 December.

SSTI. State Science and Technology Institute (2007) "14 Years of Federal Support for Academic R & D by State, 1993–2006."

Statemaster (2008) "Lifestyle Statistics. Shopping Malls."

Steingart, G. (2009) "The New American Feeling," *Der Spiegel Online*, 21 January.

Stiglitz, J. (2009) "Capitalist Fools," *Vanity Fair*, January.

Stiglitz, J. (2003) *The Roaring Nineties: Seeds of Destruction*, New York: Norton.

Stiglitz, J. (2002) *Globalization and Its Discontents,* New York: Norton.

Stiglitz, J. and L. Bilmes (2008) "The $3 Trillion War," *Vanity Fair*, April.

Stolberg, S. (2009a) "Obama Puts His Own Spin on Mix of Science with Politics," *NYT*, 9 March.

Stolberg, S. (2009b) "Obama Signs Equal-Pay Legislation," *NYT*, 29 January 2009.

Stolberg, S. (2005) "Foe of Abortion, Senator is Cool to Court Choice," *NYT*, 7 October.

Stout, D. and E. Andrews (2009) "1.2 Trillion Deficit Forecast as Obama Weighs Options," *NYT*, 7 January.

Strand, M. (2007) *Hopper*, New York: Knopf.

Strom, S. (2003) "MacArthur Foundation Gives $42 Million, Despite Economy," *NYT*, 13 January.

Suárez-Orozco, M. and M. Páez (2002) *Latinos: Remaking America*, Berkeley: University of California Press.

Sullivan, K. (2008) "US Again Hailed as Country of Dreams," *WP*, 6 November.

Tallack, D. (2000) "Architecture and Art," in R. Maidment and J. Mitchell (eds), 235–69.

Thernstrom, S. and A. Thernstrom (1999) *America in Black and White: One Nation, Indivisible,* New York: Simon & Schuster.

Tindall, G. and D. Shi (1996) *America: A Narrative History,* New York: Norton.

TNBA. The National Bowling Association (2008) "The National Bowling Association Story."

Tocqueville, A. de (1994) *Democracy in America,* London: The Everyman's Library.

Toobin, J. (2007) *The Nine: Inside the Secret World of the Supreme Court*, New York: Doubleday.

Turner, F. (1966) *The Significance of the Frontier in American History,* Ann Arbor: University of Michigan Press.

TV Decoder (2008) "Fox News Ratings Show Erosion," *NYT* blog, 28 June.

Uchitelle, L., A. Martin and S. Rosenbloom (2008) "Full of Doubts, U.S. Shoppers Cut Spending," *NYT*, 6 October.

UK Film Council (2008) "Statistical Yearbook 2007/8," Chapter 13.

Updike, J. (2005) *Still Looking: Essays on American Art*, London: Hamish Hamilton.

US Census Bureau (2009a) "Educational Attainment in the United States, 2007." Washington, DC: US Government Printing Office.

US Census Bureau (2009b) Statistical Abstract, Tables 224 and 527, "Mean Earnings by Highest Degree Earned, 2006" and "Social and Human Services". Washington, DC: US Government Printing Office.

US Census Bureau (2008a) *Income, Poverty, and Health Insurance Coverage in the United States, 2007.* Washington, DC: US Government Printing Office.

US Census Bureau (2008b) *Statistical Abstract of the United States: 2009*, Table 241. Washington, DC: US Government Printing Office.

US Census Bureau. (2008c) "American Indian and Alaska Native Heritage Month: November 2008," 17 November.

US Census Bureau (2008d) "US Census Bureau News," 28 October.

US Census Bureau (2008e) "US Census Bureau News," 26 August.

US Census Bureau (2008f) "US Census Bureau News," 14 August.

US Census Bureau (2008g) "Income, Poverty and Health Insurance Coverage in the US, 2007," August.

US Census Bureau (2008h) "US Population Estimates," July.

US Census Bureau (2004a) "Educational Attainment in the United States: 2003," June.

US Census Bureau (2004b) "Employment Status by Sex, 2000."

US Congress. National Commission on Terrorism (2000) *Countering the Changing Threat of International Terrorism.*

US Courts (2008) "2008 Year End Report on the Federal Judiciary," *Public Information Office*, 31 December.

US Courts (2001) "2000 Year End Report on the Federal Judiciary," *The Third Branch: Newsletter of the Federal Courts* 33, January 2001.

USDA. United States Department of Agriculture (2008a) "Supplementing Nutrition Assistance Program (SNAP)," 31 December.

USDA. United States Department of Agriculture (2008b) "Expenditures on Children by Families, 2007," March.

USEP. United States Election Project (2008) "Voter Turnout."

US Mayors. US Conference of Mayors (2008) "Hunger and Homelessness in America's Cities," December.

Verhovek, S. (1999) "Gates Pledges $1 Billion for Minorities," *IHT*, 17 September.

Warrick, J. and K. DeYoung (2009) "Obama Reverses Bush Policies on Detention and Interrogation," *WP*, 23 January.

Washington, G. (1796) "The Farewell Address: Transcript of the Final Manuscript," George Washington Papers, University of Virginia.

Watson, P. (2001) *A Terrible Beauty: The People and Ideas that Shaped the Modern Mind*, London: Phoenix.

Webster, N. (1789) "Dissertations on the English Language," in *The Annals of America,* Chicago: *Encyclopcedia Britannica,* 1976, 3: 375–9.

Weeks, L. (2000) "Kluge Gives $60 Million to Library of Congress," *WP*, 5 October.

Weisberg, J, (ed.) (2008) *The Best American Political Writing 2008*, New York: Columbia University Press.

Weller, C. (2006) "Drowning in Debt," *American Progress*, 11 May.

Westen, D. (2007) *The Political Brain: The Role of Emotion in Deciding the Fate of the Nation*, New York: Public Affairs.

Whitlock, C. (2009) "National Security Team Delivers Grim Appraisal of Afghanistan War," *WP*, 9 February.

Williams, W. (1966) *The Contours of American History*, Chicago: Quadrangle.

Wills, G. (2006) "A Country Ruled by Faith," *NYRB*, 16 November.

Wills, G. (1999) *A Necessary Evil: A History of American Distrust of Government,* New York: Simon & Schuster.

Winthrop, J. (1989) "A Model of Christian Charity," in N. Baym, R. Gottesman, *et al., The Norton Anthology of American Literature*, Vol. 1, New York: Norton, 31–42.

Wolfe, A. (2009) *The Future of Liberalism*, New York: Knopf.

Wolfe, A. (2006) "The Politics of Immigration. Getting In," *NR* Online, 1 May.

Wolfe, A. (1998) *One Nation After All: What Middle Class America Really Think About,* New York: Penguin.

Wood, F. (1990) *The Arrogance of Faith: Christianity and Race in America from the Colonial Era to the Twentieth Century*, Boston: Northeastern University Press.

Wood, G. (2008) *The Purpose of the Past: Reflections on the Use and Abuse of History*, New York: Penguin.

Wood, G. (1969) "The Whig Science of Politics," in J. Kirby Martin (ed.), *Colonial America: Selected Readings*, New York: Harper & Row, 330–47.

Woodward, B. (2002) *Bush at War*, New York: Simon & Schuster.

WP. Washington Post (2009) "President Bush's Approval Ratings," 20 January.

WTO. World Trade Organization (2008) "What is the WTO?"

Yardley, J. and W. Broad (2004) "Heading for the Stars, and Wondering if China Might Reach Them First," *NYT*, 21 January.

Zakaria, F. (2008a) *The Post American World*, New York: Norton.

Zakaria, F. (2008b) "The Future of American Power: How America Can Survive the Rise of the Rest," *Foreign Affairs*, June.

Zakaria, F. (2006) "How Long Will America Lead the World?" *Newsweek*, 12 June.

Zolberg, A. (2006) A *Nation by Design: Immigration Policy in the Fashioning of America*, Cambridge: Harvard University Press.

Zukin, S. (2005) *Point of Purchase: How Shopping Changed American Culture*, London: Routledge.

Index

Key: **bold**=extended discussion or concept highlighted in the text; b=box; c=caption; f=figure; n=note; t=table *=illustration; #=map.